'For those who feel uncertain about reading I would unhesitatingly recommend the *Good Reading Guide.*' *Glasgow Herald*

If you have ever wondered what to read next, your search is over. The BLOOMSBURY GOOD READING GUIDE is now in its second edition. The book's first edition was warmly greeted not only by reviewers but especially by booksellers, librarians — and readers. The first edition has sold over 25,000 copies.

The new edition is fully updated including many new writers and over 150 new works. New entries include William Boyd, Martin Amis, Anne Tyler, Peter Carey, and Jeanette Winterson. Expanded entries include Kurt Vonnegut, Margaret Atwood, Salman Rushdie, Catherine Cookson, Robert Ludlum and John Irving. It includes the 1990 Booker Prize winner.

The GUIDE builds on the approach developed for the first edition. Authors are listed A to Z, each entry detailing several works. The unique feature of the book is the network of cross-references which refer the reader from one author to another and from one work to others.

So the book really does answer the question 'What should I read next?'

Kenneth McLeish's previous books include the *Viking/Penguin Guide to the Arts in the Twentieth Century* and *Shakespeare's People A-Z*.

BLOOMSBURY GOOD READING GUIDE

NEW EDITION COMPLETELY REVISED & UPDATED

Kenneth McLeish

B L O O M S B U R Y

First published 1990

This paperback edition published 1991

Bloomsbury Publishing Ltd, 2 Soho Square, London, W1V 5DE

A CIP entry for this book is available from the British Library.

ISBN 0 7475 0862 3

10 9 8 7 6 5 4 3 2

Typeset by Alexander Typesetting Inc., Indianapolis, IN

Printed in Great Britain by Cox & Wyman Ltd, Reading, Berks

CONTENTS

INTRODUCTION

Reading is one of the most satisfying of all human skills. We can survive – people do survive – perfectly well without it, and yet many would list it high among the things which make life worth living. Even such eager readers, however, can be daunted by the sheer number of books on offer. Libraries and bookshops are stuffed with treasures; like explorers in some vast, landmarkless new continent, we hardly know where to turn.

The *Bloomsbury Good Reading Guide* seeks to answer two main questions: 'Where shall I start?' and 'Where shall I go next?' The bulk of the text is articles on some 320 authors, describing the kind of books they wrote, listing titles and suggesting books, by the same authors and by others, which might make interesting follow-ups.

There are also, scattered through the *Guide*, 19 'skeins' and over 80 'menus' of suggested reading. The menus are straightforward lists of about seven or eight books of a similar kind, ranging from **Action Thrillers** (see page 2) to **Weepies** (see page 261). The skeins, on the other hand, range wider. Each one starts with a specific book and suggests follow-ups both predictable and unexpected, a haul of reading as varied as fish in a net. E.M. Forster's *A Passage to India*, for example, leads to both Paul Theroux's *Fong and the Indians* and John Le Carré's *The Perfect Spy*. Also included as menus are a list of all Booker Prize winners since the inauguration of the prize (see page 27), and a list of 'Twelve Basic Books', essential for anyone who wants to be 'well read', suggested by readers of the *Sunday Times* (see page 236).

The *Guide* deals with prose fiction only. There is no literary criticism; I wanted to describe books, not to be clever at their expense. In particular, I tried to avoid ranking authors by 'literary merit', on assessments of whether their work is 'great' or 'light'. The length of each entry depends solely on how much needed to be said. If this had been a travel guide, New York (say) might have had more space than the commuter village up the line – but that would have had no bearing on where one might choose to live.

Throughout the text, ▷ before someone's name means that that person has a main entry of his or her own. All books mentioned in the *Guide* were written in English or are widely available in translation. We have tried to cover as wide a range of writers of English as possible and have included authors from Australia, Canada, New Zealand, the Republic of Ireland, South Africa and the USA as well as the UK. Some books may be published under different titles in the USA. If this is the case the UK title is given first, followed by the US title: Daphne du Maurier: *The Apple Tree/Kiss Me Again Stranger*. Books originally written in a foreign language are listed by their English titles. Original titles follow in brackets where they may be familiar to readers or where they may be used for some English editions.

Émile Zola: *The Boozer* (L'assommoir)
André Gide: *The Pastoral Symphony* (La symphonie pastorale)

Main author entries are listed alphabetically by surname. Each author-article contains some or all of four different strands of information:

1 a paragraph about the author's work and style in general
2 description of a particular book, a good example of the author's work
3 list of main books by the same author
4 suggestions for follow-ups
  by the same author ●
  by others ▶

In this second edition of the *Guide* we have updated entries to include books (and alas, deaths) occurring since the first publication, and we have revised entries, added new titles and added a couple of dozen authors new to the *Guide*. Some of these changes are the result of my own reading, but many came about because of letters and suggestions from readers of the *Guide*. We welcome ideas, comments and suggestions, especially for follow-ups and skeins. Please write to me, care of the publishers. We are also now publishing satellite volumes to the *Guide*, on specific types of literature. *Science Fiction* and *Murder* have been published, *Biographies and Autobiographies* is imminent, and *Children's Books* and *Travel* are in prospect.

The cut-off date for inclusion in this second edition of the *Guide* was October 1989.

Throughout the *Guide*, both first and second editions, the final choice of books and authors, the comments and the text were my responsibility; I take the blame. But many people helped, and the *Guide* has benefited from suggestions and comments from Lucy Banister, Sian Facer, Sheila Hardy, Pamela Henderson, Simon McLeish, Kathy Rooney, Stella Yates, M.H. Zool, and many correspondents to me at Bloomsbury and to the *Sunday Times*. I warmly thank them all. As always, my greatest debt is to my wife, Valerie McLeish; her inspiration and encouragement were essential to every page.

Kenneth McLeish,

October 1989

A

ACHEBE, CHINUA (BORN 1930)

Nigerian novelist.

Things Fall Apart (1958), Achebe's best-known novel, is a story of the people of Umuofia on the river Niger, and especially of Okonkwo, a rich and headstrong elder. To British readers the period seems early Victorian; to the men and women of Umuofia it would have no date, it would be part of the gentle continuum of existence. Their lives depend on the harmony between human beings and spirits, and that is preserved by a precise set of rituals and beliefs, established by precedent, explained by folk-tale and so familiar that instead of constricting the soul they liberate it. Okonkwo wins respect among his people by a magnificent wrestling-throw when he is 18, and keeps it by his hard work as a farmer, his love for the land. Then, by accident, he kills a relative, and is forced by custom to live out of the village for seven years. While he is away Christian missionaries come. They speak through interpreters, understand nothing of the people's beliefs and are followed by white commissioners whose laws destroy the society they were devised to 'civilise'. Achebe's points are blunt, and (for ex-colonialists) shamingly unanswerable. But his novel's main fascination is not political but social. External observers, however sophisticated their cameras or meticulous their anthropological methods, can only describe the surface of timeless, tribal societies: they report and explain events. Achebe, by contrast, uses a series of direct, uncomplicated scenes, reverberant as poetry, to reveal his people's souls.

Achebe's other novels are No Longer at Ease, Arrow of God

READ ON

- *A Man of the People* (a satirical, bitter farce about what happens when white imperialists leave and black politicians set up a state on 'western' lines).
- ▶ **To *Things Fall Apart:*** Amos Tutuola, *My Life in the Bush of Ghosts* (making a denser, more Homeric use of Nigerian folk-styles). ▷I.B. Singer, *Satan in Goray*. Janet Lewis, *The Trial of Sören Kvist*.
- ▶ **To Achebe's later, and politically much more savage work:** ▷V. S. Naipaul, *A Bend in the River*; David Caute, *News from Nowhere* – and, in a more hilarious but no less

and Anthills of the Savannah. Chike and the River *is a children's book, sweet as a folk-tale.*

bleak mood, ▷Evelyn Waugh, *Black Mischief*.

ACTION THRILLERS

▷Richard Condon, *The Manchurian Candidate*
Clive Cussler, *Cyclops*
▷Ken Follett, *Lie Down With Lions*
▷Frederick Forsyth, *The Day of the Jackal*
Martin Cruz Smith, *Stallion Gate*
Scott Turow, *Presumed Innocent*
Walter Wager, *Telefon*

High Adventure (p 119); Historical Adventure (p 123); Spies and Double Agents (p 231); Terrorists/Freedom Fighters (p 240)

ADAMS, DOUGLAS (BORN 1952)

British novelist.

Adams made his name with a series of genial SF spoofs, beginning with *The Hitchhiker's Guide to the Galaxy* (1979). In this, Earthman Arthur Dent, informed that his planet is about to be vaporised to make room for a hyperspace bypass, escapes by stowing away on an alien spacecraft. This is the beginning of a wild journey through time and space, in the course of which he meets the super-cool President of the Galaxy, Zaphod Beeblebrox, discusses the coastline of Norway with Slartibartfast (who won prizes for designing it), watches the apocalyptic floor-show in the Restaurant at the End of the Universe, and discovers the answer to the 'ultimate question about life, the universe and everything'. Adams himself is on a spree, spray-painting the stuffiest corners of the genre. The other *Hitchhiker* books (self-contained sequels) are *The Restaurant at the End of the Universe*; *Life, the Universe and Everything* and *So Long, and Thanks for All the Fish.* In 1987 Adams began a second series, this time starring Dirk Gently, an intergalactic private eye who has to cope not only with the usual quota of blondes and hoodlums, but with electronic monks, thinking horses, the space-time continuum and an uneasy feeling that he is no more than a bystander in his own bad dreams. The Gently books so far (appropriately, a gentler entertainment than the *Hitchhiker* series) are *Dirk Gently's Holistic Detective Agency* and *The Long Dark Teatime of the Soul.*

READ ON

- **SF spoofs in similarly lunatic vein:** Terry Pratchett, *The Colour of Magic*; ▷Harry Harrison, *The Stainless Steel Rat*; ▷Kurt Vonnegut, *The Sirens of Titan*.
- **Non-SF books featuring bewildered heroes at the centre of chaos:** Patrick Dennis, *Auntie Mame*; Charles Webb, *The Graduate*; ▷William Boyd, *Stars and Bars*; ▷Evelyn Waugh, *Decline and Fall*.

ADOLESCENCE

▷Maeve Binchy, *Echoes*
▷Colette, *The Ripening Seed*

▷Miles Franklin, *My Brilliant Career*
Jane Gardam, *Bilgewater*
▷Rumer Godden, *The Greengage Summer*
Harper Lee, *To Kill a Mocking Bird*
Sue Townsend, *The Secret Diary of Adrian Mole, aged 13¾*
▷Antonia White, *Frost in May*

Children (p 44); Eccentric Families (p 73); Growing Up: Teenagers (p 105); Parents and Children (p 193); Schools (p 220)

ALDISS, Brian (born 1925)

British novelist.

For the last 30 years Aldiss has been a major propagandist for British SF, editing anthologies, speaking at conventions and writing several non-fiction books including *Billion Year Spree* (revised version: *Trillion Year Spree*), a critical history of the genre. His own SF covers the whole range from space opera (eg *Non-stop*) to future catastrophe (eg *Hothouse*, about human life after a global catastrophe shrinks our race to two feet high), from philosophical fantasy (eg *Frankenstein Unbound* and *Moreau's Other Island*, extensions of themes from earlier SF masterpieces) to stories of alternative worlds (eg the Helliconia trilogy: see below). He is also known for non-SF novels. These range from a comic trilogy about the oversexed 1950s adolescent Horatio Stubbs (*A Hand-reared Boy*; *A Soldier Erect*; *A Rude Awakening*) to *Life in the West*, a ▷Bellow-like book about the plight of a man who has made his reputation preaching science and technology as the salvation of humanity, and is now forced, by the disintegration of his own emotional life, to give his views more intimate analysis.

The Helliconia Trilogy (1982–5)

Helliconia is one of four planets which revolve round Batalix, itself a satellite of the giant star Freyr. Helliconia seasons last not for months but for hundreds of Earth years, and the planet is inhabited by two separate and incompatible races, one adapted to winter life, the other to summer. The three novels (*Helliconia Spring*, *Helliconia Summer*, *Helliconia Winter*) explore the effects of Helliconia's enormous seasons, each long enough for whole civilisations to rise, flourish and die. Colonial wars, racism, ecology, the clash between religion, science and the arts, are underlying themes – and all the time, Helliconia is observed: watching it provides entertainment, a blend of travel-documentary and soap-opera, for the bored inhabitants of Earth.

READ ON

- *The Dark Light Years*.
- ▶ **To the Helliconia books:** ▷Ursula Le Guin, *The Left Hand of Darkness*.
- ▶ **To Aldiss' SF in general:** ▷Ray Bradbury, *The Golden Apples of the Sun*; ▷Isaac Asimov, *The Foundation Trilogy*.
- ▶ **To the Horatio Stubbs books:** Leslie Thomas, *The Virgin Soldiers*.
- ▶ **To *Life in the West*:** ▷John Fowles, *Daniel Martin*; ▷John Updike, *Roger's Version*.

Aldiss' other SF books include Earthworks, The Saliva Tree, Barefoot in the Head, Enemies of the System, The Malacia Tapestry, *and a dozen story-collections including* Starswarm, Cosmic Inferno *and* New Arrivals, Old Encounters. *His non-SF novels include* The Brightfount Diaries, The Primal Urge, The Male Response *and* Forgotten Life.

ALLBEURY, TED (BORN 1917)

British novelist.

Allbeury writes packed, fast spy thrillers, usually with cold-war settings. His titles include *A Choice of Enemies, Moscow Quadrille, The Man With the President's Mind, The Lantern Network, The Alpha List, The Crossing, Children of Tender Years* and *The Secret Whispers* (about a double agent attempting to escape from East Germany). He also uses the pseudonym Richard Butler (*Where All the Girls Are Sweeter; Italian Assets*).

READ ON

▶ Duff Hart-Davis, *The Heights of Rimring.* Ted Willis, *The Churchill Commando.* ▷Richard Condon, *The Manchurian Candidate.* ▷John Le Carré, *The Spy Who Came in from the Cold.*

ALLENDE, ISABEL (BORN 1942)

Peruvian novelist.

The House of the Spirits, Allende's first novel, was a glowing family tapestry in the manner of ▷Márquez' *One Hundred Years of Solitude*, spanning five generations and thronged with larger-than-life characters and supernatural events. Her second book, *Of Love and Shadows*, takes a narrower, more political focus, to devastating effect. Irene Beltrán, a journalist, and her photographer-lover Francisco Leal are investigating the disappearance of a disturbed, possibly saintly adolescent. In the jackbooted dictatorship in which they live, however, the child is not simply missing but 'disappeared', one of thousands snatched by the authorities who will never be seen again. Allende surrounds the four main characters – the fourth is Lieutenant Ramirez, the child's abductor – with a web of fantastic personal history in true magic-realist style. But the further the investigators thread their way through the sadism and ruthlessness of a labyrinthine fascist state, the more fact begins to swallow fairy tale. The investigators themselves begin to lose reality – their love-affair becomes a swooning parody of romantic fiction – but what they discover grows more and more uncomfortably like real South American life, like nightmare fleshed.

READ ON

- *Eva Luna.*

▶ Carlos Fuentes, *A Change of Skin.* ▷Günter Grass, *The Tin Drum.* ▷Richard Condon, *Winter Kills.* Mario Vargas Llosa, *Captain Pantoja and the Special Service* gives a more farcical view of Allende's terrifying haunted world.

ALL-ENGULFING FAMILIES

▷Anita Brookner, *Family and Friends*
▷Angela Carter, *The Magic Toyshop*
▷William Faulkner, *The Sound and the Fury*
▷John Galsworthy, *The Forsyte Saga*
Irene Handl, *The Sioux*
▷François Mauriac, *The Nest of Vipers*
▷Christina Stead, *The Man Who Loved Children*

Eccentric Families (p 73); Many Generations (p 170)

ALLINGHAM, MARGERY (1905–66)

British novelist.

Allingham wrote 'crime fiction' only in the senses that each of her books contains the step-by-step solution of a crime, and that their hero, Albert Campion, is an amateur detective whose amiable manner conceals laser intelligence and iron moral integrity. But instead of confining Campion by the boundaries of the detective-story genre, Allingham put him in whatever kind of novel she felt like writing. Some of her books (*More Work for the Undertaker, The Beckoning Lady*) are wild, ▷Wodehousian farce, others (*Sweet Danger, Traitor's Purse*) are ▷Buchanish, ▷Amblerish thrillers. Her best books are those of the 1940s and 1950s, and especially two set in an atmospheric, cobble-stones-and-alleyways London filled with low-life characters as vivid as any in ▷Dickens, *The Tiger in the Smoke* and *Hide My Eyes*.

FLOWERS FOR THE JUDGE (1936)

Strange things are happening at the old-established publishing firm of Barnabas and Company. First the junior partner turns a street-corner in Streatham and vanishes into thin air, then there is skullduggery over a priceless but obscene manuscript, and soon afterwards the firm's stuffy senior partner is murdered and Mr Campion has three intertwined mysteries on his hands.

Allingham's other Campion books include Coroner's Pidgin, Police at the Funeral, Look to the Lady *and the short-story collections* Mr Campion and Others *and* Take Two at Bedtime. *After Allingham's death, her husband* P. Youngman Carter *wrote two further Campion novels, one of which,* Mr Campion's Farthing, *is up to his wife's most sparkling standard.*

READ ON

- *Death of a Ghost* (set in London's eccentric art-community and involving – what else? – forged paintings); *Hide My Eyes*.
- ▶ ▷Michael Innes, *The Daffodil Affair*. Edmund Crispin, *The Case of the Gilded Fly*. H.R.F. Keating, *A Rush on the Ultimate*. ▷P.D. James, *An Unsuitable Job for a Woman*. Joan Smith, *Masculine Ending* is a tongue-in-cheek whodunnit starring a feminist sleuth.

ALL THE WORLD'S A STAGE
(books about theatre)

John Arden, *Books of Bale*
Richard Bissell, *Say, Darling*
Caryl Brahms and S.J. Simon, *A Bullet in the Ballet*
Bamber Gascoigne, *The Heyday*
H.R.F. Keating, *Death of a Fat God*
▷Thomas Keneally, *The Playmaker*
▷J.B. Priestley, *The Good Companions*
▷Mary Renault, *The Mask of Apollo*

ALTHER, LISA (BORN 1944)
US novelist.

Kinflicks (1976) is the 'autobiography' of Ginny Babcock, a 'typical' US adolescent in the late 1960s and early 1970s. The book sends up every cliché of the genre and of the period: Ginny spends her high school years jerking off a muscle-brained football star, discovers lesbian love at university, joins protest marches, takes up macrobiotic diets, zen and LSD, marries, has a child and divorces – and treats each experience as if she were the first person in the world ever to discover it, as if she were hypnotized by her own adventurousness. Alther intersperses Ginny's first-person narrative with chapters set ten years further on, when Ginny visits her dying mother in hospital, trying to come to terms with her feelings about herself, her family and her future. These sections give the book a harsher, more elegiac tone: the young Ginny symbolises a whole adolescent generation, as rebellious and zestful as any other but engulfed by the age they live in. Alther's second novel, *Original Sins* (1980), similarly blends satire, slapstick and irony. A 1980s equivalent to ▷Mary McCarthy's *The Group*, it traces the experience of five childhood friends as they grow to adulthood, discovering in the process civil rights, the women's movement and the pleasures and preposterousnesses of the sexual revolution. *Other Women* (1985), a less larky exploration of women's experience in the last generation, counterpoints the lives of two utterly different people, a 'flower-child' depressed at the first wiltings of middle age and the prickings of lesbianism, and her English psychiatrist.

READ ON

- **To *Kinflicks*:** ▷John Irving, *The World According to Garp*; ▷Philip Roth, *Portnoy's Complaint*; *Letting Go*; Marge Piercy, *The High Cost of Living*; Aritha van Herk, *No Fixed Address*.
- **To *Original Sins*:** ▷Mary McCarthy, *The Group*; Rona Jaffé, *Class Reunion*.
- **To *Other Women*:** ▷Alison Lurie, *Foreign Affairs*.

AMBLER, ERIC (BORN 1909)
British novelist and screenwriter.

The deadpan style of Ambler's thrillers lets him move easily from violence to farce, and he either sets his books in exotic places (the Levant, the Far East, tropical Africa), or else makes familiar European locations seem exotic as the scene of sinister and unlikely goings-on. His central characters are

READ ON

- Ambler continued Simpson's sleazy career in the appropriately-named *Dirty Story*. His minor crooks, conmen, or innocent bystanders trapped by circumstances or curiosity into a chain of bizarre and dangerous events. His supporting casts are crammed with improbable, unsavoury specimens, very few of whom are quite what they seem to be. Films and TV series have made this kind of thriller endlessly familiar. But Ambler was one of the first to write it, and he is still among the best.

THE LIGHT OF DAY (1962)

Arthur Simpson, a middle-aged, scruffy conman (played in the film version, *Topkapi*, by Peter Ustinov), is blackmailed into driving a car across the border from Greece into Turkey – and is promptly arrested and forced by the police to spy on the car's owners. They are a dangerous gang of – what? Terrorists? Drug-smugglers? Criminals? Simpson spends the whole book trying to find out, and at the same time to save his own sweaty dignity and to make as much profit as he can.

Ambler's other thrillers include Cause for Alarm, Dr Frigo, Epitaph for a Spy, Passage of Arms, The Schirmer Inheritance *and* To Catch a Spy. *He also wrote thrillers (eg* The Maras Affair; Charter to Danger*) in collaboration with* Charles Rodda, *published under the name* Eliot Reed. *They are more straightforward, but no less gripping, than his solo books.*

more serious thrillers include *The Mask of Dimitrios/Coffin for Dimitrios*, in which a bored writer sets out to track down an elusive Levantine criminal, and *The Levanter*, a story of terrorists in Palestine.

▶ **To *The Light of Day*:** David Dodge, *Bullets for the Bridegroom*; ▷Graham Greene, *Our Man in Havana*; Donald Westlake, *The Busy Body*.

▶ **To Ambler's less larky thrillers:** ▷Len Deighton, *Horse Under Water*; ▷Richard Condon, *The Manchurian Candidate*.

AMIS, KINGSLEY (BORN 1922)

British writer of novels, poems and non-fiction.

In the 1950s, when Amis' writing career began, British writers of all kinds – the 'angry young men' – had begun to rant in plays, films and novels about the unfairness, snobbishness and priggishness of life. Whingeing became an artistic form – and Amis' novels showed its funny side. The working-class hero of *Lucky Jim* tries to conform with his madrigal-singing, right-newspaper-reading, wine-savouring university colleagues, and in the process shows them up for the pretentious fools they are. The central character of *That Uncertain Feeling*, a small-town librarian, thinks that devastating sexual charm will carry him to the pinnacle of local society; the results are farcical. The hero of *Take a Girl Like You* finds it hard to persuade anyone else in his circle that 'free love' and 'the swinging sixties' are the good things glossy magazines crack them up to be. In the 1960s and 1970s Amis' farcical fires burned low. He began to affect a ponderous, self-consciously right-wing fuddy-duddiness, and abandoned satire for books of other kinds (a ghost story, a

READ ON

- *Jake's Thing*; *Stanley and the Women*.

▶ ▷Malcolm Bradbury, *Eating People is Wrong*. ▷A.N. Wilson, *Love Unknown*. Simon Raven, *The Old Gang*. ▷Tom Sharpe, *Porterhouse Blue*. ▷William Boyd, *A Good Man in Africa*. Howard Jacobson, *Peeping Tom*. William Cooper, *Scenes from Provincial Life*.

James Bond spy story and several science fiction books). In the 1980s, however, he returned to the satirical muttering which he always did better than any of his imitators – and his most recent books (eg *Jake's Thing,* about a middle-aged man trying to recapture the sexual energy of youth, and *The Old Devils*: see below) are among his funniest.

THE OLD DEVILS (1986)

A group of old men, acquaintances for over 40 years, meets daily in a Welsh bar to grumble. They are obsessed by failure, their own and the world's. They are especially vitriolic about other people's success – and their discomfort with the world is brought to a peak when one of their 'friends', a famous TV Welshman and an expert on a Dylan-Thomasish poet, comes to settle in the town.

The best of Amis' comic novels not mentioned above are One Fat Englishman, Ending Up *and* Difficulties With Girls *(a 1988 sequel to* Take a Girl Like You*). The best of his serious novels are* The Anti-Death League, *about a top-secret army unit whose aim is to abolish death, and* The Alteration, *set in a fantasy contemporary Britain in which modern science and modern religion have never happened, so that we are still organising our lives in medieval ways.*

AMIS, MARTIN (BORN 1949)

British novelist.

Amis is icily satirical, cold with rage at the physical and moral sleaziness of the human race. His characters' preoccupations are sex, food, money and success, and they are tormented by failure to win, or keep, all four. Ronald Firbank and ▷F. Scott Fitzgerald found similar prancing emptiness in the 'gay young things' of the 1920s. Amis matches those writers' bilious wit, but adds a pungent view of his own: that the entire generation born after the creation of nuclear weapons is maimed beyond cure, a race of psychotic moral mutants. Few contemporary writers treat such repulsive subject-matter so dazzlingly: Amis' novels are fictional equivalents of the raunchiest post-punk, pop-horror videos – compulsively nasty, superbly hard to like.

MONEY (1984)

This is the 'suicide note' of an obese, deranged and despairing film director, stumbling through a New York inferno of fast food, pornography, violence and moronic greed. He is a lunatic in a world gone mad; when he opens his mouth to scream, his voice is drowned in the megametropolitan carnival, the dance of death that is (for Amis, at least) contemporary America.

READ ON

- *London Fields* (about a man in apocalypse-hurtling 1999 London trying to write a novel about a woman trying to arrange her murder by a slob of a man fantasising about winning the world darts championship).
- ▶ Terence Blacker, *Fixx*, Iain Banks, *The Wasp Factory*, Madison Smartt Bell, *The Year of Silence*, ▷Saul Bellow, *Mr Sammler's Planet*.

Amis' other novels are The Rachel Papers, Dead Babies, Other People *and* Success. The Moronic Inferno *is a bilious travelogue about the USA, a marvellously raw, non-fiction counterpart to* Money. Einstein's Monsters *contains five dazzling short stories, and an introduction setting out Amis' thoughts on the way the existence of nuclear weapons has psychologically destroyed his generation.*

ANCIENT GREECE AND ROME

Greece:
▷Homer, *Odyssey*
Naomi Mitchison, *The Corn King and the Spring Queen*
▷Mary Renault, *The King Must Die*
Henry Treece, *Electra*
Rome:
▷Robert Graves, *I, Claudius*
Peter Vansittart, *Three Six Seven*
▷Thornton Wilder, *The Ides of March*
▷Marguerite Yourcenar, *Memoirs of Hadrian*

Bible (p 24); The Middle Ages (p 175); Other People, Other Times (p 192); Renaissance Europe (p 207).

ANDREWS, VIRGINIA (BORN 1933)

US novelist.

Andrews writes domestic chillers: claustrophobic stories of tense relationships in 'ordinary' US families. Her books include a quartet about the unhappy Dollenganger family: it begins with *Flowers in the Attic* (about a brother and sister kept prisoners in an attic until an inheritance is claimed), and continues with *Petal on the Wind, If There be Thorns* and *Seeds of Yesterday.*

READ ON

▶ ▷Patricia Highsmith, *The People Who Knock on the Door.*
Elizabeth Peters, *The Love Talker.*
Celia Fremlin, *The Trouble Makers.*
Josephine Tey, *The Franchise Affair.*

THE ANIMAL KINGDOM

Richard Adams, *Watership Down*
Rowena Farre, *Seal Morning*
Paul Gallico, *The Snow Goose*
▷Ernest Hemingway, *Fiesta/The Sun Also Rises*
William Horwood, *Duncton Wood*
▷Jack London, *White Fang*
Tony Weeks-Pearson, *Dodo*
Henry Williamson, *Tarka the Otter*

ANTHONY, Evelyn (born 1928)

British novelist.

'Evelyn Anthony' is the pseudonym of Evelyn Bridget Patricia Ward-Thomas. Her early books were historical romances: they include *Imperial Highness/Rebel Princess, Curse Not the King/Royal Intrigue, The Heiress/The French Bride* and *Anne of Austria/The Cardinal and the Queen*. In the 1970s she made a second name as writer of romantic thrillers and 20th-century espionage stories. These include *The Tamarind Seed, Stranger at the Gates/The Occupying Power, The Persian Ransom/The Persian Prince* and *Voices on the Wind* (in which an ex-resistance worker relives her second-world-war fight against the nazis, her love-affairs and a betrayal).

READ ON

- *Clandara* (historical romance). *The Janus Imperative*; *The Defector* (thrillers).
- ▶ **To the historical romances:** ▷Jean Plaidy, *Perdita's Prince*; ▷Dorothy Dunnett, *Queen's Play*.
- ▶ **To the thrillers:** Helen MacInnes, *The Snare of the Hunted*; ▷Mary Stewart, *Airs Above the Ground*.

ANTHONY, Piers (born 1934)

US novelist.

With R. Fuentes, Anthony has written half a dozen martial arts thrillers, including *Bamboo Bloodbath* and *Ninja's Revenge*. On his own he is a prolific SF writer. His early SF books were serious, ranging from the 'Omnivore' trilogy (*Omnivore, Orn, Ox*, 1968–76), with its parallel worlds and intelligent reptiles, to a 5-volume 'autobiography' of a future tyrant of Jupiter and the adventures of Death. His later books are quickly-read, genial fantasy in which, instead of winning through by traditional sword and sorcery methods, his heroes and heroines have to use their wits. In *A Spell for Chameleon* (1977), for example (the first of a series set in the country of Xanth), everyone except Bink (the hero) has a magic talent, and Bink's quest is to find some quality in himself which will prevent him being exiled for ordinariness.

READ ON

- *On a Pale Horse*; *Macroscope*.
- ▶ **To *A Spell for Chameleon***; Alan Dean Foster, *Spellsinger*; Terry Brooke, *The Sword of Shannara*; ▷Anne McCaffrey, *Dragonsong*.
- ▶ **To Anthony's more serious SF**: ▷Kurt Vonnegut, *Galápagos*; Phillip Mann, *Pioneers*.

ARCHER, Jeffrey (born 1940)

British novelist.

Archer writes incident-packed stories of intrigue in high and low places. His books include *Not a Penny More Not a Penny Less, A Matter of Honour* and the 1970s trilogy *Kane and Abel, The Prodigal Daughter* and *Shall We Tell the President?* (which begins with the separate but interlocking careers of two rivals in the worlds of business and politics, and continues with the daughter of one of them, who becomes the first woman president of the USA).

READ ON

- ▶ ▷Frederick Forsyth, *The Fourth Protocol*. Jon Cleary, *Spearfield's Daughter*. ▷Dick Francis, *Risk*.

ART FOR WHOSE SAKE?
(painters; fakers; patrons; art-enthusiasts)

▷Margery Allingham, *Death of a Ghost*
Michael Ayrton, *The Mazemaker*
Joyce Cary, *The Horse's Mouth*
Mary Flanagan, *Trust*
▷Wyndham Lewis, *Tarr*
▷Somerset Maugham, *The Moon and Sixpence*
Irving Stone, *The Agony and the Ecstasy*

ASIMOV, ISAAC (BORN 1920)

US writer of novels, short stories and non-fiction.

Since the age of 19, when Asimov published his first story, he has written over 300 books, ranging from Bible guides and history text-books to the SF novels and stories for which he is best known. His novels and stories live by their easy-going style, their busy plots and above all their technical swagger. His ideas are dazzlingly ingenious, and the more extraordinary the science, the more matter-of-fact its presentation. This gives his writing powerful appeal: flattered that we know more science than we thought we did, we feel that we are sharing in the wonders Asimov reveals rather than (as with most SF writers) merely gaping in astonishment.

THE FOUNDATION SAGA (1951 TO PRESENT DAY)

The first three books, a self-contained trilogy, appeared in the 1950s; Asimov began adding new novels 30 years later, and three have so far appeared. The Saga is 'space opera' (SF soap opera) on a huge scale, an account of political manoeuvrings among nations and civilisations of the far future. Hari Seldon, a professor of psychohistory (statistical and psychological prediction of the future) foresees a disastrous era of war in the galactic empire, and establishes two Foundations on the galaxy's edge, dedicated to safeguarding civilised knowledge until it is again required. The saga describes the nature and work of each Foundation, their uniting to defeat external threat (from an alien intelligence, 'the Mule') and their subsequent internecine struggles. For, like all human constructs, they are themselves prey to emotion and irrationality, to a bias which can lead towards dark as well as light.

The Foundation novels are Foundation, Foundation and Empire *and* Second Foundation. *Books in the continuation series are* Prelude to Foundation, Foundation's Edge *and* Foundation and Earth. *Asimov's other SF novels include*

READ ON

- **The best Asimov follow-ups are his robot books:** the short stories in *The Complete Robot* and the novels *The Caves of Steel*, *The Naked Sun*, and *The Robots of Dawn*.
- ▶ **To Asimov's short stories:** ▷Italo Calvino, *Cosmicomics*; ▷Robert Heinlein, *The Menace from Earth*.
- ▶ **To the Foundation saga:** ▷Frank Herbert, *Dune*; Gordon Dickinson, *Tactics of Mistake*. ▷Tom De Haan, *A Mirror for Princes* uses SF techniques to describe a mesmeric society not of the future but of the past.
- ▶ **To the Elijah Bailey books:** Larry Niven, *The Long ARM of Gil Hamilton*; Gene Wolfe, *Free Live Free* and, for anyone who finds Asimov's

Pebble in the Sky, The Stars Like Dust *and* The Currents of Space *(all on themes related to the Foundation Saga). His short SF stories are gathered in* The Early Asimov *Volumes 1-3.* Opus *is a useful anthology, an excellent sampler from his dazzling list of works.*

ideas too poker-faced, in need of sendup, ▷Douglas Adams, *Dirk Gently's Holistic Detective Agency.*

ATWOOD, MARGARET (BORN 1939)

Canadian writer of novels, short stories and poems.

Atwood is a poet as well as a novelist, and her gifts of precise observation and exact description illuminate all her work. She is fascinated by the balance of power between person and person, and by the way our apparently coherent actions and sayings actually float on a sea of turbulent unseen emotion. Her books often follow the progress of relationships, or of one person's self-discovery. The heroine of *Life Before Man*, for example, is caught up in a sexual quadrilateral (one of whose members, her lover, has just committed suicide), and our interest is as much in seeing how she copes with her own chaotic feelings as in the progress of the affair itself. In *Cat's Eye* (1989), a middle-aged painter returns to Toronto, remembers her dismal childhood and adolescence there, and finally comes to terms with the bullly who made her life miserable as a schoolchild and with that bully's appalling, manipulative mother. Many writers have tackled similar themes, but Atwood's books give a unique impression that each moment, each feeling, is being looked at through a microscope, as if the swirling, nagging 'real' world has been momentarily put aside for something more urgent which may just – her characters consistently put hope above experience – make sense of it.

THE HANDMAID'S TALE (1985)

This dazzling dystopian fiction, at once Atwood's most savage book and a departure from her usual Canadian stamping grounds, is set in the 21st-century Republic of Gilead. In this benighted state, fundamentalist Christianity rules and the laws are those of Genesis. Women are chattels: they have no identity, no privacy and no happiness except what men permit them. Offred, for example, is a Handmaid, and her life is devoted to one duty only: breeding. In Gilead, public prayers and hangings are the norm; individuality – even looking openly into a man's face or reading a woman's magazine – is punished by mutilation, banishment or death. The book shows Offred's struggle to keep her sanity and her identity in such a situation, and her equivocal relationship with the feminist Underground which may be Gilead's only hope.

READ ON

- *Surfacing* (about a woman trying to discover the truth about her relationship with her father, by re-examining her childhood in the Canadian wilderness).
- ▶ **To *The Handmaid's Tale*:** ▷George Orwell, *1984*.
- ▶ **To *Surfacing*:** ▷Angela Carter, *Heroes and Villains*; ▷George Turner, *The Sea and Summer*.
- ▶ **To *Cat's Eye*:** ▷Bernice Rubens, *Our Father*; Lynne Reid Banks, *Children at the Gate*; ▷Alison Lurie, *Imaginary Friends*.
- ▶ **To Atwood's work in general:** ▷Doris Lessing, *Martha Quest*; ▷Nadine Gordimer, *A Sport of Nature*; ▷Saul Bellow, *Herzog*.

Atwood's other novels include The Edible Woman *and* Bodily Harm. Dancing Girls *and* Bluebeard's Egg *contain short stories.* The Journals of Susannah Moodie *and* True Stories *are poetry collections, and her* Selected Poems *are also available.*

AUSTEN, JANE (1775–1817)

British novelist.

Austen loved the theatre, and the nearest equivalents to her novels, for pace and verve, are the social comedies of such writers as Sheridan or Goldsmith. The kind of novels popular at the time were epic panoramas (like those of ▷Sir Walter Scott), showing the human race strutting and swaggering amid stormy weather in vast, romantic landscapes. Austen preferred a narrower focus, concentrating on a handful of people busy about their own domestic concerns. Her books are about the bonds which draw families together and the ambitions and feelings (usually caused by grown-up children seeking marriage-partners) which divide them. Her plots fall into 'acts', like plays, and her dialogue is as precise and witty as in any comedy of the time. But she offers a delight available to no playwright: that of the author's own voice, setting the scene, commenting on and shaping events. She is like a bright-eyed, sharp-tongued relative sitting in a corner of the room watching the rest of the family bustle.

PRIDE AND PREJUDICE (1813)

Genteel Mr and Mrs Bennet and their five grown-up daughters are thrown into confusion when two rich, marriageable young men come to live in the neighbourhood. The comedy of the story comes from Mrs Bennet's mother-hen-like attempts at matchmaking, and the way fate and the young people's own inclinations make things turn out entirely differently from her plans. The more serious sections of the novel show the developing relationship between Elizabeth Bennet, the second daughter, and cold, proud Mr Darcy. She tries to 'tame' him, to show him the effects of his character on others – and in the process she both falls in love with him and is 'tamed' herself. Although secondary characters (henpecked Mr Bennet, snobbish Lady Catherine de Bourgh, Elizabeth's romantic younger sister Lydia, the dashing army officer Wickham and the conceited bore Mr Collins) steal the limelight whenever they appear, the book hinges on half a dozen magnificent set-piece scenes between Elizabeth and Darcy, the two headstrong young people we yearn to see realising their love for one another and falling into one another's arms.

Apart from a number of unfinished works (eg The Watsons;

READ ON

- *Emma* (about a young woman so eager to manage other people's lives that she fails, for a long time, to realise where her own true happiness lies); *Mansfield Park* (a darker comedy about a girl brought up by a rich, charming family who is at first dazzled by their easy brilliance, then comes to see that they are selfish and foolish, and finally, by unassuming persistence, wins through to the happiness we have always hoped for her).

▶ **To *Pride and Prejudice***: ▷Mrs Gaskell, *Wives and Daughters.*

▶ **To *Mansfield Park***: Joan Aiken, *Mansfield Revisited* – the best of many authors' attempts to use Austen's characters and equal Austen's style.

▶ **To Austen's work in general**: ▷William Thackeray, *Vanity Fair*; ▷E. M. Forster, *A Room With a View*;

Jane AUSTEN

PRIDE AND PREJUDICE *(social comedy in Regency England: choosing marriage-partners)*

'TAMING' OR 'BEING TAMED'

William **THACKERAY, VANITY FAIR**
(social comedy; girls conforming with or rebelling against society)

Edith **WHARTON, THE CUSTOM OF THE COUNTRY**
(social comedy, New York 1910s: young people prey on foolish elders)

Miles **FRANKLIN, MY BRILLIANT CAREER**
(young Australian, 1910s, preys on follies of European bourgeoisie)

ROMANCE

Georgette **HEYER, REGENCY BUCK**
(England, 1810s: will he tame her or will she tame him?)

Baroness **ORCZY, THE SCARLET PIMPERNEL**
(languid English milord is really romantic hero of French revolution)

Catherine **COOKSON, THE PARSON'S DAUGHTER**
(spirited girl 'tames' philandering husband in 19th-century English town)

Colleen **MCCULLOUGH, THE THORN BIRDS**
(Australian outback: will hero put priestly vocation before earthly love?)

COMEDY OF MANNERS

Anthony **TROLLOPE, BARCHESTER TOWERS**
(marriage and career-machinations in 19th-century English cathedral city)

H.G. **WELLS, KIPPS**
(personable young man makes his way in 1910s London society)

P.G. **WODEHOUSE, THE CODE OF THE WOOSTERS**
(problems in idyllic 1920s English country house? Ring for Jeeves . . .)

Mary **MCCARTHY, BIRDS OF AMERICA**
(likeable 1960s young American dismayed by Europe)

STYLISH, BEADY-EYED SATIRE

Mrs **GASKELL, CRANFORD**
(gossip and intrigue in small 1830s English town)

Barbara **PYM, A GLASS OF BLESSINGS**
(gossip and foolishness in 1950s London high Anglican parish)

Robertson **DAVIES, A MIXTURE OF FRAILTIES**
(intrigue and the arts in small 1950s Canadian town)

Alison **LURIE, FOREIGN AFFAIRS**
(Americans in 1970s England cling to each other for comfort and affection)

Sanditon), *Austen's output consists of six novels:* Northanger Abbey *(a spoof of romantic melodrama, unlike any of her other books),* Sense and Sensibility, Pride and Prejudice, Mansfield Park, Emma *and* Persuasion.

▷Alison Lurie, *Only Children*; the short stories of ▷Anton Chekhov and ▷Katherine Mansfield.

► The 'taming' aspect of Austen's plots has inspired a library of lighter fiction by others. The best by far – on occasion (eg in *Regency Buck* or *The Grand Sophy*) rivalling Austen's books themselves – are the Regency romances of ▷Georgette Heyer.

AUTOBIOGRAPHIES AND MEMOIRS (GHOSTED!)

Alan Brien, *Lenin: the Novel*
Margaret George, *The Autobiography of Henry VIII*
▷Robert Graves, *I Claudius*
▷Joseph Heller, *God Knows* (King David of Israel)
Stephen Marlowe, *The Memoirs of Christopher Columbus*
▷Robert Nye, *Falstaff*
Augusto Roa Bastos, *I, The Supreme* (Francia, dictator of Paraguay)

B

BAGLEY, DESMOND (1923–83)

British novelist.

Many of Bagley's best thrillers are set in Africa, and involve groups of people forced together by circumstance and battling not just outsiders and the environment but each other. In *Juggernaut* (1985), for example, an English adventurer leads a convoy through the war-torn state of Nyala. At the convoy's heart is a huge truck carrying the transformer for an oil-rig, and as it trundles across the countryside it becomes a mobile hospital, a battle-wagon and a symbol of hope for streams of refugees who flock round it like pilgrims, making their way to a new home somewhere beyond the war.

Bagley's other thrillers include The Golden Keel, High Citadel, Landslide, The Spoilers, The Freedom Trap, Flyaway, Windfall *and* Night of Error.

READ ON

- *Running Blind.*
- ▶ James Graham, *The Khufra Run*. Lionel Davidson, *The Rose of Tibet*. ▷C.S. Forester, *The Gun*.

BAILEY, PAUL (BORN 1937)

British novelist.

Bailey's novels explore despair and paranoia in spare, bleak prose: *At the Jerusalem* (1967) is set in an old people's home; in *A Distant Likeness* (1973) obsession with the crime he is investigating triggers a policeman's delusion and madness; *Peter Smart's Confession* (1977) is the testimony of an actor teetering on the edge of insanity. The hero of *Gabriel's Lament* (1986) is a middle-aged man, entirely dominated by his widower father, who finds release only after the old man dies.

READ ON

- *Old Soldiers.*
- ▶ ▷David Cook, *Happy Endings*. ▷John Updike, *The Poorhouse Fair*. ▷Susan Hill, *The Bird of Night*.

BALDWIN, JAMES (1924–87)

US writer of novels, plays and non-fiction.

In a series of non-fiction books (*Notes of a Native Son*; *The Fire Next Time*; *No Name in the Street*), Baldwin described the fury and despair of alienated US blacks, urging revolution as the only way to maintain racial identity in a hostile environment. His plays and novels tackle the same theme, but add two more, equally passionate: the way fundamentalist Christianity is a destructive force, and the quest for sexual identity in an amoral world. *Go Tell it on the Mountain* (1953) is a novel about a poor Harlem family torn apart by the pressures of born-again Christianity. *Another Country* (1962) shows people living lives of increasing desperation in a corrupt, all-engulfing and terrifying New York. *Giovanni's Room* (1956) is about an American in Paris, having to choose between his mistress and his (male) lover.

Baldwin's other novels are Tell Me How Long the Train's Been Gone, If Beale Street Could Talk *and* Evidence of Things Not Seen; *his short stories are in* Going to Meet the Man. *His plays include* The Amen Corner *and* Blues for Mr Charlie, *and his other non-fiction books are* Nobody Knows My Name, Nothing Personal *(with photos by Richard Avedon) and* A Rap on Race *(written with Margaret Mead).*

READ ON

- ▶ In Ralph Ellison, *The Invisible Man* a rootless black American travels the USA in search of identity, and finally – as the book becomes increasingly surreal – continues his quest in hell.
- ▶ A surrealist Harlem, a fantasy-land of crime, jazz, drugs and graveyard humour, is the location for Tama Janowitz's *Slaves of New York* – and also for Chester Himes' detective novels (eg *Cotton Comes to Harlem*), which, crime plots apart, are as unsparing as any of Baldwin's books.
- ▶ Maya Angelou's autobiographical sequence, beginning with *I Know Why the Caged Bird Sings*, gives sunnier reactions to equally abrasive Southern US black experience.
- ▶ Books as bleak as Baldwin's about the conjunction of sex, violence and despair: Jean Genet, *Querelle of Brest*; John Rechy, *The City of Night*; John Edgar Wideman, *A Glance Away*.

BALLARD, J.G. (JAMES GRAHAM) (BORN 1930)
British novelist.

Ballard's SF is pessimistic and satirical about the human race: each of his novels takes an aspect of the way we treat the planet, and each other, and extends it towards catastrophe. In some books (eg *The Drowned World*, about the melting of the polar ice-caps, or *The Burning World*, about the coming of permanent drought) our actions trigger natural disaster. In others (eg *Concrete Island*, about a man trapped on a motorway island, and *High Rise*, about the effects on human nature of living in ever-higher tower-blocks) we laboriously reconstruct the world as a single, megalopolitan prison-cell. His most savage, most dazzling SF novel is *The Unlimited Dream Company* (1979), a fable about human credulity. A youth who has never flown before steals a plane and crashes in the London suburbs. The people take him for a wonder-worker, even a messiah – and their credulity spirals into a religious cult involving orgiastic sex, telepathy and levitation. The story is told by the bewildered boy himself. At first disgusted and appalled, he gradually comes to believe in his own magic powers, and slowly but surely metamorphoses into the ultimate being, the god-figure everyone takes him for. Apart from SF, Ballard is best-known for *Empire of the Sun* (1984), a powerful autobiographical novel about a young teenager in a second-world-war Japanese internment camp.

Ballard's other books include The Four-Dimensional Nightmare, Hello America *(about European explorers of the future rediscovering a long abandoned USA) and* The Atrocity Exhibition/Love and Napalm: Export USA, *a tortured, surrealist meditation on politics, sex and automobile disasters.* The Voices of Time, Myths of the Near Future, Low-flying Aircraft *and the linked volume* The Vermilion Sands *are collections of short stories.*

READ ON

- *The Day of Creation* (about a scientist trying to find water in drought-stricken Africa, who sees a new river appear miraculously, becomes obsessed with it, and travels up it to find its source and hopefully understand himself).
- ▶ **To Ballard's bleak visions of human awfulness**, ▷George Turner, *The Sea and Summer*. ▷Robert Silverberg, *Master of Life and Death*. ▷Gore Vidal, *Kalki*.
- ▶ **To *The Atrocity Exhibition***: William Burroughs, *The Soft Machine*.

BALZAC, HONORÉ DE (1799–1850)
French novelist.

Photography was invented during Balzac's lifetime, and there was talk of using it to produce an encyclopedia of human types, catching each trade, profession and character in a suitable setting and at a particularly revealing moment. Balzac determined to do much the same thing in prose: to write a set of novels which would include people of every possible kind, described so minutely that the reader could envisage them as clearly as if they had been photographed. He called the project *The Human Comedy*, and although he died before completing it, it still runs to some 90 pieces of

READ ON

- *The Curé of Tours* (a similarly detailed, and almost equally moving, study of desolate old age).
- ▶ **To Balzac's power and emotional bleakness:** ▷Émile Zola, *Nana*; ▷François Mauriac,

fiction – which can be read separately – and includes over 2000 different characters.

OLD GORIOT (PÈRE GORIOT) (1834)

Goriot is a lonely old man obsessed by love for his two married daughters. He lives in a seedy Parisian boarding-house (whose contents and inhabitants Balzac meticulously describes), and gradually sells all his possessions, and even cuts down on food, to try to buy his daughters' love with presents. They treat him with a contempt he never notices – in fact everyone despises him except Rastignac, a student living in the same house. Goriot's death-bed scene, when he clutches Rastignac's hands thinking that his daughters have come to visit him at last, is one of Balzac's most moving passages, a deliberate reminiscence of King Lear's death in Shakespeare's play.

The best-known novels from The Human Comedy *are* César Birotteau *(about a shopkeeper destroyed by ambition),* Eugénie Grandet *(a love story, one of Balzac's few books with a happy ending), and* Cousin Bette *(about a man whose obsessive philandering tears his family apart).* Droll Tales *is a set of farcical short stories, similar to those in Giovanni Boccaccio's* Decameron *or* The Arabian Nights.

The Woman of the Pharisees; Theodore Dreiser, *An American Tragedy*; ▷Carson McCullers, *The Ballad of the Sad Café*; Hugh Walpole, *The Old Ladies*.

- ▶ **To his evocation of city life:** ▷Somerset Maugham, *Liza of Lambeth*; ▷Saul Bellow, *Mr Sammler's Planet*.
- ▶ **To his vision of the 'ant-hill of human aspiration', the senseless, self-destructive bustle of affairs:** ▷Charles Dickens, *Dombey and Son*; George Gissing, *New Grub Street*.

BARBER, NOEL (1911–88)

British novelist.

Barber wrote romantic thrillers, usually set in the Middle East. His books include *The Other Side of Paradise, Farewell to France* and *A Woman of Cairo* (1984), in which two lovers are drawn together and pushed apart by the pressure of events in war-torn Egypt.

READ ON

- • *Tanamera*.
- ▶ Valerie Fitzgerald, *Zemindar*. M.M. Kaye, *Shadow Moon*. ▷J.G. Farrell, *The Singapore Grip*. ▷Olivia Manning, *Fortunes of War*.

BARNES, DJUNA (1892–1982)

US novelist and short-story writer.

Nightwood (1936), Barnes' best-known novel, is a dark tale of lesbianism, adultery and madness among US exiles in Paris in the 1930s. T.S. Eliot compared it, for 'horror and doom', to Elizabethan tragedy; it is also like ▷Sartre's play *Huis Clos*, a glimpse of damned souls in an ultra-modern hell. The characters – a transvestite doctor, a womanising German baron, a frail young girl and the bisexual publicist for a travelling circus – spend their time alternately betraying one another emotionally or spending maudlin, boozy

READ ON

- ▶ ▷Jean Rhys, *Good Morning, Midnight*. ▷Angela Carter, *The Infernal Desire Machines of Doctor Hoffman*. Desmond Hogan, *A New Shirt*.

nights discussing their own and each other's erotic preferences. Barnes' style is a poetic version of the stream-of-consciousness monologues of Freud's patients, halfway between ▷Proust and Molly Bloom's soliloquy in ▷Joyce's *Ulysses*. *Nightwood* is no easy read, but it is compulsive and unforgettable.

Barnes' other fiction consists of the novel Ryder *and the story-collections* The Book of Repulsive Women, Spillway *(originally published with poems and plays, as* A Book *and* A Night Among the Horses*) and* Vagaries Malicieux. *She is also known for her plays, especially* The Antiphon.

BARNES, JULIAN (BORN 1946)

British novelist.

After two enjoyable but ordinary novels, *Metroland* and *Before She Met Me* – like early ▷Philip Roth novels transported to the UK – Barnes hit form in 1984 with *Flaubert's Parrot*. This is a dazzlingly ironical book about a biographer of ▷Flaubert so obsessed with his subject, so eager to investigate every piece of fluff on Flaubert's carpet or tea-stain on his crockery, that the quest utterly and ludicrously swallows his own identity. In 1986 Barnes followed this with a tour de force of an entirely different kind, *Staring at the Sun*. The heroine (who lives from the 1930s to the 2020s) is offered three main choices in her life, and after twice making the wrong decision (settling for the conventional) she uproots herself in old age, learns to fly and sets off to visit the Seven Wonders of the modern world. In *A History of the World in 10½ Chapters* (1989), Barnes describes a number of skin-of-the-teeth escapes for the human race, epic voyages from life-threatening reality to one mirage of the radiant future after another: Noah's Ark, the raft of the Medusa, a boatful of Jewish refugees, a film crew in the Amazon rain forest. The book also meditates on love – which, in Barnes' most ironical shaft of all, may be the solution to the human dilemma, a solution all his characters are too self-obsessed to see.

As well as novels under his own name, Barnes also writes private-eye thrillers as 'Dan Kavanagh'. They include Duffy, Going to the Dogs *and* Putting the Boot In.

READ ON

- **To *Flaubert's Parrot*:** ▷Vladimir Nabokov, *Pale Fire*.
- **To *Staring at the Sun*:** ▷David Cook, *Missing Persons*; ▷Gabriel García Márquez, *Love in the Time of Cholera*.
- **To *A History of the World in 10½ Chapters*:** ▷Michèle Roberts, *Mrs Noah*.

BATTLING WITH LIFE

(people at odds with the society around them)

▷James Baldwin, *Go Tell it on the Mountain*
▷Peter Carey, *Oscar and Lucinda*
▷Charles Dickens, *Oliver Twist*
▷Maxim Gorky, *Foma Gordeev*

▷Nathaniel Hawthorne, *The Scarlet Letter*
▷Somerset Maugham, *Liza of Lambeth*
▷John Steinbeck, *The Grapes of Wrath*
▷Émile Zola, *Nana*

Emotionally Ill-at-Ease (p 75); Perplexed by Life (p 196); Revisiting One's Past (p 209)

BECKETT, SAMUEL (1906–89)

Irish writer.

Novelist, poet and playwright, Beckett produced work both in French and English, issuing translations as he went along. Most of his novels, and his best-known play *Waiting for Godot*, first appeared in French. As a young man he was ▷Joyce's secretary, and his work owes debts to the monologue which ends *Ulysses* and to the dream-narratives of *Finnegans Wake*. His subject is the futility of human existence, and his characters (the narrators of his books) are tramps, cripples and the insane. His works would be unendurably bleak – many readers find them so – if they were not lit with a fantastical, death-defying black humour. He often wrote plays with aged silent film comedians in mind (Laurel and Hardy, Keaton), and the same kind of tatterdemalion, dignified slapstick marks his novels. Fascinating on the page, they leap even more to life when read aloud.

Beckett's main novels are Murphy, Watt *and the trilogy* Molloy, Malone Dies *and* The Unnameable. *His plays include* End Game, Krapp's Last Tape *and* Happy Days. *His poems are in* Collected Poems in English and French, More Pricks than Kicks *is a collection of early, Joycean short stories.*

READ ON

- ▶ Marguerite Duras, *The Square*. Desmond Hogan, *A New Shirt*. William Burroughs, *The Naked Lunch*.

BEERBOHM, MAX (1876–1956)

British artist and writer.

A caricaturist and satirist, Beerbohm published cartoons, parodies, essays and articles ridiculing literary and social figures of the day. His only novel, *Zuleika Dobson* (1911) is a send-up of the university-set romantic novels of Ouida (in which gels' hearts thud as they watch their heroes' rippling muscles in the rowing or boxing teams). Beerbohm turns Ouida's conventions on their heads. His Oxford undergraduates, whether gentlemen (world-weary and overbred) or scholars (weedy and obsessive) think of nothing but themselves, until Zuleika, the beautiful grand-daughter of the Warden of Judas College, sweeps into the university and every male in the place (even the statues on their pedestals)

READ ON

- • *Seven Men* (short stories).
- ▶ Nancy Mitford, *Don't Tell Alfred*. Angela Thirkell, *August Folly*. Jerome K. ▷Jerome, *Three Men in a Boat*. Noel Langley, *Cage Me a Peacock*. Oscar Wilde, *The Picture of Dorian Gray* takes

starts swooning for love of her. There are arguments, duels and suicide-pacts, and Zuleika is blind to them all. Her quarry is the Duke of Dorset, the handsomest, best-connected man in England, and her head will not rest easy, blessing the pillow it lies on, until she makes him her slave. But what, dear reader, if *she* should fall for *him* ...?

a darker view of similarly self-obsessed characters.

BEFORE THE WEDDING

Elizabeth Colegate, *Statues in a Garden*
▷Carson McCullers, *The Member of the Wedding*
David Nobbs, *A Bit of a Do*
Elizabeth North, *Worldly Goods*
▷Eudora Welty, *Delta Wedding*

BELLOW, SAUL (BORN 1915)

US novelist and playwright.

In Bellow's view, one of the most unexpected aspects of life in the modern world, and particularly in the post-Christian west, is that many people have lost all sense of psychological and philosophical identity. All Bellow's leading characters feel alienated from society. Some are content to suffer; others try to assert themselves, to invent an identity and live up to it – an attempt which is usually both bizarre and doomed. The hero of *The Adventures of Augie March* (1953), trying to model himself on one of ▷Hemingway's laconic men of action, takes his sophisticated girl-friend lizard-hunting in Mexico with a tame eagle, and is amazed when she leaves him. The hero of *Henderson the Rain King* (1959) goes on safari to darkest Africa, only to be taken prisoner by a remote people who think him a god-king and mark him for sacrifice. Devices like these warm Bellow's books, adding life and energy to what is already philosophically intriguing. His novels are compelling intellectual entertainments, thrillers of the mind.

HUMBOLDT'S GIFT (1975)

The book's hero, Charlie Citrine, is a wise-cracking, streetwise failure. He is a writer whose inspiration has run out, a husband whose wife is divorcing him and whose mistress despises him, an educated man terrified of brainwork. Unexpectedly, a legacy from a dead friend, a drunken, bawdy poet, turns out not to be the worthless pile of paper everyone imagines but a scenario which forms the basis for a hugely successful film. Wealth is now added to Citrine's problems, and he is battened on by tax officials, accountants, salesmen and an unsuccessful crook who tries to extort from him first money and then friendship. As the novel proceeds, Citrine keeps nerving himself to make the deci-

READ ON

- *Herzog* (about a panic-stricken intellectual who revisits the scenes of his past life trying to find clues to his psychological identity: cue for a magnificent travelogue through the city of Chicago, Bellow's consistent inspiration and this book's other central 'character').
- ▶ **To Bellow's theme of people searching for identity:** ▷Albert Camus, *The Fall*; ▷William Golding, *The Paper Men*; Max Frisch, *I'm Not Stiller*; ▷Jean Rhys, *Good Morning, Midnight*; Bernard Malamud, *A New Life*; ▷Margaret Atwood, *Surfacing*.
- ▶ **To his vision of the city (in his case, Chicago) as a metaphor for the**

sion – any decision – that will focus his life, and is hampered each time by ludicrous circumstances and by the contrast between his own inadequacy and the memory of his larger-than-life, dead friend.

Bellow's other full-length novels are Mr Sammler's Planet, Herzog, The Dean's December *and* More Die of Heartbreak. Dangling Man, The Victim, Seize the Day, A Theft *and* The Bellarosa Connection *are mid-length novellas, and his short stories are collected in* Mosby's Memoirs *and* Him With the Foot in his Mouth. *He has also written plays and a fascinating political memoir about a visit to Israel,* To Jerusalem and Back.

turbulence of the soul: James Plunkett, *Strumpet City* (set in pre-1914 Dublin); ▷Christina Stead, *The Beauties and the Furies* (set in 1930s Paris); Colin MacInnes, *City of Spades* (set in racially divided 1950s London).

BENNETT, Arnold (1867–1931)

British novelist and non-fiction writer.

Bennett wrote hundreds of thousands of words each year, and much of his output was pot-boiling. But his best novels and stories, set in the English Midlands (the area he called 'the Five Towns', now Stoke-on-Trent), are masterpieces. They deal in a realistic way with the lives and aspirations of ordinary people (factory hands, shop assistants, housewives), but are full of disarming optimism and fantasy. Bennett's characters have ambitions; they travel, they read, they dream. Apart from the Five Towns novels his best-known works are two books originally written as magazine-serials: *The Card* (about a bouncy young man whose japes outrage provincial society but who ends up as mayor) and *The Grand Babylon Hotel*, a set of linked stories about the guests and staff in a luxury hotel.

The Old Wives' Tale (1908)

The lives of two sisters are contrasted: vivacious Sophia and steady Constance. Sophia feels constricted by life in the Five Towns, falls for a handsome wastrel and elopes with him to Paris, where he deserts her. Constance meanwhile marries a clerk in her father's shop, and settles to a life of bored domesticity. The novel charts the sisters' lives, and includes memorable scenes of the 1870 siege of Paris in the Franco-Prussian War. Its concluding section unites the sisters, now elderly, and shows, as their lives draw to a close, that those lives were all they had, that neither achieved anything or made any impact on the world.

The Five Towns novels are Anna of the Five Towns, The Old Wives' Tale, Clayhanger, Hilda Lessways, These Twain *and* The Roll-Call. Riceyman Steps, *set in London, is grimmer and more Zolaesque.* Mr Prohack *is an entertainment, a good follow-up to* The Card. *Of Bennett's many other writ-*

READ ON

- *Clayhanger*; *Riceyman Steps*.
- ▶ ▷D.H. Lawrence, *The Rainbow*. ▷H.G. Wells, *Ann Veronica*. Theodore Dreiser, *Sister Carrie*. ▷Somerset Maugham, *Of Human Bondage*. ▷J.B. Priestley, *Angel Pavement*. Sherwood Anderson, *Winesburg, Ohio* is a set of stories echoing the feelings and lives of Bennett's characters in a small-town US setting.

ings, particularly fascinating are his Journals, *discussing such matters as his love of France, the meals he ate, the plays and novels he enjoyed, and above all his phenomenal day-to-day productivity.*

BENSON, E.F. (EDWARD FREDERIC) (1867–1940)

British novelist and non-fiction writer.

Although Benson wrote books of many kinds, he is best-known today for acid social comedies, and particularly for the 'Mapp and Lucia' series, televised with enormous success in the mid-1980s. His characters are well-to-do, middle-class Edwardians, whose chief interest in life is social one-upmanship. One's bridge-party, one's garden, one's paintings or one's recipes must simply outclass everyone else's, and if there is the slightest risk of failure, devious means must be employed.

MAPP AND LUCIA (1935)

In previous books in the series, we have already met Lucia, the social queen of Riseholme, and Miss Mapp, who holds the same position in Tilling. Now Lucia moves to Tilling for the summer with her friend Georgie Pillson, rents Mapp's beloved house Mallards, and proceeds to upstage Mapp socially at every moment and in every way. The war between the ladies is fought at garden parties, poetry evenings, dinner-parties (at which Lucia's recipe Lobster à la Riseholme is a major weapon), and finally reaches its climax – one of Benson's most preposterous inventions – on an upturned table in the English Channel.

Benson's books include school stories, biographies, reminiscences, ghost stories (collected as Spook Stories *and* More Spook Stories*), and a shoal of comic novels, similar in themes and wit to the 'Lucia' books, including the 'Dodo' series and the (slightly) more serious* Mrs Ames *and* Secret Lives.

READ ON

- *Queen Lucia*; *Paying Guests*.
- ▶ Tom Holt, *Lucia in Wartime* and *Lucia Triumphant* (sequels, as good as Benson at his best).
- ▶ Comparable authors of high social comedy, 1930s–1950s set: Gabriel Chevalier, *Clochemerle*; Nancy Mitford, *Love in a Cold Climate*; Angela Thirkell, *Before Lunch*.
- ▶ Social farce of Bensonian hilarity and sharpness, set in the present day: ▷Peter de Vries, *Reuben, Reuben*.

BIBLE:

Old Testament

▷Joseph Heller, *God Knows*
▷Thomas Mann, *Joseph and his Brethren*
▷Jeanette Winterson, *Boating for Beginners*

New Testament

▷Anthony Burgess, *The Kingdom of the Wicked*
Lloyd C. Douglas *The Big Fisherman*
Severia Huré, *I, Mary, Daughter of Israel*
Pär Lagerkvist, *Barabbas*
George Moore, *The Brook Kerith*
▷Michèle Roberts, *The Wild Girl*

Henryk Sienkiewycz, *Quo Vadis?*

Ancient Greece and Rome (p 9); Other People, Other Times (p 192)

BINCHY, MAEVE (BORN 1940)

Irish novelist.

Binchy's books are affectionate tapestries of the lives of ordinary people, often in small Irish towns in the earlier years of this century. 'Great' events happen offstage; the spotlight is on birth, friendship, marriage, death and the engrossing bustle of everyday life. Her style is gently satirical – village gossip turned into art – and her dialogue is warm with the cadences of Irish speech. Her novels include *Light a Penny Candle, Dublin Four, Firefly Summer, Silver Wedding,* and *Echoes* (1986), about a group of 1950s teenagers growing up in a quiet seaside resort. *The Lilac Bus* (1986) is a set of linked short stories about the passengers who travel regularly on a small country bus.

READ ON

- Edna O'Brien, *The Country Girls*. Elizabeth North, *Worldly Goods*. Rony Robinson, *The Beano*. Rosamunde Pilcher, *The Shell Seekers*. ▷Eudora Welty, *Delta Wedding*.
- Non-fiction – or lightly fictionalised – books of a similarly gentle, nostalgic kind: Laurie Lee, *Cider With Rosie* (nostalgic memoirs of childhood in a 1930s Gloucestershire village, of the English countryside as it used to be); Laura Ingalls Wilder, *The Little House on the Prairie* (much less schmaltzy than the TV series).

BLISH, JAMES (1921–75)

US novelist.

Blish's many SF books for children include a dozen novels based on the TV series *Star Trek*. His adult books range from space opera – for example the 'Cities in Flight' novels, in which a mechanism is devised to spin whole sections of the Earth's surface into space, where their inhabitants eagerly or apprehensively set about reinventing their own lives – to more serious works such as the 'After Such Knowledge' tetralogy, using the forms and styles of SF fic-

READ ON

- **To *A Case of Conscience***: *The Day after Judgement*, whose subject is the attempt to find a compromise between black magic, religion and modern science.

tion to discuss complex philosophical and religious ideas.

A Case Of Conscience (1959)

This book, one of the 'After Such Knowledge' tetralogy of self-contained novels, is claimed by some readers to be not only Blish's masterpiece, but one of the finest books in the SF genre. A Jesuit Earth-scientist on an unexplored, paradisal planet wonders whether the fact that he is a human being, one of God's supreme creations, gives him superiority over the alien inhabitants, who are an ethical but godless race of intelligent lizards. He decides that the planet is a creation of the Devil – and then has to face the idea that this is heresy, since only God is able to create.

The other books in the 'After Such Knowledge' tetralogy are Black Easter, Doctor Mirabilis *and* The Day After Judgement. *The 'Cities in Flight' novels are* They Shall Have Stars, A Life for the Stars, Earthman Come Home *and* A Clash of Cymbals. Blish's other books include The Seedling Stars, And All the Stars a Stage, Jack of Eagles *and* Midsummer Century. Anywhen *and* Galactic Cluster *are collections of short stories.*

- ▶ **To *Cities in Flight*:** *Jack of Eagles.*
- ▶ **To *A Case of Conscience*:** ▷Philip K. Dick, *The Transmigration of Timothy Archer.*
- ▶ **To Blish's work in general: ▷Frank Herbert,** *Dune*; ▷Isaac Asimov, *Foundation*; ▷J. G. Ballard, *The Burning World*; ▷Brian Aldiss, *The Helliconia Trilogy.*

BÖLL, Heinrich (1917–85)

German novelist and non-fiction writer.

For decades after the second world war and the 'economic miracle' which followed it, German novelists hovered over their country like doctors examining a particularly interesting patient. How could any nation be so outwardly flourishing and seem so dead inside? Were such things as student riots in the 1960s or the urban terrorism of the 1970s isolated phenomena or symptoms of a deeper-rooted sickness? Böll, a Roman Catholic, linked the malaise of society with another kind of moral disintegration, the collapse of faith – but instead of preaching or hectoring he tried to alert his readers with bitter, saturnine irony. He is at his most savage in short stories and medium-length novels: *The Safety Net* (about terrorism), *The Lost Honour of Katharina Blum* (satirising the gutter press), *The Unguarded House* (scathing about miracles, economic or religious). Böll's longer books spread his rage more widely – and paradoxically, although this makes them more relaxed, as pacy and witty as ▷Bellow's, the urbane tone makes their messages even more unsettling.

Group Portrait With Lady (Gruppenbild mit Dame) (1971)

Böll takes a 'typical' German citizen of the post-war years –

READ ON

- *Billiards at Half-past Nine* (a panoramic view of the last 50 years of German society, focussed on a single family); *The Clown* (a bleak study of one person's attempt to retain dignity and moral integrity, to say nothing of religious faith, in a society where such qualities are no longer valued).
- ▶ Robert Musil, *Young Törless.* Nathalie Sarraute, *Portrait of an Unknown Man.* J.P. Marquand, *The Late George Apley.* Janet Hitchman,

an inoffensive, dull woman in her 60s about whom the most fascinating information seems to be that she likes fresh rolls for breakfast – and tries to find out more about her by questioning her family, friends, neighbours, work-mates and old school-fellows. The method is familiar from TV documentary: a jigsaw puzzle of interlocking interviews, assembled to make a single picture. But two pictures in fact emerge: one of the woman herself and one of the teeming German society of which she is part. The book's style is brisk, witty and apparently uncontroversial, so that it is not till the end that we realise just what Böll is saying about Germany's moral plight.

Böll's other novels are And Where Were You, Adam?, Acquainted with the Night, Billiards at Half Past Nine *and* Women in a River Landscape. *His short stories are in* Absent Without Leave, Traveller, if you Come to Spa, Children are Civilians Too *and* The Casualty. What's To Become of the Boy? *is a brief, savage memoir of adolescence under the nazis;* Irish Journal *describes his stay in Ireland in the 1960s, and his affection for the Celtic, Catholic culture he found there.*

Meeting for Burial.

► **To Böll's work in general: Siegfried Lenz,** *The Heritage*; ▷Saul Bellow, *Mr Sammler's Planet.*

THE BOOKER PRIZE

The Booker Prize was established in 1968, and has become one of the most prestigious awards for British and Commonwealth writers of fiction in English. The winners so far are:

1969 ▷P. H. Newby, *Something to Answer For*
1970 ▷Bernice Rubens, *The Elected Member*
1971 ▷V. S. Naipaul, *In a Free State*
1972 John Berger, *G*
1873 ▷J. G. Farrell, *The Siege of Krishnapur*
1974 ▷Nadine Gordimer, *The Conservationist*
1975 ▷Ruth Prawer Jhabvala, *Heat and Dust*
1976 David Storey, *Saville*
1977 Paul Scott, *Staying On*
1978 ▷Iris Murdoch, *The Sea, The Sea*
1979 Penelope Fitzgerald, *Offshore*
1980 ▷William Golding, *Rites of Passage*
1981 ▷Salman Rushdie, *Midnight's Children*
1982 ▷Thomas Keneally, *Schindler's Ark*
1983 J. M. Coetzee, *The Life and Times of Michael K*
1984 ▷Anita Brookner, *Hôtel du Lac*
1985 ▷Keri Hulme, *The Bone People*
1986 ▷Kingsley Amis, *The Old Devils*
1987 Penelope Lively, *Moon Tiger*
1988 ▷Peter Carey, *Oscar and Lucinda*
1989 ▷Kazuo Ishiguro, *The Remains of the Day*
1990 ▷Antonia Byatt, *Possession*

BORGES, JORGE LUIS (1899–1987)
Argentinian short-story writer and poet.

Until the 1950s Borges worked as a librarian and was an admired poet – though, because his verse seems flat in translation, he was hardly known outside Spanish-speaking countries. But in the 1950s his 'fictions' began to appear in English, and his reputation spread world-wide. A 'fiction' is a short prose piece, ranging in length from a paragraph to a half a dozen pages. Some are short stories, in the manner of ▷Kipling, ▷Hemingway or ▷Kafka (whom Borges translated into Spanish). Others are tiny surrealist meditations, zen-like philosophical riddles or prose-poetry. A 20th-century writer produces a version of *Don Quixote* for modern times – and it is identical, word for word, to the original. A man meets a mysterious stranger by a riverside, and finds that the stranger is himself. The library of the Tower of Babel is meticulously described. A man writes about the terrifying prison which traps him – and only at the end reveals its name: the world.

LABYRINTHS (ENGLISH EDITION 1962)
This is a generous anthology of Borges' work, and gives the flavour particularly of the 'fictions'.

Borges' stories and fictions are in A Universal History of Infamy, Fictions, The Aleph, Dreamtigers, The Book of Sand *and* Doctor Brodie's Report. *His Selected Poems were published in English translation in 1972.*

READ ON

- *The Book of Imaginary Beings* (descriptions of 120 fanciful creatures from the weirder recesses of the world's imagination: the chimera, the Cheshire cat, the chonchon, the lunar hare, the elephant that foretold Buddha's birth, the 36 lamed wufniks, Haokah the thunder-god, Youwakee the flying girl, and so on).
- ▶ ▷Gabriel García Márquez, *The Innocent Erendira*. Robert Coover, *Pricksongs and Descants*. ▷Samuel Beckett, *More Pricks than Kicks*. ▷Italo Calvino, *Invisible Cities*. Michael Ayrton, *Fabrications*.
- ▶ **An unexpected parallel to Borges at his most surreal – so close at times that it seems like a send-up:** Woody Allen, *Without Feathers*.

BOWEN, ELIZABETH (1899–1973)
Irish novelist and short-story writer.

Although Bowen's themes were emotional – loneliness; longing for love; lack of communication – she wrote in a brisk and faintly eccentric style (italicising the most unlikely words, *for* example) which gives her stories an exhilarating

READ ON

- *The Heat of the Day*; *Eva Trout*.
- ▶ **To Bowen's novels:** ▷Henry James, *The*

feeling of detachment from the events and reactions they describe. She was especially skilful at evoking atmosphere in houses or locales: London streets and tube-stations during the second-world-war blitz, for example (the setting of many of her stories), become places of eerie fantasy rather than reality. Her concern, despite her characters' craving to preserve the social niceties, was to show 'life with the lid off' – and this, coupled with the unpredictability of her writing style, constantly edges her plots from actuality through dream to nightmare.

THE DEATH OF THE HEART (1938)

Portia, a naive 16-year-old orphan (in a more modern book she might be 12 or 13) goes to live with her stuffy half-brother and his brittle, insecure wife in fashionable 1930s London. Her innocence is in marked contrast to their world-weary sophistication, and they are as exasperated with her as she is with them. Then she falls in what she imagines to be love, and all parties are launched on an ever-bumpier emotional ride.

Bowen's other novels include The House in Paris, A World of Love *and* Eva Trout. *Her short stories are published in* Encounters, Ann Lee's, Joining Charles, The Cat Jumps *and the second-world-war collections* Look at All Those Roses *and* The Demon Lover.

Wings of the Dove; ▷Angus Wilson, *The Middle Age of Mrs Eliot*; ▷Iris Murdoch, *The Sandcastle*. Peter Taylor, *A Summons to Memphis* sets scenes of similar emotional ambiguity in the US mid-west.

- ▶ **To Bowen's short stories:** ▷Elizabeth Taylor, *A Dedicated Man*; ▷John Fowles, *The Ebony Tower.*

BOYD, MARTIN (1893–1969)

Australian novelist.

One of a large artistic family, Boyd originally trained as an architect, only taking up full-time writing in his 30s. He also spent much time in Europe, and writes in his autobiography of the pull between the cultural traditions of the Old World and the openness and opportunity of Australia. He turned all these themes and feelings into fiction. His principal characters are artistically sensitive people growing up in Australia, balancing the claims of family life against the need they feel to experience European art, culture and religion for themselves. He writes with malicious, ironical glee of large middle-class families, keeping up their pretensions and the façade of polite manners in what they feel is an exciting but barbarian environment. His best-known books are the 'Langton' tetralogy (1952–62): the 'biography' of Guy Langton and his extended family in the 80 years preceding the first world war. It centres on Guy's artistic and spiritual restlessness, but a major subsidiary theme is the gradual disintegration of a once tight-knit family as social opportunities in Australia increase and ties with the Old World grow less. The Langtons understand the past but have no sense

READ ON

- *The Montfords.*
- ▶ **To the theme of the disintegrating family:** ▷Thomas Mann, *Buddenbrooks.*
- ▶ **To the Australian theme:** ▷Miles Franklin, *My Brilliant Career*; ▷H.H. Richardson, *The Fortunes of Richard Mahony.*
- ▶ **To the theme of young people uneasy with their cultural background:** ▷Ford Madox Ford, *Parade's End*; ▷Willa Cather, *My*

of future opportunity; as Australia waxes, all they can do is wane.

The books in the Langton tetralogy are The Cardboard Crown, A Difficult Young Man, Outbreak of Love *and* When Blackbirds Sing. *Boyd's other novels include* Lucinda Brayford, Such Pleasure *and* The Montfords *(originally published under the pseudonym Martin Mills). His autobiographies,* A Single Flame *and* Day of My Delights, *and the travel-book* Much Else in Italy, *interestingly reflect the main themes of his fiction.*

Antonia; ▷J.D. Salinger, *The Catcher in the Rye.*

BOYD, William (born 1952)

British novelist and screenwriter.

Boyd's early books were serious farces, in the manner of ▷Waugh's *A Handful of Dust* or *Sword of Honour.* He is particularly biting about ruling-class English idiocy, and the grotesquely inappropriate settings in which it flourishes. *A Good Man in Africa* (1981) detailed the last, limp flourishes of colonialism; *An Ice Cream War* (1982) was set in the first world war; *Stars and Bars* (1984), the most farcical of all, is about an English innocent seriously at a loss in the lunatic world of the arts in the USA.

The New Confessions (1987)

The 'autobiography' of John James Todd, from inept adolescence at a hearty Scottish school, through ludicrous and ghastly first world war experiences, to a roller coaster career as one of the founding geniuses of German silent cinema. Throughout his life, Todd is obsessed by making a 9-hour epic based on Rousseau's *Confessions,* and is frustrated at every turn; by the coming of sound, the rise of Hitler, the second world war and McCarthyism. Farcical incidents, but none the less a substantial, sombre study of a man in thrall to his own glittering opinion of his past.

Boyd's other books are On the Yankee Station *(short stories) and* School Ties *(two TV scripts).*

READ ON

- **To the early books**: ▷Anthony Powell, *What's Become of Waring?*; ▷Malcolm Bradbury, *Stepping Westward.*
- **To *The New Confessions***: ▷Frederic Raphael, *California Time*; ▷Robertson Davies, *What's Bred in the Bone*; ▷Len Deighton, *Close-up*.

BRADBURY, Malcolm (born 1932)

British novelist and screenwriter.

A university professor, Bradbury writes sharp satires on academic life. The form and style of his first two novels were straightforward, but from *The History Man* onwards he began using experimental methods: fragmenting the plots into short scenes like those of TV plays, writing in the present tense, incorporating footnotes, commentaries and asides. The feeling is that each book is a game, meant to amuse the

READ ON

- *Stepping Westward* (about a naive English lecturer on an exchange visit to a liberal western US campus).
- **To *The History Man***:

author as well as the reader – a feature which sets Bradbury apart from all other 'campus' novelists.

THE HISTORY MAN (1975)

The book – far funnier than the TV series it inspired – is set in a ghastly British 'new' university, all bare concrete and graffiti. Its hero is an equally abrasive 'new' academic, the sociologist Howard Kirk. Kirk thinks that sociology is the only study relevant to the modern world, and that it should be a vehicle for radical change. He also believes in sleeping with as many female staff and students as he can entice to bed. He preaches left-wing politics in his seminars, humiliates anyone he suspects of right-wing opinions (for example young men who wear ties and call him 'Sir'), organises sit-ins and strikes, and strides happily through the destabilised, quivering society he creates all round him.

Bradbury's other novels are Eating People is Wrong, Stepping Westward, *and (the most experimental)* Rates of Exchange. Cuts *is a long short story,* Mensonge *a send-up of current French lit-crit pretentiousness and* No, Not Bloomsbury *a collection of essays, articles and reviews. He has also written TV plays and adaptations of his own and other people's books.*

▷Mary McCarthy, *The Groves of Academe*; ▷Vladimir Nabokov, *Pnin*; ▷Randall Jarrell, *Pictures from an Institution*; John Barth, *The End of the Road*.

▶ **To *Stepping Westward*:** ▷David Lodge, *Changing Places*. Michael Frayn, *Towards the End of the Morning* and Colin Douglas, *The Houseman's Tale* are 'campus' novels of a different kind, set not in universities but, respectively, in a newspaper office and a hospital. ▷Tom Sharpe, *Wilt* and its glorious, tasteless sequels are campus farce rather than comedy, entertainment for its own gross sake without a whiff of satire.

BRADBURY, RAY (BORN 1920)

US writer.

Bradbury is best known for his SF short stories, especially those in *The Martian Chronicles/The Silver Locusts* (1951), about a series of encounters between travellers from nuclear-devastated Earth and the elusive, telepathic and gentle inhabitants of Mars. His best-known novel, *Fahrenheit 451* (1953) is very different. It is a future-fantasy, set in a bland but fascist society where books are banned and burned, for fear that the ideas in them might spark political unrest. In later books, such as *Something Wicked This Way Comes* and *Death is a Lonely Business*, Bradbury wrote horror-thrillers somewhat in the manner of ▷Stephen King. *The Golden Apples of the Sun, The Illustrated Man* and *A Memory of Murder*.

READ ON

▶ **To *The Martian Chronicles*:** ▷H. G. Wells, *The First Men in the Moon*; ▷Ursula K. Le Guin, *The Word for World is Forest*.

▶ **To *Fahrenheit 451*:** ▷Aldous Huxley, *Brave New World*; ▷Robert Graves, *Seven Days in New Crete*; ▷Margaret

Atwood, *The Handmaid's Tale*.

► **To *Something Wicked This Way Comes***: ▷Stephen King, *Pet Sematary*; ▷James Herbert, *Moon*.

BRADFORD, Barbara Taylor

British novelist.

Bradford's books – many set in the north of England – are stories of characterful young women who rise in the worlds of business and society despite all obstacles. Her best-known books are *A Woman of Substance*, *Hold the Dream* and *To Be the Best*.

READ ON

- *Act of Will*.

► Nicola Thorne, *Where the Rivers Meet*. Audrey Howard, *Ambitions*. Pamela Oldfield, *The Gooding Girl*. ▷Judith Krantz, *Princess Daisy*.

BRENT OF BIN BIN: see FRANKLIN, Miles

BRONTË, Charlotte (1816–55)
BRONTË, Emily (1818–48)

British novelists.

Much has been made of the Brontës' claustrophobic life in the parsonage at Haworth in Yorkshire, and of the way they compensated for a restricted and stuffy daily routine by inventing wildly romantic stories. Their Haworth life was first described by a novelist (▷Gaskell), and is as evocative as any fiction of the time. In some ways it colours our opinion of their work: for example, if the third sister, Anne, had not been a Brontë, few people would nowadays remember her novels, which are pale shadows of her sisters' books. But Charlotte and Emily need no biographical boosting. They were geniuses, with a (remarkably similar) fantastical imagination, a robust, melodramatic view of what a 'good story' ought to be, and a pre-Freudian understanding of the dark places of the soul. Their brooding landscapes and old, dark houses may have been drawn from life, but what they made of them was an original, elaborate and self-consistent world, as turbulent as dreams.

Jane Eyre (by Charlotte Brontë, 1847)

The plot is a romantic extravaganza about a poor governess who falls in love with her employer Mr Rochester, is prevented from marrying him by the dark secret which

READ ON

- **To *Jane Eyre***: *Wuthering Heights*.
- **To *Wuthering Heights***: *Jane Eyre*.

► **To *Jane Eyre***: ▷Daphne Du Maurier, *Rebecca*; ▷Jean Rhys, *Wide Sargasso Sea*; ▷Margaret Mitchell, *Gone With the Wind*; George Douglas Brown, *The House With the Green Shutters*.

► **To *Wuthering Heights***: R.D. Blackmore, *Lorna Doone*; ▷Thomas Hardy, *Tess of the d'Urbervilles*; ▷Iris Murdoch, *The*

shadows him, and only finds happiness on the last page, after a sequence of melodramatic and unlikely coincidences. The book's power is in its counterpointing of real and psychological events. We read about storms, fires, wild-eyed creatures gibbering in attics and branches tapping at the windows – but what we are really being shown is the turmoil in Jane's own soul, the maturing of a personality. This emotional progress, magnificently described, unifies the book and transmutes even its silliest events to gold.

Unicorn (about the turbulent passions of a more modern heroine).

WUTHERING HEIGHTS (BY EMILY BRONTË, 1847)

The story begins in the 1770s, when a rich Yorkshire landowner, Earnshaw, brings home a half-wild, sullen foundling he names Heathcliff. Heathcliff grows up alongside Earnshaw's own children, and falls in love with Cathy, the daughter. But he overhears her saying that she will never marry him because she is socially above him – and the rest of the novel deals with his elaborate revenge on her whole family and the way the emotional poison is eventually neutralised. As in *Jane Eyre*, desolate moorland and lonely, rain-lashed houses are used as symbols of the passions in the characters' hearts. Heathcliff, in particular, is depicted as if he were a genuine 'child of nature', the offspring not of human beings but of the monstrous mating of darkness, stone and storm.

All three sisters wrote Wordsworthy, nature-haunted poetry. Emily's only completed novel was Wuthering Heights; *Charlotte's were* Jane Eyre, The Professor *and* Villette; *Anne's were* Agnes Grey *and* The Tenant of Wildfell Hall.

BROOKNER, ANITA (BORN 1928)

British novelist.

Brookner's novels are written in trim, witty prose, style for its own sake, a civilised delight. This exactly suits the characters of the people in her stories. They are middle-aged, upper-middle-class women (professors, librarians, novelists): well-off, well-tailored, well-organised and desperately lonely. Something has blighted their emotional lives, leaving them to order their comfortable, bleak existences as best they can, to fill their days. The books show us what brought them to their condition – usually the actions of others; husbands, parents or friends – and sometimes tell us how the problem is resolved. In 'well-made' stage and film dramas of the 1930s, women were always blinking back tears and bravely facing the future. Brookner's heroines, except that they have lost even the power to cry, try to do the same.

READ ON

- • *Hôtel du Lac.*
- ▶ Elizabeth Jane Howard, *Something in Disguise.* Edward Candy, *Scene Changing.* A. S. Byatt, *The Virgin in the Garden.* Jenny Diski, *Rainforest.* Susan Fromberg Shaeffer, *The Injured Party.*

LOOK AT ME (1983)

Frances Hinton, librarian at a medical research institute,

lives a disciplined, unvarying existence which she compares wistfully with what she imagines to be the exuberant, exciting lives of the research workers and others who use the books. She is 'taken up' by one of the most brilliant men, dazzling as a comet, and by his emotionally extrovert wife. She falls in love, and imagines that she is loved in return. But what looks like being a sentimental education in fact teaches her only that all human beings are islands, and that unless we hoard our inner lives and treasure our privacy, we will lose even what peace of mind we have.

Brookner's other novels are A Start in Life, Providence , H, A Friend from England, Latecomers *and* Lewis Percy. *She is an expert on fine art, and has published books about the painters Watteau, Greuze and David.*

BUCHAN, JOHN (1875–1940)

British novelist.

Buchan's thrillers play virtuoso variations on the same basic plot. A stiff-upper-lipped hero (often Richard Hannay) discovers a conspiracy to End Civilisation as We Know It, and sets out single-handed, or with the help of a few trusted friends, to frustrate it. He is chased (often by the police as well as by the criminals), and wins through only by a combination of physical courage and absolute moral certainty. The pleasure of Buchan's novels is enhanced by the magnificently-described wild countryside he sets them in (usually the Scottish highlands or the plains of southern Africa), and by their splendid gallery of minor characters, the shopkeepers, tramps, local bobbies and landladies who help his heroes, often at enormous (if shrugged-off) personal risk.

THE THIRTY-NINE STEPS (1915)

Richard Hannay, returning from South Africa, is told by a chance American acquaintance of a plot to invade England. Soon afterwards the American is killed and Hannay is framed for his murder. To escape two manhunts, one by the conspirators and the other by the police, he takes to the hills, and only after 300 pages of breathtaking peril and hair's-breadth escapes does he succeed in saving his country and clearing his name.

Buchan's other thrillers include Huntingtower, John MacNab *and* Witchwood *(all set in Scotland), and the Hannay books* Greenmantle, Mr Standfast *and* The Three Hostages. *He also wrote lively biographies (of ▷Scott, the emperor Augustus and Oliver Cromwell), and an autobiography,* Memory Hold-the-Door.

READ ON

- *Greenmantle*; *Mr Standfast*; *Prester John* (an African adventure as exciting and bizarre as anything by ▷H. Rider Haggard, whose *She* makes an excellent follow-up).
- ▶ Erskine Childers, *The Riddle of the Sands*. ▷Geoffrey Household, *Rogue Male*. ▷Ken Follett, *Storm Island/The Key To Rebecca*. ▷Helen MacInnes, *The Snare of the Hunted*. Craig Thomas, *Firefox*. ▷Robert Ludlum, *The Gemini Contenders*.

BUCK, Pearl S. (Sydenstricker) (1892–1973)

US writer.

The daughter of US missionaries in China, Buck taught in that country in her twenties, began writing in her thirties, and won the Nobel Prize for Literature in 1938. As well as novels, she published plays, children's books, essays, political studies, memoirs and travel books. She is best known for her 1930s trilogy *The Good Earth, Sons* and *A House Divided,* an enormous family saga about farmers in China coping with the land, the weather, political upheavals, and above all with the stresses and strains of family life, their own personalities and the relationships between incompatible characters and people from different generations.

Buck's other novels include This Proud Heart, Dragon Seed, Imperial Woman *and* Letter from Peking. The Exile *and* Fighting Angel: Portrait of a Soul *are biographies of her parents, fascinating accounts of religious fervour in an alien land.*

READ ON

- *This Proud Heart.*
- ▶ Mikhail Sholokhov, *And Quiet Flows the Don* (on remarkably similar themes, and with an equally epic sweep, but set in the USSR). ▷Eleanor Dark, *The Timeless Land* and its sequels (about the first European settlers in Australia); Lewis Grassic Gibbon, *A Scots Quair* (set in Scotland).

BURGESS, Anthony (born 1917)

British novelist and non-fiction writer.

Originally a composer, Burgess began writing books in his mid-30s, and since then has poured out literary works of every kind, from introductions to ▷Joyce (*Here Comes Everybody/Re Joyce*) to filmscripts, from opera libretti to book-reviews. Above all he has written novels, of a diversity few other 20th-century writers have ever equalled. They range from fictionalised biographies of Shakespeare (*Nothing Like the Sun*) and the early Christian missionaries (*The Kingdom of the Wicked*) to farce (the four Enderby stories, of which *Inside Mr Enderby* is the first and *Enderby's Dark Lady* is the funniest), from experimental novels (*The Napoleon Symphony,* about Napoleon, borrows its form from Beethoven's Eroica Symphony) to semi-autobiographical stories about expatriate Britons in the Far East (*The Malaysian Trilogy*). The literary demands of Burgess' books vary as widely as their contents: the way he finds a form and style to suit each new inspiration is one of the most brilliant features of his work.

A Clockwork Orange (1962)

In a grim future Britain, society is divided into the haves, who live in security-screened mansions in leafy countryside, and the have-nots, who swagger in gangs through the decaying cities, gorging themselves on violence. The book is narrated by the leader of one such gang, and is written in a private language, a mixture of standard English, cockney

READ ON

- *Earthly Powers* (a blockbuster embracing every kind of 20th-century 'evil', from homosexual betrayal to genocide, and the Church's reluctance or inability to stand aside from it).
- ▶ **To *A Clockwork Orange*:** ▷Aldous Huxley, *Brave New World*; ▷Margaret Atwood, *The Handmaid's Tale*; ▷Russell Hoban, *Riddley Walker.*
- ▶ **To Burgess' historical novels:** John Hersey, *The Wall*; ▷Michèle Roberts, *The Wild Girl.*
- ▶ ***To The Malaysian Trilogy*:** ▷Paul

slang and Russian. (Burgess provides a glossary, but after a few pages the language is easy enough to follow, and its strangeness adds to the feeling of alienation which pervades the book.) The young man has committed a horrific crime, breaking into a house, beating up its owner and raping his wife, and the police are 'rehabilitating' him. His true 'crime', however, was not action but thought – he aspired to a way of life, of culture, from which his class and lack of money should have barred him – and Burgess leaves us wondering whether his 'cure' will work, since he is not a brute beast (as the authorities claim) but rather the individuality in human beings which society has chosen to repress.

Burgess' other novels include a reflection on what he sees as the death-throes of modern western civilisation, 1985, *and a gentler, ▷Priestleyish book about provincial English life earlier this century,* The Piano-players. Little Wilson and Big God *is autobiography,* Urgent Copy *and* Homage to Qwert Yuiop *are collections of reviews and literary articles and* The Devil's Mode *is a collection of short stories.*

Theroux, *Jungle Lovers*.

▶ **To the Enderby comedies:** ▷David Lodge, *Small World*; ▷Peter De Vries, *Reuben, Reuben*.

C

CALVINO, ITALO (1923–85)

Italian novelist and short-story writer.

Calvino's first works followed the grim neo-realist tradition of the late 1940s, treating contemporary subjects in an unsparing, documentary way. But in the 1950s he decided to change his style, to write (as he put it) the kind of stories he himself might want to read. These were fantastic, surrealist tales, drawing on medieval legend, fairy stories, SF and the work of such 20th-century experimental writers as ▷Kafka and ▷Borges. The style is lucid and poetic; the events, however bizarre their starting-point, follow each other logically and persuasively; the overall effect is magical. In *Cosmicomics* huge space-beings play marbles with sub-atomic particles and take tea with one another as decorously as any Italian bourgeois family. The people in *The Castle of Crossed Destinies* are struck magically dumb, and have to tell each other stories using nothing but tarot cards. In *Invisible Cities* Marco Polo invents fantasy-cities to tickle the imagination of Kubla Khan. Calvino's wide-eyed, bizarre fantasy has been imitated but never surpassed; he is one of the most entrancing writers of the century.

OUR ANCESTORS (1951–9)

This book contains a full-length novel (*The Baron in the Trees*) and two long stories. In *The Baron in the Trees* a boy abandons the ground for the treetops and – in one of Calvino's most sustained and lyrical tours-de-force – lives an entire, fulfilled life without ever coming down to earth. In *The Cloven Viscount* a medieval knight is split in two on the battlefield – and each half goes on living independently, one good, one bad, deprived of the link which made them a

READ ON

- *Invisible Cities*; *Cosmicomics*.
- ▶ John Gardner, *Vlemk the Box-painter* (a long medieval allegory, in the collection *The Art of Living and Other Stories*, which otherwise contains modern tales). ▷Thomas Mann, *The Holy Sinner*. T.H. White, *The Sword in the Stone*.
- ▶ **Good short-story follow-ups:** ▷Jorge Luis Borges, *Fictions* ; ▷Martin Amis, *Einstein's Monsters*; ▷Angela Carter, *The Bloody Chamber*.

whole human being and gave them moral identity. In *The Non-Existent Knight* an empty suit of armour takes on its own identity, fighting, discussing tactics, brawling – and forever yearning after the reality of life, the psychological and emotional fullness which it/he can never know.

Calvino's neo-realist books are The Path to the Nest of Spiders *(a novel) and* Adam, One Afternoon *(short stories). His fantasies are collected in* T Zero, Cosmicomics, Invisible Cities, Our Ancestors, The Castle of Crossed Destinies, Mr Palomar *and* The Watcher and Other Stories. Italian Folk-Tales *reworks traditional material in a similar, uniquely personal way.*

CAMUS, ALBERT (1913–60)

French novelist and non-fiction writer.

Throughout his life, in newspaper articles, plays, essays and novels, Camus explored the position of what he called *l'homme revolté*, the rebel or misfit who feels out of tune with the spirit of the times. His characters recoil from the values of society. They believe that our innermost being is compromised by conformity, and that we can only liberate our true selves if we choose our own attitude to life, our day-to-day philosophy. Camus compared the human condition to that of Sisyphus in Greek myth, forever rolling a stone up a hill only to have it crash back down every time it reached the top – and said that the way to cope with this situation was to abandon ambition and concentrate on the here and now. But despite his uncompromising philosophy, his books are anything but difficult. His descriptions of sun-saturated Algeria (in *The Outsider*), rainy Amsterdam (in *The Fall*) or disease-ridden, rotting Oran (in *The Plague*) are fast-moving and evocative, and he shows the way inner desolation racks his heroes with such intensity that we sympathise with every instant of their predicament and long, like them, for them to break through into acceptance, into happiness.

THE PLAGUE (1947)

Plague ravages the Algerian town of Oran. Quarantined from the outside world, the citizens cope with their tragedy as best they can, either clinging to the outward forms of social life (petty city ordinances; the formalities of religion) or pathetically, helplessly suffering. (For Camus' original readers, the novel was an allegory of France under wartime nazi occupation.) At the heart of the story are Dr Rieux (the story-teller) and a group of other intellectuals. Each has different feelings about death, and for each of them the plague is not only a daily reality, an external event which has to be

READ ON

- *The Fall*.
- ▶ ▷Saul Bellow, *The Victim*. ▷Hermann Hesse, *Rosshalde*. ▷William Golding, *The Spire*. Carlo Gébler, *Work and Play*. Simone de Beauvoir, *The Mandarins*. Paul Bowles, *The Sheltering Sky*. More extrovert books, cloaking the philosophy in action and comedy respectively: ▷Graham Greene, *A Burnt-Out Case*; ▷Joseph Heller, *Something Happened*.

endured, but a philosophical catalyst, forcing them to decide what they think about the world and their place in it.

As well as in novels, Camus set out his philosophy in two substantial essays, The Rebel *(L'homme revolté) and* The Myth of Sisyphus. *His plays are* Caligula, Cross Purpose, The Just Assassins *and* State of Siege *(a stage version of* The Plague*).* Exile and the Kingdom *is a collection of short stories.*

CAREY, PETER (BORN 1943)

Australian novelist.

A common theme of Australian writers, from ▷Miles Franklin to ▷Patrick White, from ▷Eleanor Dark to ▷Thomas Keneally, is the way discovering the vastness of the continent opens up psychological chasms in the souls of their leading characters. Carey follows this grand tradition, but instead of concentrating on Australian vistas, as most of these other writers do, he focuses on the inner torment and turmoil of his people, their precarious grasp on the condition of humanity. Many critics compare him to ▷Dickens, for depth of characterisation and richness of detail and incident. He is certainly just as good, and (because he never moralises so openly) he is many times more readable.

OSCAR AND LUCINDA (1988)

Oscar Hopkins is a freak of nature; a clumsy, obstinate Anglican clergyman with a genius for gambling. Lucinda Leplastrier is an heiress who buys a glassworks in the hope that it will be her ticket to equality with men. Alas, for this is the 1850s, both are constricted by the manners and bigotries of their time. They end up in Sydney, planning to transport a glass-and-steel church deep into the outback – a gamble as ludicrous and as pointless as anything else in their anguished, unsatisfied lives. They think that they are taking on the whole continent of Australia; in fact their battles are chiefly against themselves.

Carey's other novels are Bliss *and* Illywhacker. The Fat Man in History *is a collection of short stories.*

READ ON

- *Illywhacker* (the 'autobiography' of an outrageous boaster and liar, who has, it seems, personally supervised the entire history of white people in Australia).
- ▶ Equally powerful studies of self-exploration: ▷Patrick White, *Voss*; ▷Thomas Keneally, *The Playmaker*; Tony Weeks-Pearson, *Dodo*.
- ▶ Equally lacerating about religion faced by the hugeness of the world (this time in 17th-century Canada): ▷Brian Moore, *Black Robe*.
- ▶ ▷David Cook, *Sunrising*, imagines the 19th century with a mixture of unblinking power and simple compassion very similar to Carey's.

CARR, PHILIPPA (BORN 1906)
British novelist.

'Philippa Carr' is one of the pseudonyms of ▷Eleanor Hibbert. She writes historical romances, showing the effect of great events on ordinary people's lives. Her best-known books are the *'Daughters of England' series*; other titles include *The Witch from the Sea, Sara Band of Two Sisters* and *Lament for a Lost Lover.*

READ ON

- Jane Aiken Hodge, *Judas Flowering.* Juliette Benzoni, *'Catherine' series.* Pamela Bennetts, *A Dragon for Edward.*

CARTER, ANGELA (BORN 1940)
British novelist and non-fiction writer.

Carter's inspiration includes fairy tales, Jung's theory of the collective unconscious, horror movies and the fantasies of such writers as ▷Poe and ▷Shelley. Above all, she is concerned with female sexuality and with men's sexual predations on women. Her books range from Gothic reworkings of fairy tales (*The Bloody Chamber*) to such surrealist nightmares as *The Passion of New Eve* (see right). The novels begin with dream-images, and spiral quickly into fantasy. In the opening chapter of *The Magic Toyshop* (1967), for example, 15-year-old Melanie walks in a garden at night in her mother's wedding dress – a common, if none too reassuring dream. Soon afterwards, however, Melanie's parents die, she is fostered by a mad toymaker-uncle, and the book climaxes when she is forced to re-enact the myth of Leda and the Swan with a life-sized puppet-swan. At first sight such stories seem little more than an upmarket literary equivalent of the occult, sex-and-sadism shockers of James ▷Herbert or Stephen ▷King. But Carter's books are less titillating than psycho-political. They are nightmare-visions, designed to induce self-examination and to lead to change.

NIGHTS AT THE CIRCUS (1984)
Walser, a reporter, is investigating the claims of Fevvers, a winged trapeze artist who may or may not be an angel disguised as a blowsy, turn-of-the-century circus artiste. The story begins with wide-eyed accounts of Fevver's early life in a brothel, the object of strange and violent male lusts, and continues as she and Walser tour Russia with Colonel Kearney's magical, surrealist circus. At first *Nights at the Circus* seems to be jollying up Carter's usual fascination for digging in the darker corners of society, and its gusto and wit continue to the end. But as the story proceeds, events become ever more sinister, and human endeavour is shown more and more to be a hopeless, grubby farce.

Carter's other novels are Shadow Dance, Several Perceptions, Heroes and Villains, Love *and* The Infernal Desire

READ ON

- *The Passion of New Eve.* In a near-future USA where armies of blacks, feminists and pubescent children are waging guerrilla war, the young man Evelyn hides in the California desert, only to be kidnapped by devotees of the multi-breasted, all-engulfing Earth Mother, who rapes him, castrates him and remakes him as a woman, Eve.
- **To *Nights at the Circus*:** ▷David Cook, *Sunrising*; ▷Charles Dickens, *Nicholas Nickleby*; Bamber Gascoigne, *The Heyday*.
- **To Carter's work in general**: D.M. Thomas, *The White Hotel.* ▷Margaret Atwood, *The Handmaid's Tale*; ▷Jeanette Winterson, *Sexing the Cherry*; ▷Gore Vidal, *Myra Breckinridge.*

Machines of Dr Hoffman. The Sadeian Woman *is non-fiction, a study of the social and sexual potential of women.* Fireworks *collects short stories (among her most disturbing works), and* Nothing Sacred *collects essays and journalism.*

CATHER, Willa (1876–1947)

US novelist.

Most of Cather's books are set in the south-western USA, and are about settlers (often European immigrants) coming to terms with the wilderness. But there is no Hollywood melodrama: her interests are in the contrast between civilised feelings and the wild natural environment, in psychological growth and change. In two characteristic books, *My Antonia* and *A Lost Lady*, the central female characters (the ones who change) are described by men who have watched them, and loved them, from a distance since childhood – a device which allowed Cather the objective, emotional distance from her characters which she preferred. This objectivity, and the elegance of her style, are two of the most enjoyable features of her books. Her sentences seem placid and unhurried: every event, every description seems to be given the same measured treatment. But nothing is extra. Every phrase has emotional or philosophical resonance, and after a few pages the reader is drawn into the narrative, hypnotised by nuance.

Death Comes For The Archbishop (1927)

Based on true events, and on diaries and letters by real people, this novel tells of two French Catholic missionaries to New Mexico in the second half of the 19th century. The book is partly about landscape, and contains magnificent descriptions of the desert. But it is mainly concerned with relationships: between the two priests, friends for many years, between the humans and their animals (who have to carry them on long, lonely desert journeys from one Christian settlement to another), and between the missionaries' ancient European culture and the stripped-to-essentials, 'primitive' habits of life and mind of their New Mexican flock. The book's title is not a promise of high drama. It refers to a Holbein painting, and suggested to Cather the feeling of frozen movement, of life arrested at the instant of recording, which she found in paintings and tried to recapture in her prose.

Two of Cather's novels, The Song of the Lark *and* Lucy Gayheart, *are about young women torn between the claims of family life and an artistic, musical career.* O Pioneers!, *like* My Antonia, *is about foreign immigrants settling in the wilderness. The main character of* The Professor's House *is a*

READ ON

- *Shadows on the Rock* (a similarly quiet book about the impact of the American wilderness on Europeans, this time 17th-century explorers in Quebec).
- ▶ Janet Lewis, *The Trial of Sören Kvist.* ▷Hermann Hesse, *Rosshalde*. George Moore, *The Brook Kerith* (about Joseph of Arimathea). ▷Patrick White, *A Fringe of Leaves*. Neil M. Gunn, *The Well at the World's End*.

successful academic who suddenly feels that he has failed, that lack of danger (emotional, intellectual or physical) has blighted his life. Other novels are One of Ours *and* My Mortal Enemy. Obscure Destinies *is a collection of short stories.*

CHANDLER, RAYMOND (1888–1959)

US novelist.

In the 1930s Chandler (an ex-businessman and journalist) began writing gangster-stories for magazines, treating violence, prostitution and betrayal in the cynical, hard-boiled style popular in films of the time. His ambition was to replace the kind of detective novels then fashionable (stories of bizarre crimes solved by wildly eccentric detectives, distantly modelled on Sherlock Holmes: see ▷Christie; ▷Sayers) with books about realistic crimes, investigated in a plausible way by a detective who would be ordinary, with recognisable human hopes, fears and reactions. Philip Marlowe (Chandler's private-eye hero) is an honest, conscientious man who sweats, cowers and lusts just like anyone else. He narrates the stories himself, in a wisecracking, deadpan style – 'The next morning was bright, clear and sunny. I woke up with a motorman's glove in my mouth, drank two cups of coffee and went through the morning papers' – which has made two generations of literary critics fawn over Chandler, claiming him, somewhat snobbishly, as one of the few 'true novelists' in US crime fiction.

FAREWELL, MY LOVELY (1940)

Marlowe, as often, is drifting with nothing particular to do when he is picked up (literally, by the scruff of the neck) by a muscle-bound ex-convict called Moose Malloy. From this simple event, as ripples spread on a pond, the story grows to take in a priceless necklace, kidnapping, blackmail and murder – and at its heart, like the still centre of a whirlwind, Marlowe slouches from clue to clue, a martyr to his own curiosity, pushing open every door and investigating each alleyway even though he knows, from long experience, that painful or nasty surprises are all he'll find.

Chandler's Marlowe novels are The Big Sleep, Farewell My Lovely, The High Window, The Lady in the Lake, The Little Sister, The Long Goodbye *and* Playback. Killer in the Rain *is a collection of short stories.*

READ ON

- *The Big Sleep*; *The Lady in the Lake.*
- ▶ ▷Dashiell Hammett, *The Maltese Falcon.* ▷Ernest Hemingway, *To Have and Have Not.* Ross MacDonald, *The Drowning Pool.* John Milne, *Shadow Play* (set in the London underworld). James Hadley Chase, *No Orchids for Miss Blandish* is a sombre, bleak book, Chandler without the wisecracks. Greg MacDonald, *Fletch* is the first of a series starring a pleasingly farcical private eye, a would-be Marlowe who succeeds only in being himself.

CHATWIN, BRUCE (1940–89)

British novelist and travel writer.

A journalist, Chatwin wrote precise, brisk prose – and it utterly belies the content of his books. Neither fiction nor

READ ON

- ▶ *The Viceroy of Ouidah* (about a

fact, they straddle the borders between dream and reality, reportage and philosophy. He was fascinated by nomads and the dispossessed, and inserted himself into his work as narrator, as rudderless and amazed as any of his characters. *In Patagonia*, ostensibly a travel book, is a magpie's nest of history, anecdote, reflection and self-revelation, set in a South America which seems to shimmer between fantasy and reality. *On the Black Hill*, ostensibly a novel, is a meditation on loneliness and the interaction between landscape and personality, set in the remote Welsh hills. Chatwin's masterpiece, *The Songlines* (1987), is a 'novel' about a white man, 'Bruce Chatwin', travelling in central Australia to investigate the Aboriginal 'songlines', the paths invisibly traced by the world's ancestors as they sang dream-reality into being. The book is raw with rage about both the whites ('caring people' and 'trash' alike) and the feckless, hopeless Aboriginals – and most savage of all about its dogged, put-upon central character, a 1960s hippie floundering out of his depth and out of his time, lost in someone else's dream.

Chatwin's other novels are The Viceroy of Ouidah *and* Utz. What Am I Doing Here *is a fascinating collection of his journalism.*

slave-trader exporting 'black gold' from West Africa to Brazil).

▶ ▷Keri Hulme, *The Bone People*, ▷Chinua Achebe, *Things Fall Apart*, Carlos Fuentes, *The Old Gringo*.

CHEEVER, John (1912–82)

US novelist and short-story writer.

Most of Cheever's stories appeared in the New Yorker between 1945 and 1975. The majority of his characters are prosperous New England commuters. They have beautiful houses in tidy neighbourhoods, their children go to good schools, and they can afford European holidays (often in Italy). But they are walking wounded: their emotions may be intact, but their hearts and consciences have been sliced away. They lacerate one another with sexual affairs, rows, petty-minded gossip and dispiriting, single-minded malice. The reason is that they believe that they are living in the American Dream – and by the day, by the minute, they find that it is a mirage. Cheever narrates their empty lives in sleek, ironic prose: his dialogue is particularly good at suggesting overtones of menace or longing in commonplace remarks.

The Stories (1978)

This book of 61 stories contains all but a few teenage pieces. Most of the stories are set in commuter villages – fine examples are 'The Country Husband' or 'The Trouble of Marcie Flint' – but a few place their characters' wasted, tragic lives in lakeside summer homes (eg 'The Day the Pig Fell into the Well') or in a favourite Cheever location, Italy,

READ ON

- Cheever's two Wapshot novels are set in the same world and among the same kind of bewildered characters as his stories. The Wapshot family, however, contains wonderful eccentrics, and the novels consequently spill into slapstick farce.

▶ **To Cheever's novels:** ▷John Updike, *The Centaur*; ▷Peter De Vries, *The Tunnel of Love*.

▶ **To the stories:** Peter Taylor, *Happy Families Are All Alike*; ▷Katherine

where his people gape at the culture and civilisation they miss in their own drab lives. (Good examples are 'The Bella Lingua' and 'A Woman Without a Country'.)

Cheever's novels are The Wapshot Chronicle, The Wapshot Scandal, Bullet Park, Oh What A Paradise it Seems *and* Falconer *(on an uncharacteristic subject: the rehabilitation of a murderer in a 'correctional facility'). His story-collections are* The Way Some People Live*;* The Enormous Radio*;* The Housebreaker of Shady Hill*;* Some People, Places and Things that will not Appear in my Next Novel*;* The Brigadier and the Golf Widow *and* The World of Apples.

Mansfield, *Bliss*; ▷L.P. Hartley, *The Killing Bottle*; Stanley Baron, *Americans and People*.

CHEKHOV, Anton (1860–1904)

Russian short-story writer and playwright.

Chekhov paid his way through medical school by writing short comic articles for magazines; in his mid-twenties he began publishing more elaborate pieces, and by the time he was 40 (and turning from stories to plays) he was considered one of the finest of all Russian prose-writers. Many of his stories are first-person monologues – he said that he was inspired by the sort of things people tell doctors during consultations, or penitents murmur at confession – and, like such monologues, they often reveal far more than the speaker intends. We hear symptoms, as it were, and from them diagnose a whole sick life. In other stories it is as if Chekhov were sitting beside us, drawing our attention to people moving about in the distance, and commenting in a quiet, compassionate way on their motives and feelings. Sympathetic detachment is the essence of his art: reading his stories (like watching his plays) is like looking through a window into other people's lives.

Lady With The Little Dog (1899)

Chekhov's best-known story – perhaps because it seems exactly to match the ironical, tragi-comic mood of his plays – tells of two people who begin a casual holiday love-affair, find that they can't live without each other, and are then forced to do just that.

Chekhov's stories are published (by Oxford University Press) in a fine translation by Ronald Hingley, who catches every nuance of the original graceful style.

READ ON

- Of Chekhov's plays, the nearest in mood to his stories are *Uncle Vanya* and *The Seagull*. (Michael Frayn's translations are recommended.)
- ▶ ▷Ivan Turgenev, *Sportsman's Sketches*. Guy De Maupassant, *Miss Harriet*. ▷Katherine Mansfield, *In a German Pension*. Seán O'Faoláin, *Foreign Affairs*. ▷Katherine Anne Porter, *The Leaning Tower*.

Children

▷David Cook, *Sunrising*
▷William Golding, *Lord of the Flies*
▷L.P. Hartley, *Eustace and Hilda*
Richard Hughes, *A High Wind in Jamaica*

Nancy Mitford, *The Blessing*
▷Marcel Proust, *Swann's Way* (part 1 of *Remembrance of Things Past*)
▷Mark Twain, *The Adventures of Tom Sawyer*

Adolescence (p 3); Parents and Children (p 193)

CHRISTIE, AGATHA (1890–1976)
British novelist.

Ingenuity is the essence of Christie's detective stories. She confined herself largely to two detectives, pompous Poirot and elderly, inquisitive Miss Marple. Nowadays, as well as her plots, it is the period detail of her books which fascinates: her English villages, spa hotels, 1930s cruise-ships and above all country houses are caught (as Poirot might put it) like ze flies in ze amber. She chronicles a vanished pre-second-world-war, upper-middle-class Britain with an accuracy which is enhanced rather than diminished by the staginess of her characters and plots.

MURDER AT THE VICARAGE (1930)
This typical Miss Marple story is set in a picture-postcard English village riven by gossip and inhabited by as unlikely a collection of eccentrics as even Christie ever threw together. Everyone could be guilty of murder, and Miss Marple's investigation is so gently persistent, so self-effacingly officious, that one trembles in case she ends up as victim rather than as sleuth.

MURDER IN MESOPOTAMIA (1936)
A nurse goes to look after the neurotic wife of an archaeologist on a dig, and is thrown into the middle of intrigue, suspicion, rancorous insult and finally, inevitably, murder. At the end of it all Poirot applies his 'little grey cells' to unearthing means, motive and opportunity as painstakingly as an archaeologist trowelling treasure.

Among the best-known of Christie's 83 detective novels are The Murder of Roger Ackroyd, Ten Little Niggers/Ten Little Indians/Then There Were None, Murder on the Orient Express *and* The Crooked House. *She also wrote stage plays (including* The Mousetrap), *an excellent second-world-war espionage thriller (*N or M*), and six romantic novels under the pseudonym Mary Westmacott.*

READ ON

- **To *Murder at the Vicarage***: *A Murder is Announced*;
- **To *Murder in Mesopotamia***: *Death on the Nile*.
- ▶ Patricia Wentworth, *Miss Silver Investigates*. Gladys Mitchell, *Come Away, Death*. Dorothy Simpson, *The Night She Died*. Cyril Hare, *An Ill Wind*. The detective stories of Erle Stanley Gardner (eg *The Case of the Howling Dog*) and ▷Georges Simenon (eg *Maigret's Pipe*) describe a similar mixture of patient sleuthing and brilliant deduction; their settings (California and Paris) are as much part of their appeal as Christie's English villages and creepy country mansions are of hers.

Agatha CHRISTIE

Julian **SYMONS, THE END OF SOLOMON GRUNDY**
(murder, obsession and madness in the English suburbs)

Friedrich **DÜRRENMATT, THE PLEDGE**
(maniacal child-killer stalks – and is stalked – across idyllic Swiss countryside)

Patricia **HIGHSMITH, STRANGERS ON A TRAIN**
(two men agree to commit 'perfect murder' for each other – and everything goes wrong)

PSYCHOLOGICAL CRIME

POLICE PROCEDURAL

H.R.F. **KEATING, FILMI, FILMI, INSPECTOR GHOTE**
(mild Bombay police inspector; murder at the film studio)

Lesley **EGAN, CRIME AT CHRISTMAS**
(no holiday for the men of Glendale Police Department, Los Angeles)

Nicholas **FREELING, CASTANG'S CITY**
(who gunned down Deputy Mayor of small French town?)

Rex **STOUT, WHERE THERE'S A WILL**
(orchid-loving, gourmet recluse; murderous family)

Dorothy L. **SAYERS, THE NINE TAILORS**
(lordly super-sleuth; death in a remote church tower)

Gladys **MITCHELL, TWELVE HORSES AND THE HANGMAN'S NOOSE**
(elderly, lizard-like Dame; death at the riding stables)

DETECTIVES OF CHARACTER

TEN LITTLE NIGGERS/TEN LITTLE INDIANS

(one murderer, nine potential victims, all cooped up together – who is who?)

CRIME PUZZLES

Josephine **TEY, DAUGHTER OF TIME**
(hospitalised woman investigates 'crimes' of English King Richard III)

Carter **DICKSON, THE RED WIDOW MURDERS**
(locked-room mystery in old, dark house)

Freeman Wills **CROFTS, DEATH OF A TRAIN**
(railway timetables; cast-iron alibis; Inspector French investigates)

MURDER – WHERE?

Delano **AMES, CORPSE DIPLOMATIQUE**
(blackmail and murder in Brown's Hotel in Nice)

Cyril **HARE, WHEN THE WIND BLOWS**
(murder in the Markshire Orchestral Society, where 'harmony' is a word unknown)

Pamela **BRANCH, MURDER'S LITTLE SISTER**
(who is trying to murder the bitchiest agony aunt in London?)

PRIVATE SLEUTHING

A. Conan **DOYLE, THE HOUND OF THE BASKERVILLES**
(Sherlock Holmes and the fiend that stalks the moor)

Edmund **CRISPIN, THE MOVING TOYSHOP**
(Oxford poetry professor; death at a vanishing toyshop)

Harry **KEMELMAN, THURSDAY THE RABBI WALKED OUT** *(Rabbi Small; murder of anti-semitic millionaire in Barnard's Crossing, Massachusetts)*

CITIES: NEW WORLD

▷Saul Bellow, *Herzog* (Chicago)
Paul Gallico, *Mrs Harris in New York*
▷Mordecai Richler, *The Apprenticeship of Duddy Kravitz* (Montreal)
▷George Turner, *The Sea and Summer* (Melbourne, 1990)
▷Jerome Weidman, *Fourth Street East* (New York, 1920s)
Donald Westlake, *Gangway* (San Francisco)
▷Edith Wharton, *The Age of Innocence* (New York, 1880s)

CITIES: OLD WORLD

▷Margery Allingham, *The Tiger in the Smoke* (London)
▷Lawrence Durrell, *The Alexandria Quartet*
▷Mrs Gaskell, *Amos Barton* (Manchester)
▷Victor Hugo, *Notre Dame de Paris*
▷Christopher Isherwood, *Goodbye to Berlin*
John Lear, *Death in Leningrad*

CLARKE, ARTHUR C. (ARTHUR CHARLES)

(BORN 1917)
British writer of novels, short stories and non-fiction.

Apart from ▷Asimov, Clarke is the best 'real' scientist among SF writers. His subject is space travel, and his 1940s and 1950s non-fiction books and articles predicted, in accurate detail, many things which have since happened, such as the invention of communications satellites, the first Moon-landing and the development of laser space-weaponry. Like ▷Verne, he begins a fictional story with existing scientific fact or theory, and then extends it logically; even his wildest fantasies thus seem rooted in the possible. His main themes are the colonization from Earth of other planets and visits to Earth by explorers from distant galaxies. His stories bustle with the detail of space-travel and setting up home in alien environments, and he is particularly interested in the psychological stress on people faced with the unknown, and with the relationship between human beings and high technology. These ideas outweigh sometimes wooden character-drawing and creaky plots.

THE SANDS OF MARS (1951)

Martin Gibson, a world-famous writer of SF and on space-travel, is invited to make his first-ever real space journey,

READ ON

- *Rendezvous with Rama* (as so often with Clarke, the straightforward development of a stunningly simple idea: that human beings land on and explore a vast alien starship on a mysterious, million-year voyage. A psychologically more elaborate follow-up to this is ▷Stanislaw Lem, *Solaris*.)
- ▶ ▷Jules Verne, *The First Men in the Moon*. ▷H.G. Wells, *The War of the*

to report on a project for 'greening' Mars, making it fit for human habitation. The book is a straightforward account of Gibson's reactions to what he sees, and to the relationship between reality and his own writings. One might imagine that events since 1951 would have superceded Clarke's imaginings – but although some of the detail now seems old hat (for example Gibson's reactions to weightlessness), the meticulousness of other descriptions, especially of the way humans cope with daily life on Mars, still fascinates.

Clarke's short stories are admired: one, 'The Sentinel', *is regularly claimed to be the finest SF story ever written. (It was the basis of the film* 2001, *and led to the novel-sequence* 2001: a Space Odyssey, Odyssey Two *and* 2061: Odyssey Three.*) A good story collection is* The Nine Billion Names of God. *Clarke's novels include* Childhood's End, A Fall of Moondust *and* Imperial Earth. Astounding Days *is autobiography, excellent on why Clarke writes, and how his career began.*

Worlds. ▷Robert Heinlein, *Have Space-suit, Will Travel*. ▷James Blish, *Earthman Come Home* (first of the 'Cities in Flight' series).

CLASSIC DETECTION

G.K. Chesterton, *The Innocence of Father Brown*
▷Michael Innes, *Stop Press*
▷P.D. James, *The Skull Beneath the Skin*
Harry Kemelman, *Tuesday the Rabbi saw Red*
Emma Lathen, *Banking on Death*
▷Ngaio Marsh, *Surfeit of Lampreys*
Gladys Mitchell, *Laurels are Poison*

Great Detectives (p 104); Murder Most Mind-Boggling (p 181); Police Procedural (p 198); Private Eyes (p 202)

COLETTE (SIDONIE GABRIELLE) (1873–1954)

French novelist.

In the 1900s Colette's works were condemned as pornographic; in the 1970s she was claimed by the women's movement as one of the founders of feminism. The reason in each case is the same. Her themes are the awakening of sensual feelings in adolescence, the way in which young women first discover their sexual power, and the attempts by middle-aged people (of both sexes) to rejuvenate themselves by preying on innocence. Her stories are not explicitly sexual, but she writes in an impressionistic style in which sun, flowers, insects, animals and the textures of skin, grass and clothes blur into a kind of drowsy, erotic reverie, a counterpart to the awakening feelings of her characters. Adult experience is always just ahead – and few of

READ ON

- *A Lesson in Love* (La naissance du jour).
- ▶ Françoise Sagan, *Bonjour Tristesse*. Edna O'Brien, *The Country Girls* (and its sequels *The Lonely Girl* and the magnificent *Girls in Their Married Bliss)*. David Garnett, *Aspects of Love*. ▷Vladimir Nabokov,

her young people notice, as the reader does, that every adult in Colette's books is a tragic figure, ineffectual or cynical. Youth, in the end, is the only worthwhile possession in life, and it is daily, hourly, squandered for experience.

THE RIPENING SEED (LE BLÉ EN HERBE) (1923)

Colette's own favourite among her books, this tells of the relationship between two teenagers, Philippe and Vinca. They have been friends from childhood, and their families have spent the summer months every year together at the seaside. Now, in Vinca's sixteenth and Philippe's seventeenth year, the young people feel a new tension in their relationship – an anxiety about each other, and about themselves, which is not helped when Philippe is seduced by another, older summer visitor.

The most substantial of Colette's works is the 'Claudine' series of novels, about a young girl growing up in the early years of this century. Another pair of books, Chéri *and* The Last of Chéri, *is on a favourite theme, the corrupting effects of a young man's first sexual experience. Her other books, many based on her own experience and family, include* Sido, My Apprenticeship *and* The Tendrils of the Vine. *Her collected short stories were published in English in 1984.*

Ada and ▷André Gide, *The Immoralist*, though their purposes and plot-development are very different, catch the same sensual and poetic mood as Colette. ▷Carson McCullers, *The Member of the Wedding* is a harsher view of the awakening of a young girl to adult feelings. Charles Webb, *The Graduate* is a riotous send-up of the young man/ older woman theme.

COMEDY THRILLERS

Delano Ames, *Murder, Maestro, Please*
▷Eric Ambler, *The Light of Day*
Laurence Block, *The Burglar Who Quoted Spinoza*
Pamela Branch, *The Wooden Overcoat*
▷Richard Condon, *Prizzi's Honour*
Greg Macdonald, *Fletch*
Andrew Taylor, *Caroline Type*
Donald Westlake, *A New York Dance*

COMPTON-BURNETT, IVY (1884–1969)

British novelist.

After a single false start (*Dolores*, an imitation of George ▷Eliot, later disowned), Compton-Burnett produced 19 comic novels in a uniquely bizarre, uncompromising style. Each book is set in a large late-Victorian or early-Edwardian household, ruled by a tyrant (one of the parents or some elderly, inflexible relative). Isolated by wealth from the outside world, the family members – often grown-up, middle-aged children – bicker, snub and plot against one another, powerless and embittered. There are family secrets to be revealed – incest, murder, insanity – and no member of the household, neither family nor servants, is a 'normal',

READ ON

▶ The uniqueness of Compton-Burnett's style means that no other writers' works are truly similar. Stories of claustrophobic families, however, in artificial 'high styles' of their own and equally compulsive,

unwarped human being. The books are written largely in dialogue, spectacularly wooden and artificial. Compton-Burnett's detractors find her novels unreadable; her fans think them hilarious.

Compton-Burnett's novels are Pastors and Masters, Brothers and Sisters, Men and Wives, More Women than Men, A House and its Head, Daughters and Sons, A Family and a Fortune, Parents and Children, Elders and Betters, Manservant and Maidservant, Two Worlds and their Ways, Darkness and Day, The Present and the Past, Mother and Son, A Father and his Fate, A Heritage and its History The Mighty and their Fall, A God and his Gifts *and* The Last and the First.

are: Samuel Butler, *The Way of All Flesh* (a book which influenced Compton-Burnett herself); ▷Edith Wharton, *The Age of Innocence*; Jean Cocteau, *The Children of the Game* (Les enfants terribles); Molly Keane, *Good Behaviour;* ▷Mervyn Peake, *Titus Groan*.

CONDON, Richard (born 1915)

US novelist.

Condon's black comedies treat horrifying matters – insanity, kidnapping, assassination – in a deadpan way, as if part of everyday experience. His characters live each moment with unflustered obsession, shopping, for example, for hand-grenades with the same matter-of-fact orderliness as for peaches or toothpaste. Condon is fascinated by wealth and power, and his books are set among politicians, financiers, mafia godfathers, generals and film-studio executives. It is a world in which power always corrupts, money never brings happiness and the devil always, delightfully, wins every trick.

Any God Will Do (1966)

The hero, Francis Vollmer, is a bank executive in pre-1914 New York – and a maniac. Convinced that he is the unacknowledged son of a European aristocrat, he embezzles a fortune, learns French (and, in the process, the skills of cooking and acrobatic sex), changes his identity and sets out to find and claim his inheritance. Despite a wonderfully boring literal mind – he talks like an encyclopedia-entry on any subject, given only a trigger-word such as 'wine' or 'symphony' – he is irresistible to women, and his quest for identity is intertwined with a love-affair which might have brought him happiness if he had not, underneath all his suaveness, been as crazy as the man in every lunatic asylum who thinks himself Napoleon.

Condon's novels include The Whisper of the Axe, Arigato, The Vertical Smile, Mile High, The Manchurian Candidate *and* The Oldest Confession.

READ ON

- *Prizzi's Honour*; *Prizzi's Family*; *Prizzi's Glory* (comedies about an upwardly-mobile mafia hit-man, a murderer with cultural aspirations).

- ▶ ▷Jerome Weidman, *Other People's Money*. ▷Thomas Mann, *Confessions of Felix Krull*. ▷John Irving, *The Hotel New Hampshire*.

CONRAD, JOSEPH (1857–1924)
Polish/British novelist.

Born in Poland, Conrad ran away to sea at 17 and ended up a captain in the merchant navy and a naturalised British subject. He retired from the sea at 37 and spent the rest of his life as a writer. There was at the time (1890s–1910s) a strong tradition of sea-stories, using the dangers and tensions of long voyages and the wonders of the worlds sailors visited as metaphors for human life. Most of this writing was straightforward adventure, with little subtlety; Conrad used its conventions for deeper literary ends. He was interested in 'driven' individuals, people whose psychology or circumstances force them to extreme behaviour, and the sea-story form exactly suited this idea. His books often begin as 'yarns', set in exotic locations and among the mixed (and mixed-up) human types who crew ocean-going ships. But before long psychology takes over, and the plot loses its straightforwardness and becomes an exploration of compulsion, obsession and neurosis.

HEART OF DARKNESS (FROM YOUTH, 1902)
This 120-page story begins as a 'yarn': Marlow, a sea-captain, tells of a journey he once made up the Congo river to bring down a stranded steamer. He became fascinated by stories of an ivory-merchant, a white man called Kurtz who lived deep in the jungle and was said to have supernatural powers. Marlow set out to find Kurtz, and the journey took him deeper and deeper into the heart not only of the 'Dark Continent', but into the darkness of the human soul. (Francis Ford Coppola's 1970s film *Apocalypse Now* updated this story to the Vietnam War, making points about US colonialism as savage as Conrad's denunciation of the ivory-trade.)

Conrad's major novels are Lord Jim, The Nigger of the Narcissus, Nostromo, The Secret Agent *and* Under Western Eyes. *His short-story collections (an excellent introduction to his work) are* Tales of Unrest, Youth, Typhoon, A Set of Six, 'Twixt Land and Sea, Within the Tides *and* Tales of Hearsay.

READ ON

- *Typhoon* (which deals with corruption and exploitation of a different kind, this time using as its metaphor a passenger steamer caught in a typhoon in the China Sea); *The Secret Agent* (about the conflict between innocence and corruption among a group of terrorists in 1900s London).
- ▶ ▷Herman Melville, *Billy Budd, Foretopman*. ▷Graham Greene, *The Comedians*. Lionel Davidson, *Making Good Again*. B. Traven, *The Treasure of the Sierra Madre*. ▷Paul Theroux, *The Mosquito Coast*. John Kruse, *The Hour of the Lily*. ▷J.G. Ballard, *The Drowned World* is an SF novel of Conradian intensity.

COOK, DAVID (BORN 1940)
British novelist.

Many of Cook's books are compassionate stories about the kind of people usually shunned by society (and by novelists): a depressive widow and a catamite in *Albert's Memorial*, child molesters in *Happy Endings* and *Crying out Loud*, a Downs Syndrome sufferer in *Walter*. The combination of

READ ON

- *Missing Persons* (a warm-hearted comedy about two elderly ladies who refuse to give in to clinical descriptions of awful events and warm-heartedness allowed him to take even greater risks in his finest novels, *Winter Doves* (in which two inhabitants of a mental home, Walter and a would-be suicide, fall in love and run away to seek happiness together), and *Sunrising* (see below).

SUNRISING (1984)

This book steps aside from the late-20th-century inadequates of Cook's other novels. It is set in the 1830s, and tells of three orphaned children who befriend each other and travel in search of a home. The descriptions of rural England, of the Oxford Goose Fair and especially of the London slums are as gripping as anything in ▷Dickens (but far less wordy), and the story is radiant with humanity. Despite the miseries and deprivation the children suffer, they find help and friendship, ordinary human decency, at every turn.

old age. One sets up as a private detective, the other goes to find a lover and a new home in Tuscany).

- **To *Sunrising*:** ▷Charles Dickens, *Oliver Twist*; Richard Hughes, *A High Wind in Jamaica*; ▷J.G. Ballard, *Empire of the Sun*.
- **To *Missing Persons*:** Julian Barnes, *Staring at the Sun*.
- **To Cook's other books:** ▷Susan Hill, *I'm the King of the Castle*; ▷Paul Bailey, *At the Jerusalem*; ▷Ian McEwan, *The Child in Time*.

COOKSON, CATHERINE (BORN 1906)

British novelist.

'Catherine Cookson' is a pseudonym of Ann McMullen. Her books are warm-hearted romances about 'ordinary people'. She set most of them in the north-east of England (Tyneside) where she was born, and showed how her characters coped with the harsh conditions of 19th-century life in the area. Apart from her style, which is matter-of-fact, not moralising – it has learned lessons from 20th-century film and TV documentary – her books are in the unsentimental tradition of such great 'social' novels as those of ▷Mrs Gaskell or ▷George Eliot. She grouped many of her novels in series, for example the 'Mary Ann' books (beginning with *A Grand Man*) and the Mallen trilogy (*The Mallen Girl, The Mallen Litter* and *The Mallen Streak*). The heroine of *Tilly Trotter, Tilly Trotter Wed* and *Tilly Trotter Widowed* (a characteristic series, written in the 1960s) is a poor but spirited girl in 1930s County Durham who becomes the mistress of the owner of the 'big house', emigrates to America when he dies, and returns in middle age to find happiness at last in her beloved native country.

Cookson's other books include The Invisible Cord, The Gambling Man, The Black Candle *and* The Harrogate Secret.

READ ON

- Catherine Gaskin, *Sarah Dane*, Maria Joseph, *Gemini Girls*. ▷Danielle Steel, *The Promises*, ▷George Eliot, *The Mill on the Floss*, ▷Mrs Gaskell, *North and South*.

Let Me Make Myself Plain *is an anthology of writings, her own and other people's, which were originally spoken as Epilogues on Tyne Tees Television, and which sum up her philosophy of life. She also writes as Catherine Marchant; titles include* Heritage of Folly, The Fen Tiger, The Mists of Memory, Miss Martha Mary Crawford *and* The Slow Awakening.

COUNTRY HOUSES

Mazo de la Roche, *Jalna*
▷E.M. Forster, *Howards End*
▷Hermann Hesse, *Rosshalde*
▷Eudora Welty, *Delta Wedding*
▷Michael Innes, *Old Hall, New Hall*
▷Evelyn Waugh, *Brideshead Revisited*
▷P.G. Wodehouse, *Summer Lightning*

Dark Old Houses (p 56)

COX, RICHARD (BORN 1931)

British novelist.

Cox was a defence correspondent, and is an expert on aerial warfare. His best-known thrillers (eg *The Time It Takes*, about mercenaries in central Africa) have a flying background, but everything he writes is enriched by his knowledge of modern weapons-systems and global politics.

READ ON

- *The KGB Directive.*
- ▶ Ernest K. Gann, *The Aviator*. Spencer S. Dunmore, *The Sound of Wings*. ▷Frederick Forsyth, *The Dogs of War*. Tom Clancy, *The Cardinal of the Kremlin*.

CULTURE-CLASH

▷Chinua Achebe, *Things Fall Apart*
▷E.M. Forster, *A Passage to India*
Brian Glanville, *Along the Arno*
▷William Golding, *The Inheritors*
▷Henry James, *The Europeans*
Joseph Olshan, *A Warmer Season*
▷Evelyn Waugh, *The Loved One*
▷H.G. Wells, *Kipps*

D

DARK, Eleanor (born 1901)

Australian novelist.

Dark's novels are psychological meditations like those of Virginia ▷Woolf, showing the movement of their characters' minds as they react to apparently ordinary events. The theme of *Prelude to Christopher* (1934) is that we are the prisoners of our past, that we carry the burden of previous actions and understandings – as Dark put it – the way snails carry their shells. *Sun Across the Sky* and *Waterway* each focus on a single day, during which a group of characters reaches a moment of self-realization and psychological crisis which results in violent, tragic action. *Return to Coolami* (1936) is about the relationship of four people on a 300-mile drive through New South Wales; although the book is marvellously evocative of the Australian landscape (a recurring pleasure in Dark's work), the exploration is really of character not countryside and physical travelling is a metaphor for the journey of the soul. In the 1940s Dark applied similar techniques of psychological investigation to a historical subject, writing a novel-trilogy (*The Timeless Land*; *Storm of Time*; *No Barrier*) about the first European settlements in Australia. The counterpoint of lyrical descriptions of what (to the whites) was a virgin, beautiful land with analyses of the soul's turbulence caused by their amputation from their European culture and families gives these books extraordinary power; only ▷William Golding and ▷Patrick White so strikingly combine the epic and the intimate.

Dark's other novels are Slow Dawning, The Little Company *and the lighter* Lantana Lane, *the anecdotal story of a farming family in Queensland.*

READ ON

- **To Dark's psychological novels:** ▷Virginia Woolf, *The Waves*; ▷Nadine Gordimer, *The Conservationist*; ▷Anita Brookner, *A Misalliance*.
- **To the historical trilogy:** ▷William Golding, *Darkness Visible*; ▷Thomas Keneally, *The Playmaker*; ▷Patrick White, *Voss*; ▷William Faulkner, *Sartoris*.
- **To *Lantana Lane*:** ▷Miles Franklin (writing as 'Brent of Bin Bin'), *Up the Country*.

Dark Old Houses

▷Jane Austen, *Northanger Abbey*
Robert Bloch, *Psycho*
▷Charlotte Brontë, *Jane Eyre*
▷Daphne Du Maurier, *Rebecca*
Dinah Lampitt, *Sutton Place*
▷Mervyn Peake, *Gormenghast*
Horace Walpole, *The Castle of Otranto*

Country Houses (p 54)

DAVIES, Robertson (born 1913)

Canadian novelist, journalist and playwright.

The deceptively gentle, expansive tone of Davies' satires belies their extraordinary subject-matter: it is as if ▷Jane Austen had reworked ▷Rabelais. Davies' books are comedies of manners, many set in small university towns riven with gossip and pretension. *Tempest-tost* (1951) is about an amateur production of Shakespeare's *The Tempest* all but sabotaged by the unexpected, lacerating love of the middle-aged leading man for the girl who plays his daughter. *A Mixture of Frailties* (1958) describes the chain of bizarre events after a woman leaves money to educate a girl in the arts, unless and until the woman's son sires a male heir. In each novel of the 'Deptford trilogy' (1970–75) a different narrator tries to explain the circumstances leading up to the death of a man killed by a stone wrapped in a snowball. What each man does, however, is reveal his own tangled life-history and his bizarre enthusiasms (which range from medieval saints to Houdini, from the history of vaudeville to experiments into 'the collective unconscious').

The 'Cornish' Trilogy (1982)

The books in this trilogy, about members of the wealthy, eccentric Cornish family, are *The Rebel Angels, What's Bred in the Bone* and *The Lyre of Orpheus.* Hovering over the events, as puppeteers loom over marionettes, are guardian angels, devils and spirits of medieval mischief; we humans are not alone. Alternate chapters of *The Rebel Angels* are told by Father Darcourt, a professor of Biblical Greek at a small, Roman Catholic, Canadian university, and Maria Magdalene Theotoky, a research student. The university is a quiet place, dedicated to placid scholarship and barbed common-room gossip. But Ms Theotoky is researching Rabelais, and the plot suddenly erupts with priceless manuscripts, bizarre lusts, devil worship, scatology, and a storm of passion and deceit against which no grove of academe

READ ON

- *A Leaven of Malice.*
- ► **To *Rebel Angels*:** ▷David Lodge, *Small World*; ▷Anthony Burgess, *Enderby's Dark Lady.*
- ► **To *What's Bred in the Bone*:** ▷Richard Condon, *Any God Will Do*; ▷Thomas Mann, *The Confessions of Felix Krull.*
- ► **To *The Lyre of Orpheus*:** ▷Randall Jarrell, *Pictures from an Institution*; D.J. Enright, *Academic Year.*
- ► **To Davies' work in general:** ▷John Irving, *A Prayer for Owen Meany*; Howard Jacobson, *Peeping Tom*; Aritha van Herk, *No Fixed Address.*

could stand unbowed. *What's Bred in the Bone* is the life-story of Francis Cornish, art expert, multi-millionaire, war-time spy and loner, whose search for himself, and for love, is hampered by his guardian devil Maimas. *The Lyre of Orpheus* tells of the recreation, in 20th-century Canadian academe, of a lost Arthurian opera by the devil-inspired 19th-century romantic composer E. T. A. Hoffmann. The style in all three books is urbane, placid narrative, but the contents are sown with mines. If ▷Jane Austen rules the tone of Davies' earlier trilogies, in this one ▷Rabelais keeps blowing raspberries.

The books in the 'Deptford trilogy' are Fifth Business, The Manticore *and* World of Wonders. *Davies' other novels include a third trilogy, in a similarly urbane and hilarious vein,* The Salterton Trilogy. The Diary of Samuel Marchbanks, The Table Talk of Samuel Marchbanks *and* Marchbanks' Almanac, *are collections of humorous journalism, and Davies' plays include* A Jig for the Gipsy, Hunting Stuart *and the political satire* Question Time.

DEEP SOUTH, USA

Harper Lee, *To Kill a Mocking Bird*
▷Carson McCullers, *The Ballad of the Sad Café*
▷Margaret Mitchell, *Gone With the Wind*
▷Mark Twain, *The Adventures of Huckleberry Finn*
▷Alice Walker, *The Color Purple*
▷Eudora Welty, *Delta Wedding*
▷Thomas Wolfe, *Look Homeward, Angel*

Places (p 197): Small Town Life, USA (p 227)

DEFOE, Daniel (1660–1731)

British novelist and non-fiction writer.

A journalist, Defoe wrote over 500 essays, poems, political satires and other works, including a history of England, a handbook of good manners and a guide-book to Britain. In his 60s he began writing what he called 'romances': books which purported to be the autobiographies of people who had led unusual or adventurous lives (pirates, whores, treasure-hunters) but which were really fiction and among the earliest English novels. Apart from his characters' proneness to theological and philosophical reflection (eminently skippable), his books lack the ponderousness of later 18th-century fiction. His fast-moving, simple prose and his journalist's talent for description give his work a freshness which belies its age.

READ ON

- *The Farther Adventures of Robinson Crusoe.*
- ▶ ▷Henry Fielding, *Tom Jones.* ▷William Golding, *Pincher Martin*; *Rites of Passage.* ▷Patrick White, *Tarr.* Michel Tournier, *The Other Friday* and Jane Gardam, *Crusoe's Daughter* play

ROBINSON CRUSOE (1719)

The germ of this story came from the autobiography of a real-life sailor, Alexander Selkirk, who was marooned on a desert island in 1704. As often in his works, Defoe was fascinated by the idea of the confrontation between civilisation and barbarism, in this case by how a 'modern' European, filled with the knowledge and aspirations of the Age of Reason, might cope if all the trappings of civilisation were stripped from him. Crusoe is allowed nothing but a few tools and other possessions saved from the shipwreck, and the resources of his own ingenuity. Later, after Crusoe has lived alone for 26 years, Defoe provides him with a companion, the 'savage' Friday, and so lets us see 'civilised' humanity through innocent, unsophisticated eyes.

Defoe's 'romances' include Moll Flanders *(set in the 18th-century criminal underworld),* The Life and Adventures of Mr Duncan Campbell *(whose hero is a deaf-and-dumb conjurer),* Captain Singleton *(whose hero is a pirate),* Memoirs of a Cavalier *and* Memoirs of Captain George Carleton *(whose heroes are swashbuckling soldiers-of-fortune), and – more serious –* A Journal of the Plague Year, *a day-by-day, first-person account of life during the Great Plague of London in 1664.*

fascinating games with *Robinson Crusoe*'s themes and plot, Tournier by retelling the story from Friday's point of view, and Gardam by focussing on a reclusive girl fixated on *Robinson Crusoe* who makes it her chief emotional resource. C.S. Lewis, *Out of the Silent Planet* is a similar novel of survival, set on the planet Mars, and J.M. Coetzee, *Foe* gives an alternative account of how *Robinson Crusoe* came to be written, and of the 'real' events which might have inspired it – Friday and Crusoe are the sole survivors from a wrecked slave-ship.

DE HAAN, TOM (BORN 1964)

British novelist.

At one level, De Haan's *A Mirror for Princes* (1987) is a swaggering medieval tale, as crammed as a Breughel painting. Its setting is Brychmachrye, a glittering, barbarous feudal court. Its pages jostle with tyranny, intrigue, incest and delight in the earthier human pleasures. Its dialogue wastes no words, and the central element of its plot – the relationship between the poetry-loving third son of a tyrant and his hard-fighting, hard-wenching brothers while they wait for the old king to die – is hardly unfamiliar. But the book's title gives the game away: appearances are deceptive. *A Mirror for Princes* is set not in reality but in an imagined, timeless world of De Haan's own invention. The medieval detail, however fascinating, is no more important than the wimples and hautboys in religious paintings of the period. The book is a sustained meditation on power and love, a moral and

READ ON

- *The Child of Good Fortune* (a 'prequel', about a poet living in Brychmachrye just after the *coup d'état*, longing for revolution but unable to bring himself to lead it).
- ► Pär Lagerkvist, *The Dwarf*. Helen Waddell, *Héloïse and Abelard*. ▷Thomas Mann, *The Holy Sinner*.

philosophical allegory in the manner of ▷Hesse's *The Glass Bead Game*. The combination of this and red-blooded action is magnificently handled; *A Mirror for Princes*, De Haan's first novel, is a masterpiece.

DEIGHTON, LEN (BORN 1929)

British novelist.

In the 1960s, fired by dislike of snobbish spy fantasies of the James Bond school, Deighton produced a series of books (beginning with *The IPCRESS File*) showing spies as ordinary human beings, functionaries of a ridiculous and outdated bureaucracy in which requisitions for paper-clips could take precedence over analyses of the danger of nuclear war. He devised for them a documentary, 'dossier' technique, flooding the text with lists, letters, memoranda, meeting-transcripts, diary-entries and technical notes – and went on to use it in a series of devastatingly authentic-seeming novels on non-spy subjects. Although his material is fictional, it reads like fact, like the transcript of a TV documentary which shows us people's thoughts and feelings as meticulously as what they do and say.

BOMBER (1970)

In direct contrast to the stiff-upper-lip, jolly-good-show British war-films of the 1950s, Deighton gives a blunt, detailed idea of what it was probably like to prepare for and make an RAF bombing-raid in 1943. He is particularly interested in the tensions between service and civilian personnel, the class-divisions between officers and other ranks and the bumbling and paper-chasing which contrasted with, and sometimes jeopardised, the bravery of actual combat.

Deighton's spy novels include Funeral in Berlin, Horse Under Water, Spy Story *and the trilogy* Berlin Game, Moscow Set, London Match. Spy Hook *and* Spy Line *are the first two books in a new, follow-up series.* Close-up *is a black satire on the film business.* Only When I Larf *is a comedy about confidence tricksters. His 'dossier' novels include* SS-GB, *a nightmarish vision of what might have happened if Britain had lost the second world war and were now under nazi rule.*

READ ON

- *Goodbye Mickey Mouse* (a detailed, convincing – and, in its implications for Western defence, horrifying – novel about USAF personnel manning a nuclear-weapons airfield in the UK).
- ▶ **To the spy-stories:** ▷John Le Carré, *The Spy Who Came in from the Cold*; Adam Hall, *The Quiller Memorandum*. (Hall also writes Deightonish war-stories under the name Elleston Trevor).
- ▶ **To Deighton's flying-stories:** Gavin Lyall, *Midnight Plus One*; Peter George, *Red Alert* (about the accidental triggering of the nuclear holocaust).

DEPRESSION AND PSYCHIATRY

▷Lisa Alther, *Other Women*
▷Paul Bailey, *Peter Smart's Confessions*
Roy Brown, *The Siblings*
▷Jonathan Kellerman, *Shrunken Heads*
▷Doris Lessing, *The Golden Notebook*
▷H.H. Richardson, *Maurice Guest*
▷J.D. Salinger, *Franny and Zooey*

Paul Sayer, *The Comforts of Madness*
▷Antonia White, *Beyond the Glass*

Madness (p 166); On the Edge of Sanity (p 190)

DE VRIES, PETER (BORN 1910)
US novelist and journalist.

De Vries worked for the *New Yorker*, and his novels satirise a favourite target of that magazine, the upwardly-mobile suburbanites he himself called 'globules of metropolitan life'. His characters live in trim stockbroker villages on Long Island or in Connecticut. The husbands commute into New York to work; the wives stay at home to mind their beautiful houses, tend their lawn-sprinklers, go to coffee mornings and PTA meetings and bore each other to death. Evenings and weekends are given up to self-improving parties (at which people read modern poetry and make bitchy remarks about each other's clothes) and to furtive, desperate love-affairs. Most of De Vries' books are first-person novels, and his narrators enliven them with aphorisms, wisecracks, puns and parodies of everything from TV commercials to the *Reader's Digest*. It is an empty, panic-stricken society, pathetically narcissistic – but instead of merely sending it up, as many other *New Yorker* writers and cartoonists do, De Vries shows it with compassion as well as wit. His books may be slapstick, but they end in tears.

THE TUNNEL OF LOVE (1954)
The story is told by Dick, the cartoons editor of a New York magazine called *The Townsman*. He is happy in his work and his marriage, but affects to be bored, constantly making world-weary jokes which no one else appreciates, and fantasising about a Maine hideaway called Moot Point at which he woos beautiful women in the manner of Cary Grant, Clark Gable or George Sanders. He and his wife are asked to sponsor their neighbours as a suitable couple to adopt a child – and the more Dick finds out about the husband, a womanising cartoonist, the more he himself is tangled in lust, deceit and sexual compromise.

De Vries' comic novels include Comfort Me with Apples, Through the Fields of Clover, Reuben Reuben, Mrs Wallop, I Hear America Swinging, Into Your Tent I'll Creep, Sauce for the Goose, Madder Music *and* The Prick of Noon. The Blood of the Lamb *is serious, about the death of a child.*

READ ON

- *The Mackerel Plaza*; *Let Me Count the Ways*.
- ▶ ▷John Updike, *The Witches of Eastwick*. ▷Iris Murdoch, *A Severed Head*. ▷Kingsley Amis, *That Uncertain Feeling*. Martin Amis, *The Rachel Papers*. George Axelrod, *Where Am I Now – and Do I Need Me?*

DICK, PHILIP K. (KENDRED) (1928–82)

US novelist and short-story writer.

Dick used standard SF ideas – androids, alternative worlds, aliens – to write novels about the hinges between fantasy and reality, madness and sanity, wish and acceptance. For a time in the 1960s, thanks to books like *The Three Stigmata of Palmer Eldritch* (1964), which deals with the effects of mind-altering drugs on our perception of reality – and with the nature of that perception – he had a huge cult following. However, his novels are less ponderous than this suggests, being told in a deadpan, quirky style as wittily unpredictable (granted the different genre) as Hitchcock's films. His characters often teeter on the brink of insanity, struggling to understand the world in which they feel trapped. In one classic novel, *Do Androids Dream of Electric Sheep?* (1968; later filmed as *Bladerunner*), their dilemma is entirely real, as they are not human beings at all but androids aspiring to humanity. SF fans make high claims for Dick, and he is certainly a master of the genre. But his metaphorical transformation of well-worn ideas, and his bizarre humour, make him a pleasure not only for addicts, but for readers who would not normally cross the road to read SF.

THE MAN IN THE HIGH CASTLE (1962)

The basis of this plot is the standard SF idea of rewriting history. The Axis powers have won the second world war, and the Japanese rule the USA. Or do they? Is this world real? Is this history real? While we find out, Dick feeds us a cocktail of Fascism, Zen, individual schizophrenia and mass paranoia; a heady, uniquely Dickian mix.

Dick's other novels include The Penultimate Truth, A Maze of Death, Eye in the Sky, Ubik, Martian Time-Slip, A Scanner Darkly *(about how the dual life of a future-Earth narcotics agent causes him to lose hold of his own identity),* The Broken Bubble *and* Valis, *about what happens when an ancient, extra-terrestrial satellite beams directly into the hero's brain the news that reality ended in 74* AD.

READ ON

- **To *The Man in the High Castle***: *Radio Free Albemuth.*
- **To *Valis***: *The Transmigration of Timothy Archer.*
- ▶ **To the novels exploring extreme or variable states of mind**: Gene Wolfe, *The Fifth Head of Cerberus*; K. W. Jeter, *The Glass Hammer*; William Burroughs, *The Naked Lunch*.
- ▶ **To Dick's world in general**: ▷John Fowles, *The Magus*; ▷Brian Aldiss, *Reports on Probability A*; ▷Franz Kafka, *The Trial*.

DICKENS, CHARLES (1812–70)

British novelist.

In his early 20s Dickens worked as a journalist, writing reports of law court proceedings and Parliamentary debates, and short essays on the life and manners of the time (later collected as *Sketches by Boz*). It was not until the success of his first novel *Pickwick Papers*, when he was 25, that he made writing a full-time career. He composed large parts of his novels in dialogue, and was proud of his gift for showing

READ ON

- *Nicholas Nickleby*; *Oliver Twist*.
- ▶ Novels of 'growing up', using a biographical framework to give a picture

Charles DICKENS

Victor **HUGO, Les Misérables**
(1820s France: honest man convicted to galleys escapes and rebuilds his life)

Anthony **TROLLOPE, The Last Chronicle of Barset**
(1860s England: honest man wrongly accused of theft; student making his way in London)

Edith **WHARTON, The House of Mirth**
(1880s New York heiress rejects ways of society to 'be herself')

J.B. **PRIESTLEY, Angel Pavement**
(1920s London firm taken over, developed and ruined by confidence-trickster)

John **O'HARA, The Lockwood Concern**
(1930s Pennsylvania family becomes wealthy by violence, destroys itself)

James **BALDWIN, Go, Tell It on the Mountain**
(1950s Harlem: son of slum family learns about sex, racism and born-again Christian love)

'DICKENSIAN' NOVELS: BLEAK SIDE OF LIFE

David **COOK, Sunrising**
(1830s England: three children rescued from degradation in rural and urban slums)

Mark **TWAIN, The Adventures of Huckleberry Finn** *(1860s Mississippi: boy's adolescence on river and in riverside communities)*

H.G. **WELLS, The History of Mr Polly**
(1890s England: middle-aged 'drop-out' has many adventures, finds happiness)

Thomas **MANN, The Confessions of Felix Krull, Confidence Man** *(1900s Europe: confidence-man's cheerful, amoral adventures among the bourgeoisie)*

Angus **WILSON, The Middle Age of Mrs Eliot**
(1950s widow travels world in search of happiness)

Saul **BELLOW, The Adventures of Augie March**
(1930s Chicago: zestful account of slum boy using his wits to make his way)

'DICKENSIAN' NOVELS: CHEERFUL SIDE OF LIFE

(dark childhood, miserable growing-up and eventual happiness in 19th-century London)

LEARNING HOW TO BE GROWN-UP

William **THACKERAY, PENDENNIS**
(1840s London: after many escapades, young man finds literary success)

W. Somerset **MAUGHAM, OF HUMAN BONDAGE**
(1890s London school days, Paris student life and eventual happiness of lonely young man)

Johann Wolfgang von **GOETHE, THE APPRENTICESHIP OF WILHELM MEISTER**
(1790s Europe: young man runs away to be an actor, experiences real life, 'finds' himself)

André **GIDE, THE COUNTERFEITERS**
(1920s Paris: young people growing up, initiated into life and love)

Mordecai **RICHLER, THE APPRENTICESHIP OF DUDDY KRAVITZ**
(1930s Montreal: young man moves from rags to riches, loses his soul)

Lisa **ALTHER, KINFLICKS**
(1960s USA: young woman learns about sex, love, feminism, protest-politics and 'dropping out')

character through speech alone; he also gave his minor characters (pot-boys, shop-customers, carters, oystermen, toddlers) turns of speech or physical eccentricities to make them instantly memorable – another theatrical technique. This character-vividness is matched by a sustained commentary on human nature and society: Dickens consistently savaged the humbug and petty-mindedness of the middle classes who bought his books, and said that human happiness comes not from law, religion, politics or social structures but from gratuitous, individual acts of kindness. In his later books, notably *Great Expectations* and *Our Mutual Friend*, savagery predominated over sentimentality to an extent rivalled only in ▷Zola.

DAVID COPPERFIELD (1849–50)

Dickens' own favourite among his novels, this tells the story (in the first person, as if an autobiography) of a boy growing up: his unhappy childhood and adolescence, his first jobs and first love-affair, and the way he finally transmutes his experience into fiction and becomes a writer. As often in Dickens' books, subsidiary characters seem to steal the show: the grim Murdstones, the optimistic Micawbers, salt-of-the-earth Peggotty, feckless Steerforth and above all the viperish hypocrite Uriah Heep. But the book's chief interest is the developing character of Copperfield himself: apparently passive, at other people's mercy, he learns and grows by each experience, maturing before our eyes.

Dickens' novels, in order of publication, are Pickwick Papers, Oliver Twist, Nicholas Nickleby, The Old Curiosity Shop, Barnaby Rudge, Martin Chuzzlewit, Dombey and Son, David Copperfield, Bleak House, Hard Times, Little Dorrit, A Tale of Two Cities, Great Expectations, Our Mutual Friend *and* Edwin Drood. *His shorter works include* A Christmas Carol, A Child's History of England *and three collections of articles,* Sketches by Boz, American Notes *and* The Uncommercial Traveller.

(documentary, satirical or both at once) of society: ▷Henry Fielding, *Tom Jones*; ▷Somerset Maugham, *Of Human Bondage*; ▷Mark Twain, *Huckleberry Finn*; ▷James Joyce, *Portrait of the Artist as a Young Man*.

▶ **To Dickens' more savage social novels:** ▷Mrs Gaskell, *North and South*; ▷John Steinbeck, *The Grapes of Wrath*; ▷Patrick White, *Riders in the Chariot*.

▶ **To his more relaxed tableaux of human life:** ▷H.G. Wells, *Kipps*; ▷Angus Wilson, *Anglo-Saxon Attitudes*.

DICKINSON, PETER (BORN 1927)

British novelist and children's writer.

Although Dickinson's crime novels contain their quota of murders and clues, they centre on the unravelling of mysteries of a different kind. Each is set in a self-contained, bizarre society about which we long to learn more – and the further his detective investigates the crime, the deeper we are drawn into the surrounding atmosphere. *Sleep and His Brother* is set in a community of brain-damaged, psychically sensitive children, and the only being who knows the identity of the murderer is a 'talking' chimpanzee. *The Seals* is

READ ON

- *The Lively Dead.*

▶ **To Dickinson's crime-novels:** ▷Michael Innes, *The Daffodil Affair*; H.R.F. Keating, *Death and the Visiting Firemen*; Gladys Mitchell, *The*

about a crazy religious community waiting for the apocalypse on a remote Scottish island. In *King and Joker* someone commits murder in a Buckingham Palace inhabited by an egalitarian, trendy-left royal family whose dark secrets give the book its fun. In later novels, Dickinson abandoned the crime format to explore wider themes, especially of identity. The mysteries in *A Summer in the Twenties, The Last House-Party* and *Hindsight*, for example, are not murders but long-forgotten love-affairs, betrayals and family secrets whose effects stain the lives of the present generation.

SKIN DEEP (1968)

A tribe of people from Papua New Guinea lives in a terraced house in London, carrying out stone-age rituals in the attics. Their chief is murdered, and the community begins to fall apart. Superintendent Pibble must not only find the murderer, but reassure the tribespeople – and to do that he must try to enter their minds and understand their culture.

Dickinson's adult novels include A Pride of Heroes, The Lizard in the Cup, The Poison Oracle, The Lively Dead, One Foot in the Grave, *and* Skeleton-in-Waiting. *He has also written children's books:* Tulku, Annerton Pit *and an SF trilogy,* The Changes.

Twenty-third Man.

- ▶ **To his non-crime books:** Macdonald Harris, *The Balloonist*; Bamber Gascoigne, *The Heyday*; ▷John Irving, *A Prayer for Owen Meany.*

DONALDSON, STEPHEN (BORN 1947)

US novelist.

Donaldson's major work, the 2600-page Thomas Covenant series (1977–84), is adventure-fantasy inspired by – and as good as – ▷Tolkien's *The Lord of the Rings*. Thomas Covenant, a leper, is transported to a distant country in the grip of the evil Lord Foul. He finds that his wedding-ring is a powerful magic talisman, but is at first reluctant to use it because he believes himself psychologically tainted by his illness – in fact he wonders if the Land and its plight are not fantasies of his own sick mind. The novels chart his spiritual agonising, his recruitment of a band of helpers and followers, and his epic battles against Lord Foul.

The Thomas Covenant books are Lord Foul's Bane, The Illearth War, The Power That Preserves, The Wounded Land, The One Tree, White Gold Wielder *and the brief* Gildenfire. Daughter of Regals *is a collection of short stories, a good introduction to Donaldson's work.*

READ ON

- • *The Mirror of the Dreams* and its sequel *A Man Rides Through.*
- ▶ ▷David Eddings, *Pawn of Prophecy* (first of the Belgariad quintet). Jack Vance, *Lyonesse*. R.A. MacAvoy, *Damiano*. Gene Wolfe, *The Book of the New Sun*. ▷Tom de Haan, *The Child of Good Fortune.*

DONLEAVY, J.P. (JAMES PATRICK) (BORN 1926)

Irish novelist.

Beginning with *The Ginger Man* (1955), Donleavy has writ-

READ ON

- ▶ Flann O'Brien, *At*

ten a series of bawdy, boozy 'biographies', like shaggy-dog stories reworked by ▷Joyce. Nothing much happens to his heroes: they wander amiably through life, spending much time in bed and even more in pubs, and endlessly, riotously reflecting on the meaning of life and love. His other novels include *A Singular Man, The Beastly Beatitudes of Balthazar B, The Destinies of Darcy Dancer, Gentleman,* and *Are You Listening, Rabbi Löw?*. *Meet My Maker, the Mad Molecule* is a collection of short stories.

Swim-Two-Birds. ▷John Kennedy Toole, *A Confederacy of Dunces*. Robert Coover, *Pricksongs and Descants* (short stories).

DOSTOEVSKI, Fyodor (1821–81)

Russian novelist.

Dostoevski admired ▷Balzac and ▷Dickens, and set out to describe Russian characters and society in a similar way, creating atmosphere by a series of vivid evocations (verbal snapshots) of everything from people's skin and clothes to the texture of furniture or the gleam of rain on cobblestones. His characters are a gallery of 'types', particularly strong on the destitute, the suffering and the inadequate. He was fascinated by people driven to extreme behaviour by despair or lack of external moral guidance, such as the teaching of his own Christian faith. Raskolnikov, the central character of *Crime and Punishment*, makes himself a moral outsider by committing murder. Myshkin in *The Idiot* is so tormented by the thought of his own inadequacy that he becomes the imbecile he thinks he is. Every member of the Karamazov family (in *The Brothers Karamazov*) is morally tainted, and only the youngest, a novice monk, is able to wrestle with his own evil nature and win. If Dostoevski had been a 20th-century writer, his pessimistic view of human existence might have led him to surrealist black comedy (see ▷Kafka); as it was, the psychological intensity of his books is closer to stage tragedy (*King Lear* or *Medea*, say) than to prose fiction, and has a similar all-engulfing power.

Crime and Punishment (1866)

Raskolnikov, a student, driven to neurotic frenzy by his powerlessness to change the injustice of the world, decides to demonstrate the freedom of his soul by a single gratuitous act: murder. Instead of being liberated, however, he is enslaved by his own guilt-feelings, and the book describes, in a remorseless and clinical way, the disintegration of his personality. The part of his 'conscience' is embodied in Inspector Petrovich, who harries him like a Fury from ancient myth, goading and cajoling him to admit his guilt and so to purge his soul.

Dostoevski's other books include Notes From the House of the Dead *(based on his own prison-camp experiences: he was*

READ ON

- *The Idiot*; *The Brothers Karamazov*.
- ▶ ▷Victor Hugo, *Les misérables*. ▷Nathaniel Hawthorne, *The Scarlet Letter*. ▷Joseph Conrad, *Under Western Eyes*. ▷Albert Camus, *The Fall* (La chute). ▷Vladimir Nabokov, *Despair*. ▷Georges Simenon, *Act of Passion*. ▷François Mauriac, *The Nest of Vipers* (Le Nœud de Vipères). ▷Paul Bailey, *A Distant Likeness* reverses one of the themes of *Crime and Punishment*: obsession with a crime triggers self-condemnation and madness not in the criminal but in the investigating officer.

a political dissident), Winter Notes on Summer Experiences *(a horrified account of the degenerate Europe he found while visiting the London World Exhibition of 1862), and the novels* Notes from Underground, The Gambler *and* The Possessed.

Down To Earth
(the implacability of nature)

Stella Gibbons, *Cold Comfort Farm*
▷Thomas Hardy, *The Woodlanders*
▷Geoffrey Household, *Rogue Male*
▷Paul Theroux, *The Black House*
Mary Webb, *Precious Bane*
▷Fay Weldon, *The Heart of England*
▷Edith Wharton, *Ethan Frome*

The Rhythm of Nature (p 210)

DOYLE, Arthur Conan (1859–1930)
British writer of novels, short stories and non-fiction.

A doctor with very few patients, Doyle began writing to improve his income. His main interest was military history, and he regarded his historical novels (eg *The White Company*, the story of a band of 14th-century knight-errants, or the Brigadier Gerard books, set during the Napoleonic Wars) as his best work. His Sherlock Holmes stories were meant as potboilers, and throughout his life he claimed (while still going on writing them) to be embarrassed by their success. The Holmes stories were published by *Strand Magazine* in the UK and by *Harper's* in the USA; these papers also serialised Doyle's Professor Challenger novels (beginning with *The Lost World*), about a flamboyant scientific genius and explorer, a blend of the heroes of ▷Verne and Rider ▷Haggard.

The Memoirs Of Sherlock Holmes (1893)
In each of the 11 stories in this collection, Holmes is presented with a problem which seems insoluble – at least so far as his friend and chronicler Dr Watson can see – and solves it by a mixture of dazzling deductive reasoning and melodramatic adventure. He is a master of disguise, an expert shot and boxer, a drug-taker, a neurotic introvert, a plausible liar who uses every trick to trap his suspects – and Doyle's style has a single-mindedness, an obsessiveness, which perfectly suits both Holmes' character and the mysteries he is set to solve.

Doyle's Holmes books are the novels A Study in Scarlet, The

READ ON

- *The Case Book of Sherlock Holmes.*
- ▶ Nicholas Meyer, *The Seven-per-cent Solution* (one of the most convincing of many Holmes stories by others since Doyle went out of copyright). G.K. Chesterton, *The Father Brown Stories*. Gladys Mitchell, *Twelve Horses and the Hangman's Noose.* John Dickson Carr, *The Emperor's Snuff Box.*

Sign of Four, The Hound of the Baskervilles *and* The Valley of Fear, *and the short-story collections* Adventures of Sherlock Holmes, The Return of Sherlock Holmes, His Last Bow *and* The Case Book of Sherlock Holmes. *The Challenger books include* The Poison Belt *and* The Land of Mist, *and Doyle's historical novels, apart from those mentioned, include* Micah Clarke *(set during the Monmouth Rebellion of 1685 and its bloody aftermath).*

DRABBLE, MARGARET (BORN 1939)

British novelist and non- fiction writer.

An admirer of ▷Eliot and ▷Bennett, Drabble has updated their fictional ideas to the present day. Her books are crammed with the detail of everyday lives – fetching children from school, making gravy, taking inter-city trains, washing tights – and are about 'ordinary' people: housewives, librarians, teachers, midwives. But Drabble, like Eliot and Bennett, is also interested in intellectual ideas, in describing the spirit of the times as well as their domestic detail. Without being feminist, her books centre on women's experience. They tell us how middle-class girls of the late 1950s felt about their lives, how they went on in the 1960s to balance marriage, motherhood and careers, and how they coped in the 1970s and 1980s with teenage children and rocky marriages. It is fiction so honest that it seems almost like autobiography: every one of Drabble's women shares an outlook, a tone of voice, which sounds (rightly or wrongly) like the author's own.

THE RADIANT WAY (1987)

The lives of three women of similar age (late 40s) and background (educated middle-class) are contrasted, in a brilliantly-evoked mid-1980s Britain. All were born in the north of England; Liz has moved south and made a career as a Harley Street psychiatrist; her sister has stayed at home to look after their senile mother; Alix and her husband, failing to make a success in London, are returning north to regenerate their lives. The characters' contrasting experience, and their middle-aged views of the way their younger ambitions have worked out, match the political and social feelings Drabble sees as typical of Britain in the 1980s, when the young adults of the flower-power generation are just beginning to feel that life has passed them by.

Drabble's novels are The Garrick Year, The Millstone, Jerusalem the Golden, The Waterfall, The Realms of Gold, The Ice Age, The Radiant Way *and* A Natural Curiosity. *She has also written biographies of Wordsworth and Bennett.*

READ ON

- *A Natural Curiosity* is a sequel to *The Radiant Way*. *The Garrick Year* is tougher; a moving study, set in the 1960s, of a woman trying to manage both marriage, to a rising actor, and the claims of her own career.
- ▶ Penelope Mortimer, *The Pumpkin Eater*. Deborah Moggach, *Close to Home*. ▷Margaret Atwood, *The Edible Woman*. Joan Didion, *The Book of Common Prayer*. Mary Flanagan, *Trust*.
- ▶ **Earlier books foreshadowing Drabble's concerns:** ▷George Eliot, *Middlemarch*; ▷Arnold Bennett, *Hilda Lessways*; ▷Virginia Woolf, *Mrs Dalloway*.

Dreaming Spires

(books set in Cambridge and Oxford Universities)

▷Max Beerbohm, *Zuleika Dobson*
Glyn Daniel, *The Cambridge Murders*
Alan Judd, *The Noonday Devil*
▷Barbara Pym, *Crampton Hodnett*
▷Dorothy L. Sayers, *Gaudy Night*
▷Tom Sharpe, *Porterhouse Blue*
▷C.P. Snow, *The Affair*

Higher (?) Education (p 122)

DUMAS, Alexandre (1802–70)

French writer of novels, plays, short stories and non-fiction.

In his 20s Dumas worked as a civil-service clerk; it was not until he was 29 that he was able to take up writing full-time. From then till his death, working with a team of assistants, he poured out over 250 plays, novels, essays, books on history, travel and cooking and no less than 22 volumes of memoirs. He was one of the most popular authors of his century, and the genre he specialised in, swashbuckling historical romance, was a favourite for 120 years, a forerunner of both modern spy stories and fantasy.

The Three Musketeers (1844–5)

At the beginning of the 17th century d'Artagnan, a young country squire, goes to Paris to seek adventure. He makes friends with three of the King's musketeers (by the unusual method of challenging each of them to a duel on the same day) and the four become inseparable. D'Artagnan is accepted for royal service, and the musketeers throw themselves into the political intrigues centring on weak king Louis, his unhappy queen and her arch-enemies Cardinal Richelieu and the seductive, treacherous Milady. The story involves stolen jewels, masquerades, bluff and double bluff, and the musketeers gallop the length and breadth of France, duelling, drinking, wenching and making a thousand skin-of-the-teeth escapes. Although the book's style is old-fashioned, its breathless plot, its good humour and above all the wisecracking, bantering friendship between the four central characters, give it irresistible gusto. After a few dozen pages of acclimatisation, it may prove hard to put it down.

Although Dumas was best-known – and is now best-remembered – for his Musketeers adventures, he wrote fine novels set in other periods, notably The Queen's Necklace *and* The

READ ON

- Dumas continued the Musketeers' adventures in *Twenty Years After*, *The Vicomte of Bragelonne* and *The Man in the Iron Mask*.
- ▶ **Swashbuckling stories:** Rafael Sabatini, *Captain Blood*; Jeffery Farnol, *The Broad Highway*; Stanley J. Weyman, *Gentleman of France*; Baroness Orczy, *The Scarlet Pimpernel*.
- ▶ **The idea of buddies united against the world is repeated, in a similar tongue-in-cheek way, in** ▷Len Deighton, *Only When I Larf* (about 1960s conmen) and Donald Westlake, *Gangway!* (about 1860s San Francisco crooks).

Countess of Charny *(both of which take place during the French Revolution) and* The Count of Monte Cristo, *about a man falsely imprisoned for helping the defeated Napoleon, who escapes, discovers hidden treasure and proceeds to hunt down the people who betrayed him.*

DU MAURIER, DAPHNE (1907–89)

British novelist and non-fiction writer.

Although Du Maurier wrote novels and stories of many kinds, she is best known for a series of atmospheric romances set in the English West Country (Cornwall, Devon and Somerset) and drawing on the moorland landscape and seafaring associations of the area. In her best-loved book, *Rebecca* (1938), a girl marries an enigmatic young widower and goes to be mistress of his large country house Manderley, only to find it haunted by the mystery of his first wife's death. Solving that mystery (against the wishes of the sinister housekeeper Mrs Danvers) is the only way to bring happiness to the young girl (who is unnamed) and peace to her tormented husband – and the search leads her into a psychological labyrinth as threatening as the corridors of the dark old house itself.

Du Maurier's romances include Jamaica Inn, Frenchman's Creek, My Cousin Rachel *and* Mary Anne. *Her other novels include* The King's General, The Parasites, The Glassblowers *and* The House on the Strand. The Apple Tree/Kiss Me Again Stranger, The Breaking Point *and* Early Stories *are collections of short stories. She also wrote plays, biographies (of her family, Branwell Brontë and Francis Drake) and an autobiography,* The Shaping of a Writer/Myself When Young.

READ ON

- Philippa Gregory, *The Favoured Child*. Jane Gardam, *Crusoe's Daughter*. ▷Charlotte Brontë, *Jane Eyre*. ▷Susan Howatch, *Penmarric*. ▷Frank Yerby, *A Woman Called Fancy*. Catherine Darby, *Rowan Garth*.

DUNNETT, DOROTHY (BORN 1923)

British novelist.

Dunnett is best-known for two enormous historical sagas, swashbuckling romances set in the 15th and 16th centuries. The hero of the 'Lymond' books is a Scottish soldier of fortune whose adventures take him as far as Malta, the Ottoman Empire and Russia (where he serves in the army of Ivan the Terrible). Back home, he becomes the protector of the infant Mary Queen of Scots and is embroiled in the religious and political intrigues of the English Tudor court. A second series (beginning with *Niccolò Rising* and continuing with *The Spring of the Ram* and *Race of Scorpions*) is in progress. It is the story of an equally charming adventurer, this time set in Renaissance Italy (Florence at the time of the Medicis and Savonarola) and Germany (during the reli-

READ ON

- Reay Tannahill, *The World, the Flesh and the Devil*. ▷Tom De Haan, *A Mirror for Princes*. Margaret Irwin, *Still She Wished for Company*. ▷Jean Plaidy, *The Plantagenet Prelude* and its sequels: the Plantagenet Saga. Frans Bengtsson,

gious wars triggered by Martin Luther's condemnation of the Roman Catholic Church). Dunnett's other books include *King Hereafter* (a novel about the historical Macbeth, King of Scotland) and a series of romantic thrillers set in the present day, all of whose titles – at least in the UK editions – include the name 'Dolly'. (These were originally published under the pseudonym 'Dorothy Halliday'.)

The Lymond books, in order, are The Game of Kings, Queen's Play, The Disorderly Knights, Pawn in Frankincense, The Ringed Castle *and* Checkmate. *The 'Dolly' books are* Dolly and the Singing Bird/The Photogenic Soprano, Dolly and the Cookie Bird/Murder in the Round, Dolly and the Doctor Bird/Match for a Murderer, Dolly and the Starry Bird/Murder in Focus *and* Dolly and the Nanny Bird.

The Long Ships (set in Viking times). ▷R.L. Stevenson, *Kidnapped* and its sequels (set in 18th-century Scotland, during the Jacobite uprisings).

DURRELL, LAWRENCE (1912–90)

British writer of novels, poems and non-fiction.

Durrell lived most of his life out of Britain, in Greece, Egypt and France. As well as fiction, he wrote poetry and half a dozen non-fiction books about Greek islands: they are among his most enjoyable work, allowing scope for the impressionistic descriptions of landscape and character and the ruminations on love and life which sometimes clog his novels. In his fiction, he uses experimental forms, constantly varying each story's structure and standpoint; this sets up a dialogue between writer and reader, a feeling of collaboration, which is one of the most exhilarating aspects of his work.

THE ALEXANDRIA QUARTET (1957–60)

Each book in the quartet, *Justine*, *Balthazar*, *Mountolive* and *Clea*, tells us part of the story: they give different viewpoints of the same events, and it is not till the end that every motive, every action, every twist of character becomes clear. The people are a group of friends and lovers, English, Greek and Egyptian, living in the turmoil of late-1930s Alexandria. At the centre is Darley, a teacher and would-be writer who observes events, partakes, but cannot explain. A main 'character' is the city of Alexandria itself. Durrell/Darley pretends to be giving accurate pictures of its souks, bars, palaces, brothels and crumbling embassies, but it is a dream-city, a fantasy-land where reality is subjective and events are only what you make of them.

As well as The Alexandria Quartet, *his novels include* The Black Book, The Dark Labyrinth/Cefalù *and the five-novel 'Avignon quincunx',* Monsieur, Livia, Constance, Sebastian *and* Quinx. *Durrell's* Collected Poems *are published, and*

READ ON

- *Tunc* and *Numquam* (a pair of Siamese-twin novels) are similarly dreamlike, setting bizarre events and characters in a blur of countries and climaxing magnificently, if unexpectedly, under the dome of St Paul's Cathedral, London.
- ▶ Stuart Evans, *Centres of Ritual* (and its sequels: the 'Windmill Hill' sequence). ▷Nathaniel West, *The Dream Life of Balso Snell*. D.M. Thomas, *Birthstone*. ▷Olivia Manning, *The Balkan Trilogy* (set in Bucharest and Athens during the second world war); *The Levant Trilogy* (set in Cairo).

Antrobus Complete *is a collection of satirical stort stories about diplomats, like TV sitcom frozen on the page. His island books include* Prospero's Cell *(about Corfu, also the subject of his brother Gerald's* My Family and Other Animals*),* Reflections on a Marine Venus *(about Rhodes) and* Bitter Lemons *(about Cyprus).*

E

ECCENTRIC FAMILIES

H.E. Bates, *The Darling Buds of May*
▷Ivy Compton-Burnett, *A House and its Head*
▷John Irving, *The Hotel New Hampshire*
Nancy Mitford, *The Pursuit of Love*
▷Vladimir Nabokov, *Ada*
Peter Tinniswood, *A Touch of Daniel*
▷Virginia Woolf, *To the Lighthouse*

All-engulfing Families (p 5); Many Generations (p 170); Parents and Children (p 193)

ECO, UMBERTO (BORN 1932)

Italian novelist.

The framework of Eco's first novel, *The Name of the Rose* (1983) is a murder mystery. A 14th-century monk, William of Baskerville, using methods of deduction which anticipate those of Sherlock Holmes, solves seven murders in the monastery he happens to be visiting. On this simple frame Eco weaves a wonderful tapestry of philosophy, intellectual jokes, extraordinary lore about monasticism, alchemy and religious belief. Although *The Name of the Rose* tweaks and stimulates the intellect, it is anything but hard to read – largely due to Eco's beautifully clear prose and to his affection for even the tiniest detail of medieval life.

READ ON

- *Foucault's Pendulum*.
- ► Helen Waddell, *Peter Abelard*. ▷William Golding, *The Spire*. ▷Hermann Hesse, *The Glass Bead Game*. ▷Tom De Haan, *A Mirror for Princes*.

EDDINGS, DAVID (BORN 1931)

US novelist.

After one modern adventure story, *High Hunt*, Eddings concentrated on fantasy. His best-known work is the 'Belgariad quintet' (1982–4), a ▷Tolkien-influenced saga of good and evil, magic and mysticism – but laced, unlike *The Lord of the Rings*, with a strong sense of the absurd. The books in the series are *Pawn of Prophecy*, *Queen of Sorcery*, *Magician's Gambit*, *Castle of Wizardry* and *Enchanter's Endgame*. Eddings is currently writing a second series (The 'Mallorean' quintet, beginning with *Guardians of the West*): further adventures of his hero Garion, who begins as a scullion, graduates to be sorcerer's apprentice and ends up a fully-fledged wizard.

READ ON

- ▶ Alan Dean Foster, *Spellsinger*. ▷Piers Anthony, *A Spell for Chameleon*. T.H. White, *The Once and Future King*. ▷J.R.R. Tolkien, *Lord of the Rings*.

THE ELDERLY

▷Kingsley Amis, *Ending Up*
▷Honoré de Balzac, *Old Goriot*
▷Julian Barnes, *Staring at the Sun*
▷David Cook, *Missing Persons*
▷Tove Jansson, *Sun City*
▷Muriel Spark, *Memento Mori*

ELIOT, GEORGE (1819–80)

British novelist.

'George Eliot' was the pen-name of Marian Evans, a farm-manager's daughter. She grew up in the stifling provincial pieties of middle-class Victorian England, but after her father's death became an atheist and freethinker, travelled abroad and set up home in London. She was at the heart of the liberal intellectual circles of her time: a supporter of Darwin, an admirer of ▷William Morris and other early socialists. A similar receptivity to new ideas and disdain for convention mark her novels. They deal with the kind of moral issues (such as whether a 'good life' can be lived without religion, or if sexual happiness is essential to a successful marriage) which were rarely discussed in polite Victorian company and were even less common in literature. At the same time her books teem with realistic detail of provincial society, minutely observed. The combination of exact documentation of behaviour and character with unashamed discussion of ideas normally left unspoken was a heady one: she was one of the most widely read authors of her day.

MIDDLEMARCH (1871–2)

Two people try to break free from the petty-minded boredom of the English provincial town of Middlemarch. Doro-

READ ON

- • *The Mill on the Floss* (about a brother and sister who are idyllically happy together as children, grow apart in adult life, and are finally, tragically reunited).
- ▶ **Matching Eliot's concern for the individual stifled by society:** ▷Gustave Flaubert, *Madame Bovary*; ▷Mrs Gaskell, *North and South*; ▷Thomas Hardy, *Jude the Obscure*; Benjamin Disraeli, *Sybil*.
- ▶ **To *Daniel Deronda*:** ▷Henry James,

thea Brooke marries because of intellectual infatuation, only to find that her husband (an elderly scholar) is a domestic tyrant. Tertius Lydgate, a doctor struggling to introduce new medical ideas in a society which is deeply suspicious of them, marries for love, only to find that his wife's brainless following of fashion destroys his bank-balance, his self-confidence and his social position.

Apart from Romola, *set in 15th-century Florence, all Eliot's novels have 19th-century English locations and characters. Her first book,* Scenes from Clerical Life, *contains three mid-length stories; it and the short novel* Silas Marner *(about a freethinking country weaver tormented for his beliefs and for a crime he did not commit) are the most accessible of all her works. Her full-length novels are* Adam Bede, The Mill on the Floss, Felix Holt, Middlemarch *and* Daniel Deronda.

EMOTIONALLY ILL-AT-EASE

▷Anita Brookner, *Look at Me*
Anita Desai, *Baumgartner's Bombay*
▷George Eliot, *Middlemarch*
▷Gustave Flaubert, *Madame Bovary*
▷E.M. Forster, *Howards End*
▷Elizabeth Jolley, *Milk and Honey*
▷Rosamond Lehmann, *The Ballad and the Source*
▷Mary McCarthy, *The Company She Keeps*
▷John Updike, *Marry Me*

Battling with Life (p 20); Perplexed by Life (p 196)

Portrait of a Lady; Janet Lewis, *The Trial of Sören Kvist.*

► **Contemporary books combining social observation with 'issues' in an Eliotish way, though their styles are entirely different:** ▷Margaret Drabble, *The Millstone*; ▷Katharine Anne Porter, *Pale Horse, Pale Rider*; Winifred Holtby, *South Riding*; Simone De Beauvoir, *The Mandarins.*

F

FANTASY ADVENTURE

▷Stephen Donaldson, *'Thomas Covenant' series*
▷A. Conan Doyle, *The Lost World*
▷David Eddings, *'Belgariad' quintet*
C.S. Lewis, *Out of the Silent Planet*
▷Michael Moorcock, *The Warhound and the World's Pain*
Terry Pratchett, *The Colour of Magic*
▷J.R.R. Tolkien, *The Lord of the Rings*
▷Jules Verne, *Journey to the Centre of the Earth*
Patricia Wrightson, *The Ice is Coming*

Fantasy Societies (p 76); High Adventure (p 119)

FANTASY SOCIETIES

▷Tom De Haan, *A Mirror for Princes*
Michael Frayn, *Sweet Dreams*
Alasdair Gray, *Lanark*
Tanith Lee, *The Storm Lord*
▷Ursula Le Guin, *Malafrena*
▷Anne McCaffrey, *Dragonflight*
▷Robert Silverberg, *Lord Valentine's Castle*
▷Jonathan Swift, *Gulliver's Travels*
▷H.G. Wells, *The Time Machine*
Gene Wolfe, *The Book of the New Sun*

Future Societies (p 89)

FARMER, PHILIP JOSÉ (BORN 1918)

US novelist.

Each of Farmer's SF novels is the exploration of a single, brilliantly surreal initial idea: in *Dayworld*, for example, that the world's overpopulation leads to each human being being allowed one day per week of 'life' and having to spend the other six in cold storage. His best-known work is the 'Riverworld' series (1972–80; the individual titles are *To Your Scattered Bodies Go*; *The Fabulous Riverboat*; *The Dark Design*; *The Magic Labyrinth*; *Gods of Riverworld*). Riverworld is a planet on which every human being ever born, from the dawn of history to beyond the present day, has been granted a second life and the chance of moral self-reformation. The series tells how three people, Samuel Clemens (alias Mark ▷Twain), Richard Burton (translator of the *Kama Sutra*) and Alice Hargreaves (née Liddell: the inspiration for *Alice In Wonderland*) explore Riverworld and try to discover the nature and purpose of the experiment of which they – to say nothing of King John of England, plotting a political coup – are part.

Farmer's other books include three separate novels dealing with the pull between love and sex: Flesh, The Lovers *and* A Feast Unknown, Night of Light *(about religious experience), and the dazzling short-story collection* The Book of Philip José Farmer.

READ ON

- *Jesus on Mars.*
- ▷Michael Moorcock, *Warlord of the Air*. ▷Frank Herbert, *The Dosadi Experiment*. ▷Isaac Asimov, *Foundation*.

FARRELL, J.G. (JAMES GORDON) (1935–79)

British novelist.

After three contemporary novels, including *The Lung* (1965, based on his own experience), about the onset of polio, Farrell took all his themes from history. *Troubles* (1970), set in Ireland after the first world war, is a barbed account of the Irish freedom-struggle against the English, and draws uncomfortable parallels with the present-day situation in Northern Ireland. *The Siege of Krishnapur* (1973), equally vitriolic and farcical – its tone is close at times to ▷Heller's *Catch-22* – is set in 1850s India, during the so-called 'Mutiny'. *The Singapore Grip* (1978) is a blockbuster about the Japanese capture of Malaysia in the second world war – for Farrell, the beginning of Britain's eclipse as a global power. Taken together, the three books are an indictment of Britain's attitude towards its empire: not so much thuggishness as boneheaded indifference, the unconcern of those who never imagine that others might resent their rule.

READ ON

- **To *Troubles*:** Liam O'Flaherty: *The Informer*; Bernard MacLaverty, *Cal*.
- **To *The Siege of Krishnapur*:** ▷John Masters, *Nightrunners of Bengal*; Idries Shah, *Kara Kush*; Gita Mehta, *Raj*.
- **To *The Singapore Grip*:** ▷J.G. Ballard, *Empire of the Sun*; Timothy Mo, *An Insular Possession*.

FAULKNER, William (1897–1962)

US novelist and short-story writer.

Faulkner's work deals obsessively with a single theme: the moral degeneracy of the US Deep South. His characters are the descendants of the cotton barons of the time before the Civil War, and of the slaves who worked for them. The whites live in crumbling mansions, dress in finery handed down from previous generations and bolster their sagging self-esteem with snobbery, racism and drink. The blacks either fawn, as if slavery had never been abolished, or seethe in decaying slums on the edge of town. The air itself seems tainted: despair, lust, introversion and murder clog people's minds. It is a society without hope or comfort, and Faulkner describes it in a series of moral horror stories, compulsive and merciless.

The Sound And The Fury (1929)

The novel's theme is how moral decadence overwhelms two generations of the white Compson family. We see a brother and sister, Caddy and Quentin, growing up as bright, happy adolescents, full of hope for the future, only to fall victims to the family taint and spiral into incest, nymphomania and suicide. One of their brothers, Jason, a morose bully, succeeds his father as head of the family and becomes a miser and a tyrant; their other brother Benjy has a mental age of two. In the second half of the book we see the corruption threatening to engulf Caddy's and Quentin's incestuous daughter, and her attempts to break free from the family curse. Large sections of the book are told as first-person narratives, by Caddy, Jason, Quentin and – eerily, a tour de force of writing, demanding concentration in the reader – the idiot Benjy. A final strand of claustrophobia is added by the Compsons' negro servants: watching, always-present, like the chorus of a particularly fraught Greek tragedy.

Faulkner's short stories are in two fat volumes, Collected Stories *and* Uncollected Stories. *His main Southern novels, a series set in the imaginary Yoknapatawpha County, Mississippi, are* Sartoris, Absalom, Absalom!, The Unvanquished *and the trilogy* The Hamlet, The Town *and* The Mansion. *His other books include* Intruder in the Dust, The Sound and the Fury, Light in August, The Rievers *and two books in experimental styles,* As I Lay Dying *and* Requiem for a Nun.

READ ON

- *Sartoris* (about the family of a Southern Civil War general coming to terms with defeat); *Intruder in the Dust* (a comparatively sunny book about an adolescent awakening to adulthood).
- **Good Deep South follow-ups:** ▷Carson McCullers, *The Ballad of the Sad Café*; William Styron, *Lie Down in Darkness*; Harper Lee, *To Kill a Mockingbird*; Tenessee Williams, *Short Stories*.
- **More cheerful:** ▷Eudora Welty, *Delta Wedding*; Calder Willingham, *Eternal Fire*.
- **Good follow-ups on the theme of the degenerate, collapsing family:** ▷Thomas Mann, *Buddenbrooks*; Giuseppi Tomaso di Lampedusa, *The Leopard*; ▷Ivy Compton-Burnett, *Mothers and Sons*.
- **Good stylistic follow-ups:** ▷James Joyce, *Ulysses*; ▷Virginia Woolf, *To the Lighthouse*. ▷Thomas Pynchon, *Gravity's Rainbow*.

FIELDING, Henry (1707–54)

British novelist and playwright.

Fielding's first successes were with satirical stage comedies: *Rape upon Rape* (a farce) and *The Tragedy of Tom Thumb* (a parody of melodramatic tragedy). But his plays were too political for the authorities, who closed them down. He turned to fiction, announcing that he meant to write an English equivalent of *Don Quixote*. His books are life-stories, involving charming young people in a series of escapades as they journey from country-house to inn, from farmyard to theatre-box, from law-court to bedroom, gathering experience and outwitting would-be predators at every step. Fielding's novels are long and leisurely: it is as if he is taking a stroll through English society, high and low, and everything he sees or hears reminds him of an anecdote, genial, unhurried and preposterous.

Tom Jones (1749)

Tom Jones is a foundling brought up by kindly Squire Allworthy. He is a personable, amorous young man, and his immorality finally makes Allworthy send him into the world to seek his fortune. The novel tells Tom's adventures, in and out of bed, as he wanders through England enjoying life as it comes, torn by the thought of his true-love Sophia Western, but still ready to be seduced by every pretty girl he meets. The story is told in short chapters, like extended anecdotes, and Fielding keeps breaking off to address the reader directly, telling jokes, pointing morals and commenting on the life and manners of the time.

Fielding's other novels are Joseph Andrews *and* Amelia. A Journey from This World to the Next *and* The Life and Death of Jonathan Wild the Great *are short, savage satires: the second, for example, treats a notorious, real-life highwayman as if he were an epic hero.* Journal of a Voyage to Lisbon *is a fascinating travel-diary about crossing the Bay of Biscay in a leaky, storm-tossed ship.*

READ ON

- *Joseph Andrews* (a parody of the heroine-in-moral-danger novels of ▷Samuel Richardson is the story of a young man so beautiful that every woman he meets longs to entice him into bed).
- ▶ Bob Coleman, *The Later Adventures of Tom Jones* (a 1986 sequel to *Tom Jones*, taking Tom to colonial America, where he is embroiled not only in love-affairs but in the War of Independence). Apuleius, *The Golden Ass* (in the ▷Robert Graves translation). Miguel de Cervantes Saavedra, *Don Quixote*. ▷Laurence Sterne, *Tristram Shandy*.
- ▶ **Later books in a similarly relaxed, satirical vein:** ▷H.G. Wells, *Kipps*; ▷Thomas Mann, *Confessions of Felix Krull*; ▷Mary McCarthy, *Birds of America*; ▷Saul Bellow, *The Adventures of Augie March*.

THE FILM BUSINESS

Dirk Bogarde, *West of Sunset*
▷Len Deighton, *Close Up*
▷Peter De Vries, *The Prick of Noon*
H.R.F. Keating, *Filmi, Filmi, Inspector Ghote*
▷Frederic Raphael, *California Time*
Terry Southern, *Blue Movie*
▷Nathaniel West, *The Day of the Locust*
Donald Westlake, *Who Stole Sassi Manoon?*

FITZGERALD, F. SCOTT (FRANCIS SCOTT)

(1896–1940)
US novelist and short-story writer.

In the USA of the 1920s the earnestness which had been needed to win the first world war was replaced by giddy exhilaration. Jazz, bootleg liquor, drugs and sex seemed to be not merely pleasures, but symbols of a new, liberated age – and the fact that that age was clearly doomed, that the dancing would end in tears, gave every party, every spending-spree, an edge of extra excitement, as if people were roller-skating on the brink of the abyss. Fitzgerald, rich, handsome, athletic and talented, not only wrote about this doomed high society, but was one of its leaders. In the 1930s, when the inevitable reckoning came – the Great Depression, was parallelled in Fitzgerald's life by his wife's madness and his own alcoholism and bankruptcy – his books not unnaturally turned sour and sad. But his 1920s stories and novels told the legend of the 'jazz age' with such glittering force that it is easy, now, to believe that all America, and not just a few thousand sophisticates, lived like that.

THE GREAT GATSBY (1925)

In a millionaire community on Long Island, the enigmatic bachelor Gatsby gives huge all-night parties at his mansion, orgies of dancing, drugs and sex, the season's most fashionable events. His fascinated neighbour, the book's narrator Nick Carraway, makes friends with him and begins unravelling the secrets of his personality. Carraway's intervention triggers revelations about Gatsby's criminal past, and a love-affair between Gatsby and the wife of a wealthy oaf, Tom Buchanan; these in turn lead to further tragedy. At the end of the book Carraway sits alone outside Gatsby's deserted house, reflecting on the emptiness of the lives he has just described.

Fitzgerald's 1920s novels are This Side of Paradise, The Beautiful and Damned *and* The Great Gatsby. Tender is the Night, *bitterly autobiographical, describes the life of an alco-*

READ ON

- *The Beautiful and Damned* (about the doomed marriage of two bright young things, leaders of jazz-age society: a book given ferocious ironical point for today's readers by what we know of the decay to come in Fitzgerald's own marriage).
- ▶ ▷Evelyn Waugh, *Vile Bodies*. ▷Anthony Powell, *Afternoon Men*. Anita Loos, *Gentlemen Prefer Blondes*. ▷Thornton Wilder, *Theophilus North*. Ronald Firbank, *Valmouth*. Vita Sackville-West, *The Edwardians*. Andrew Sinclair, *The Breaking of Bumbo*. ▷Martin Amis, *Success* applies Fitzgerald's tone of hopeless, cynical black farce to a much later 'doomed' generation: our own, and ▷William

holic doctor and his insane wife on the French Riviera, and the unfinished The Last Tycoon *is a satire on the Hollywood for which he wrote rubbish to earn money in his last desperate months of life.* Tales of the Jazz Age *and* Taps at Reveille *are collections of short stories.*

Thackeray, *Vanity Fair* takes a similar view of 19th-century English middle-class society.

FLAUBERT, GUSTAVE (1821–80)

French novelist.

Many of Flaubert's contemporary writers – even such 'realists' as ▷Balzac and ▷Dickens – believed that 'fiction' involved larger-than-life characters, events or emotions. Flaubert's ambition, by contrast, was to hold up a mirror to ordinary people in humdrum situations, to take the boring events of commonplace lives and make them interesting. He also avoided heightened language, wit, irony and the other devices novelists used to enliven their narrative. He worked to make his prose evenly-paced and unobtrusive, taking its tensions and climaxes from the flow of events themselves. In modern times, similar techniques have been used in 'fly-on-the-wall' TV documentaries, where a camera-crew records unscripted scenes from daily life – and if nothing else, these programmes have shown just how tempestuous and extraordinary everyday lives can be.

MADAME BOVARY (1857)

Emma, a romantic and foolish young woman, dreams of being swept away on clouds of ecstasy, either by a handsome lover or into the arms of the Church. She marries a small-town doctor, and finds the routine of provincial life stifling and unfulfilling. She tries to bring excitement into her life by flirting, and is gradually trapped in pathetic and grubby love-affairs, stealing from her husband to pay for her ever more eccentric whims. In the end, destroyed by her inability to live up to her own dreams, she kills herself – and everyone else's life goes on as if she had never existed.

Flaubert's novels of ordinary French life are Madame Bovary, Sentimental Education (L'Éducation sentimentale) *and the unfinished* Bouvard and Pécuchet. Salammbô *applies the same techniques to a story of the Carthage of Hannibal's time, to bizarre effect, as if an archaeological treatise had been jumbled up with the script for a Hollywood epic film.* The Temptation of St Anthony *seeks to describe all the temptations, of flesh, spirit and will, which might assail a devout Catholic believer;* Three Stories *contains 'A Simple Heart', one of the most moving of all Flaubert's works.*

READ ON

- *Sentimental Education* (about a young man who tries, like Emma Bovary, to spice his boring life with grand passions, and fails. A secondary strand in the book is the political situation leading up to the 1848 revolution – something as busy and sterile, in Flaubert's opinion, as his hero's attempts to find meaning in existence).
- ▶ ▷Italo Svevo, *A Life*. ▷Arnold Bennett, *Hilda Lessways*. ▷Joseph Heller, *Something Happened*. ▷Elizabeth Taylor, *A Wreath of Roses*. ▷Iris Murdoch, *Under the Net*. ▷R.K. Narayan, *The English Teacher*, though set in a society (provincial India) and a period (the 1950s) remote from *Madame Bovary*, and less than a quarter as long, magnificently

matches Flaubert's insight into the way that the joys and sorrows of small lives, no less than large, can tear the heart.

FLEMING, IAN (1908–64)
British novelist.

Fleming's James Bond books are like comic strips for adults: Bond is a super-hero who saves the world from spectacularly nasty, psychopathic master-criminals. Bond wins through by a mixture of supreme physical prowess and late-Edwardian one-upmanship somewhat bizarre in the 1960s setting. Adult tastes are catered for less by psychological insight or intellectual depth than by frequent sex-scenes (Bond, as well as everything else, is a super-stud) and by laconic, hardboiled wit. In everything but plot – over-the-top technology, larky dialogue, high-gloss violence – the Bond films give the exact flavour of Fleming's books.

GOLDFINGER (1959)
Auric Goldfinger has two obsessions: gold and power. He plans to smash the vaults of Fort Knox with a nuclear missile and use the stolen gold to finance world domination. Only Bond can stop him – and the book shows in deadpan, second-by-second detail how he does it.

Other Bond novels include Moonraker, Thunderball, From Russia With Love, Diamonds are Forever, Dr No, On Her Majesty's Secret Service, You Only Live Twice *and* The Man With the Golden Gun. Octopussy *is a collection of short stories.*

READ ON

- *From Russia With Love.*
- In the 1960s, until ▷Deighton and ▷Le Carré took the spy-story in a different direction, there were a million Bond imitations and spoofs, of which some of the jolliest are by John Gardner, Fleming's official successor as chronicler of Bond. (A good example of Gardner at his best is *Scorpius*). Peter O'Donnell, *Modesty Blaise* all but out-Flemings Fleming, with the added zest that the supersexed superspy is a woman.
- **More recent follow-ups:** ▷Robert Ludlum, *The Matarese Circle*; Joe Poyer, *The Chinese Agenda*.

FOLLETT, KEN (BORN 1949)
British novelist.

Follett's novels are fast-action thrillers, many with industrial-espionage or wartime themes. His books include *The Bear Raid* (about stock-market espionage), *Storm Island/The Key to Rebecca* (a fight for survival on an uninhabited

READ ON

- Palma Harcourt, *A Matter of Conscience*. Clive Egleton, *Troika*.

island during the second world war) and *The Man from St Petersburg* (about the secret negotiations between the powers before the first world war, and moving, with biting social relevance, from scenes set in the London slums to the whispers and backstabbings of an opulent Imperial court).

George Markstein, *Soul Hunters.*

FORD, Ford Madox (1873–1939)

British novelist and non-fiction writer.

Although Ford produced books of all kinds, from biographies to historical novels (*The Fifth Queen*, a Tudor trilogy), he is best remembered for *Parade's End* and *The Good Soldier*. *The Good Soldier* (1915) is a ▷Jamesian story aboul two couples who meet in a German hotel and become emotionally and sexually entwined, with devastating results for both themselves and the innocent young ward of one of them. The four novels of *Parade's End* (1924–8) tell how a country landowner, a young man rooted in the social and moral attitudes of the past, is forced by experience (as an officer in the first world war and as a reluctant participant in the freer sexual atmosphere of the post-war years) to slough off the skin of Victorian morality and come to terms, a dozen years later than everyone else, with 20th-century values.

READ ON

- ▶ Vita Sackville-West, *The Edwardians*. Isabel Colegate, *The Shooting Party*. ▷C.P. Snow, *Strangers and Brothers*. ▷Kazuo Ishiguro, *An Artist of The Floating World* (setting the 'coming-to-terms' theme in post-war Japan). Richard Aldington, *The Hero*. Frank Swinnerton *(Nocturne)*; and Elizabeth M. Roberts *(The Time of Man)* are novelists much like Ford, and almost equally neglected.

FORESTER, C.S. (Cecil Scott) (1899–1966)

British novelist.

Forester is best-known for his 'Hornblower' novels, about a career officer in the British navy of Nelson's time. The books are rich in the detail of life on wooden fighting ships, and the historical background is meticulous; Forester however gives Hornblower 20th-century sensibilities (he is for example sickened by floggings and horrified by the brutality of war) which both flesh him out as a character and draw the reader into the story. The Hornblower series has overshadowed Forester's other books, which include two superb novels set during the Napoleonic Wars (*Death to the French*; *The Gun*), the psychological crime stories *Payment Deferred* and *Plain Murder*, and the comedy-thriller *The African Queen*, memorably filmed in the 1950s with Katharine Hepburn and Humphrey Bogart.

READ ON

- *The African Queen* (about a prissy missionary and a rough-diamond ship's captain who take a leaky old boat full of dynamite downriver in second-world-war Africa to blow up an enemy convoy – and fall in love on the way).
- ▶ **To Forester's**

BROWN ON RESOLUTION (1929)

This tense thriller is about a man captured by an enemy ship during the first world war and taken to the remote island of Resolution, where he escapes and tries, single-handed, to hinder the refitting of the warship before he himself can be tracked down and killed.

*The core of the Hornblower series is a trilogy of books (*The Happy Return, Flying Colours, Ship of the Line*) often published together as* Captain Horatio Hornblower. *Other books in the series fill in details of Hornblower's career, tracing his adventures over a quarter of a century. Typical titles are* Mr Midshipman Hornblower, Hornblower and the Atropos, Hornblower in the West Indies *and* Lord Hornblower.

thrillers: ▷Geoffrey Household, *Watcher in the Shadows*; ▷Graham Greene, *Gun for Sale/This Gun for Hire*.

▶ **To the Hornblower books:** Bernard Cornwell, *Sharpe's Honour* (one of a series about an army officer at the time of the Peninsular War); Alexander Kent, *Richard Bolitho, Midshipman*. George Macdonald Fraser, *Flashman* and its sequels turn the whole idea splendidly upside-down, telling us the outrageous grown-up career of the caddish bully from *Tom Brown's Schooldays*.

FORSTER, E.M. (EDWARD MORGAN) (1879–1970)

British novelist.

All Forster's novels were written in the 1900s (though *A Passage to India* was not published until 1924), and all are concerned with the crippling emotional reticence he considered typical of the Edwardian age. Outwardly extrovert and competent, the Edwardians (Forster thought) were afraid of intimacy. They replaced it with 'manners', and often even members of the same family, even husbands and wives, were inhibited from showing towards each other the kind of genuine feelings they revealed towards God, the flag or their pampered pets. Forster's plots all turn on the disastrous results of emotional inexperience, of people blundering about in each other's sensibilities. In *Where Angels Fear to Tread* an Edwardian family's inability to believe that an Italian can have true paternal feelings for his baby leads to a doomed expedition to Italy to kidnap the child. In *Howards End* a note from one friend to another, confessing love (in fact one snatched kiss in a garden) leads to a hurricane of emotional misunderstanding and disapproval which involves

READ ON

- *A Room With a View* (about the emotional awakening of a snobbish English girl visiting Italy for the first time and realising that there is a real world beyond Edwardian English convention).

▶ ***To A Passage to India*:** ▷Ruth Prawer Jhabvala, *Heat and Dust*; Paul Scott, *The Raj Quartet*; M.M. Kaye, *The Far Pavilions*.

E.M. FORSTER

A PASSAGE TO INDIA *(1910s English girl confused by experience of the Raj)*

IMPERIALISM, GOOD AND BAD

Rudyard **KIPLING, KIM**
(adventures of Anglo-Indian boy in heyday of Raj)

Timothy **MO, AN INSULAR POSSESSION**
(Blockbusting novel about English imperialism in Hong Kong)

James **BLISH, A CASE OF CONSCIENCE**
(should mineral-rich planet be exploited at expense of native inhabitants' life and culture?)

Kingsley **AMIS, RUSSIAN HIDE AND SEEK**
(life in Orwellian Britain, part of Russian 'evil empire')

CONFUSED EMOTIONS

R.K. **NARAYAN, THE VENDOR OF SWEETS**
(devout Hindu in rural India dismayed by son's 'progressive' ways)

V.S. **NAIPAUL, A HOUSE FOR MR BISWAS**
(Indian Hindu in Jamaica caught between dependence on his wife's all-engulfing family and his longing to lead his own life)

L.P. **HARTLEY, THE GO-BETWEEN**
(small boy in 1910s England carries love-messages, emotions he only dimly understands)

Willa **CATHER, MY ANTONIA**
(daughter of 19th-century Bohemian immigrants growing up in rural Nebraska)

Paul **THEROUX, FONG AND THE INDIANS**
(Indian shopkeeper struggling to survive in rural, tribal Africa)

BETWEEN TWO WORLDS

Ruth Prawer **JHABVALA, HEAT AND DUST**
(Englishwoman contrasts modern India with her aunt's 1920s experience)

Henry **JAMES, THE AMBASSADORS**
(Rich 1900s Americans take 'culture' to Europe, find it more civilised than they expected)

John **LE CARRÉ, THE PERFECT SPY**
(memoirs of elderly double agent, trying to discover where his loyalty lies)

James **CLAVELL, SHÔGUN**
(American becomes samurai in 17th-century Japan)

TWILIGHT OF EMPIRE

Paul **SCOTT, STAYING ON**
(plight of English in India after independence)

Peter **VANSITTART, THREE SIX SEVEN**
(Romanised Britons watching advance of barbarism after 4th century collapse of Roman power)

P.H. **NEWBY, THE PICNIC AT SAKKARA**
(English teacher in 1950s Egypt confused by collapse of British Empire)

Morris **WEST, THE AMBASSADOR**
(US ambassador in Vietnam, appalled by his country's actions there)

Gerald **SEYMOUR, FIELD OF BLOOD**
(undercover SAS officer hunts IRA suspect in present-day Belfast)

a dozen people and three generations. The central character in *The Longest Journey* tries to 'connect' emotionally with his newly-discovered, no-good step-brother, and in the process destroys first his marriage and then himself. Forster, himself an emotional introvert (a self-deprecating homosexual), offers no solutions. But few writers have better described the problem: his intuition for emotional nuance and his compelling characterisation (especially of women), give his books fascination despite their narrow focus.

▶ **To Forster's work in general:** ▷Henry James, *The Wings of the Dove*; ▷Marcel Proust, *Within a Budding Grove* (the second part of *Remembrance of Things Past)*; ▷L.P. Hartley, *The Go-Between*; ▷Somerset Maugham, *East and West*.

▶ **Fascinating books showing culture-clash going the other way** (people used to 'abroad' being discomforted by contemporary Britain): ▷Paul Theroux, *The Black House*; ▷P.H. Newby, *Leaning in the Wind.*

A PASSAGE TO INDIA (1924)

Adela Quested leaves for India to get to know her fiancé Ronny before she marries him. Her openness of manner, and especially the way she treats Indians as equals, offends the stuffy British community. For her part, she is overwhelmed by India, and her stupefaction leads her to a moment of mental confusion during which she accuses an Indian friend, Dr Aziz, of molesting her on a visit to the Malabar Caves. In court, oppressed by the certainty of the English that Aziz must be guilty, she reruns the events at Malabar in her mind, and suddenly recants. Her behaviour has, however, made apparent the unbridgeable gulf between Indians and English under the Raj, not to mention the lack of communication between 'free spirits' such as herself and her more hidebound contemporaries.

Forster's other fiction includes the novel Maurice *(about a homosexual friendship; written in the 1910s but not published until the 1970s) and three collections of short stories,* Celestial Omnibus, The Eternal Moment *and* The Life to Come.

FORSYTH, FREDERICK (BORN 1938)

British novelist.

Forsyth worked as a BBC reporter and a war correspondent, and his thrillers are as immediate and waffle-free as good news-stories. They often include real people and events; only the hair-trigger tension of his plots makes actuality look tame. In *The Odessa File* (1972), for example, a journalist covering the hunt for a war-criminal uncovers a nazi arms-smuggling conspiracy to help Arab terrorists in Israel. The details are fiction, but the story is as fresh as this morning's news.

Forsyth's novels are The Day of the Jackal, The Devil's Alternative, The Fourth Protocol, The Dogs of War *and* The Negotiator. The Shepherd *is a short novel;* No Comebacks *is a collection of short stories.*

READ ON

▶ Walter Wager, *Telefon*. ▷Ted Allbeury, *The Crossing*. Daniel Easterman, *The Seventh Sanctuary*. ▷Ian Fleming, *From Russia With Love*.

FOWLES, JOHN (BORN 1926)

British novelist.

Obsession and delusion are Fowles' main themes. The deranged hero of *The Collector* 'collects' a pretty girl as one might a butterfly. The heroes of *Daniel Martin* and *Mantissa* are authors deserted by the Muse, one a screenwriter corrupted by success, the other a novelist undergoing creative therapy at the hands (and other parts) of a seductive, feminist goddess. *A Maggot*, set in the 18th century, reworks a real-life murder investigation to take in erotic obsession, witchcraft, religious mania and flying saucers. Fowles further blurs the boundary between 'truth' and 'fiction' by using experimental techniques. He shifts between past and present, makes authorial asides and comments, and gives us two, three or half a dozen alternative versions of the same events. As with ▷Durrell, this experimentalism is coupled with ornate prose (sometimes in brilliant imitation of 18th and 19th century styles); few modern best-selling writers offer such a packed experience.

THE FRENCH LIEUTENANT'S WOMAN (1969)

The book's heart is a straightforward 19th-century story about the obsessive love-affair between a rich man and an outcast, the 'French Lieutenant's Woman' of the title. They meet in the seaside town of Lyme Regis; their affair scandalises society; she runs away; he pursues her. Fowles' prose, likewise, is for much of the time straightforward and solid in the 19th-century manner. But he also plays games with the reader. He keeps interrupting the story to tell us things about Lyme Regis (home of Mary Anning the fossil-collector), Darwin, Freudian psychology and the social customs of Victorian London. He claims that he has no idea what will happen next, that this is the characters' story, not his. He supplies alternative endings, so that we can choose our own. These devices give the book an unexpectedness in marked contrast to its sober 19th-century heart – it is as if someone reading us ▷Eliot or ▷Thackeray kept breaking off to perform conjuring tricks.

Apart from novels, Fowles has published a story-collection, The Ebony Tower, *and* The Aristos, *a set of philosophical meditations.*

READ ON

- ***The Magus*** (revised version): about a man trying obsessively to find out if what he thinks he experiences is real or fantasy. Much of it involves magic, and takes place on a mysterious Greek island – or seems to, for our perception of 'truth' and 'fiction' is as shifting as the character's.
- ▶ **To *The French Lieutenant's Woman*:** John Barth, *The Sot-weed Factor*; John Berger, *G*; ▷William Golding, *Rites of Passage*; Thornton Wilder, *The Bridge of San Luis Rey*.
- ▶ **To *The Magus*:** ▷Lawrence Durrell, *The Dark Labyrinth/Cefalù*; D.M. Thomas, *The White Hotel*.

FRANCIS, DICK (BORN 1920)

British novelist.

Francis writes brilliantly-paced, characterful thrillers, most of them about blackmail, fraud and revenge among jockeys, owners, trainers, bookies and others involved in the racing

READ ON

- ▶ John Francome, *Slaughterhorse*. Grant Adamson,

business. In *Break In* (1986), for example, champion steeplechaser Kit Fielding sets out to discover why someone is trying to ruin his brother-in-law, the trainer Bobby Allardeck – and at once himself becomes the target of newspaper smears, bribery, entrapment and attempted murder.

Francis' novels include Dead Cert, Blood Sport, Forfeit, Bonecrack, Slay-Ride, Risk, Whip Hand, Proof, Straight *and* The Edge. The Sport of Queens *is autobiography, fascinating about his own racing days.*

Wild Justice. ▷Jeffrey Archer, *A Matter of Honour.* Nicolas Freeling, *The Dresden Green.*

FRANKLIN, MILES (1879–1954)

Australian novelist.

'Miles Franklin' was one of the pseudonyms of Stella Miles Franklin. She wrote optimistic tales of pioneer farming life in Australia, in a cheerful, bustling style; her novels are like literary patchwork quilts. Under the name Miles Franklin she is best-known for *My Brilliant Career* (1901), its sequel *My Career Goes Bung* (1946) – the story of a breathlessly enthusiastic adolescent, Sybylla Melvyn, as she learns about life, the arts and love on outback farms and in the big city – and *All That Swagger* (1936), a more serious panorama of outback life. Under a second pseudonym, 'Brent of Bin Bin', Franklin published six lighter novels on the same lines, 'snapshots of ordinary life' modelled on the writings of Mark ▷Twain. Their titles are *Up the Country, Ten Creeks Run, Back to Bool Bool, Cockatoos, Prelude to Waking,* and *Gentlemen at Gyang Gyang.* One editor (Carmen Callil) called her an 'unsophisticated genius', prone to 'ebullient outpourings'; the description is exact.

Franklin's other books under her own name include the novels Some Everyday Folk and Dawn, Old Blastus of Bandicoot *and* Bring the Monkey *and the autobiographical memoir* Childhood at Brindabella. *Under the pseudonym* 'Mrs Ogniblat l'Artsau' *she published one novel,* The Net of Circumstance.

READ ON

- ▷Mark Twain, *The Adventures of Tom Sawyer.* H.E. Bates, *The Darling Buds of May.* Betty MacDonald, *The Egg and I.* Laura Ingalls Wilder, *The Little House on the Prairie.*
- **Exactly matching Franklin's bouncy, happy style, though its theme and location are entirely different:** ▷Jerome K. Jerome, *Three Men in a Boat.*

FREEMANTLE, BRIAN (BORN 1936)

British novelist.

As well as his own name, Freemantle uses the pseudonyms Richard Gant and Leslie Street. His books include thrillers (*Goodbye to an Old Friend; Face Me When You Walk Away*) and a series of spy-stories (eg *Clap Hands, Here Comes Charlie*) featuring the amiable down-and-out Charlie Muffin, whose past life and whose character are as fascinating as the missions he undertakes.

READ ON

- ▷Len Deighton, *Horse Under Water.* Roy Lewis, *A Certain Blindness.* Sara Woods, *Cry Guilty.* John Wainwright, *All On a Summer's Day.*

FRIENDS (?) AND NEIGHBOURS
(gossip; bitchiness; one-upmanship)

▷E.F. Benson, *Mapp and Lucia*
▷Peter De Vries, *The Mackerel Plaza*
▷Mrs Gaskell, *Cranford*
▷Sinclair Lewis, *Main Street*
▷Barbara Pym, *A Glass of Blessings*
▷John Updike, *Couples*

The Human Comedy (p 127)

FUTURE SOCIETIES

▷Margaret Atwood, *The Handmaid's Tale*
▷Angela Carter, *The Passion of New Eve*
▷Philip K. Dick, *The Man in the High Castle*
▷Robert Graves, *Seven Days in New Crete*
▷Aldous Huxley, *Brave New World*
▷Walter M. Miller, *A Canticle for Leibowitz*
▷William Morris, *News from Nowhere*
▷George Orwell, *1984*
▷George Turner, *The Sea and Summer*
▷John Wyndham, *The Chrysalids*

Fantasy Societies (p 76)

G

GALSWORTHY, JOHN (1867–1933)

British novelist and playwright.

In the 1960s an adaptation of Galsworthy's *The Forsyte Saga* was the most popular British TV series ever shown till then. It spawned a thousand imitations – series and books about rich families quarrelling over multi-million pound businesses and living wretched private lives have become a genre in themselves. Some critics say that this is unfair to Galsworthy, who was regarded as a heavyweight writer in his day (of plays as well as novels). But although he intended his first Forsyte book (*The Man of Property*) as a serious novel, as soon as the Forsytes became popular he quite happily extended it into a saga, adding another dozen novels and short stories.

THE FORSYTE SAGA (1922)

This contains three novels and two short stories. Its subject is the way money-making and commercial endeavour atrophy the emotions. Three generations of Forsytes are morally tainted by their family's business success, in particular Soames and his unhappy wife Irene. Every boardroom victory is balanced by a bedroom defeat; children inherit not only wealth, but the poisoned character which goes with it. There is more than a whiff of Victorian moralising about it all: in Galsworthy the bad always end unhappily (and so do the good). But unlike many later family-business sagas, his books offer three-dimensional characters, and he is particularly good at showing the ebb and flow of relationships between the sexes. *To Let*, the third volume of the saga, a Romeo and Juliet story with a devastating final twist, is a fine example of

READ ON

- *A Modern Comedy*.
- ▶ ▷Anthony Trollope, *Can You Forgive Her?* (and its sequels: the 'Palliser' family saga). ▷Thomas Mann, *Buddenbrooks* (an equally withering, but jollier, account of the decline of a powerful mercantile family). ▷C.P. Snow, *The Conscience of the Rich* (a moving study of the son of a family dynasty at odds with his parents). ▷Henry James, *The Spoils of Poynton* (a study of property as 'the middle-class deity'). ▷Christina Stead, *House of All Nations*.

this, one of Galsworthy's most satisfying books.

Apart from the Forsyte books (two trilogies – The Forsyte Saga; A Modern Comedy *– and the short-story collections* Four Forsyte Stories *and* On Forsyte Change*), Galsworthy's novels include* The Island Pharisee, Fraternity *and the trilogy* End of the Chapter, *a saga about the Charwell family (cousins of the Forsytes).*

▶ **Of the dozens of family-business blockbusters which followed the TV success of *The Forsyte Saga*, the juiciest are:** Harold Robbins, *The Adventurers*; ▷Judith Krantz, *Princess Daisy* and ▷Barbara Taylor Bradford, *A Woman of Substance.*

GASKELL, MRS (ELIZABETH CLEGHORN) (1810–65)

British novelist.

For a century after her death, Gaskell was chiefly remembered for a biography of her friend Charlotte ▷Brontë, and for *Cranford*, a gently malicious book about middle-class life in a provincial town. (It reads like a collaboration between ▷Austen and ▷Trollope, without being quite as good as either.) But she was actually a novelist of a far tougher kind. She was a friend of ▷Dickens and ▷Eliot, and shared their interest in social themes, particularly the way men treat women and the plight of the urban poor. She lived in Manchester, and wrote pungently about life among the 'dark Satanic mills' (as Blake had called them) which her southern readers had till then imagined were figments of the revolutionary imagination. Her novels were discussed in Parliament and led to social reform, a result which greatly pleased her. They survive today less as social documents than as powerful stories of people struggling against their environment or the indifference of others.

MARY BARTON (1848)

Mary's father is a mill-hand employed by the unfeeling Henry Carson. He is also a staunch fighter for worker's rights. When the mill-owners ignore their workers' requests for better treatment, the men decide to murder Carson as a warning to his class, and nominate Barton to fire the gun. Mary's beloved Jem Wilson is arrested for the crime, and Mary has to face the agony of proving his innocence by incriminating her father.

Gaskell's novels Ruth, Cousin Phyllis *and* Wives and Daughters *concern the relationship between the sexes.* Sylvia's Lovers, *an unsmiling tale set in 18th-century Whitby, is about a man snatched by the press gang.* Mary Barton *and* North and

READ ON

- *North and South* (in which a southern minister goes to preach God's word in a northern mill-town, and his wife and daughter become involved in the class-struggle – a concern greatly complicated when the daughter falls in love with a mill-owner's son).

▶ ▷Charlotte Brontë, *Shirley*. ▷Charles Dickens, *Hard Times*. ▷Émile Zola, *Germinal*. ▷Arnold Bennett, *Clayhanger*. ▷D.H. Lawrence, *Sons and Lovers*. ▷Jack London, *The People of the Abyss* (about slum life), David Storey, *Radcliffe* and Upton Sinclair, *The Jungle* carry Gaskell's themes into the 20th century.

South *are about class war.* Lois the Witch, *a long short story, is set during the Salem witch-hunts of the 17th century.*

▶ Lewis Grassic Gibbon, *A Scots Quair* (partly in Scots dialect, but comprehensible) is a saga of three generations coping with harsh conditions, on West highland crofts and in industrial Glasgow during the 1920s General Strike.

GIDE, André (1861–1951)

French novelist, poet and non-fiction writer.

In Plato's dialogues, Socrates tries to reach the core of a philosophical argument by elimination: each wrong assumption, each false trail is considered and rejected until what is left is 'truth'. Gide admired Plato – his favourite among his own works was *Corydon*, a set of four Platonic dialogues discussing homosexuality – and he used Socrates' methods in his fiction. His heroes seek the truth about themselves, the core of their being, and they do it by considering and rejecting all religious, social, sexual and intellectual conventions. Sometimes a quest results in the happiness of self-knowledge, but often the young men – Gide was not over-interested in young women – find, when they reach the core of themselves, that there is nothing there at all. Gide's contemporaries found his moral stripteases shocking, and condemned him as a pornographer; nowadays the most striking thing about his books is their spare, limpid style, which makes even more startling the things they say.

The Immoralist (1902)

Michel, a young intellectual, nearly dies of tuberculosis, and his brush with death changes his character. He rejects his former convention-ridden life in favour of living each moment for itself, of doing exactly what he pleases. As his personality flowers, that of his beloved wife begins to wither, leaving him to agonise over whether his actions have led to psychic liberation or to a surrender to selfishness.

Gide's other fiction includes Strait is the Gate *(La porte étroite),* The Vatican Cellars, Isabelle, The Pastoral Symphony *(La Symphonie pastorale) and* The Counterfeiters. *His non-fiction works on similar themes include* If it Die *(Si le grain ne meurt),* Et nunc manet in te/Madeleine *and* Journals.

READ ON

- *Strait is the Gate*; *The Pastoral Symphony*. *The Vatican Cellars* is a more extrovert, ironic romp involving murder, the kidnapping of the Pope and a frantic chase across Europe. *The Counterfeiters* is about a group of secondary schoolboys in Paris, their adolescent friendships and the adults who initiate them into grown-up life.

▶ **To Gide's short, philosophical books:** ▷Hermann Hesse, *Peter Camenzind*; Joris-Karl Huysmans, *Against Nature*; Frederick Rolfe, *The Desire and Pursuit of the Whole*; ▷Aldous Huxley, *Eyeless in Gaza*.

▶ **To *The***

***Counterfeiters*:** ▷Colette, *A Lesson in Love*; ▷Marcel Proust, *Cities of the Plain* (the fourth part of *Remembrance of Things Past)*.

- **More modern books on Gidean themes:** ▷Iris Murdoch, *The Flight from the Enchanter*; ▷Ian McEwan, *The Comfort of Strangers*; Alan Hollingshurst, *The Swimming Pool Library*.

GODDEN, Rumer (born 1907)

British novelist.

Godden has written over 100 books. Her novels, written in a placid, unflurried style, explore the lives of people in emotional turmoil or the clash between cultures. She is particularly known for her sensitive books about adolescents (*The Greengage Summer*, *The Battle of the Villa Fiorita*), about the religious life (*Black Narcissus*; *This House of Brede*; *Five for Sorrow, Ten for Joy*) and about India, where she lived and taught for many years (*Breakfast with the Nikolides*; *The River*, *The Dark Horse*).

Godden's other novels include A Fugue in Time/Take Three Tenses, A Candle for St Jude, Kingfishers Catch Fire *and* The Peacock Spring, Shiva's Pigeons *(written with Jon Godden) and* A House with Four Rooms *are autobiography. She has also written many children's books, including* The Rocking Horse Secret *and* A Kindle of Kittens.

READ ON

- **To Godden's books about India:** ▷Ruth Prawer Jhabvala, *Heat and Dust*.
- **To her books about young people:** ▷L.P. Hartley, *The Go-Between*; ▷Colette, *The Ripening Seed*.
- **To her novels in general:** R.F. Delderfield, *To Serve Them All My Days*; ▷John Mortimer, *Summer's Lease*.

GOETHE, Johann Wolfgang von (1749–1832)

German writer of novels, poems, plays and non-fiction.

Goethe's genius expressed itself in restless intellectual energy: he never heard an idea without wanting to develop it. He took the nearest convenient form – Shakespearean or Greek tragedy, letters, biography – and crammed it with philosophical and political reflections, discussions and suggestions. During his lifetime he was regarded as an innovator, forming European thought; by hindsight he seems

READ ON

- *The Travels of Wilhelm Meister* takes Meister and his son on a ramble through Europe. They sample every kind of human

rather to have caught ideas in the air – humanism, romanticism, political libertarianism – expanded them and given them wide circulation. Like Shakespeare, he distilled the spirit of his age – and this feeling, the sense that in reading him we are communing with the 18th and early 19th centuries at their sanest and most stimulating, is one of the main pleasures of his work.

THE APPRENTICESHIP OF WILHELM MEISTER (1796)

This enormously long, leisurely novel is the spiritual and moral 'biography' of Wilhelm Meister. As a young man, fascinated by the stage (and by Marianne, an actress), he gives up his business career and runs away to join an acting company. He takes part enthusiastically in their lives, and observes both their sorrows (symbolised by the brutal treatment of Mignon by her trapeze-artist 'protector') and their triumphs (symbolised by a production of Hamlet in which he takes part). He decides that this life – 'the world' – is not for him, and leaves. In the castle of Lothario he experiences both earthly pleasures ('the flesh') and religious conversion ('the spirit') and rejects them. Finally, matured by all his experiences, he decides to devote his life to education, to passing on all he knows, 'the balance that makes a human being', to his young son.

Goethe is best-known for his poetry, and for such plays as Egmont, Iphigenie in Tauris, Götz von Berlichingen/Ironhand *and* Faust. *Apart from* Wilhelm Meister, *his novels are* The Sorrows of Young Werther *and* Elective Affinities.

society, and their experiences make this book a reflection on 'manners' and politics, just as *The Apprenticeship of Wilhelm Meister* dealt with individual human personality. *The Sorrows of Young Werther*, in letter-form, tells the story of a young man tormented by love for his friend's fiancée. *Elective Affinities* is a heartless, amoral book (anticipating ▷Gide) about a married couple each of whom has a love-affair.

- ▶ **To *Wilhelm Meister:*** Miguel de Cervantes Saavedra, *Don Quixote*. ▷Thomas Mann, *The Magic Mountain*.
- ▶ **To *Elective Affinities*:** ▷George Eliot, *Daniel Deronda*; ▷Christina Stead, *The Man Who Loved Children*.
- ▶ **To *The Sorrows of Young Werther*:** ▷Hermann Hesse, *Gertrud*.

GOGOL, NIKOLAI VASILEVICH (1809–52)

Russian writer of novels, short stories and plays.

The despair which seems to hover over much Russian fiction was replaced in Gogol by hilarity: he was a 20th-century surrealist ahead of his time, a forerunner of ▷Kafka and Ionesco. His best-known work, the stage-farce *The Government Inspector*, is about a confidence trickster mis-

READ ON

- ▶ Gogol's sinister brilliance is matched in the short stories of ▷Kafka, Saki and

taken for a high official by a village of pompous fools. In one of his stories a nose takes on a malign, satirical life independent of its owner's will; in another a man saves for years to buy a new coat, only to be mugged and robbed the first time he wears it. Gogol's preferred form was the short story: he was terrified of writer's block. He struggled for a dozen years to finish his one long book, *Dead Souls*, and in 1852, convinced by a religious adviser that the second (unpublished) half of the book was 'sinful' and that if he went on writing he would go to hell, he burned the manuscript and fasted until he died.

DEAD SOULS (1842)

In 19th-century Russia landowners estimated their wealth not only by the acres they owned, but also by the number of their serfs, or slaves. Chichikov, a confidence-trickster, realises that serfs who die between official censuses are not legally dead until the next census, and so still count as property. He travels the length and breadth of Russia, buying 'dead souls' from landowners, and becomes – on paper at least – one of the wealthiest men in the country. Gogol uses this simple story as the basis for a set of farcical character-studies: he saw the book as a portrait-gallery of contemporary Russia, and filled it with short, self-contained comic episodes. He also wrote, with ironical pointedness, that Chichikov's journey stands for the journey of every human being through life: we move on, never sure of what is coming next, relieved each time that whatever it was we did, we got away with it.

Gogol's most surreal short stories are 'Diary of a Madman', 'Nevski Prospekt', 'The Portrait', 'The Nose' *and* 'The Overcoat'. *His collections* Evenings on a Farm, Mirgorod *and* Arabesques *are more farce than surrealism, short sketches about tongue-tied suitors, credulous peasants and feather-headed, pretty girls.*

Roald Dahl; his gentler comic stories are like ▷Chekhov's.

▶ **Good follow-ups to *Dead Souls*:** Ivan Goncharov, *Oblomov* (about a man so alienated from the world that he decides to spend the rest of his life in bed); ▷Franz Kafka, *America*; ▷Jaroslav Hašek, *The Good Soldier Švejk*; Bernard Malamud, *The Fixer*; Miguel de Cervantes Saavedra, *Don Quixote*.

GOLDING, WILLIAM (BORN 1911)

British novelist.

From his first novel (*Lord of the Flies*, 1954, about choirboys reverting to savagery after being marooned on a desert island) onwards, Golding has explored the dark side of human nature. He believes that homo sapiens is corrupt, that we destroy more than we create, that we are devilish without redemption. But instead of baldly stating this philosophy, he dresses it in allegories of the most unusual and fantastical kind. He pictures the devil engulfing not only choirboys on an island, but also (in other novels) a drowning sailor, a tribe of neanderthal people, the dean of a medieval

READ ON

- *The Inheritors* (a brilliantly-imagined story of the coming of homo sapiens, seen from the standpoint of the gentle ape-people they exterminate).

▶ **To *The Spire*:** ▷Hermann Hesse,

William GOLDING

LORD OF THE FLIES *(choirboys lost on desert island revert to satanic evil, humanity's dark side)*

SURVIVING

Daniel **DEFOE, ROBINSON CRUSOE**
(18th-century shipwrecked sailor builds new life on desert island)

Jonathan **SWIFT, GULLIVER'S TRAVELS**
(18th-century sailor tries to teach European 'culture' in fantasy lands he visits)

James Vance **MARSHALL, WALKABOUT**
(English children marooned in Australian outback, taught survival by Aboriginal boy)

EVIL AND CHILDREN

Susan **HILL, I'M THE KING OF THE CASTLE**
(devil-child, jealous of rival, torments the life from him)

Stephen **KING, CARRIE**
(bullied girl in junior high school uses Devil's power to take revenge)

John **WYNDHAM, THE MIDWICH CUCKOOS**
(alien race seeks to capture England by breeding race of hyper-intelligent, soulless children)

Henry **JAMES, THE TURN OF THE SCREW**
(neurotic governess tries to protect two innocent charges against half-sensed, wholly evil ghosts)

THE DEVIL

Fay **WELDON, THE HEART OF ENGLAND**
(evil forces in Glastonbury countryside interfere with yuppie lives)

John **UPDIKE, THE WITCHES OF EASTWICK**
(bored Connecticut housewives play with witchcraft – and raise the Devil)

James **BLISH, BLACK EASTER**
(nuclear scientist enlists Devil's help in bringing about Armageddon)

THE WILDERNESS

Patrick **WHITE, VOSS**
(half-crazy explorer leads doomed 19th-century expedition into heart of Australia)

Joseph **CONRAD, HEART OF DARKNESS**
(African jungle used as metaphor for the evil in humanity)

C.S. **LEWIS, PERELANDRA**
(battle for survival – and against unrelenting evil – on the empty planet Venus)

Brian **MOORE, THE BLACK ROBE**
(17th-century Jesuit among 17th-century Indians: bloody, hopeless culture-clash)

cathedral, a boy growing up in 1960s Britain, and a group of 18th-century people sailing towards Australia. He evokes these situations with absolute conviction: few writers are better at suggesting the feel, taste, smell and sound of things, the texture of experience.

THE SPIRE (1964)

Inspired by a vision, medieval Dean Jocelin commissions for his cathedral a 400-foot spire. He intends it as proof of human aspiration towards God; his enemies see it as a symbol of vanity, the devil's work; the master-builder points out that as the cathedral's foundations are inadequate, the tower will bring the whole building crashing down. Jocelin overrides all objections, the work proceeds – Golding gives fascinating, vertigo-inducing detail of medieval building techniques – and the higher the spire rises the more people are destroyed. In the end the struggle between God and the devil takes over Jocelin's own self. In truly medieval manner, his brain and body become a battleground, and the issue moves from the tower to questions of his own moral integrity and saintliness.

Golding's novels are Lord of the Flies, Pincher Martin, Free Fall, The Spire, The Pyramid, Darkness Visible, *the trilogy (about an ill-assorted cargo of passengers on a voyage to 18th-century Australia),* Rites of Passage, Close Quarters, *and* Fire Down Below, *and* The Paper Men. The Scorpion God *is a collection of three long stories, one based on his stage-comedy* The Brass Butterfly, *about a crazy inventor trying to interest a decadent Roman ruler of Egypt in steam power.*

Narziss and Goldmund (which parallels both the good/evil theme and the medieval craft-background of *The Spire)*. John Barth, *Giles Goat-boy* (a fantasy, partly satirical, about a professor who brings a child up with no company but goats, trying to avoid contaminating him with human original sin). ▷Anthony Burgess, *Earthly Powers*. ▷Umberto Eco, *The Name of the Rose*.

- **To *Lord of the Flies*:** Marianne Wiggins, *John Dollar*.
- **To the Australian trilogy:** ▷Thomas Keneally, *The Playmaker*.

GOOD AND EVIL
(the devil at large)

Mikhail Bulgakov, *The Master and Margharita*
▷John Fowles, *A Maggot*
▷Stephen King, *Carrie*
▷Ian McEwan, *The Comfort of Strangers*
Neville Shulman, *Exit of a Dragonfly*
▷I.B. Singer, *Satan in Goray*
▷John Updike, *The Witches of Eastwick*
▷Fay Weldon, *The Life and Loves of a She-Devil*

Something Nasty . . . (p 230)

GORDIMER, NADINE (1923)

South African novelist and short-story writer.

Gordimer makes life in South Africa (and especially among the tormented liberal whites who are her main characters)

READ ON

- *The Late Bourgeois World* (a grim study

an objective background for subjective choice. Her concerns are the diversity of human nature, and the way our moral and psychological personality is revealed in what we do. She also, magnificently, evokes the vastness and beauty of Africa. Like other South African writers (notably Alan Paton and Laurens van der Post) she gives the continent a kind of mystical identity; its indigenous inhabitants understand this completely, but it gives the incoming whites (who can only dimly perceive it) an unsettling sense of their own inadequacy, as if they are made second-class citizens not by other people's laws but by the very place they live in.

A Sport Of Nature (1987)

From adolescence rich, white Hillela is dominated by politics and sex, and combines the two: sex is a source of power, politics give orgasmic satisfaction. She is attracted by, and attracts, powerful men of all professions and races – and progressively moves out of the orbit of whites to a leading position in the black revolutionary movement. The book ends with the success of the revolution, the establishment of majority rule – and with doubts sown in the reader's mind about Hillela herself. Has she really identified as wholly with the blacks as she hoped, or does she remain the 'sport of nature', or freak, of the book's title?

Gordimer's other novels are The Lying Days, A World of Strangers, Occasion for Loving, The Late Bourgeois World, A Guest of Honour, Burger's Daughter, The Conservationist *and* July's People. *Her story-collections include* Not For Publication, Livingstone's Companions *and* A Soldier's Embrace.

of white liberals in a police state. Max, tortured into betraying his friends, commits suicide, and Liz (his divorced wife) is left to choose between continuing in bourgeois complacency, doing nothing about the situation but wring her hands, and joining the black revolutionary movement).

▶ André Brink, *Rumours of Rain* (about redneck Afrikanerdom). J.M. Coetzee, *In the Heart of the Country*. David Caute, *News From Nowhere*. ▷Isabel Allende, *Of Love and Shadows*. ▷John Le Carré, *The Little Drummer Girl*. Alan Paton, *Cry, the Beloved Country* (a moving book about the harmony between ancient Zulu culture and the land, and the discord brought by invading whites; it is mirrored, from a different country and a different point of view, by ▷Chinua Achebe, *Things Fall Apart)*.

GORKY, Maxim (1868–1936)

Russian writer of novels, short stories and plays.

Gorky (a pseudonym meaning 'bitter') was left to fend for

READ ON

- *Yegor Bulitchev and*

himself at the age of eight, and spent his childhood as a barge-hand, washer-up, thief, beggar, tramp and journalist. This 'apprenticeship', as he called it, affected the style and content of his writing. He saw himself as a colleague and heir of ▷Dostoevsky and ▷Tolstoy, and aimed to write the same kind of panoramic, allegorical works as theirs. But whereas their world was that of landowners and the bourgeoisie, his was one of serfs, vagabonds, criminals and other members of what he called society's 'lower depths'. He despised the middle class, and wrote with contempt of their dependence on money, gentility and religion, the very forces which were destroying them. His preoccupations led him to friendship with Lenin, and to enthusiastic support for the 1917 revolution. Many of his post-1917 books are grandiose and propagandist, and his revolutionary sympathies have diminished his reputation in capitalist countries. But his early work places him squarely in the company of the great 19th-century writers he admired.

FOMA GORDEEV (1899)

Foma, the son of an illiterate barge-owner who has made a fortune conveying goods on the Volga, has been brought up in his godfather's cultured, bourgeois home. His father tries to take him into the business, to educate him in the ways of the world, and for a time Foma thrives. But when the old man dies and he inherits, his head is turned and he lives a life of increasing debauchery, ending up as a lunatic and a drunkard. He is a man without identity: he takes on the moral colouring of the society around him, and is destroyed.

Gorky is known for plays (such as The Lower Depths *and* Smug Citizens*) as well as for prose fiction. His novels include* Mother, Foma Gordeev, The Artamonov Affair, The Life of Klim Samgin *and the post-revolutionary tetralogy* Bystander, The Magnet, Other Fires *and* The Spectre. *His short stories are headed by* 'Twenty-six Men and a Girl', *which normally gives its name to collections. His best-known work, in or out of the USSR, is the autobiographical trilogy* My Childhood, My Apprenticeship *and* My Universities.

Others (a black comedy about a dying merchant fawned on by hypocrites who anticipate rich pickings when he dies). *My Childhood* (the first volume of Gorky's autobiography, a scalding account of his life as a barge-hand, the background to *Foma Gordeev).*

► ▷Fyodor Dostoevski, *The Gambler* (a harsh account of aristocratic folly and obsession in Tsarist Russia, the kind of decadence Gorky vociferously denounced). Jean Genet, *Querelle of Brest* (the story of a boy's brutal upbringing among criminals and gansters in France between the two world wars). ▷Jerome Weidman, *I Can Get It For You Wholesale* (about a young man making his way by guile in the business world of post-Depression New York – and the moral disintegration of character which is the price he pays).

GRAHAM, WINSTON (BORN 1911)

British novelist.

Although Graham has written books of many kinds, from

READ ON

► ▷Emily Brontë,

historical romances to thrillers, he is best-known for the brooding, atmospheric 'Poldark' saga, about feuding families in 18th and 19th century Cornwall.

The first Poldark book was *Ross Poldark/Renegade*, and the series includes *Demelza, Jeremy Poldark, Warleggan/The Last Gamble* and *The Black Moon*. Graham's best-known thriller is *Greek Fire*.

Wuthering Heights. Arthur Quiller-Couch ('Q'), *Troy Town*. ▷Daphne Du Maurier, *My Cousin Rachel*. R.D. Blackmore, *Lorna Doone*.

GRASS, GÜNTER (BORN 1927)

German writer of novels, plays and non-fiction.

In his twenties Grass worked as a graphic artist, stage designer and jazz musician; he took up writing full-time only after his novel *The Tin Drum* was a best-seller, when he was 32. Politics are the main subject of his books: he grapples with what has happened in Germany over the last half-century, and what is happening now. He uses a framework of absurdity, blending real events with wild black fantasy, collapsing history (so that time is like a well from which you draw not systematically but at random), and making his characters allegorical figures like the people in cartoons. The leading character in *The Tin Drum* (1959), for example, symbolising the German people, is a child who chooses to stop growing at the age of three, and who spends forty years banging a toy drum and giggling as the procession of nazism and post-war reconstruction passes by. For Grass, the human condition is 'absurd': not only ridiculous but morally and philosophically out of focus. His books offer no solutions, but they point out the problems with enormous, malicious glee.

THE FLOUNDER (1977)

The wife and husband from a Grimm fairy-tale move through the entire history of the human race, popping up in this period or that, playing each role by the conventions of its time, and endlessly, affably arguing about gender dominance. They are aided or hindered by a talking fish from the same fairy-tale: it takes now her side, now his. Finally the fish is ordered to defend itself before a late 20th-century feminist tribunal, and the whole male/female business is thrashed out in a hearing as preposterous as the trial in Alice in Wonderland. The fact that this book is about sexual rather than German politics makes it one of Grass' most accessible novels to non-German readers, and it is also wonderfully enlivened with puns, poems, satires and recipes. The pleasures of human life have not had such a going-over since ▷Rabelais.

Grass's other novels include the 'Danzig trilogy' (The Tin

READ ON

- *The Tin Drum* is the most accessible of the 'Danzig' novels, and although its theme (nazism) gives it a harsher tone than *The Flounder*, it is equally hilarious and bizarre.
- **Other books similarly reinventing the human race, tossing all human knowledge and invention into a single fantastic melting-pot:** ▷Thornton Wilder, *The Eighth Day*; ▷Kurt Vonnegut, *Galápagos*; ▷J.G. Ballard, *The Unlimited Dream Company*; ▷Jeanette Winterson, *The Passion*.

Drum, Dog Years *and* Local Anaesthetic*)*, From the Diary of a Snail, Cat and Mouse, The Meeting at Telgte, Headbirths *and* The Rat.

GRAVES, ROBERT (1895–1985)

British novelist, poet and non-fiction writer.

Graves' main interests were myth and poetry. He wrote a best-selling version of the Greek myths, a controversial account of the Bible stories as myth, and *The White Goddess* (1948–52), a study of poetic inspiration. Throughout his life he composed poetry (much of it autobiographical), and his love-poems in particular are much admired. He claimed that his novels were potboilers, written to finance 'real' work, but their quality and craftsmanship belie this description. Most are historical, reimagining characters of the past – from the author of the *Odyssey* to Jesus – as people with markedly 20th-century sensibilities, able to view the events of their own lives, as it were, with hindsight. His books are like psychological documentaries, as if we are looking directly into his characters' minds.

I, CLAUDIUS (1934)

This novel and its sequel *Claudius the God* purport to be the autobiography of the fourth Roman emperor. A spastic and an epileptic, he is regarded by everyone as a fool and ignored; he thus survives the myriad political and dynastic intrigues of the first 50 years of the Roman empire, the reigns of his three dangerous predecessors. He is finally made emperor himself, in a palace coup – and proceeds to rule with a blend of wisdom, guile and ruthlessness which he describes with fascinated relish. The story ends – typically for Graves – with a real document, an account by a Roman satirist of the 'Pumpkinification of Claudius', the arrival of the stammering, limping fool of an emperor in Olympus, home of the gods and of his own terrifying, deified relatives.

Graves' other novels include Count Belisarius *(set in 6th-century Byzantium),* Sergeant Lamb of the Ninth *and* Proceed, Sergeant Lamb *(about the American War of Independence),* Wife to Mr Milton *(set in Puritan England, and written in a brilliant pastiche of 17th-century prose),* Homer's Daughter *(set in prehistoric Greece), and* King Jesus *(about the life and death of Christ).* Seven Days in New Crete *is an urbane future-fantasy, and* Goodbye to All That *is autobiography, moving from a tormented account of Graves' time as an officer in the first world war to malicious glimpses of Oxford life and the literary London of the 1920s.*

READ ON

- *The Golden Fleece/Hercules, My Shipmate* (a novelised account of the expedition of Jason and the Argonauts to find the Golden Fleece, with ingenious, rational explanations of such magic events as the escape from the Clashing Rocks, the yoking of bronze bulls and the sowing of serpents' teeth).
- **To *I, Claudius*:** ▷Mary Renault, *The King Must Die*; ▷Marguerite Yourcenar, *Memoirs of Hadrian*; Naomi Mitchison, *The Corn King and the Spring Queen*; Joan Grant, *Winged Pharaoh*.
- **Books of similar gusto, on non-classical subjects:** Frederick Rolfe, *Hadrian the Seventh* (about a waspish inadequate who is elected Pope); Augusto Roa Bastos, *I The Supreme* (the 'autobiography' of a deranged 19th-century Paraguayan dictator; ▷Gore Vidal, *Kalki* (about an insane Vietnam

Robert GRAVES

Norman **MAILER, ANCIENT EVENINGS**
(memories of chief minister of warrior-pharaoh Rameses II)

Gore **VIDAL, CREATION**
('memoirs' of Persian diplomat who knew Socrates, Buddha and Confucius)

Joan **GRANT, WINGED PHARAOH**
(Grant describes her own previous existence in ancient Egypt)

Joseph **HELLER, GOD KNOWS**
('memoirs' of Old Testament King David)

Marguerite **YOURCENAR, MEMOIRS OF HADRIAN**
(reflections of 14th Roman Emperor and philosopher)

Hilda **DOOLITTLE (*'H.D.'*), HEDYLUS**
(Samos, 3rd century BC: ex-courtesan, lover and poet-son meditate delicately on life, love, the arts and politics)

John **ARDEN, SILENCE AMONG THE WEAPONS**
('memoirs' of actor's agent mixed up with Roman dictator Sulla in 1st century BC)

Peter **VANSITTART, THREE SIX SEVEN**
(twilight of Roman Britain, late 4th century)

Anthony **BURGESS, THE KINGDOM OF THE WICKED**
(Luke, Paul and other early Christian missionaries)

I, CLAUDIUS

(4th Roman Emperor's 'memoirs' of his bloodthirsty forebears)

Henry **TREECE, MEDEA**
(powerful evocation of myth-witch, scorned wife who murdered her children)

Mary **RENAULT, THE MASK OF APOLLO**
('memoirs' of actor-spy in 4th century BC Greece)

Peter **GREEN, ACHILLES HIS ARMOUR**
(Alcibiades, the Oscar Wilde of ancient Athens)

Mario **VARGAS LLOSA, THE WAR OF THE END OF THE WORLD** *(19th-century South American religious community, communist, waiting for the Apocalypse)*

Augusto Roa **BASTOS, I, THE SUPREME**
('memoirs' of Francia, 19th-century dictator of Paraguay)

Gabriel García **MÁRQUEZ, THE AUTUMN OF THE PATRIARCH** *(deathbed monologue of fanatical, deranged South American dictator)*

Nicholas **MONSARRAT, RUNNING PROUD**
(one of Columbus' sailors shipwrecked in New World, is taken for a god)

Carlos **FUENTES, TERRA NOSTRA**
('memoirs' of Philip II of Spain, in deranged old age)

Stephen **MARLOWE, THE MEMOIRS OF CHRISTOPHER COLUMBUS** *(early disappointments and ironic triumph of unscrupulous adventurer-explorer)*

veteran who imagines himself Kalki, the Hindu god whose coming will end the present cycle of human existence).

GREAT DETECTIVES

John Dickson Carr, *Death Watch*
▷Agatha Christie, *Death on the Nile*
▷A. Conan Doyle, *The Hound of the Baskervilles*
▷Dorothy L. Sayers, *Murder Must Advertise*
▷Georges Simenon, *Inquest on Bouvet*
Rex Stout, *Plot it Yourself/Murder in Style*

GREENE, GRAHAM (BORN 1904)

British writer of novels, plays and non-fiction.

In the 1930s Greene wrote several thrillers influenced by ▷Buchan and by action-films of the time: they include *Stamboul Train* (set on the Orient Express), *A Gun for Sale/This Gun for Sale* (about the manhunt for a political assassin) and *The Confidential Agent* (about left-wing politics in a right-wing state). This work culminated in atmospheric film-scripts, of which the best (later novelised) was *The Third Man*. But thrillers – and, later, comedies such as *Our Man in Havana*, *Travels With My Aunt* and *Monsignor Quixote* – always took second place, at least in Greene's own estimation, to his Catholic novels. These are all concerned with people tormented by their own moral failure and by the longing for God's forgiveness. The settings are often the tropics; the political situations are unstable; the heroes are second-rank functionaries despised by their superiors. Two novels, *Brighton Rock* (1938, about a petty criminal in 1930s Brighton) and *The Human Factor* (1978, about the minor-public-school loyalties and betrayals of the British Intelligence Services), set similar searches for grace in a soulless, down-at-heel Britain. Despite the Catholic overtones of these books, which non-believers may find unconvincing, Greene's plots are fascinating, and his evocation of character and place is marvellous.

THE HEART OF THE MATTER (1948)

Scobie, Captain of Police in a God-forsaken African colony during the second world war, is a decent, honest man. His wife Louise, tormented by memories of their dead daughter and by her own isolation from the rest of the British community, begs him to send her away to South Africa – and

READ ON

- *The Power and the Glory* (a lacerating story, set in Mexico during a left-wing revolution, about a drunken, self-hating priest who struggles against his own fear and the persecution of the revolutionaries to take God to the peasants).
- ▶ 'Psychic thrillers', similarly showing people driven to the edge of breakdown and beyond, by circumstances, their surroundings or consciousness of their own moral failings: ▷Malcolm Lowry, *Under the Volcano*; ▷Joseph Conrad, *Nostromo*; B. Traven, *The Treasure of the Sierra Madre*; ▷Georges Simenon, *The Stain on the*

because of a mixture of pity for her misery and anguish at his inability to make her happy, he breaks police rules and borrows money from a suspected diamond-smuggler. From that lapse onwards, everything Scobie does ends in disaster, and there is nothing he can do but watch himself, appalled but helpless, as he plunges remorselessly towards damnation.

Greene's other novels include The End of the Affair, The Quiet American, A Burnt-out Case, The Comedians, The Honorary Consul, Doctor Fischer of Geneva *and* The Captain and the Enemy. *His short stories (many of them 'comedies of the sexual life', as he called them) are collected in* Twenty-one Stories *and* May We Borrow Your Husband? *He has also written travel books and plays.*

Snow.

▶ **Short stories:** ▷Somerset Maugham, *Creatures of Circumstance*; ▷V. S. Pritchett, *Collected Stories*; ▷Ernest Hemingway, *Men Without Women.*

GROWING UP: TEENAGERS

Lynne Reid Banks, *The Writing on the Wall*
▷Elizabeth Bowen, *The Death of the Heart*
▷Willa Cather, *The Song of the Lark*
▷Charles Dickens, *David Copperfield*
▷André Gide, *The Counterfeiters*
▷Rose Macaulay, *They Were Defeated*
▷Mary McCarthy, *Birds of America*
▷Iris Murdoch, *The Flight from the Enchanter*
▷J.D. Salinger, *The Catcher in the Rye*

Adolescence (p 2); All-engulfing Families (p 5); Children (p 44); Growing Up: Young Adults (p 105)

GROWING UP: YOUNG ADULTS

▷Lisa Alther, *Kinflicks*
▷Ford Madox Ford, *Parade's End*
▷Johann Wolfgang von Goethe, *The Apprenticeship of Wilhelm Meister*
▷Nadine Gordimer, *A Sport of Nature*
▷Marcel Proust, *Within a Budding Grove* (part 2 of *Remembrance of Things Past)*
▷Philip Roth, *Goodbye, Columbus*
Charles Webb, *The Graduate*

Growing Up: Teenagers (p 105); Emotionally Ill-At-Ease (p 75); Perplexed by Life (p 196)

H

HAGGARD, H. RIDER (HENRY RIDER) (1856–1925)

British novelist.

Haggard's novels are adventure fantasies set in wildly exotic locations: the geysers and glaciers of Iceland (*Erik Brighteyes*), the South American jungle (*Montezuma's Daughter*) or – most commonly of all – Darkest Africa, a continent of the imagination as fabulous as the setting of Sindbad's adventures in *The Arabian Nights*. In *King Solomon's Mines* (1885), Haggard's best-known book, Allan Quatermain leads a safari in search of the fabulous treasure beyond Africa's Solomon Mountains, a treasure which has already claimed a thousand lives. Desert heat, jungle, hostile warrior-tribes and ice-caves in the mountains must all be faced, to say nothing of black magic, cannibalism and the guile and treachery of members of Quatermain's own party. Hokum? The best.

READ ON

- *She*; *Allan Quatermain*; *Ayesha: The Return of She*.
- ▶ ▷John Buchan, *Prester John*. ▷A. Conan Doyle, *The Lost World*. James Hilton, *Lost Horizon*. ▷Wilbur Smith, *Shout at the Devil*. Edgar Rice Burroughs, *A Princess of Mars*.

HAILEY, ARTHUR (BORN 1920)

British/Canadian novelist.

Hailey's books are well-researched, fast-paced adventures set not in jungles or jet-set ski-resorts but in the no less exotic surroundings of a luxury hotel (*Hotel*), an international airport (*Airport*), the US government (*In High Places*) or Wall Street (*The Moneychangers*). In all of them, the fascination is as much in the detail of the location as in action: his books are fly-on-the-wall documentary, thriller and soap opera rolled into one. The hero of *Overload* (1979), a power-company executive, claims that his employers' greed

READ ON

- ▶ Burton Wohl, *The China Syndrome*. Paul Erdman, *The Silver Bears*. Paul Gallico, *The Poseidon Adventure*.

and carelessness will lead to a breakdown of the entire electrical network of California. He becomes involved with ecological fringe-groups, citizen-protection societies, terrorists, big-business troubleshooters and muck-raking newspaper-reporters – and as the novel pounds towards its climax, he is proved to have been a truer prophet of disaster than even he suspected.

HALL, Rodney (born 1936)

Australian novelist.

In *Kisses of the Enemy* (1989), Hall's most ambitious novel, Rabelaisian comedy and magic realism prance hand in hand. Hall's idea is simple; a few years hence, US multinational interests buy Australia and install a puppet president, who gradually turns into a bloated, self-gratifying dictator. Nothing stands in his way – neither his wife and family, groups of terrorists for democracy, nor ghosts and demons from the past. Hall tells the story in a deadpan style which none the less seems always about to burst language at its seams. He is like a messenger of doom who finds difficulty keeping a straight enough face to blurt it out. The novel is that rare thing, dystopian farce – a feast of a book with a distinctly bitter aftertaste.

READ ON

- *Captivity Captive* (a book of an entirely different kind, as if ▷D. H. Lawrence and ▷Gabriel García Márquez had collaborated to tell the story of a remote, outback murder in the 1890s).
- ▶ **To *Kisses of the Enemy***: ▷Peter Carey, *Illywhacker* ; ▷Isobel Allende, *Of Love and Shadows*; ▷Robertson Davies, *The Rebel Angels*.
- ▶ **To *Captivity Captive***: ▷Katharine Susannah Prichard, *Coonardoo*; Mike Nicol, *The Powers that Be*; Janet Lewis, *The Trial of Sören Kvist*.

HAMMETT, Dashiell (1894–1961)

US writer of novels, short stories and screenplays.

A former private detective, Hammett wrote stories and serials for pulp magazines, and later became a Hollywood scriptwriter. He perfected the 'private eye' story, in which kidnappings, thefts and murders are investigated by laconic, wisecracking individuals who are always just on the side of the angels and just one step ahead of the police. His best-known detectives are Sam Spade (made famous by Humphrey Bogart), the urbane Nick Charles (made famous in William Powell's 'Thin Man' films) and 'The Continental

READ ON

- ▶ ▷Raymond Chandler, *The Lady in the Lake*. James M. Cain, *No Orchids for Miss Blandish*. Ross Macdonald, *The Drowning Pool*. Peter Coffin, *The Search for My Great*

Op'. Hammett's novels are *The Dain Curse, Red Harvest, The Maltese Falcon, The Glass Key* and *The Thin Man*; his story-collections include *The Continental Op, A Man Called Spade* and *A Man Called Thin.*

Uncle's Head. Andrew Bergman, *The Big Kiss-off of 1944.* ▷Norman Mailer, *Tough Guys Don't Dance.*

HARDY, Thomas (1840–1928)

British novelist and poet.

As a young man Hardy worked as an ecclesiastical architect, sketching and surveying country churches. This work intensified his love of the old ways of the countryside, patterns of life and customs which dated from feudal times. This is the background to his novels (which are all set in south-western England, the ancient kingdom of Wessex). He describes the minutiae of farming and village life with the exactness of a museum curator, and his characters' habits of mind are rooted in the ebb and flow of the seasons, in the unending cycle of tending for their animals and caring for the land. Life is unhurried but inexorable: Hardy's people are owned by their environment. They are also subject to a range of violent passions and emotions – Hardy thought of human beings as the playthings of destiny – and the placid continuum of existence is the setting for such irrational psychological forces as jealousy, intolerance and revenge. Hardy's bleakness and pessimism were much criticised, and in 1895 he gave up novels to concentrate on poetry. Paradoxically, for all the sombreness of their events, his novels are valued now mainly for their feeling of the harmony between human beings and nature: a kind of rural innocence which has long since disappeared.

Far From The Madding Crowd (1874)

The shepherd Gabriel Oak works for Bathsheba Everdene, and loves her. Bathsheba's head is turned by dashing Sergeant Troy, who marries her and then deserts her, letting her believe that he is dead. Bathsheba now agrees to marry Boldwood, a yeoman farmer, unimaginative and dull, who has secretly loved her for years. Then Troy comes back and claims his wife – provoking a crisis and the resolution of the uneasy relationship between Oak and Bathsheba which has simmered all this time.

Hardy's other novels include Under the Greenwood Tree, A Pair of Blue Eyes, The Return of the Native, The Trumpet-Major, The Mayor of Casterbridge, The Woodlanders, Tess of the d'Urbervilles *and* Jude the Obscure. *He wrote an epic drama set during the Napoleonic Wars,* The Dynasts, *and several books of poetry including* Satires of Circumstance, Moments of Vision *and* Winter Words.

READ ON

- *The Mayor of Casterbridge*; *Tess of the d'Urbervilles.*
- ▶ **Books on similar themes, in a similar style:** ▷George Eliot, *Adam Bede*; ▷Mrs Gaskell, *Ruth*; ▷Edith Wharton, *Ethan Frome*; Melvyn Bragg, *The Hired Man.*
- ▶ **Further away in period or manner, but equally atmospheric:** ▷John Fowles, *The French Lieutenant's Woman*; ▷Sigrid Undset, *Kristin Lavransdatter*; Oliver Onions, *The Story of Ragged Robyn.*

HARRISON, Harry (born 1925)
US novelist and short-story writer.

Although Harrison has written serious SF (eg the fast-moving adventure-series *Deathworld I*, *Deathworld II* and *Deathworld III*), he is best-known for farce, and especially for his books about The Stainless Steel Rat. In a future where technology has made crime all but redundant, James Bolivar di Griz, the Stainless Steel Rat, is a spectacular exception to the rule. He sees himself as a public benefactor, keeping the police on their toes, giving employment to insurance clerks and bringing colour and excitement to TV newscasts. In the first book of the series, *The Stainless Steel Rat*, the galactic police decide that the only way to cope with him is to recruit him and send him to catch the lovely interplanetary criminal Angelina.

The Stainless Steel Rat books include The Stainless Steel Rat's Revenge, The Stainless Steel Rat Saves the World, The Stainless Steel Rat Wants You! *and* The Stainless Steel Rat for President. *Harrison's other novels include* Bill, the Galactic Hero, Planet of the Damned, Star Smashers of the Galaxy Rangers, *and the more serious* Make Room, Make Room! *and* Mechanismo. Two Tales and Eight Tomorrows, Prime Number *and* One Step from Earth *are collections of short stories.* Great Balls of Fire *is a study of sex in SF.*

READ ON

- *Star Smashers of the Galaxy Rangers*; *The Technicolor Time Machine*.
- **To Harrison's comedies:** ▷Kurt Vonnegut, *Cat's Cradle*; Robert Sheckley, *The Status Civilization*; Jack Trevor Story, *Morag's Flying Fortress*.
- **To *Make Room, Make Room!*:** ▷George Turner, *The Sea and Summer*; John Brunner, *Stand on Zanzibar*.

HARTLEY, L.P. (Leslie Poles) (1895–1972)
British novelist and short-story writer.

An admirer of ▷James and ▷Forster, Hartley wrote a dozen decorous, restrained novels about emotional deprivation and the way childhood experience shadows a person's whole existence. His best-known books are the 'Eustace and Hilda' trilogy (*The Shrimp and the Anemone*, *The Sixth Heaven* and *Eustace and Hilda*, 1944–7), about a brother and sister whose emotional interdependence, innocent-seeming when they are children, blights their later lives, and *The Go-Between* (1953), about a boy on holiday during an idyllic Edwardian summer. Carrying messages between two doomed lovers (the daughter of the 'big house' and a tenant farmer), he is emotionally crippled by the passions he senses but hardly understands. *Facial Justice* (1960) is an uncharacteristic but fascinating book, a future-fantasy set in a drab post-nuclear world where there is no fear, no pain, no unkindness – and no room for individuality or emotion.

Hartley's other main novels are The Boat, A Perfect Woman, The Hireling *and* The Brickfield. *His short-story collections include* The Killing Bottle *and* The Travelling Grave.

READ ON

- ▷Henry James, *What Maisie Knew*. ▷Anita Brookner, *H Bowen, The Death of the Heart*. Jane Gardam, *A Long Way from Verona*. Philip Larkin, *Jill*.

HAŠEK, JAROSLAV (1883-1923)

Czech novelist and journalist.

Hašek spent most of his youth as a dropout and a half-baked political activist (for which, for six months, he was imprisoned by the Russians as a spy). He served, reluctantly, in the first world war, was invalided out and became a satirical journalist. His masterpiece, the 700-page comic novel *The Good Soldier Švejk,* makes hilarious use of all his early experiences. Švejk is the town drunk, a dog-catcher, who is conscripted into the Austrian army as the lowliest of privates. A moon-faced, brainless lump, he obeys every fatuous order and follows every regulation to the letter. The book follows his farcical army career, during which he rises to the dizzy heights of chaplain's batman, takes part in the first world war and sees the first skirmishes of the Russian revolution. He understands nothing of what is going on: food, drink and staying out of trouble are all that interest him. Hašek uses Švejk's blankness like a mirror, showing up officers, politicians and bureaucrats for the fools they are.

All earlier English translations of The Good Soldier Švejk *have been outclassed by Cecil Parrott's, written in the 1970s. Parrott has also published a selection of Hašek's lunatic journalism,* Jaroslav Hašek: the Red Commissar.

READ ON

▶ ▷François Rabelais, *Gargantua* is the nearest match for Hašek's farcical gusto, and Von Grimmelshausen, *Simplex Simplicissimus* is about a Middle Ages precursor of Švejk. Of more modern books, Eric Linklater, *Private Angelo* is a genial satire on the second world war; Thomas Berger, *Reinhart in Love* is a similarly light-hearted novel about a Švejkish US 'little man'. ▷Thomas Mann, *The Confessions of Felix Krull, Confidence Man,* about a confidence-trickster travelling the spas and luxury hotels of Europe in the 1900s, though it lacks Hašek's devastating view of war and politics, exactly parallels his wide-eyed, amiable style.

HAWTHORNE, NATHANIEL (1804–64)

US novelist.

Much of Hawthorne's writing was excellent but minor – examples are *A Wonder Book* and *Tanglewood Tales,* sensitive retellings of Greek myth for children. He was triggered into greatness by discovering, in an old chest in Salem, Massachusetts, documents about his family's part in the Salem witchhunts of the mid 17th-century. Soon afterwards, he wrote *The Scarlet Letter* – and revealed his true genius for the first time.

READ ON

- *The House of the Seven Gables* (a similarly remorseless novel about a New England family cursed for generations because of their forebears'

THE SCARLET LETTER (1850)

This study of intolerance and humbug is set among the first Puritan settlers in the USA. Hester Prynne has spent two years in Boston, waiting for her elderly husband to join her from England. In the meantime she has borne a love-child, Pearl, and the Puritans pillory her and brand her an adulteress, making her wear the scarlet letter 'A' embroidered on her clothes. Her husband arrives, discovers that her secret lover is a minister of the church, and mercilessly persecutes him for refusing to admit his guilt. Hester's husband and lover pursue their enmity to the end; they ignore Hester herself, who in the meantime lives an unobtrusive but truly Christian life helping the neighbours who once ill-treated her.

persecution of an innocent man for witchcraft). *The Blithedale Romance* (a satire, based on Hawthorne's own experience, about life in a Massachusetts utopian community).

► ▷Aldous Huxley, *The Devils of Loudon* (about an outbreak of hysteria and demonic possession in a medieval French village). ▷I.B. Singer, *Satan in Goray* (set in a medieval community of Polish Jews harrassed by pogroms and torn apart by the appearance of a false Messiah). André Brink, *Rumours of Rain* (about ignorance and intolerance in present-day South Africa). Robert Coover, *The Origin of the Brunists* (a fascist allegory about the growth of a ruthless religious sect).

HEINLEIN, ROBERT (1907–88)

US novelist.

Heinlein's 1930s and 1940s writings were a bridge between early SF (▷Verne and ▷Wells) and the present day. They are straightforward stories of space-travel and the colonisation of distant planets, and much of their detail has been overtaken by events. In the 1960s his novel *Stranger in a Strange Land* had a cult following, because it seemed to be

READ ON

- *Job* (a Bible-inspired story of a human being tormented by a practical-joking, malicious God and finally befriended by

advocating a mystical union of humankind brought about by flower-power, free love and hallucinatory drugs. His 1970s and 1980s books range from the serious *I Will Fear No Evil* to the ironical farce *Job*, akin to the bleakly hilarious fantasies of ▷Joseph Heller and ▷Kurt Vonnegut. They have been condemned (particularly by admirers of *Strangers in a Strange Land*) as excessively right-wing and over concerned with sex. His best known books, the heart of his achievement, are a series of independent but linked novels about Lazarus Long, a man who has the ability to live forever, and who ends up as a kind of universal patriarch; everyone in existence is one of his descendants. Heinlein explores the personal and social problems of such a person, stirring in exotic and fascinating plot-ideas. In *Time Enough to Love* (1973), for example, Lazarus Long, bored with life and contemplating suicide, is distracted by being allowed to try the forbidden experience of time travel. He goes back to 1917, fights in the first world war, meets himself as a six-year-old and falls in love with his own mother.

Other books including Lazarus Long are Methuselah's Children, The Number of the Beast *and* The Cat Who Walks Through Walls. *Heinlein's other novels include* The Day After Tomorrow *and* To Sail Beyond the Slushpile. *His short stories, including such classics as 'The Man Who Sold the Moon' and 'The Green Hills of Earth', are in the two-volume omnibus* The Past Through Tomorrow.

the Devil).

► ▷Isaac Asimov, *Foundation*. ▷Philip José Farmer, *Riverworld*. ▷Kurt Vonnegut, *Galápagos*. ▷John Updike, *Roger's Version*.

HELLER, JOSEPH (BORN 1923)

US novelist.

Throughout the 1950s, the escalation of the nuclear-arms race produced in many people a feeling of desperate impotence. Faced with imminent apocalypse, the only possible option seemed to be hysterical, cynical laughter. By the early 1960s this mood was common in plays, comedians' routines, cartoons and satirical magazines, and Heller's first novel *Catch-22* expressed it perfectly. On the surface a wild farce about airmen in the second world war, it shows human beings as both trapped in a detestable destiny and paradoxically liberated, by the absence of hope or choice, to do exactly as they please, to turn reality into fantasy. Until *Catch-22*, this had been a theme for serious novels (for example those of ▷Camus, ▷Sartre or ▷Hemingway); Heller made it comedy, leading a trend which has since spread from the arts into our general attitude to both our 'leaders' and the way we live.

CATCH-22 (1961)

A group of US bomber-pilots is stationed on a Mediterra-

READ ON

- Two other Heller novels centre on characters who are trapped. *Something Happened* (1974) shows a man in thrall to his own boringness; in *God Knows* (1984) the Old Testament King David is shackled by knowledge of the world's whole future history, and by his relationship with a wisecracking, cynical and unhelpful God. ('Where does it say nice?' asks God.

nean island during the second world war. Every time a man thinks he has flown his quota of bombing-missions, high command doubles the number. There is no escape, and the reason is Catch-22: if you're sane enough to ask to be grounded because what you're doing is crazy, you're sane enough to fly. For all its bleak philosophy, *Catch-22* is brilliantly funny, particularly in its deadpan reporting of the lunatic, gung-ho US top brass, of Milo Minderbinder's extension to infinity of the rules of free-market enterprise (profiteering on everything from eggs to his comrades' lives), and of such pitiful victims of destiny as Major Major Major Major, a man haunted by his name. Robert Altman's film *M*A*S*H*, and the dazzling TV series which followed it, caught an exactly similar mood; *Catch-22* is like all *M*A*S*H*'s most ludicrous, lacerating scenes gathered into one glorious, agonising whole.

Heller's other novels are Something Happened, Good as Gold, God Knows *and* Picture This. No Laughing Matter *is non-fiction, a blackly funny account of Heller's recovery from near-fatal illness.*

'Where does it say I have to be nice?').

▶ ▷Jaroslav Hašek, *The Good Soldier Švejk*. ▷Wyndham Lewis , *Childermass*. ▷Philip Roth, *Portnoy's Complaint.*

HEMINGWAY, Ernest (1898-1961)

US novelist and short-story writer.

Few great writers provoke such love/hate reactions as Hemingway: it seems impossible to read him without judging him. The reason is that although he wrote some of the most evocative, persuasive prose of the century – as direct and compelling as a journalist's reports – many people find his subject-matter and philosophy of life repellent. He believed that creatures, including human beings, are at their noblest when fighting for survival, and his novels and stories are therefore about boxing, big-game hunting, deep-sea fishing, bull-fighting and above all war. Hemingway himself realised that his macho philosophy belonged more to the Middle Ages than the 20th century, and most of his books are tinged with failure. His heroes rarely succeed in 'proving' themselves, their wars are futile, the emphasis is on pain, despair and death. But the dream remains, and is Hemingway's own dream. He spent his leisure time in exactly the activities he describes – precise details of how to fight bulls, hunt big game, box or fish are what he does best – and in 1961, feeling too old and sick to continue, he shot himself.

A Farewell To Arms (1929)

A US ambulance driver in Italy during the first world war is wounded and taken to hospital, where he falls in love with an English nurse. While he convalesces the couple are deliriously happy, but then he is commanded back to the front. She tells him that she is pregnant, and they decide that their

READ ON

- *The Old Man and the Sea* describes a duel to the death between the old Cuban fisherman Santiago and a gigantic marlin, the biggest fish he has ever tried to catch in his life. The book is short, and concentrates on Santiago, struggling not only with the marlin but against his own failing powers, and kept going only by determination and a lifetime's skill.

▶ ▷Graham Greene, *The Power and the Glory*. ▷Norman Mailer, *The Naked and the Dead*. ▷George Orwell,

Joseph HELLER

Len **DEIGHTON, BOMBER**
(meticulous planning for a bombing-run over Germany in World War II)

Neville **SHUTE, LANDFALL**
(breakdown of young pilot who sinks 'one of ours' by mistake)

Stephen **CRANE, THE RED BADGE OF COURAGE**
(young volunteer horrified but exhilarated by battle conditions in American Civil War)

WAR IS HELL

Andrew **SINCLAIR, GOG**
(giant from past washed up in Scotland, travels to London, horrified at 20th-century 'civilisation')

IT'S A MAD, MAD WORLD

Günter **GRASS, THE TIN DRUM**
(nazism as an insane circus-parade watched by a gleeful, baby-brained adult)

Budd **SCHULBERG, WHAT MAKES SAMMY RUN?**
(Sammy claws his way to the top; scum always floats)

Richard **CONDON, MILE HIGH**
(US power politics; a farcical orgy of sex, drugs, blackmail and murder)

Jerzy **KOSINSKI, BEING THERE**
(lame-brain gardener taken for political guru and saint)

Terry **SOUTHERN, CANDY**
(virgin innocent abroad – neither innocent nor virgin for long)

Catch-22

(lunacy of war; USAF bomber base on fantasy mediterranean island in World War II)

ANTI-WAR NOVELS

Mario **VARGAS LLOSA, THE CITY AND THE DOGS/ THE TIME OF THE HERO**
(farcical tragedy of young cadets in 1950s Peruvian military academy)

Norman **MAILER, THE NAKED AND THE DEAD**
(World War II US conscripts brutalised by conditions of service on a hopeless Pacific mission)

Erich Maria **REMARQUE, ALL QUIET ON THE WESTERN FRONT**
(lives of four young men disrupted and ruined by brutality of World War I trench warfare)

CRAZINESS OF COMMAND

Richard **HOOKER, M*A*S*H**
(US doctors in Korea fighting insane conditions, boredom and gung-ho top brass)

Leslie **THOMAS, THE VIRGIN SOLDIERS**
(over-sexed, bewildered British conscripts in Far East)

Thomas **PYNCHON, GRAVITY'S RAINBOW**
(what is top secret World War II establishment for? What is meaning of life? Should war (and sex) not be more fun that this?)

Jaroslav **HAŠEK, THE GOOD SOLDIER ŠVEJK**
(World War I batman obeys every order, believes every lie, keeps out of trouble)

Herman **WOUK, THE CAINE MUTINY**
(crew court-martialled for mutinying against insane World War II minesweeper captain)

Peter **GEORGE, RED ALERT**
(chain of command follies and failures triggers World War III)

only course is 'a farewell to arms', escaping from the war to neutral Switzerland.

Hemingway's other novels are The Torrents of Spring, The Sun Also Rises/Fiesta *(which includes a superb description of bull-running during the festival at Pamplona),* Death in the Afternoon *(about bull-fighting),* The Green Hills of Africa, To Have and Have Not, For Whom the Bell Tolls *(set during the Spanish civil war),* Across the River and Into the Trees *and* The Old Man and the Sea. *Several unrevised, unfinished books were published posthumously: the best-known is the novel* Islands in the Stream. *His short-story collections include* In Our Time, Men Without Women *and* Winner Take Nothing.

Homage to Catalonia. ▷Jack London, *The Sea-wolf.* ▷Hammond Innes, *Campbell's Kingdom.* Alistair Maclean, *The Guns of Navarone.*

HERBERT, Frank (1920–86)

US novelist.

Herbert's work is dominated by the 2000-page (6-novel) 'Dune' series (1965–85), an SF epic whose scope and complexity dwarf all rivals. Dune is a desert planet, inhabited by gigantic sand-worms which produce mélange, a substance which inhibits aging and gives knowledge of the past and future. The saga (each of whose novels is self-contained) tells how Paul Atreides inherits Dune, has to win it from his enemies and then colonise it. It describes the 'greening' of a planet where water is the most precious of all commodities, and recounts the wars between the Atreides family and other interests (especially the powerful Bene Gesserit sisterhood, which is dedicated to harnessing the pure power of thought and so dispensing with science and technology). The books are partly a swaggering multi-generation saga, the apotheosis of space-opera, and partly a detailed and moving account of the inter-relationship between the colonists and their planet. The effort of controlling but not destroying the environment produces in them a feeling of near-mystic communion with natural forces which contrasts strongly with the snarling and bickering of their relations with one another.

The first Dune trilogy is Dune, Dune Messiah *and* Children of Dune*; the second is* God Emperor of Dune, Heretics of Dune *and* Chapterhouse of Dune. *Herbert's many other books include* The Dragon in the Sea, The Whipping Star, The Dosadi Experiment, The Green Brain *and* The Santaroga Barrier.

READ ON

- **Good SF follow-ups:** ▷Brian Aldiss, *Helliconia Spring* and its sequels; ▷Ursula Le Guin, *The Left Hand of Darkness.*
- **Good non-SF follow-ups:** Frans Bengtsson, *The Long Ships* (about Vikings exploring the surface of our own planet); Jean M. Auel, *Earth Children* (a saga of the distant past, about human beings learning to control their environment and discovering ways of civilisation); Nicholas Monsarrat, *Running Proud* (about one of Columbus' sailors shipwrecked and forced, by the tribe who find him, to invent himself as a godlike personality, with deeds to match).
- National Lampoon,

Doon is a splendid send-up of all Herbert's ideas – replacing mélange, for example, with a wonder-drug called Coke.

HERBERT, JAMES (BORN 1943)

British novelist.

Herbert's supernatural chillers, among the most frightening in the business, include *The Dark*, *The Domain*, *The Fog*, *The Rats*, *Shrine*, *The Spear*, *The Survivor*, *Sepulchre* and *Moon* (about a boy on an island who dreams of a sadistic, supernatural creature – at the same time as it dreams of him).

READ ON

▶ ▷Stephen King, *It*. Margaret Bingley, *Devil's Child*. Dean R. Koontz, *Whispers*. Robin Cook, *Mutation*. Stephen Gallagher, *Oktober*.

HESSE, HERMANN (1877-1962)

German/Swiss novelist and non-fiction writer.

A poet and mystic, Hesse was influenced by Jung's ideas of the unconscious and the collective unconscious, and later by Buddhist philosophy. His most famous mystical novel, *The Glass Bead Game/Magister Ludi* (Das Glasperlenspiel), is about a future utopia where all questions about life, morality and personality are covered by a monastic philosophical system centred on a zen-like game involving coloured beads and an abacus. Hesse's reputation for gentle, philosophical woolliness has obscured his true worth. His novels before *The Glass Bead Game* are spare, moving accounts of how people in psychological turmoil reach peace with themselves, either through their own efforts or with the help of friends and loved ones. He is something of a special taste, but few writers' works so reward their devotees.

ROSSHALDE (1914)

Veraguth, a world-renowned painter, is suffering creative block. His marriage is breaking down, and he and his wife stay together out of love for Rosshalde, their beautiful country estate, and devotion to their young son Pierre. Veraguth's problems seem beyond cure – until unexpected tragedy forces him to come to terms with himself, and so to find peace at last.

Hesse's major novels are Gertrud, Peter Camenzind, Under the Wheel/The Prodigy, Siddhartha *(about Buddha)*, Steppenwolf, Narziss and Goldmund *and* The Glass Bead Game.

READ ON

- *Gertrud* (1910, the story of a tragic love-triangle between a girl and two young men who are close friends). *Steppenwolf* (1927) and *Narziss and Goldmund* (1930) are both about the divided self. In *Steppenwolf* a hopeless, middle-aged recluse is 'brought back' by the spiritual energy of three young people who may be dream-figures from his subconscious. In *Narziss and Goldmund* (set in medieval Europe) the conflict between flesh and spirit is symbolised by the two main characters,

*He also published shorter, more mystical fiction (*Knulp; Klingsor's Last Summer*), poetry, short stories, essays and letters.*

close friends, one carnal, one spiritual.

- **To *Rosshalde*:** ▷André Gide, *The Pastoral Symphony*.
- **To *The Glass Bead Game*:** ▷Tom De Haan, *A Mirror for Princes*.
- **To *Narziss and Goldmund*:** Georges Bernanos, *Diary of a Country Priest*.
- **To *Steppenwolf*:** D.M. Thomas, *The White Hotel*.
- **To Hesse's work in general:** ▷Heinrich Böll, *The Clown*; ▷Kazuo Ishiguro, *An Artist of the Floating World*.

HEYER, GEORGETTE (1902–74)

British novelist.

Apart from a handful of detective stories (eg *Envious Casca*; *Detection Unlimited*), all Heyer's novels are historical. Some centre on real events (*The Infamous Army*, for example, is about the battle of Waterloo); others, notably *Beauvallet* (1929), *The Tollgate* (1954) and *The Unknown Ajax* (1959), are heady tales of smugglers, highwaymen and other members of the 18th-century underworld. The bulk of her books are light-hearted, frothy romances. A hero and heroine who detest or distrust one another are thrown together by circumstances and fall in love. Often she 'tames' him or he 'tames' her; sometimes masquerade (such as posing as lady's maids or cads) is involved. Heyer's knowledge of Regency ways was exhaustive: every garment, vehicle, gesture and turn of phrase seems exactly and delightfully right. Her novels are fast-moving, uncomplicated entertainment. She perfected the Regency genre, and within it she is unsurpassed.

Heyer's best-known romances are The Masqueraders, These Old Shades, Devil's Cub, Regency Buck, Friday's Child,

READ ON

- **To the novels based on real events:** Margaret Irwin, *Young Bess* (first of a trilogy about Queen Elizabeth I of England); ▷Jean Plaidy, *The Spanish Bridegroom*.
- **To the adventure novels:** ▷Daphne Du Maurier, *Jamaica Inn*; Jane Aiken Hodge, *Rebel Heiress*; ▷Mary Stewart, *This Rough Magic* (set in modern Greece).
- **To the romances:** ▷Jane Austen, *Mansfield Park*; Sheila Walsh, *The*

The Foundling, The Grand Sophy, Bath Tangle, Sprig Muslin *and* Cotillion. Pistols for Two *contains short stories.*

Rose Domino; Clare Darcy, *Eugenia*; Bob Coleman, *The Further Adventures of Tom Jones.*

HIBBERT, Eleanor (BORN 1906)

British novelist.

Hibbert has written all her books under pseudonyms: Eleanor Burford ▷Philippa Carr, Elbur Ford, ▷Victoria Holt, Kathleen Kellow, ▷Jean Plaidy and Ellalice Tate.

HIGGINS, Jack (BORN 1929)

British novelist.

'Jack Higgins' is one of the pseudonyms of Henry Patterson, who also writes thrillers as Martin Fallon, James Graham, Hugh Marlow and Harry Patterson. The Higgins books are pacy, violent and full of character. They include *The Last Place God Made, A Prayer for the Dying, The Eagle Has Landed* (about a plot to assassinate Churchill in the second world war), *Hell is Always Today, The Dark Side of the Street, Solo* and *A Season in Hell* (1989), about a young ex-SAS officer taking revenge on drug-barons who have killed two apparently harmless young addicts.

READ ON

▶ ▷Len Deighton, *Berlin Game*. Alexander Fullerton, *Regenesis*. Colin Forbes, *Terminal*. Gerald Seymour, *Kingfisher*.

High Adventure

▷Desmond Bagley, *The Golden Keel*
▷Alexandre Dumas, *The Three Musketeers*
▷H. Rider Haggard, *King Solomon's Mines*
▷Anthony Hope, *The Prisoner of Zenda*
▷Hammond Innes, *Campbell's Kingdom*
Rafael Sabatini, *Captain Blood*
▷Wilbur Smith, *Shout at the Devil*
B. Traven, *The Treasure of the Sierra Madre*

Action Thrillers (p 2); Spies and Double Agents (p 231); Terrorists/Freedom Fighters (p 240)

Georgette HEYER

Clare **DARCY, ELYZA**
(plain girl disguises herself as boy to find romance)

Caroline **COURTNEY, DUCHESS IN DISGUISE**
(spurned wife disguises herself to win husband's love)

Jane **AUSTEN, SENSE AND SENSIBILITY**
(love-affairs of two sisters; sensible Elinor and impulsive, romantic Marianne)

Joan **AIKEN, MANSFIELD REVISITED**
(spirited girl 'tames' brother-in-law's snobbish family)

REGENCY ENGLAND

Henry **FIELDING, TOM JONES**
(escapades of foundling wandering 18th-century England to find truth about himself)

P.G. **WODEHOUSE, BILL THE CONQUEROR**
(Percy Pilbeam's havoc-strewn career as editor of 'Society Spice')

Iris **MURDOCH, A SEVERED HEAD**
(sexual merry-go-round in 'swinging' 1960s London)

Mary **WESLEY, THE VACILLATIONS OF POPPY CAREWE** *(rich heiress reviews young men in her life to find the 'best' – i.e. least obviously eligible – husband. Love intervenes.)*

COMEDY OF MANNERS

Mary **STEWART, NINE COACHES WAITING**
(English governess in France, caught in family feud, saves charges from death, finds love)

Helen **MACINNES, RIDE A PALE HORSE**
(US journalist at Prague conference approached by would-be defector)

Anne **BRIDGE, THE GINGER GRIFFIN**
(intrigue and unhappiness in pre-Revolutionary China)

Jane Aiken **HODGE, POLONAISE**
(love and politics in 1810s Poland, caught between Russia and Napoleon)

ROMANTIC MYSTERY

Regency Buck

(dislike turns to love in Regency English high society)

PERIOD ROMANCE

Norah **LOFTS, THE BRITTLE GLASS**
(independent girl grows up in 18th-century Fens, a place of smugglers, gipsies and highwaymen)

T.N. **MURARI, TAJ**
(love of Indian Shah Jahan and his wife, for whom he built the Taj Mahal)

Kathleen **WINSOR, FOREVER AMBER**
(love and adventure in 17th-century, Restoration England)

Rosalind **LAKER, WHAT THE HEART KEEPS**
(two immigrants to 1900s USA fall in love, make life together in Wild West and early Hollywood)

20TH-CENTURY ROMANCE

M.M. **KAYE, THE FAR PAVILIONS**
(love across the races in dying days of British Raj in India)

Margaret **PEMBERTON, NEVER LEAVE ME**
(successful Californian looks back on doomed wartime love-affair with German officer, when she works for French Resistance)

Caroline **FIRESIDE, GOODBYE AGAIN**
(will heroine sacrifice glamorous film career for love?)

Erich **SEGAL, LOVE STORY**
(two college students fall idyllically, tragically, in love)

HIGHER (?) EDUCATION

▷Robertson Davies, *The Rebel Angels*
▷J.P. Donleavy, *The Ginger Man*
Richard Gordon, *Doctor in the House*
Howard Jacobson, *Coming from Behind*
▷Randall Jarrell, *Pictures from an Institution*
▷Alison Lurie, *The War Between the Tates*
▷Mary McCarthy, *The Groves of Academe*
▷Tom Sharpe, *Wilt*

Dreaming Spires (p 69)

HIGHSMITH, PATRICIA (BORN 1921)

US novelist and short-story writer.

Except for ***The People Who Knock on the Door*** (1982, about the disintegration of an 'ordinary' US family whose father becomes a born-again Christian) Highsmith's books are all psychological thrillers. They show the planning and commission of horribly convincing, 'everyday' crimes, and the way murder erodes the murderer's moral identity. Few writers screw tension so tight in such functional, unemotional prose. Highsmith's most chilling insight is how close the criminally insane can be to people just like ourselves.

RIPLEY'S GAME (1974)

Ripley, who appears in several Highsmith books, is a charming American psychopath who lives in France. In this book, out of boredom, he sets up circumstances to snare an entirely innocent man into committing murder. But the murder-victim is a mafia boss, and soon assassins begin to hunt down both Ripley and his dupe. The plot is exciting, but Highsmith's main concern is the comparison between Ripley's icy amorality and the conscience-racked flailings of the man he corrupts.

Other Ripley books are The Talented Mr Ripley, Ripley Under Ground *and* The Boy Who Followed Ripley. *Highsmith's other novels include* Strangers on a Train, The Two Faces of January, The Story Teller/A Suspension of Mercy, The Tremor of Forgery, Edith's Diary *and* Found in the Street. The Snailwatcher/Eleven, The Animal-lover's Book of Beastly Murder, The Black House, Mermaids on the Golf Course *and* Tales of Natural and Unnatural Catastrophes *contain short stories.*

READ ON

- The central character of *The Glass Cell* (a typical non-Ripley book) is a man released from prison after six years during which his character has been brutalised and his moral integrity destroyed. Tormented by the possibility of his wife's unfaithfulness, he sets out to discover the truth.
- ▶ Julian Symons, *The Man Who Killed Himself*. ▷Georges Simenon, *The Hatter's Ghosts*. Greg MacDonald, *Running Scared*. ▷Ruth Rendell, *Live Flesh*. ▷P.D. James, *The Skull Beneath the Skin*. Celia Fremlin, *Appointment with Yesterday*; *Don't Go to Sleep in the Dark* (short stories).

HILL, Reginald (born 1936)

British novelist.

Hill writes thrillers and adventure stories under the pseudonyms Dick Morland (*Heart Clock*), ▷Patrick Ruell and Charles Underhill (*Captain Fantom*). Under his own name he writes affable, joky detective stories, featuring slobbish Inspector Dalziel and his bushy-tailed, over-eager assistant Pascoe. Hill's books include *A Clubbable Woman, An Advancement of Learning, A Fairly Dangerous Thing, A Very Good Hater* and the cheekily-named *Another Death in Venice.*

READ ON

- ▶ Colin Watson, *One Man's Meat*. Joyce Porter, *Who the Hell Was Sylvia?*. Ira Wallach, *The Absence of a Cello.*

HILL, Susan (born 1942)

British writer of novels, short stories and non-fiction.

Except for *The Woman in Black,* a ghost-story in classic 19th-century style, all Hill's novels and stories are about predatory emotional relationships. One partner (spouse, friend, lover or acquaintance) can only survive by engulfing the other, and the process is agonising and deliberate, an erosion of spirit without hope or help. Her least bleak book is *In the Springtime of the Year* (1974), in which a young woman devastated by the death of her husband is rescued from despair by the tranquil daily round of country life. Hill's themes may be sombre, but she writes with delicacy and compassion: in the end, the tears we shed are for the human condition itself, a predicament which is like a third partner in the stories, a malign presence feasting on victims and predators alike.

I'M THE KING OF THE CASTLE (1970)

Mr Hooper, a lonely widower, invites Mrs Kingshaw to be housekeeper of his large Victorian mansion. He hopes that his ten-year-old son and hers will become friends. But the boy Hooper resents Kingshaw's invasion of his psychological kingdom, and torments him. The psychopathic child, possessed by the devil, was a familiar figure in pulp fiction and films of the 1970s (a good example is the 'Omen' film series); Hill turns the same subject into art.

Hill's other main novels are A Change for the Better, Gentleman and Ladies, Strange Meeting *and* The Bird of Night, *a sombre book about a manic-depressive artist and the friend who tries to help him.* The Albatross *and* A Bit of Singing and Dancing *contain short stories.*

READ ON

- • *The Bird of Night*
- ▶ **To *I'm the King of the Castle*:** ▷Henry James, *The Turn of the Screw*; ▷John Wyndham, *Chocky*; ▷William Golding, *Lord of the Flies.*
- ▶ **To *In the Springtime of the Year*:** Penelope Lively, *Perfect Happiness.*
- ▶ Hill's grim compassion, and her unblinking descriptions of the desolation of the soul, are matched in ▷Carson McCullers, *Reflections in a Golden Eye;* James Agee, *A Death in the Family* and ▷John Updike, *The Centaur.*

HISTORICAL ADVENTURE

Peter Carter, *The Black Lamp*
Bernard Cornwell, *Sharpe's Regiment*

Frederick Couens, *Gnur Bodi*
▷C.S. Forester, *Mr Midshipman Hornblower*
George Macdonald Fraser, *Flashman*
▷Homer, *Odyssey*
▷R.L. Stevenson, *Kidnapped*

Action Thrillers (p 2); Spies and Double Agents (p 231); High Adventure (p 119)

HOBAN, RUSSELL (BORN 1925)

US/British novelist.

Hoban first made his name with children's books and with *Turtle Diary* (1976), a novel about two lonely people drawn together by their ambition to return the turtles from the London Zoo to the sea. His chief fame, however, is for *Riddley Walker* (1980). This is a future-fantasy, set in England generations after the nuclear holocaust. The society is primitive – making fire is still a problem, never mind organising the rule of law – and the survivors are haunted by memories of the time before the bomb. Rags of old culture, technology and morality flap in their minds, as inexplicable and as powerful as myth. Their language, similarly – the one the book is written in – is shredded, reconstituted English: words coalesce, grammar has collapsed, new metaphors sprout like weeds. Although this style is difficult at first, it becomes perfectly comprehensible after a few pages, and before long the broken, patched-together words begin to seem like poetry, as Riddley, the story-teller, struggles to find ways to describe the pictures inside his mind.

READ ON

- *The Lion of Boaz-Jachin and Jachin-Boaz*; *The Medusa Frequency*.
- ▶ ▷William Golding, *Pincher Martin*. ▷George Turner, *Vaneglory*. ▷Anthony Burgess, *A Clockwork Orange*. Robie Macauley, *A Secret History of Time to Come*.

HOLT, VICTORIA (BORN 1906)

British novelist.

'Victoria Holt' is one of the pseudonyms of ▷Eleanor Hibbert. She writes romantic mystery and suspense. In *Secret for a Nightingale*, for example, a 19th-century English girl marries for love in India, and finds out only after her return to England that her husband has not told her everything about himself.

Holt's two dozen other books include Mistress of Mellyn, The Bride of Pendorric, The Shivering Sands, Lord of the Far Islands, The India Fan *and* My Enemy the Queen.

READ ON

- ▶ ▷Norah Lofts, *The Wayside Tavern*. Naomi Jacob, *'Gollantz' saga*. Cynthia Harrod-Eagles, *'Dynasty' series*. Caroline Courtney, *Guardian of the Heart*. Sarah Woodhouse, *The Indian Widow*.

HOMER (C 9TH CENTURY BC)

Greek epic poet.

Although Homer's *Odyssey* was composed to be declaimed, section by section, at royal feasts, the depth of its charac-

READ ON

- ▶ ▷Robert Graves, *Homer's Daughter* (a

ter-drawing and its psychological perception transcend such fragmented performances: in a good prose translation (such as E.V. Rieu's) it is as complex and fascinating as any modern novel. Its plot, taken from Greek myth, recounts Odysseus' supernatural adventures on his way home from the Trojan War and his epic battle with the suitors who have plagued his wife Penelope during his absence. But it is also the story of Odysseus' own development, of the way his experiences mould and mature his personality. Each of his encounters – with the flesh-eating giant Polyphemus, the Lotus-eaters, the Sirens, the seductress Calypso, Circe, Nausicaa – changes him, teaches him more about himself, until he is ready to prove himself to his enemies, his people and his patient wife. The *Iliad*, similarly, uses the framework of myth (the quarrel between Achilles and Hector during the Trojan War) to discuss such themes as ambition, pride, courage, the place of destiny in human lives and the glory and futility of war.

fantasy about the events leading up the composition of the Odyssey); ▷Mary Renault, *The King Must Die*; Henry Treece, *Electra*.

▶ **Books using Homeric style or themes:** Virgil, *Aeneid*; Petronius, *Satyricon* (a parody of the Odyssey set among the pimps, prostitutes, hermaphrodites, fake prophets and pimps of a fantasy ancient Rome); Miguel de Cervantes Saavedra, *Don Quixote*; ▷Lev Tolstoy, *War and Peace*. The themes and structure of the *Odyssey* inspired ▷James Joyce, *Ulysses*.

HOPE, ANTHONY (1863–1933)

British novelist.

In *The Prisoner of Zenda* (1894) Hope invented the 'Ruritanian' adventure-story, a colourful escapist yarn set in some fantasy foreign kingdom. Rudolf Rassendyl, an upper-class Englishman on holiday in the middle European country of Ruritania, is astonished to find that he is an exact double of the king, and even more surprised when the king is kidnapped just before his coronation, and Rassendyl is asked to impersonate him. As the story proceeds, the kidnappers (the king's ambitious brother and his henchman Rupert of Hentzau, the finest swordsman in Ruritania) try to foil the coronation-plans, and Rassendyl (who has meanwhile fallen in love with Flavia, the future queen) breaks into Zenda Castle to rescue the imprisoned king. The novel has been filmed a dozen times, and has inspired one of the cinema's favourite clichés: two men, one debonair, one saturnine, duelling up and down the steps of an ancient castle, slicing candles in half, parrying thrusts with three-legged stools and matching each rapier-thrust with a dazzling shaft of wit.

READ ON

- *Rupert of Hentzau* (the sequel); *Sophy of Kravonia*.

▶ Jane Barry, *The Conscience of the King*. Marjorie Bowen, *The Viper of Milan*. Rafael Sabatini, *Captain Blood*. ▷A. Conan Doyle, *The White Company*. P.C. Wren, *Beau Geste*.

HOUSEHOLD, GEOFFREY (1900–88)

British novelist.

Household's thrillers follow squarely in the steps of ▷Buchan, pitting single individuals against the might of sinister corporations, political groups or foreigners, and letting them win by persistence, guts and an invincibly late-Edwardian code of gentlemanly behaviour. Many of his heroes are themselves hunted, and have to 'hole up' either in seedy urban lodgings or in the countryside, where they live by the survival strategies of a commando training manual. The mixture of boys' comic-strip yarns and adult terror is common in English thrillers; in Household's hands it is unsurpassed.

Household's best-known books are Rogue Male, Rogue Justice, The High Place, A Rough Shoot, A Time to Kill, Watcher in the Shadows *and* The Courtesy of Death.

READ ON

- John Welcome, *Run for Cover*. ▷Graham Greene, *A Gun for Sale/This Gun for Hire*. Hugh McCutcheon, *A Hot Wind from Hell*. James Graham, *A Game for Heroes*. William Haggard, *Closed Circuit*. Lionel Davidson, *The Sun Chemist*.

HOWATCH, SUSAN (BORN 1940)

British novelist.

After a number of atmospheric romances (*The Dark Shore, The Waiting Sands, April's Grave, The Devil on Lammas Night*), Howatch made a second reputation with multi-generation family sagas, setting internal rivalries and alliances against the background of historical events. Her books include *Cashelmara, The Rich Are Different* and *Penmarric* (the story of a British family from Victorian times to the second world war).

READ ON

- Jean Stubbs, *Kits Hill*. Mary Pearce, *The Appletree Saga*. Jessica Stirling, *The Spoiled Earth*.

HUGO, VICTOR (1802–85)

French novelist, poet and playwright.

Although Hugo was principally a poet and dramatist, he is also remembered for four panoramic historical novels. *Notre Dame de Paris* (1831), set in medieval times, is about the beautiful foundling Esmeralda, the men who try to seduce her, and the deformed Quasimodo, bell-ringer at Notre Dame cathedral, who loves her. The book's detail of Parisian low life is matched in *Les misérables* (1862), about a noble-hearted convict and the corrupt policeman who persecutes him. *The Toilers of the Sea* (1866) allegorises the eternal struggle between human beings and nature into a story of Guernsey fishermen, fighting both the elements and each other. *Ninety-three* (1873) is about royalist resistance in the French Revolution. Hugo's novels are long and prone to philosophising, but they make up for it by the energy of their plots, the melodramatic attraction of their characters – not for nothing is the Hunchback of Notre Dame a Hollywood favourite – and the extraordinary feeling they give

READ ON

- **To *Notre Dame de Paris*:** ▷Alessandro Manzoni, *The Betrothed* (I promessi sposi).
- **To *Les misérables*:** Heinrich Mann, *The Blue Angel/Small Town Tyrant*.
- **To *The Toilers of the Sea*:** ▷Charles Dickens, *Hard Times*.
- **To *Ninety-three*:** ▷Alexander Solzhenitsyn, *August, 1914*.

that every event, every story, is just one glimpse of the teeming anthill of human life.

► **To the more swaggering elements of Hugo's style:** ▷Lew Wallace, *Ben-Hur;* ▷Alexandre Dumas, *The Man in the Iron Mask*; Mika Waltari, *Sinuhe the Egyptian.*

HULME, KERI (BORN 1947)

New Zealand novelist and short-story writer.

Hulme's first novel *The Bone People* was the outsider which won the Booker Prize for 1985. It counterpoints the story of a woman's attemps to 'thaw' an autistic child with an extended reflection on Maori legend and culture. For Hulme, the Maoris are like disabled people in a fit society, and she invests their presence and their culture with the resonance of myth. Her prose-style is uncompromising and experimental, full of fragmented dialogue, stream-of-consciousness narrative and abrupt shifts in time and place. In 1987 *The Bone People* was followed by *The Windeater (Te Kaihau)*, a collection of short stories written over the previous decade. They share the preoccupations, themes and style of *The Bone People* – with an added ingredient, radical feminism – but their shortness makes them easier to read, an excellent introduction to Hulme's work. Despite, or perhaps because of, Hulme's stylistic experiments, the impact of these stories is both overwhelming and unforgettable.

READ ON

► Ian Wedde, *Symme's Hole.* ▷Bruce Chatwin, *The Songlines.* Kathy Acker, *Blood and Guts in High School.* Sheila Watson, *The Double Hook*. Amos Tutuola, *Pauper, Brawler and Slanderer.*

THE HUMAN COMEDY

▷Jane Austen, *Pride and Prejudice*
▷John Cheever, *The Wapshot Chronicle*
▷Peter De Vries, *The Tunnel of Love*
▷David Lodge, *The British Museum is Falling Down*
▷Alison Lurie, *Real People*
▷Barbara Pym, *A Glass of Blessings*
▷William Thackeray, *Vanity Fair*
Angela Thirkell, *High Rising*
▷H.G. Wells, *Tono-Bungay*

Dreaming Spires (p 69); Friends (?) and Neighbours (p 89); Higher (?) Education (p 122)

HUNTER, EVAN (BORN 1926)

US novelist.

Hunter writes under his own name and under the pseud-

READ ON

► Donald Westlake,

onyms ▷Ed McBain, Richard Marsten (*Rocket to Luna*; *Vanishing Ladies*) and Hunt Collins (*Cut Me In*). As Hunter he has written children's books, plays, screenplays (notably *The Birds*, for Hitchcock), tough novels of New York life (eg *The Blackboard Jungle*, 1954, about an idealistic teacher in a slum high school), and thrillers, many of them agreeably laced with farce. His books (many of them filmed) include *Buddwing*, *The Paper Dragon*, *Last Summer*, *Nobody Knew They Were There*, *Hail to the Chief*, *Where There's Smoke* and *Every Little Crook and Nanny*.

The Mercenaries. ▷Richard Condon, *Prizzi's Honour*. Colin Dunne, *Black Ice*.

HUXLEY, ALDOUS (1894–1963)

British novelist and non-fiction writer.

Huxley's early books were glittering satires on 1920s intellectual and upper-class life, accounts of preposterous conversations at country-house costume parties and in such unlikely meeting-places as publishers' offices or the Egyptian Room at the British Museum. His characters are intelligent, creative, fascinating and empty; haunted by the pointlessness of existence, they pass their time flirting, gossiping, swapping philosophical ideas and planning all kinds of japes and pranks. In the 1930s, beginning with *Brave New World*, he changed his approach. Instead of focussing his satire on a single section of British society, he turned on the human race at large, and wrote a series of increasingly bitter books demolishing all our ambitions to make a better society by science, philosophy, religion, socialism or (in the late 1950s, at the germination-stage of flower-power) hallucinatory drugs. His books are a witty, cold dazzle of ideas; enjoyable as you read them, they leave an acid aftertaste.

BRAVE NEW WORLD (1932)

In a soulless future world, genetic engineering programmes people from birth for their status in society, and removes all aggressive or unproductive instincts. Individuality, creativity and personality are sacrificed in the causes of material prosperity, good health and freedom from anxiety. Only a small group of 'savages' – people like us – survives, in a community in New Mexico, and one of them escapes and is brought into the 'real world', with tragic results. As in all his novels, Huxley tells this tale soberly and without comment: the flatness of his prose brilliantly intensifies the horror of what he is saying. Nothing truly terrible happens – and that is the most terrible thing of all.

In chronological order, Huxley's novels are Crome Yellow, Antic Hay, Those Barren Leaves, Point Counter Point, Brave New World, Eyeless in Gaza, After Many a Summer, Time Must Have a Stop, Ape and Essence, The Genius and

READ ON

- *Ape and Essence* (about a California-dwelling group of survivors from the nuclear holocaust, primitives visited by a horror-struck scientist from New Zealand).
- ▶ **To Huxley's social satires:** ▷F. Scott Fitzgerald, *The Beautiful and Damned* (from the 1920s); ▷Anthony Powell, *Venusberg* (from the 1930s); ▷Martin Amis, *Money* (from the 1980s).
- ▶ **To *Ape and Essence*:** ▷Paul Theroux, *O-Zone*.
- ▶ **To Huxley's later books:** Frederik Pohl and C.M. Kornbluth, *The Space Merchants*; ▷L.P. Hartley, *Facial Justice*; Michael Frayn, *Sweet Dreams*.

the Goddess *and* Island. Limbo, Mortal Coils, The Little Mexican, Two or Three Graces *and* Brief Candles *are collections of short stories, all of them early.*

I

INDIA

▷J.G. Farrell, *The Siege at Krishnapur*
Valerie Fitzgerald, *Zemindar*
▷E.M. Forster, *A Passage to India*
▷Ruth Prawer Jhabvala, *Heat and Dust*
▷Rudyard Kipling, *Kim*
T.N. Murari, *Taj*
▷R.K. Narayan, *The Vendor of Sweets*
▷Salman Rushdie, *Midnight's Children*

INNES, Hammond (born 1913)
British novelist.

Innes writes tough action thrillers, often with a background of the services, mining, oil drilling or seafaring. One of his major interests, reflected in many books, is the balance between human beings and the natural environment. His books include *Wreckers Must Breathe/Trapped, The Blue Ice, Maddon's Rock/Gale Warning, Campbell's Kingdom, The Mary Deare/The Wreck of the Mary Deare, Atlantic Fury, Solomon's Seal* and *Medusa* (1989), about a British skipper whose lone task it is to counteract revolution on the island of Minorca and stop the Russians establishing a strategically vital deep-water harbour in the Mediterranean. The problem is that the revolutionaries have captured the girl he loves.

READ ON

- *Levkas Man*. Innes also writes thrillers under the name 'Ralph Hammond' (*Isle of Strangers/Island of Peril*; *Saracen's Gold/Cruise of Danger*.
- ▶ ▷Desmond Bagley, *Bahama Crisis*. Duncan Kyle, *Whiteout!* Lionel Davidson, *The Sun Chemist*.

INNES, MICHAEL (BORN 1906)

British novelist.

'Michael Innes' is the pseudonym of the Oxford don J.I.M. Stewart. His 50 detective novels set bizarre puzzles in the unhurried world of Oxford colleges, English country houses, fine art auction-rooms and elegant Tuscan villas. Well-bred, exquisitely educated people cheat, lie and kill without ruffling a hair and with a well-turned quotation always on their lips. The blend of privilege and nastiness is brilliant, and the pace of Innes' writing enhances it. When brutality happens it is fast, unexpected and breathtaking; when Innes' detectives Appleby or Honeybath investigate the speed is gentle and unflustered, allowing plenty of time to savour every epigram, every devious conversational nuance, every glass of port. Stewart's novels and stories under his own name use similar locations, the same placid style and an even more twinkly-eyed cultural affectation, but instead of murders they concern such gentler matters as friendship (especially between old and young), family feuds, love-affairs and unexpected inheritances.

OPERATION PAX/PAPER THUNDERBOLT (1951)

In a private clinic in the quiet Oxford countryside something extremely sinister – brainwashing? conditioning by drugs? plotting world domination? – is going on. A petty criminal, kidnapped by the experimenters as a human guinea-pig, escapes and hides in Oxford, where the action at once involves East European refugees, eccentric dons, the pupils of a prep school for especially brainy boys, and John Appleby's pretty young sister Jane. The investigation climaxes in the 'stacks' of the Bodleian Library, a pile of eight million books in a cavernous vault under Radcliffe Square.

Innes' earlier novels (more convoluted and fantastical than his later books) include Death at the President's Lodgings, Lament for a Maker, Appleby on Ararat, The Weight of the Evidence, A Night of Errors *and* The Journeying Boy. *At the heart of Stewart's books is a quintet of novels of Oxford life,* The Gaudy, Young Patullo, A Memorial Service, The Madonna of the Astrolabe *and* Full Term. Myself and Michael Innes *is J.I.M. Stewart's autobiography.*

READ ON

- *The Daffodil Affair.*
- **To Innes' detective stories at their larkiest:** Edmund Crispin, *The Moving Toyshop*; Rex Stout, *Too Many Cooks*; Carter Dickson, *The Ten Teacups*; Gladys Mitchell, *Laurels Are Poison*.
- **To J.I.M. Stewart's novels:** ▷C.P. Snow, *The Masters*; ▷Anthony Powell, *Afternoon Men*.

IRELAND

▷Maeve Binchy, *Echoes*
▷J.G. Farrell, *Troubles*
Jennifer Johnston, *The Captains and the Kings*
▷James Joyce, *Portrait of the Artist as a Young Man*
Molly Keane, *Good Behaviour*
Patrick McGinley, *The Trick of the Ga Bolga*

Edna O'Brien, *The Country Girls*
Flann O'Brien, *At Swim-Two-Birds*
James Plunkett, *Strumpet City*

IRVING, John (born 1942)

US novelist.

At first glance, Irving's novels seem little more than surreal black comedies, magic realism exported from South to North America. In fact, nothing that happens in his books is unbelievable. His tales may lose nothing in the telling, but they are always plausible. The main characters of *Setting Free the Bears* plot to release the inmates of the Vienna Zoo. The hero of *The World According to Garp* is a writer whose terror of death leads him to imagine appalling catastrophes for his loved ones – only to have even more, unimagined horrors actually occur. The family in *The Hotel New Hampshire* turns a derelict girls' school into a hotel (complete with dancing bear), and later, when business falls off, moves to Austria where the hotels are smaller, the bears are cleverer, and terrorists are threatening to take over the Vienna Opera. Irving, in his deadpan way, constantly implies – and who can deny it? – that there is nothing eccentric here, that he is recording the bizarreness of life itself.

The Cider House Rules (1985)

Homer Wells, brought up in a rural Maine orphanage and abortion clinic run by the saintly ether-addict Dr Larch, struggles against his destiny, which is to become a gynaecologist and take his mentor's place. He runs away, becomes the manager of a cider-farm, falls in love with his best friend's wife and lives a life of confused obscurity – but he constantly feels the pull back to the clinic and to Melony, a homicidal feminist who hero-worships him and is waiting her chance to murder him.

Irving's other novels are The Water-Method Man *and* The 158-Pound Marriage.

READ ON

- *A Prayer for Owen Meany* (about the friendship of two boys, one of whom (Owen Meany) is a charming freak gifted with second sight and the ability to transform other people's lives).
- ▶ **To *The Cider House Rules*:** Richard Brautigan, *Trout Fishing in America*; ▷Robertson Davies, *What's Bred in the Bone*.
- ▶ **To *A Prayer for Owen Meany*:** G. H. Morris, *Grandmother, Grandmother, Come and See*.
- ▶ **To Irving's work in general:** ▷Salman Rushdie, *Midnight's Children*; ▷Russell Hoban, *Turtle Diary*; Jack Trevor Story, *Morag's Flying Fortress*.

ISHERWOOD, Christopher (1904–86)

British/US writer of novels, screenplays and non-fiction.

Isherwood was a university teacher in California, a writer of plays, films and non-fiction books (chiefly autobiographical or on Hindu mysticism). His novels and stories are all based on personal experience. The best-known (*Mr Norris Changes Trains/The Last of Mr Norris*, 1935; *Goodbye to Berlin*, 1939; *The Berlin Stories*, 1946) are set in 1930s Berlin, a

READ ON

- *Prater Violet*; *A Meeting by the River*.
- ▶ ▷Ruth Prawer Jhabvala, *Heat and Dust*. ▷Mary

seedy, decadent city haunted by German defeat in the first world war and by the gathering power of nazism. They are first person stories, told by a naive young language teacher amused, perplexed and vaguely terrified by the human tragicomedy he reports. They have been filmed, made into a stage-play (*I Am a Camera*) and a hit musical (*Cabaret*). In a similarly rueful vein, Isherwood's novel *A Single Man* (1964) describes the emptily busy life of a lonely homosexual teaching English literature at a US university.

McCarthy, *Birds of America*. Michael Frayn, *The Russian Interpreter*. Francis King, *The Custom House*. ▷Angus Wilson, *Setting the World on Fire*.

ISHIGURO, Kazuo (born 1954)

Japanese/British novelist.

Ishiguro was educated in England and writes in English. His first two books are gentle, poetic studies of the effects on present-day Japanese of earlier 20th-century events. The central character of *A Pale View of Hills* (1982), a middle-aged woman living in England, is driven by her daughter's suicide to a prolonged reverie about her own childhood in Nagasaki, and her attempt to rebuild her life and her emotional relationships after the city's atomic destruction in 1945. Oni, the elderly protagonist of *An Artist of the Floating World* (1986), was a prominent propagandist for Japanese militarism in the 1930s, and now, in his own 60s, has to come to terms with the collapse of his professional life, his ostracism by younger colleagues, and the way his own children's moral values, typical of the new Japan, seem to deny everything he ever believed in or affirmed. Ishiguro's Booker Prize winning third novel, *The Remains of the Day* (1989), by contrast, is told in the first person by an English butler, humourless and pernickety, looking back on a life which has been busily self-important but which has denied him all human contact, all opportunity for emotional growth.

READ ON

▶ ▷R.K. Narayan, *The English Teacher/Grateful to Life and Death*. ▷Willa Cather, *The Professor's House*. ▷Graham Greene, *The Quiet American*.

ISRAEL

Lynne Reid Banks, *Children at the Gate*
Lionel Davidson, *A Long Way to Shiloh*
John Le Carré, *The Little Drummer Girl*
Blaine Littall, *Via Dolorosa*
Clive Sinclair, *Cosmetic Effects*
Leon Uris, *Exodus*

J

JAGGER, Brenda (1937–86)
British novelist.

Jagger wrote historical romances, many of them in series and most set in Yorkshire. Her books include the trilogy *Clouded Hills, Flint and Roses* and *Sleeping Sword*, and *A Song Twice Over* (1985), about two early Victorian women, one poor, one rich, who fall in love with the same man.

READ ON

- ▶ ▷Maeve Binchy, *Light a Penny Candle*. Alice Adams, *Superior Women*. ▷Georgette Heyer, *False Colours*.

JAMES, Henry (1843–1916)
US/British novelist and short-story writer.

As well as novels, James wrote plays, essays, travel-books, literary criticism and a dozen volumes of short stories. In his fiction he returned again and again to the same theme: the conflict between decadence and innocence. James identified decadence with the 'old culture' of Europe, and innocence with the late 19th-century USA; his books often involve visitors from one continent experiencing and coming to terms with the other. Because he was not religious – he was brought up as a rationalist – the moral struggle of his plots is usually less between overt 'good' and 'evil' than between different standards and manners, and he also liked to tease out every strand of meaning in a situation, to explain and theorise about his characters' motives and the possible outcome of each choice they make. Untangling this, especially in his last three, most intricately stylised novels (*The Wings of the Dove, The Ambassadors* and *The Golden Bowl*), is one of the chief pleasures of his work.

READ ON

- • *Portrait of a Lady* (about the moral and social consequences of a young American's decision to settle in England and Italy); *The Ambassadors* (a long, ironical novel about how Europe changes a group of Americans, young and middle-aged, rich and poor, friends and strangers).
- ▶ ▷Marcel Proust, *Swann's Way* (part I

THE WINGS OF THE DOVE (1902)

Kate Croy lives with her snobbish aunt, who plans to make a 'great' marriage for her. But Kate is secretly engaged to a penniless journalist, Merton Densher. Millie Theale, a young, rich American, visits Kate's aunt to be introduced to London society, and becomes Kate's friend. Millie is frail, and it is soon apparent that she is dying. She goes to Venice, where she welcomes all her friends in a decaying palazzo on the Grand Canal. Kate persuades Merton to try and comfort Millie's last months by pretending that he loves her; Kate hopes that Millie will then leave money to Merton which will enable them to marry. So everyone will be happy. But another of Millie's suitors, the unprincipled Lord Mark, tells Millie of Merton's and Kate's secret engagement – a revelation which brings tragedy to all three principal characters.

James' other novels include Daisy Miller, Portrait of a Lady, Washington Square, The Bostonians, The Spoils of Poynton *and* The Tragic Muse. *Of his 100 short stories and novellas, the best-known are* The Turn of the Screw *(about two children haunted by a sinister dead couple),* The Real Thing *and* The Lesson of the Master.

of *Remembrance of Things Past).* ▷E.M. Forster, *A Room with a View.* ▷Edith Wharton, *The Reef.* ▷Muriel Spark, *The Mandelbaum Gate.* ▷Stendhal, *Scarlet and Black.* ▷Elizabeth Bowen, *Eva Trout.*

JAMES, P.D. (PHYLLIS DOROTHY) (BORN 1920)

British novelist.

Although James is often described as the 'Queen of Crime', Agatha ▷Christie's heir, she is more like a cross between ▷Sayers and ▷Highsmith. The crimes in her books are brutal, are committed by deranged, psychopathic people, and are described in chilling, unblinking prose as objective as a forensic report. Her principal detective, Adam Dalgliesh, is a poet and aesthete, combining brilliant detective instincts with a liberal conscience and a dandyish distaste for what he does. Although the books at first seem long and leisurely, James racks tension inexorably tighter until her dénouement: not a cosy Christieish explanation round the library fire, but a scene of pathological, cathartic violence.

A TASTE FOR DEATH (1986)

A lonely spinster, taking flowers to decorate her local church, finds the throat-cut corpses of a tramp, Harry Mack, and a prominent Tory MP, Sir Paul Berowne. Berowne has been the subject of recent slanderous accusations, and Dalgliesh's investigation must begin by deciding whether he was murdered or committed suicide after killing Mack. The story gradually sucks in various members of Berowne's large and mutually hostile family, his servants and his mistress – and as well as showing us this, and describing the

READ ON

- *Devices and Desires.*

► ▷Ngaio Marsh, *Surfeit of Lampreys.* ▷Margery Allingham, *The Tiger in the Smoke.* ▷Patricia Highsmith, *Ripley Under Ground.* ▷Ruth Rendell, *A Sleeping Life.* Margaret Millar, *Mermaid.*

police work in exact, unhurried detail, the book also concerns itself with the lives and preoccupations of Dalgliesh's assistants, especially Inspector Kate Miskin, the newest member of the team.

James' other novels are Cover Her Face, A Mind to Murder, Death of an Expert Witness, Unnatural Causes, Shroud for a Nightingale, An Unsuitable Job for a Woman, The Black Tower, Innocent Blood *and* The Skull Beneath the Skin.

JANSSON, Tove (born 1917)

Finnish novelist and children's writer.

Jansson is best-known for her 'Moomin' books for children: humorous fantasies about gentle balloon-creatures with magic powers. *The Summer Book* (1972), for adults, is a short, beautiful novel about a young child's relationship with her grandmother. The two of them quietly investigate their world – much of the book takes place on a peaceful island in the Gulf of Finland where the family are spending the summer – and share their feelings. They have two kinds of innocence: the child's freshness and the grandmother's paring-down of a lifetime's experience. The mood is placid and evocative, and for all its shortness the book is one of the half-dozen most poetic evocations of childhood composed this century.

READ ON

- *Sun City*.
- ▶ **Childhood memoirs of similar poetic intensity:** Laurie Lee, *Cider With Rosie*; Flora Thompson, *Lark Rise to Candleford*; W.H. Hudson, *Far Away and Long Ago*; ▷Vladimir Nabokov, *Speak, Memory*; Gerald Durrell, *My Family and Other Animals*.

Japan

▷J.G. Ballard, *Empire of the Sun*
James Clavell, *Shōgun*
▷Kazuo Ishiguro, *An Artist of the Floating World*
James Melville, *The Wages of Zen*
Yukio Mishima, *Confessions of a Mask*
Murasaki Shikibu, *The Tale of Genji*

JARRELL, Randall (1914–65)

US poet, children's writer and novelist.

Jarrell's main fame is for poetry and a well-loved children's book, *The Animal Family* (1965). His only adult novel, *Pictures from an Institution* (1954), is one of the funniest of all campus comedies. It takes place in a progressive women's college in the 1950s. The girls are dewy-eyed innocents, passionate for life and learning; the faculty-members are wild eccentrics, whether they be Dr Rosenblum the advanced Austrian composer, Jerrold and Flo Whittaker the

READ ON

- ▶ D.J. Enright, *Academic Year*. ▷Anthony Burgess, *Enderby's Dark Lady*. ▷Kingsley Amis, *Lucky Jim*. ▷Robertson Davies, *The Rebel Angels*.

hippie sociologists, Gertrude the experimental novelist (and her down-trodden husband and greatest fan Sidney) or President Robbins himself, formerly an Olympic swimmer and now a fundraising superman. There is no real plot: the book runs through one eventful year, and the fun is in Jarrell's mixture of malice, magnificent one-liners and affection for even his most absurd characters.

JEROME, JEROME K. (KLAPKA) (1859–1927)

British novelist and journalist.

Jerome, an actor, wrote humorous pieces while waiting to go on stage; after the success of *Three Men in a Boat* in 1889 he became a full-time writer. *Three Men in a Boat* is the story of a boating holiday on the Thames undertaken by three London clerks (to say nothing of the dog). The book's deadpan humour – what Jerome calls its 'hopeless and incurable veracity' – depends on magnifying life's small problems (such as opening a tin without a tin-opener, or being in the same house as a courting couple without embarrassing them) to epic proportions, and on losing no opportunity for reflections on life, liberty, the pursuit of happiness, and the heroes' invincible conviction that middle-class Victorian young Britons, such as themselves, are the goal to which all human evolution has been tending.

READ ON

- *Three Men on the Bummel*; *My Life and Times* (autobiography).
- ▶ George and Weedon Grossmith, *The Diary of a Nobody*. ▷Max Beerbohm, *Zuleika Dobson*. A.G. Macdonell, *England, Their England*. Stephen Leacock, *Literary Lapses*. Giovanni Guareschi, *The House that Nino Built*.

JHABVALA, RUTH PRAWER (BORN 1927)

British novelist and screenwriter.

In a series of placid, gently ironical novels and screenplays (beginning with *Shakespeare Wallah* (1965), for the Merchant-Ivory partnership), Jhabvala has become a main European chronicler of India since the Raj. She is less interested in public events than in emotions, and particularly in the interface between two mutually uncomprehending cultures, Indian and European. In her best-known book, *Heat And Dust* (1975, filmed 1983), a young Englishwoman visits modern India to find out about her aunt's unhappy love-affair there 60 years before. The story cuts between the two periods, contrasting the modern character's apparently sophisticated racial and cultural awareness with the aunt's naivety and immaturity, and making points about attitudes (of Indians towards the English and vice versa) both during the Raj and in our own day.

Jhabvala's novels include To Whom She Will, The Nature of Passion, Esmond in India, The Householder, Get Ready for Battle, A Backward Glance, A New Dominion, Three Conti-

READ ON

- *Esmond in India*.
- ▶ ▷E.M. Forster, *A Passage to India*. Paul Scott, *Staying On*. Rabinadrath Tagore, *The Home and the World*. Anita Desai, *Games at Twilight* (short stories).

nents *and* In Search of Love and Beauty *(set in the USA, and influenced by her experience scripting ▷Henry James'* The Europeans *for Merchant-Ivory).* Like Birds Like Fishes, A Stronger Climate, An Experience of India, Out of India *and* How I Became a Holy Mother *are collections of short stories.*

JOLLEY, ELIZABETH (BORN 1923)

Australian novelist.

Jolley's characters are outwardly respectable: doctors, teachers, farmers, musicians, novelists. But without exception, they are emotionally arid, driven by the need for human contact to eccentric behaviour which is all the more unsettling for being both gentle and genteel, and which invariably ends in tears. *Palomino* (1980) is about a doctor, 'struck off' for murdering a patient, who forms a doomed lesbian friendship with a young girl she meets on a cruise. In *Milk and Honey* (1984) a cello-playing prodigy is driven by sexual longing to irrational and finally self-destructive action. The heroine of *Foxybaby* is an 'advanced' novelist working on a film with a group of adult students in a macabre outback school. In *The Sugar Mother* (1989) a lonely professor, abandoned for a year by his gynaecologist wife, becomes the sexual and emotional prey of an ambitious mother and her ugly but ever-willing daughter. Critics praise Jolley for her fine style and waspish black humour. Those qualities give her books zest and pace, but the predominant feeling remains one of melancholy, of pity for her characters, not mockery. Her work is easy and enjoyable to read, but distinctly unsettling to think about afterwards.

MISS PEABODY'S INHERITANCE (1983)

Miss Peabody, a lonely London spinster, writes a fan letter to a writer in Australia, and is rewarded by not so much letters in return as passages from the new novel the author is working on. This involves the headmistress of a financially rocky girls' boarding school in the outback, who is travelling in Europe with a colleague, a lesbian mistress of long standing, and a lumpish schoolgirl *protégé*. As the correspondence proceeds, Miss Peabody becomes so absorbed in the fictional story that the reality of her own life begins to blur irredeemably with fiction. She begins to reinvent her own reality – a process which continues until the book's last, most deliciously ironical line.

Jolley's other novels include Mr Scobie's Riddle, The Newspaper of Claremont Street, The Well *and* My Father's Moon. Stories *and* Woman in a Lampshade *are collections of*

READ ON

- *The Sugar Mother.*
- ▶ William Trevor, *Mrs Eckdorff in O'Neill's Hotel.* ▷Anita Brookner, *Look at Me*, ▷Alison Lurie, *The Truth About Lorin Jones*, ▷ELizabeth Bowen, *Eva Trout*, Alice Thomas Ellis, *The 27th Kingdom.*

*short stories. (*Stories *originally appeared as two volumes,* Five Acre Virgin *and* The Travelling Entertainer.*)*

JONG, ERICA (BORN 1942)
US novelist and poet.

Although Jong is primarily a poet, she became world-famous for two bleak prose satires on our contemporary obsession with sex. The novels are the autobiography of Isadora. In *Fear of Flying* (1974) she spends her time cock-hunting: the Holy Grail, she tells us, is the 'zipless fuck', sex without commitment, and she searches for it in locker-rooms, on trains and planes, on beaches, in hotel rooms and wherever else multiple orgasms beckon. In *How to Save Your Own Life* (1978) she has fame and wealth (as the author of a best-selling dirty book), and walks the treadmill of personal appearances, tours and the jetset life while still (metaphorically and literally) unzipping every man in sight. But by now the sex is even more mechanical; the pleasure is no smaller but lasts less long, and Isadora is increasingly obsessed by the void in her own life where love should be. Jong's novels have sold because of their frequent, explicit descriptions of sexual coupling – no position is left untried – and because they were at the forefront of the battle to have women's sexuality treated as openly as men's. But they also, chiefly, satirise contemporary US life and values. The zipless fuck is a metaphor for instant gratification of every kind, and the books' insistent theme is that there is much, much more to life.

Serenissima *is a fantasy about a woman transported back in time to 16th-century Venice, where she has a passionate affair with a young English playwright and poet who later immortalises her as 'the dark lady'. Jong's poetry-collections include* Fruits and Vegetables, Half-Lives, Loveroot, Here Comes *and* At the Edge of the Body.

READ ON

▶ ▷Lisa Alther, *Kinflicks*. Marilyn French, *The Women's Room*. ▷Jean Rhys, *Good Morning, Midnight*. Aritha van Herk, *No Fixed Address*.

JOURNALISM

▷Heinrich Böll, *The Lost Honour of Katharina Blum*
Max Davidson, *Wellington Blue*
Michael Frayn, *Towards the End of the Morning*
George Gissing, *New Grub Street*
▷Rose Macaulay, *Potterism*
▷William Thackeray, *Pendennis*
▷Evelyn Waugh, *Scoop*

James JOYCE

IRELAND

James **PLUNKETT, STRUMPET CITY**
(Dublin life and troubles – of all kinds – before World War I)

Molly **KEANE, GOOD BEHAVIOUR**
(large Anglo-Irish family collapsing under its own eccentricity)

Flann **O'BRIEN, AT SWIM-TWO-BIRDS**
(homosexual biographer doing research, finds himself being engulfed by his subject and by memories of his own past life)

SELF-DISCOVERY

Virginia **WOOLF, MRS DALLOWAY**
(middle-class Englishwoman preparing for dinner-party reviews –and reveals – her whole existence and inner self)

Marcel **PROUST, THE GUERMANTES WAY**
(Part III of Remembrance of Things Past *– the effects of death – of love and the death of the beloved)*

Iris **MURDOCH, THE SANDCASTLE**
(middle-aged schoolmaster, besotted with young artist, finds his whole life toppling round his ears)

Joseph **HELLER, SOMETHING HAPPENED**
(empty man, New York business executive, reviews the reasons for the failure of his career and family life)

John **FOWLES, THE MAGUS**
(man seeks true meaning of experience: is our life as real as it seems, or a series of illusions – and if illusion, how well-disposed is the illusionist?)

ULYSSES

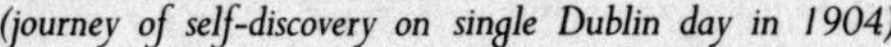

(journey of self-discovery on single Dublin day in 1904)

Alexander **THEROUX, D'ARCONVILLE'S CAT**
(jilted by sophomore lover, D'Arconville leaves US Deep South to 'find himself' in Venice)

John **BARTH, GILES GOAT-BOY**
(US professor tries to bring up child free of original sin)

Salman **RUSHDIE, MIDNIGHT'S CHILDREN**
(Saleem and family, 'handcuffed to India', experience the 80-year evolution of independence and self-renewal)

Laurence **STERNE, TRISTRAM SHANDY**
('autobiography' of 18th-century English gentleman turns into the longest, richest shaggy-dog story ever told)

'JOYCEAN' NOVELS:

BIG, EXPERIMENTAL, ALL-ENCOMPASSING

Italo **SVEVO, THE CONFESSIONS OF ZENO**
(explaining to his psychiatrist why he can't give up smoking, Zeno tells the tale of his extraordinary, inadequate existence)

Joyce **CARY, THE HORSE'S MOUTH**
(eccentric artist determines to live bohemian existence, boozy and bawdy, reinventing his own character from day to day)

John Kennedy **TOOLE, A CONFEDERACY OF DUNCES**
(self-confessed genius bestrides New Orleans like an anarchic, flatulent colossus, finds it too small to accommodate his appetite for mischief)

Anthony **BURGESS, EARTHLY POWERS**
('memoirs' of aged homosexual novelist, who has been at heart of all human betrayal and bitchiness since the 20th century began)

Robertson **DAVIES, WHAT'S BRED IN THE BONE**
(odyssey of art-forger, thief and conman, as discovered from his will)

Saul **BELLOW, HUMBOLDT'S GIFT**
(Chicago)

J. D. **SALINGER, THE CATCHER IN THE RYE**
(New York)

Lawrence **DURRELL, THE ALEXANDRIA QUARTET**

Eleanor **DARK, WATERWAY**
(Sydney)

CITIES

JOYCE, JAMES (1882–1941)

Irish novelist and short-story writer.

Although Joyce settled in Italy at 27, and spent the rest of his life there, he never left the Ireland of his memory: his work is a ceaseless exploration of Irish scenery, education, history, religion, habits of thought and patterns of daily life. His early writings – the short stories in *Dubliners* (1914) and the novel *Portrait of the Artist as a Young Man* (1915), based on his own school and university life – are stylistically straightforward. They are also notable for precise evocation of sensation and atmosphere. By giving a mosaic of tiny impressions (the feel of wooden desks in a schoolroom, the taste of mud on a rugby field, the smell of gas-lamps in student digs) Joyce builds up a detailed picture which is both factually and emotionally compelling. (▷Proust used a similar idea in the childhood sections of *Remembrance of Things Past.*) In his two long novels, *Ulysses* (1922) and *Finnegans Wake* (1939), Joyce developed this mosaic structure further: *Ulysses* relates the events of a single day, *Finnegans Wake* a man's thoughts and dreams during a single night. Parts of these books are stream-of-consciousness monologues, a tumble of apparently unrelated sentences threading a path through the maze of one person's mind. Joyce often seems to be collapsing language itself: syntax splits apart; words blur into one another; each page is a kaleidoscope of puns, parodies, half-quotations, snatches of song and snippets from half a dozen languages. Some people find this style unreadable; for others it is endlessly rewarding, a mesmeric impression of the jumble of thought itself.

ULYSSES (1922)

The book follows two people, Leopold Bloom and Stephen Dedalus, from dawn to midnight on a single day in Dublin in 1904. At one level what they do is ordinary: they shave, go to the privy, eat, drink, argue in bars, go to a funeral, borrow money, flirt with girls on a beach, visit Dublin's red-light area. But Joyce also shows us their thoughts, the fragmentary responses and impressions evoked by each real incident. The book ends with a 60-page 'interior monologue', the inconsequential, erotic reverie of Bloom's wife Molly as she lies beside him, drifting into sleep.

Joyce's works are Dubliners; Portrait of the Artist as a Young Man *(based on an earlier, unfinished novel,* Stephen Hero, *which has also been published);* Ulysses; Finnegans Wake; Chamber Music *and* Pomes Penyeach *(poetry).*

READ ON

▶ Ralph Ellison, *Invisible Man*. ▷Malcolm Lowry, *Under the Volcano*. ▷Thomas Wolfe, *Look Homeward, Angel*. ▷Virginia Woolf, *Mrs Dalloway*. ▷John Kennedy Toole, *A Confederacy of Dunces* is a kind of comic Ulysses, set in New Orleans, and both Joyce's experimental writing and the whole concept of Irishness are spectacularly sent up in Flann O'Brien, *At Swim-Two-Birds*.

K

KAFKA, FRANZ (1883-1924)

Czech novelist and short-story writer.

In the 1920s and 1930s people regarded Kafka as an unsmiling neurotic who depicted the human condition as a bureaucratic hell without explanation or compassion: 'Kafkaesque' was a synonym for 'nightmarish'. Kafka, by contrast, always regarded himself as a humorist, in the line of such surrealist East European jokers as ▷Gogol. Each of his novels and stories develops a single idea to ludicrous, logical-illogical extremes. In 'Metamorphosis' a man has to cope with the fact that he has turned into a gigantic beetle overnight. The prison-camp commander of 'In the Penal Colony' is so eager to show off a newly-invented punishment-machine that he turns it on himself. In 'The Burrow' a creature designs a defence-system of underground tunnels so complex and so perfect that it becomes the whole meaning of existence: it engulfs its own creator. The central figure of *The Trial* (*Der Prozess*) is arrested one morning although he has done nothing wrong, spends the book trying to discover the charges against him, and is finally executed without explanation. It is easy to treat such tales as psychological or political allegories. But it is also possible to read them as jokes, grimly funny anecdotes invented just for the hell of it. Perhaps keeping his face straight was Kafka's best trick of all.

THE CASTLE (DER SCHLOSS) (1926)

An ordinary, unremarkable man, K, arrives in a strange town to take up the post of Land Surveyor. He finds that no one is expecting him, that the town and the castle which dominates it are a labyrinthine bureaucracy where everyone is responsible only for passing the buck to someone else,

READ ON

- *The Trial*; *America* (the story of a naive young German who goes to the USA thinking that its streets are paved with gold, and goes on believing it despite being cheated and betrayed by everyone he meets).
- ▶ **Echoing Kafka's humour:** ▷Jaroslav Hašek, *The Good Soldier Švejk*; ▷Joseph Heller, *Catch-22*; ▷Nathaniel West, *The Dream Life of Balso Snell*; Joe Orton, *Head to Toe*.
- ▶ **Echoing the idea of a 'Kafkaesque', nightmare society:** Rex Warner, *The Aerodrome*; Alasdair Gray, *Lanark*; Max Frisch, *I'm Not*

and each favour done, each door opened, leads only to more confusion. K's efforts to reach the heart of the mystery, to be given some official confirmation of his existence, are doomed, hilarious and have the logic not of reality but of a very bad dream indeed.

Kafka's novels are The Trial, The Castle *and* America. *Of the many collections of his stories, the best is* Kafka's Shorter Works, *translated by* Malcolm Pasley.

Stiller; ▷George Orwell, *1984*.

KAVANAGH, Dan: see BARNES, Julian

KELLERMAN, Jonathan (born 1949)

US novelist.

Like his hero, Alex Delaware, Kellerman is a professional psychologist, and his compulsive, chilling thrillers depend on unlocking the secrets in apparently demented minds. In *When the Bough Breaks/Shrunken Heads* (1985), for example, Delaware is working with a disturbed seven-year-old girl who may have witnessed a murder, and uncovers a story of pederasty, child prostitution and murder. In *Over the Edge* (1987) a disturbed young man is the chief suspect in a case of multiple knife-murders, and Delaware must turn every stone in wealthy Los Angeles society to prove the boy's innocence. Kellerman's themes are grim and his books are long, but his writing is mesmeric; to begin each novel is to guarantee reading it through to the shattering, surprising end.

READ ON

- *Blood Test.*
- ▶ ▷Sara Paretsky, *Bitter Medicine*. Robert B. Parker, *Looking for Rachel Wallace*. ▷Stephen King, *Pet Sematary*.

KENEALLY, Thomas (born 1935)

Australian novelist and playwright.

Although Keneally has written books on many subjects, including the partly-autobiographical *Three Cheers for the Paraclete* (1968), about a young Roman Catholic losing his faith, he is best-known for 'faction': powerful fictional treatments of the issues and personalities behind real events. Apart from *Blood Red, Sister Rose* (1974), about Joan of Arc, his books are set in comparatively recent times, usually at decisive moments in the history of a people or continent – and Keneally gets under the skin of the participants, showing how great events happen for what are usually far smaller and more personal reasons (a quarrel; a cold in the head) than the awareness of grand political or strategic trends which historians would suggest. He is not, however, a 'historical' novelist, simply telling tales about the past. His concentration on issues gives his stories universal resonance: we are constantly shown the relevance of the events he describes to our present-day situation or attitudes. His best-

READ ON

- *The Playmaker* (in which convicts transported to 18th-century New South Wales, under the guidance of a confused, would-be liberal army lieutenant, rehearse and perform – of all things – Farquhar's Restoration comedy *The Recruiting Officer*).
- ▶ E.L. Doctorow, *The Book of Daniel*. Lionel Davidson,

known books are *The Chant of Jimmie Blacksmith* (1971, about racial confrontation in 19th-century Australia), *Gossip from the Forest* (1973, set during the 1918 Armistice negotiations), *Confederates* (1979, about Stonewall Jackson's campaigns in the American civil war) and *The Playmaker* (1987, see Read On).

Making Good Again. William Styron, *Sophie's Choice.*

SCHINDLER'S ARK (1982)

Schindler is a bragging, boozing opportunist who makes a fortune in Poland during the second-world-war German occupation, buying up the businesses of dispossessed Jews. We read about his black-market deals, his backslapping relationship with the authorities, his parties and his mistresses – and gradually discover that his lifestyle is a façade, that his true activity is saving thousands of Jews from the gas-chambers.

Keneally's other novels include A Dutiful Daughter, Bring Larks and Heroes *(set in 19th-century New South Wales),* Season in Purgatory *(about Tito and the Yugoslavian partisans during and after the second world war),* A Victim of the Aurora, A Family Madness, Passenger, The Cut-Rate Kingdom *and* Asmara. *He has also written films, stage plays, children's books and a fascinating account of his travels in Australia,* Outback.

KING, STEPHEN (BORN 1946)

US novelist.

King writes horror-stories: tales of obsession, insanity and the supernatural made even more terrifying by the ordinary US suburbs, schools and factories where they take place. His books (many made into blockbuster films) are *The Dead Zone, Carrie, Salem's Lot, Firestarter, The Shining, The Stand, Christine, Pet Sematary, Cujo, It, The Tommyknockers, Misery* and *The Dark Half* (1989), about a thriller writer forced by supernatural powers to commit sadistic and horrific crimes. *Night Shift* and *Skeleton Crew* are collections of ghoulish short stories. King also writes as 'Richard Bachman' (whose *Thinner,* about a man tormented by a gipsy's curse, is not for readers who find it hard to sleep).

READ ON

- **To King's novels:** ▷James Herbert, *Sepulchre*; Richard Matheson, *The Shrinking Man*; ▷Ruth Rendell, *Live Flesh* – and, from an earlier generation, ▷H.G. Wells, *The Island of Doctor Moreau.*
- **To his short stories:** ▷Edgar Allan Poe, *Tales of Mystery and Imagination*; ▷Patricia Highsmith, *Mermaids on the Golf Course*; Roald Dahl, *Kiss, Kiss*; ▷Angela Carter, *Fireworks.*

Thomas KENEALLY

NOVELS ARISING FROM REAL EVENTS

E.L. **DOCTOROW, THE BOOK OF DANIEL**
(lives of children of US immigrants executed for espionage)

John **FOWLES, A MAGGOT**
(witchcraft, murder and possible UFOs in 18th-century England)

Tony **WEEKS-PEARSON, DODO**
(extermination of dodo brings culture-shock to native inhabitants of idyllic Pacific island)

Frederick **FORSYTH, THE DAY OF THE JACKAL**
(plot to assassinate General de Gaulle of France)

Martin Cruz **SMITH, STALLION GATE**
(Mexican magic versus development of first atomic bomb)

THE AUSTRALIAN PAST

Bruce **CHATWIN, THE SONG LINES**
(writer travels modern Australia, investigating Aboriginal sacred places)

William **GOLDING, CLOSE QUARTERS**
(life on 1790s convict-ship sailing from England to Australia)

Eleanor **DARK, THE TIMELESS LAND**
(first white settlers in Australia)

Patrick **WHITE, A FRINGE OF LEAVES**
(shipwrecked 1910s woman learns survival by assimilating Aborigine culture)

FRONTIERS OF CIVILISATION

Nathaniel **HAWTHORNE, THE SCARLET LETTER**
(religious hysteria and persecution in Puritan New England)

Chinua **ACHEBE, THINGS FALL APART**
(Nigerian tribal life, the rhythms of civilisation, disrupted by coming of white missionaries)

Brian **MOORE, BLACK ROBE**
(Jesuit priest in 17th-century Huron Indian country: irreconcilable culture-clash)

The Playmaker

(1780s Australia: English officer guides convicts through production of a Restoration comedy)

CONVICTS

Victor **HUGO, LES MISÉRABLES**
(19th-century France: honest man wrongly convicted to the galleys tries to rehabilitate himself)

Alexander **SOLZHENITSYN, ONE DAY IN THE LIFE OF IVAN DENISOVICH**
(20th-century USSR: unsparing account of life in labour-camp for dissidents)

Charles **DICKENS, LITTLE DORRIT**
(19th-century England: corrupting effects of money, and life in the Marshalsea Debtors' Prison)

John **CHEEVER, FALCONER**
(20th-century USA: life in 'correctional facility' as experienced by mentally unstable, middle-class wife-murderer)

PLAYS AND PLAY ACTORS

Robertson **DAVIES, TEMPEST-TOST**
(amateurs in 1950s Canadian university town)

Paul **BAILEY, PETER SMART'S CONFESSIONS**
(testimony of unsuccessful, mentally unstable actor)

Virginia **WOOLF, BETWEEN THE ACTS**
(thoughts and feelings of everyone involved in village historical pageant)

Noël **LANGLEY, THERE'S A PORPOISE CLOSE BEHIND US** *(sour success of 'bright young things' on 1930s London stage)*

AUSTRALIAN LIFE: THE FUNNY SIDE

Elizabeth **JOLLEY, THE FUNNY SIDE**

Peter **CAREY, ILLYWHACKER**

Howard **JACOBSON, REDBACK**

KIPLING, RUDYARD (1865–1936)

British short-story writer and poet.

Kipling learned his craft working for English-language newspapers in India in the 1880s. He wrote reports, stories and poems about the British soldiers and administrators, their servants and the snake-charmers, fortune-tellers and other characters of the towns they lived in. Later, during the Boer War, he worked as a correspondent in South Africa, where he was a friend of Cecil Rhodes. Under the circumstances, it would have been hard for him not to reflect the imperialist attitudes of his age, first sunny confidence and then the jingoistic panic which overtook it in late Victorian times. But he is a more rewarding writer than this suggests. His sympathies were always with subordinates – with private soldiers rather than generals, servants rather than employers, children rather than adults. He wrote well about all three: his stories for and about children, in particular, are magnificent. Something like half of each collection – most books contain both stories and poems – is nowadays hard to take, not least where he writes in baby-talk (as in the *Just-So Stories*, O best-beloved) or uses funny spellings to evoke Cockney or Irish speech. But every archness is balanced by a gem of insight or sensitivity. In this, too, he was characteristic of his time.

KIM (1901)

This episodic novel is the story of a British orphan brought up as a beggar in Lahore, who becomes first the disciple of a wandering Buddhist priest and then an agent of the British secret service. He travels throughout India, and Kipling uses his adventures as a framework for descriptions of everyday scenes and characters, of 'such a river of life as nowhere else exists in the world'.

Kipling's collections include Barrack-room Ballads, The Seven Seas *and* The Years Between *(verse),* Soldiers Three *(stories), and the mixed prose-and-verse collections* Many Inventions, Traffics and Discoveries, A Diversity of Creatures *and* Debits and Credits. *His novels are* The Light That Failed *and* Captains Courageous, *and his children's books include the* Just-so Stories, *the* Jungle Book, Puck of Pook's Hill *and the public-school yarn* Stalky and Co. Something of Myself *is a guarded autobiography.*

READ ON

- *Plain Tales from the Hills*; *Debits and Credits*.
- ▶ **To Kipling's stories about children:** ▷Katherine Mansfield, *Bliss and Other Stories*.
- ▶ **To his stories about colonial adults:** ▷Somerset Maugham, *Orientations*; the short stories of Noël Coward.
- ▶ ▷John Masters, *Nightrunners of Bengal*, and ▷J.G. Farrell, *The Siege of Krishnapur*, about the 1857 Indian 'Mutiny', match Kipling's insight into the heyday of the Raj.

KOSINSKI, JERZY (BORN 1933)

Polish/US novelist and non-fiction writer.

Kosinski settled in the USA in his 20s, and all his fiction is in English. He writes of contemporary life with horrified dis-

READ ON

- *Steps* (the random thoughts and

dain, as if he were a being from an alien planet describing some bizarre and repulsive civilisation – indeed, the SF of such writers as ▷Moorcock or ▷Vonnegut is the closest parallel to his experimental, fantastical style. His best-known book (because of the Peter Sellers film made from it) is *Being There* (1971), about a non-person, a man of miniscule intelligence whose ideas are received entirely from television or from gardening, and whose monosyllabic mutterings are taken by all around him as profound moral and political philosophy. Chance (the hero) ends up as adviser to the US president, and we are left uncomfortably wondering if he may not also be the only sane person in a lunatic society. Kosinski's other novels also centre on outsiders. The central character of *The Painted Bird* (1965) is a swarthy orphaned child in peasant Poland, regarded by everyone as an alien (a Jew or a gipsy) and rejected. The hero of *The Devil Tree* (1973) is a young man isolated from society both by immense inherited wealth – he could buy and sell whole countries – and by his own adolescent fantasy that he is the only person in the world obsessed by sex. In *Cockpit* (1975) and *Blind Date* (1977) the central characters are secret agents isolated from the real world not only by their trade but by their own burgeoning, uncommunicated thoughts.

conversations of a youth growing up in a country he hates and from which he is planning to emigrate as soon as chance allows).

▶ ▷Michael Moorcock, *The English Assassin*. Milan Kundera, *The Book of Laughter and Forgetting*. ▷Saul Bellow, *Mr Sammler's Planet*. Patrick McGinley, *The Trick of the Ga Bolga*. ▷I.B. Singer's short stories, although their subjects are entirely unlike Kosinski's, share his feeling that the world is a terrifying, alien environment in which human beings survive – if they do survive – only by chance or because of their own uncompromisingly lateral stance to life.

KRANTZ, Judith
US novelist.

In the 1970s Krantz took the 'novel of affairs' genre (big-business as sex; sex as big business) perfected a generation earlier by such writers as Harold Robbins, and refurbished it for modern tastes. The businesses of which she writes are multi-national corporations; the wealth is megabucks; the sex is as near pornography as respectable publishers will print. Only the morality remains the same: non-existent. Krantz's books (*Princess Daisy*; *Scruples*; *Mistral's Daughter*; *I'll Take Manhattan*, *We'll Meet Again*) are like dirtied-up versions of such TV soaps as *Dallas* or *Dynasty*: superb escapism.

READ ON

▶ Shirley Conran, *Lace*. Jackie Collins, *Lucky*. Sally Quinn, *Regrets Only*. Sidney Sheldon, *Bloodlines*. Sally Beauman, *Destiny*.

L

Larger Than Life

▷Peter Carey, *Illywhacker*
▷Robertson Davies, *What's Bred in the Bone*
Howard Jacobson, *Redback*
▷Robert Nye, *Falstaff*
Petronius, *Satyricon*
▷François Rabelais, *Gargantua*
▷Laurence Sterne, *Tristram Shandy*

LAWRENCE, D.H. (David Herbert) (1885-1930)

British writer of novels, short stories, plays and poems.

For 70 years Lawrence's radicalism has outraged as many people as it has enthralled. He thought that every matter of concern to human beings, and moral and ethical issues in particular, could be settled by rational discussion, if people would only be honest about themselves. His novels deal with such matters as female emancipation, the class struggle, atheism, sexual liberation and pacifism – not explicitly but as part of an ongoing advocacy of nakedness, of people at their best when stripped of inhibition and convention. Lawrence regarded his plain speaking as a way of shedding light in dark corners, a return to the innocence of the Garden of Eden; his enemies thought it shocking. Nowadays, when his rawness seems less threatening, his books stand up not only for moral earnestness – they read at times like humourless, secular sermons – but for their acute presentation of people and society in turmoil, of attitudes to life which the second world war and the nuclear age have made seem unimaginably remote.

READ ON

- *The Rainbow*.
- ▶ ▷George Eliot, *Middlemarch*. ▷Thomas Hardy, *Jude the Obscure* (especially close to *Women in Love* in its treatment of tensions between the sexes). David Storey, *Radcliffe*. Melvyn Bragg, *The Maid of Buttermere*. ▷Thomas Wolfe, *Look Homeward, Angel*. Henry Roth, *Call It Sleep*. ▷James Baldwin,

SONS AND LOVERS (1913)

Paul Morel is the son of ill-matched parents, an ex-schoolteacher and an illiterate, alcoholic miner. Morel's mother is determined to help her son escape from the physical grind and intellectual atrophy of pit-village life and fulfil his ambition to be a writer. Her love for him is, however, a force for darkness not liberation. It inhibits both his self-discovery and his relationship with other people (especially the young farm-girl Jessie, who encourages his writing), and it is only when he breaks free of his mother – a protracted, agonising process, a second birth – that he is able to fulfil the destiny she has planned for him.

Lawrence's other novels include The Rainbow *and its sequel* Women in Love, Aaron's Rod, Kangaroo, The Plumed Serpent *and* Lady Chatterley's Lover. *He also published poems, travel books (eg* Sea and Sardinia; Mornings in Mexico*), plays, books on history and literature, and collections of short stories (eg* England, My England; The Woman Who Rode Away*).*

Go Tell it on the Mountain.

LE CARRÉ, JOHN (BORN 1931)

British novelist.

For over a century, writers from ▷Verne to ▷Fleming depicted espionage as a swashbuckling, Robin Hood activity with clear rules, absolute moral standards and a penchant for flamboyance. But in the 1960s this view changed. The Cuban missile crisis all but led to world annihilation; the Berlin Wall was built; a series of well-publicised defections revealed that spies were secretive, unremarkable men, morally hesitant and trapped by their own profession. Betrayal, not derring-do, was their stock-in-trade; east, west, north, south, they were as indistinguishable as civil service clerks. This is the atmosphere of Le Carré's books. His characters are not James Bonds, swaggering forth to smash conspiracies of global domination; in dark back streets and rainy woods they nibble away at one another's loyalties, hardly even certain of their own. It is a world of remorseless moral erosion, and Le Carré chillingly shows how – even now, when Cold War attitudes are rapidly becoming obsolete – it functions entirely for itself, inward-looking and self-perpetuating, with minimal relevance to real life.

READ ON

- *A Perfect Spy.*
- ▶ **To the spy-stories:** ▷Ruth Rendell, *Talking to Strange Men*; ▷Graham Greene, *The Human Factor*; John Lear, *Death in Leningrad.* Julian Semyonov, *Tass is Authorized to Announce* is a cold-war spy-story of Le Carré-esque complexity, seen from the Russian side.
- ▶ **To *The Naive and Sentimental Lover*:** ▷John Fowles, *Daniel Martin*; ▷Frederic Raphael, *April, June and November.*
- ▶ **To *The Little Drummer Girl*:** ▷Doris Lessing, *The*

THE RUSSIA HOUSE (1989)

Barley, a shambolic publisher, visiting Leningrad at the dawn of the Gorbachev era and *glasnost*, makes friends with a Soviet scientist who has a devastating manuscript to sell – and is co-opted into the secret service and sent to persuade the scientist to defect. Unfortunately, he proceeds to fall in

John LE CARRÉ

THE PERFECT SPY *('autobiography' of upper-echelon British spy – and double-agent)*

Robert **LUDLUM, THE PARSIFAL MOSAIC**
(can 'burnt-out' agent's secret knowledge prevent World War III?)

John **LEAR, DEATH IN LENINGRAD**
(ex-spy Ashweald revels in Leningrad – but there is a price to pay)

John **TRENHAILE, THE MAHJONG SPIES**
(can Chinese Intelligence stop KGB destabilising Hong Kong?)

Ted **ALLEBURY, THE SECRET WHISPERS**
(double agent escaping from eastern to western Europe)

Martin Cruz **SMITH, STALLION GATE**
(can Mexican folk magic halt 1945 race to develop atomic bomb?)

Michael **MOLLOY, THE KID FROM RIGA**
(can SAS officer give up his career for love? In the meantime . . .)

Walter **WAGER, TELEFON**
(brainwashed assassins, 'sleepers', await trigger phone-calls to terrorise USA)

Jack **HIGGINS, CONFESSIONAL**
(KGB agent sent to Belfast to stir things up)

Ian **FLEMING, DOCTOR NO**
(super-agent 007 outwits psychopathic master-criminal)

Len **DEIGHTON, HORSE UNDER WATER**
(drugs, spies, master-criminals, all boiled together in Marrakesh)

Eric **AMBLER, THE MASK OF DIMITRIOS/COFFIN FOR DIMITRIOS** *(hero tracks down elusive, deadly master-criminal)*

Philip **MACDONALD, THE LIST OF ADRIAN MESSENGER**
(10 people on list, marked for death. What is the link – and can they be saved in time?)

A. J. **QUINNELL, IN THE NAME OF THE FATHER**
(who is killing off ageing world leaders, one by one?)

love with the scientist's ex-lover, and is forced for the first time in his life to come to terms with his character, his life-style and his loyalties.

Le Carré's other spy-books are The Spy Who Came in from the Cold, The Looking Glass War, A Small Town in Germany, *and the trilogy* The Search For Karla *(containing the three 'Smiley' books* Tinker Tailor Soldier Spy, The Honourable Schoolboy *and* Smiley's People. *His other books are the detective stories* Call for the Dead *and* A Murder of Quality, The Naive and Sentimental Lover *(about a bored middle-aged man given the chance to reconstruct his life) and* The Little Drummer Girl *(about a young idealist in the Middle East who turns to terrorism).*

Good Terrorist; David Ignatius, *Agents of Innocence*.

LE GUIN, Ursula (born 1929)

US novelist.

Le Guin made her name writing space opera (the 'League of All Worlds' series), and the prize-winning 'Earthsea' trilogy for children. In the late 1960s she broadened her scope, using the framework of alternative-world fantasy to discuss social, ecological and political themes. Although many of her books are still technically SF, set in the future and on other planets, she also lets people from the past and the present break through into magical kingdoms whose values and customs are ironical variations on our own. This happens literally in *Threshold* (1980): a supermarket checkout operator crosses the freeway into a wood, finds himself in another realm with its own time and its own reality – and meets and falls in love with a girl, another escapee from reality. The hero of *Malafrena* (1980) becomes a revolutionary leader in an alternative world in which the political ferment of post-Napoleonic Europe is blended with the religious outlook of Germany in Luther's time and with psychological and ecological concerns of the late 20th century. *Always Coming Home* (1984) is set among a pastoral tribe living peaceful, Zen-like lives in a far-future California.

The Left Hand Of Darkness (1969)

Genly Ai, an ambassador from the Ekumen, visits Gethen, a planet in the grip of an ice age, to persuade its inhabitants to join the League of Known Worlds. The novel alternates between his diary of his visit, and his accounts of the Gethenians' myths, political intrigues (in one of which he is himself caught up), and above all the way the people cope with life in a society without gender roles.

Le Guin's other novels include Rocannon's World, Planet of Exile, City of Illusions, The Lathe of Heaven *and* The Dis-

READ ON

- *The Left Hand of Darkness*.
- ▶ ▷Tom De Haan, *A Mirror for Princes*. ▷Stephen Donaldson, *Lord Foul's Bane* (first in the 'Chronicles of Thomas Covenant' series). Ian Watson, *The Gardens of Delight*. C.S. Lewis, *Perelandra*.

possessed. The Wind's Twelve Quarters *and* Orsinian Tales *are collections of short stories. The Earthsea trilogy (as magical as her adult fantasies, but with a child as hero) is* A Wizard of Earthsea, The Tombs of Atuan *and* The Farthest Shore.

LEHMANN, ROSAMOND (BORN 1901)

British novelist.

The ideas behind Lehmann's novels were strengthened by reading Jung and by psychic research after her daughter's death in the 1950s. She believes that we are not alone, that each person is part of a greater whole: the experience and knowledge of all human beings who have ever existed. We can enter into that experience, make use of it, during the rites of passage from one stage of existence to another – birth, adolescence, marriage, death – when the subconscious is particularly receptive. Lehmann's heroines are people on the brink of self-discovery; they are either innocents or victims of life, and the novels describe, in a lucid way far removed from the exoticism and mysticism of their events, how self-knowledge is achieved and how it changes the heroine's life, for bad or good.

THE BALLAD AND THE SOURCE (1944)

Ten-year-old Rebecca, picking bluebells in the garden of the old house beside the churchyard, is invited inside by the owner, Mrs Jardine, who knew Rebecca's grandmother and becomes Rebecca's friend. Rebecca listens enthralled to Mrs Jardine's tales of 'the old days' – and the more terrible the stories (they are accounts of passion, adultery, betrayal and hatred in Mrs Jardine's own young life), the more Rebecca is ensnared. Mrs Jardine is not so much like a witch casting a spell – though this is how Rebecca's alarmed mother sees her – as a Sibyl from the remote past, revealing the true nature of human emotional existence.

Lehmann's other novels are Dusty Answer, Invitation to the Waltz *and its sequel* The Weather in the Streets, The Echoing Grove *and* A Sea-Grape Tree. The Gipsy's Baby *collects short stories, and* The Swan in the Evening *is an autobiographical memoir centring on her reactions to her daughter's death.*

READ ON

- In *A Sea-Grape Tree* (the sequel to *The Ballad and the Source*) Rebecca, now grown-up and betrayed by men exactly as Mrs Jardine had been, goes to a Caribbean island to sort out her life and is affected not only by the people she meets there but by spirit-visitors from her past, including Mrs Jardine herself.
- ▶ ▷Rose Macaulay, *The World My Wilderness*. ▷Iris Murdoch, *The Philosopher's Pupil*. ▷Virginia Woolf, *Mrs Dalloway*. ▷Alison Lurie, *Imaginary Friends*. Rebecca West, *The Thinking Reed*. Jane Gardam, *Crusoe's Daughter*.

LEM, STANISLAW (BORN 1921)

Polish novelist.

Lem's novels are ▷Kafkaesque SF, a blend of black humour and psychological mysticism. His best-known books are *The Cyberiad, His Master's Voice, The Invincible, One Human*

READ ON

- *The Futurological Congress* (a spoof of his own work).

Minute, *Fiasco* and – thanks to Tarkovsky's mesmeric film – *Solaris* (1961), about astronauts orbiting a planet which is covered by a sentient sea, able to sense the nerve-impulses of living beings which land on it, and then make clones.

▶ ▷Robert Silverberg, *Tom O'Bedlam*. Jack Vance, *The Blue World*. Robert Irwin, *The Arabian Nightmare*.

LEONARD, Elmore (born 1925)

US writer.

Until Leonard became a full-time author in 1967, he worked in advertising, and his prose is as pacy and straight-to-the-point as that would suggest. He has written westerns, but is best known for edgy, witty crime thrillers with a twist of plot and blood-hammering suspense on every page. His books include *Glitz*, *52 Pick-up*, *Unknown Man No. 89*, *Bandits*, *The Switch*, *Touch* (1987), centring on a mysterious man in downtown Detroit who 'bleeds from five wounds', heals people and works miracles, and *Freaky Deaky* (1988), about a couple of old friends, an ex-urban terrorist and an explosives expert, who join up to settle a few old scores.

READ ON

▶ ▷Jonathan Kellerman, *Over the Edge*. Richard Stark, *Slayground*. Colin Dunne, *Rat-Catcher*.

LESSING, Doris (born 1919)

British novelist and non-fiction writer.

Lessing was brought up in Rhodesia (now Zimbabwe), but her involvement in progressive politics made it an uncomfortable place to live, and she moved to London in 1949. In the same year she published her first novel, *The Grass is Singing*, about relationships between the races, and followed it in 1952 with the semi-autobiographical *Martha Quest*, the first in a five-book series (the other volumes, published over the next 17 years, are *A Proper Marriage*, *A Ripple from the Storm*, *Landlocked* and *The Four-gated City*). The sequence took her heroine from girlhood to marriage in white Rhodesia, from political virginity to radical activism, from Africa to London, from youth to age. Martha becomes a feminist; she samples and rejects the 'swinging sixties'; she tries religion and mysticism; she watches, and reports on, the last hours of the human race as we writhe towards the apocalypse. The books are in a straightforward 'as-told-to' style: they have the power of documentary rather than fiction. Two other Lessing novels, *The Golden Notebook* (1962, about an unhappy writer coming to terms with herself as a person and with her place in a male-dominated society) and *Briefing for a Descent into Hell* (1971, about nervous breakdown), have similar intensity. Lessing's (Jungian)

READ ON

▶ **To *Canopus in Argus*:** Olaf Stapledon, *Last and First Men*.

▶ **To Lessing's work in general:** Margaret Laurence, *A Jest of God*. ▷Patrick White, *The Solid Gold Mandala*. ▷Margaret Drabble, *Jerusalem the Golden*. Stanley Middleton, *Harris' Requiem*. Marilyn French, *The Women's Room*. Simone de Beauvoir, *She Came to Stay*. ▷H.H. Richardson, *The Fortunes of Richard Mahony*.

psychological interests, and her fascination with Sufi mysticism, influence much of her other work, especially the five-volume sequence 'Canopus in Argus' (1979–83), which uses an SF format to explore ideas not so much of outer as of inner space, the alternative realities inside the mind.

The 'Canopus in Argus' novels are Shikasta; The Marriage Between Zones Three, Four and Five; The Sirian Experiments; The Making of the Representatives for Planet 8 *and* Documents Relating to the Sentimental Agents in the Volyen Empire. *Lessing's other fiction includes the novels* Memoirs of a Survivor, The Summons before the Dark *and* The Good Terrorist, *and the short-story collections* The Habit of Loving, A Man and Two Women *and* African Stories.

LEWIS, SINCLAIR (1885-1951)

US novelist.

In the 1920s Lewis won prizes for a series of satirical novels on aspects of US life. They are exhaustively researched, and use a fly-on-the-wall technique, reporting actions and speech in an objective-seeming way which conceals Lewis' own devastating authorial point of view. His theme was that the more honest, the more naive people seem, the more they are concealing humbug, and he was especially scathing about the US middle and professional classes. *Main Street* (1920) and *Babbitt* (1922) are slices of life in typical middle US towns: gossip-ridden, bigoted, censorious and unimaginative. *Dodsworth* (1929) is about a wimpish rich businessman trying to discover his soul (and put new life into his flagging marriage) by travelling in Europe. *Arrowsmith* (1925) is a comparatively serious study of a young doctor interested in bacteriological research. *Elmer Gantry* (1927), perhaps the most relevant of Lewis' books today, is about a religious charlatan, a born-again preacher who uses his charms to seduce women and embezzle money.

The best of Lewis' other novels – his later work tends slackly to repeat former themes – are It Can't Happen Here *(about fascism in the late 1930s USA) and* Gideon Planish *(a savage satire about big business and philanthropy).*

READ ON

- **To the satires:** Hamilton Basso, *The View from Pompey's Head*; ▷John Updike, *Rabbit, Run*; ▷Jerome Weidman, *The Center of the Action*; ▷Thornton Wilder, *Heaven's My Destination*; ▷Heinrich Böll, *Billiards at Half Past Nine*; ▷Saul Bellow, *Mr Sammler's Planet.*
- **To *Arrowsmith*:** ▷C.P. Snow, *The Search.*

LEWIS, WYNDHAM (1882-1957)

British writer and artist.

Lewis spent his life outraging the bourgeoisie, first as a wild avant-garde artist and then as a fiercely opinionated essayist on art and politics, a member of Mosley's British fascist

READ ON

- **To the satires:** Richard Aldington, *Seven Against*

party and an outspoken Hitler-supporter. His novels were prancing satires in the manner of ▷Huxley or ▷Waugh. *Tarr* (1918) and *The Apes of God* (1930) send up art-snobs and the dealers and phoney artists who prey on them. *The Revenge for Love* (1937) is about society people playing at politics but understanding nothing of a real tragedy (the Spanish Civil War) going on under their noses. The hero of *Self-condemned* (1954), a middle-aged professor tired of European life, retreats to a Canadian hotel, only to find it fuller of frauds and fools than the world he has left. Lewis' most stinging satire is the trilogy *The Human Age* (1928–55). It is about Armageddon, and shows the Day of Judgement not in lofty Christian terms but as a dusty, sweaty carnival, human beings prancing or shuffling to their doom at the whim of a cackling, deformed Showman – the gatekeeper of eternity is not St Peter but Mr Punch.

Reeves; ▷Anthony Powell, *What's Become of Waring?*; ▷Aldous Huxley, *Antic Hay*; Julian Symons, *The Immaterial Murder Case*.

- **To Lewis' more apocalyptic comedies:** Joyce Cary, *The Horse's Mouth*; ▷Patrick White, *The Twyborn Affair*; Stuart Evans, *The Caves of Alienation*.

LODGE, David (BORN 1935)

British novelist.

In the 1960s Lodge wrote half a dozen tragi-comic novels about young people perplexed by the pull between their Catholic upbringing and the urges of the Swinging Sixties; the funniest is *The British Museum is Falling Down*. In the 1970s he began to write campus comedies, many set in an imaginary Midlands new university, Rummidge. These include *Changing Places* (in which an innocent Rummidge lecturer changes places for a year with brash, oversexed Maurice Zapp of Euphoria State University, USA), *Small World* (about a young man pursuing a beautiful girl at a succession of ludicrous academic conferences) and *Nice Work* (1988) (in which an uptight feminist lecturer and a chauvinist captain of industry are set to 'shadow' each other for a year).

Lodge's other novels include Ginger, You're Barmy *and* How Far Can You Go? *He has also written academic books, chiefly on the writing of fiction and on structuralism.*

READ ON

- **To the Catholic books:** Auberon Waugh, *The Foxglove Saga*.
- **To the campus comedies:** ▷Malcolm Bradbury, *The History Man*; Howard Jacobson, *Coming From Behind*; ▷Mary McCarthy, *The Groves of Academe*.

LOFTS, Norah (1904–86)

British novelist.

Lofts wrote historical romances, many set in East Anglia. *The Brittle Glass* (1942) is typical: the story of Sorrel Kingabay, the red-haired, independent daughter of a Norfolk trader in the early 1700s, when smugglers and highwaymen still roamed the English Fens.

Lofts' other novels include many set in romantic or sinister old houses: The Town House, The House at Old Vine, The

READ ON

- Oliver Onions, *The Story of Ragged Robyn*. ▷Daphne Du Maurier, *Jamaica Inn*. Sarah Woodhouse, *Daughter of the Sea*.

House at Sunset, Gad's Hall, Haunted House. *Her other romances include* Jassy *and* Day of the Butterfly, *and her thrillers (written under the name Peter Curtis) are* Dead March in Three Keys, Lady Living Alone *and* The Devil's Own.

LONDON, JACK (1879–1916)

US novelist, short-story and non-fiction writer.

In his teens London worked as a docker, a seal-hunter, an oyster pirate (stealing from other fishermen's oyster-beds) and a customs officer; he also tramped across the United States and took part in the Klondike Gold Rush. At 19 he settled down to writing, aiming to produce 1000 words a day, and began turning out he-man articles and short stories, heavy on adventure and light on character. His human beings (most of them fur-trappers, gold-miners or fishermen) take a two-fisted approach to life. Brutality rules, and survival is only guaranteed until someone stronger or brighter comes along. However blinkered London's view of life – he managed, at the same time, to be a fervent socialist and a fascist convinced that fair-haired, blue-eyed Aryans were the master-race – he wrote of it with breath-taking, blood-hammering effectiveness. His descriptions of fights, and of men battling against enormous natural hazards, set a model which many tough-guy writers have imitated, but none surpassed.

CALL OF THE WILD (1903)

Buck, a St Bernard dog, is stolen from his home in California and taken to the Klondike as a sledge-dog. He passes from owner to owner, each more brutal than the last, until he finds kindness at the hands of John Thornton. But Thornton is killed, Buck's last link with human beings is broken and he escapes to the wild and becomes the leader of a pack of wild dogs.

London's novels include Before Adam *(about the prehistoric ancestors of homo sapiens),* The Sea-wolf *(a ▷Conradian account of the struggle between a brutal sea-captain and the city couple he kidnaps) and* The Iron Heel *(a story of the future, recounting the struggle of a group of urban guerrillas to overthrow a dictatorship which has overrun Chicago). His story-collections include* Children of the Frost, The Road, When God Laughs, The Strength of the Strong *and* Island Tales. John Barleycorn *is an autobiographical novel about a writer battling alcoholism.*

READ ON

- *White Fang* (a mirror-image of *The Call of the Wild*: the story of a wild dog drawn to the human race, who is betrayed and ill-treated by every owner – the description of his life as a fighting-dog is particularly harrowing – until he ends up at last with a master he can trust).
- **To *The Call of the Wild*:** Richard Adams, *The Plague Dogs*; Romain Gary, *White Dog*; ▷H.G. Wells, *The Island of Doctor Moreau*.
- **To London's books about humans:** ▷Ernest Hemingway, *The Old Man and the Sea*; *To Have and Have Not*; ▷Maxim Gorky, *Foma Gordeev*; ▷Joseph Conrad, *Typhoon*.
- **To his short stories:** Ring Lardner, *Round Up: the Stories/Collected Short Stories*.

LOWRY, MALCOLM (1909–57)
British novelist.

Lowry began experimenting with drugs and drink at Cambridge, and by the time he was 20 he was irretrievably addicted. He spent the rest of his life bumming across the world, in rehabilitation clinics, or in self-imposed isolation while he struggled to turn his experiences into fiction. The only novel published during his lifetime – it took him 20 years to write it – was *Under the Volcano* (1947). This tells of the last two days in the life of an alcoholic British consul in revolution-torn Mexico, and interwines memory, dream and reality in the manner of ▷Joyce's *Ulysses*. His posthumous novels are *Lunar Caustic*, set in a 'drying-out' clinic in New York, and *Dark as the Grave Wherein my Friend is Laid*, about a boozy, doom-ridden tour of Mexico.

READ ON

- ▶ ▷Joseph Conrad, *Heart of Darkness*. ▷F. Scott Fitzgerald, *Tender is the Night*. ▷Fyodor Dostoevski, *The Idiot*. ▷Lawrence Durrell, *The Black Book*. ▷Ernest Hemingway, *Islands in the Stream*.

LUDLUM, ROBERT (BORN 1927)
US novelist.

Ludlum also writes as Jonathan Ryder (*The Cry of the Halidon*; *The Rhineman Exchange*). His thrillers (many based on real-life incidents) are suspenseful, tough-talking and racy: they include *The Scarlatti Inheritance, The Gemini Contenders, The Matarese Circle, The Osterman Weekend, The Parsifal Mosaic* and *The Icarus Agenda* (1988), in which a mild US congressman has to save a group of 200 hostages from Islamic fundamentalists bent on world domination.

READ ON

- • *The Parsifal Mosaic*; *Trevayne*.
- ▶ Allen Drury, *The Roads of Earth*. Fred Taylor, *Walking Shadows* (set among German officers during the second world war). ▷John Le Carré, *A Perfect Spy*.

LURIE, ALISON (BORN 1926)
US novelist.

The people in Lurie's novels are all terribly nice: well educated, well-off, well dressed, liberal and compassionate. Their lives are like placid pools – and into each of them Lurie drops the acid of discontent (usually something to do with sex) and invites us to smile as the water seethes. Her funniest books are set on university campuses: *Love and Friendship* (1962) is about two people trapped in an affair (and what everyone else thinks about it); *The War Between the Tates* shows the gradual collapse of a 'perfect' marriage under threat from a combination of adultery and student politics. The people of *Imaginary Friends* are participants in or investigators of a bizarre religious cult. The narrator of *Only Children* is a child, who reports on the sexual imbroglios of the adults around her with a wide-eyed gravity which arises less from innocence than from a precocious understanding

READ ON

- • *The War Between the Tates*.
- ▶ **To *Foreign Affairs*:** ▷Mary McCarthy, *The Company She Keeps*; Joan Didion, *A Book of Common Prayer*; ▷Philip Roth, *The Professor of Desire*.
- ▶ **To *The War Between the Tates*:** Susan Fromberg Shaeffer, *The Injured Party*; ▷Anne Tyler, *Dinner*

Alison LURIE

US CAMPUS LIFE

Randall **JARRELL, PICTURES FROM AN INSTITUTION**
(send-up of life in 'progressive' US women's university, 1950s)

Mary **MCCARTHY, THE GROVES OF ACADEME**
(political satire: protest-movement when university president tries to sack incompetent lecturer)

Malcolm **BRADBURY, STEPPING WESTWARD**
(naive Englishman takes up post on 'liberated' Californian campus)

Vladimir **NABOKOV, PNIN**
(sad Russian émigré tries to adjust to US university ways, while clinging to culture of 'old country')

UNCOMFORTABLE IN AMERICA

Franz **KAFKA, AMERICA**
(innocent young German immigrant discovers fantasy-land)

William **BOYD, STARS AND BARS**
(shy Englishman plunged into fast-lane US business life)

Peter **DE VRIES, REUBEN, REUBEN**
(boozy, hard-wenching poet cuts a swathe through crackerbarrel Massachusetts community)

Evelyn **WAUGH, THE LOVED ONE**
(the US funeral business will never seem the same again)

John **UPDIKE, BECH, A BOOK**
(problems of US author: family, publishers, fans, lecture-audiences, reporters, writer's block . . .)

The War Between the Tates

(tragi-comic collapse of 'civilised' marriage on 'liberal' US university campus)

ACADEMIC FOLLIES

David **LODGE, Small World**
(international conference-circuit)

Robertson **DAVIES, The Rebel Angels**
(Canadian Rabelais – researcher raises the Devil)

Kingsley **AMIS, Lucky Jim**
(1950s English culture-snobbery in small-town university)

Howard **JACOBSON, Coming from Behind**
(English provincial and polytechnic life – as in 'you don't have to be mad to work here, but it helps')

Max **BEERBOHM, Zuleika Dobson**
(life and love among 1910s Oxford dreaming spires)

NON-ACADEMIC FOLLIES

J.B. **PRIESTLEY, Low Notes on a High Level**
(classical music snobs at 1950s BBC – who will get first performance of famous Scandinavian composer's latest symphony?)

Paul **BRYERS, Coming First**
(trendy TV producer works hard not to be male chauvinist)

Hilary **MANTEL, Vacant Possession**
(rollercoaster black satire: 'madwoman' drives yuppie English family crazy)

Patrick **DENNIS, Auntie Mame**
(high society – conventional and bizarre – 1950s USA: eccentric aunt takes over 'education' of shy orphan nephew)

not only of what is going on but of the sort of butter-won't-melt-in-*my*-mouth cuteness adults expect from little girls.

FOREIGN AFFAIRS (1984)

Three Americans are visiting England: Vinnie, a 54-year-old professor, Fred, a hunky young academic, and Chuck, a middle-aged, none-too-bright businessman on a package tour. The novel shows Vinnie's attempts to bring into the two men's lives the same kind of decorous, unflustered order she herself enjoys – and the way her own values crumple under the strain of real emotion.

Lurie's other novels are Real People, *a comedy about artists coping with inspirational blocks and sexual passion in a 'creative colony',* A Nowhere City, *a serious book about a woman trying to cope with unfocussed psychological panic, and* The Truth About Lorin Jones, *about a woman writing the biography of a painter, whose life becomes totally entangled with the facts and emotions she is researching.*

at Homesick Restaurant.

- **To *Love and Friendship*:** ▷David Lodge, *Small World.*
- **To *Only Children*:** ▷Henry James, *What Maisie Knew.*
- **To Lurie's work in general:** ▷Anita Brookner, *Look at Me*; Alice Thomas Ellis, *The Birds of the Air.*

M

MACAULAY, Rose (1881–1958)

British novelist.

In the 1920s Macaulay wrote deadpan satires (*Potterism, Crewe Train, Told by an Idiot*). In the 1930s, beginning with *They Were Defeated* (see below), she began to concentrate on the sympathetic side of her art, writing about people (young girls especially) who are racked by the need to choose between the life of the mind and that of the flesh: their intellectual or spiritual ambitions are ambushed by sexual infatuation. The second world war, and a succession of private misfortunes, made Macaulay give up novel-writing for a dozen years, but she returned triumphantly in her mid-70s with *The World My Wilderness* (about a confused girl trying to discover her psychological identity after the second world war) and a riotous, malicious romp about love (sacred and profane), *The Towers of Trebizond.*

They Were Defeated (1932)

In 17th-century, Puritan England, Dr Conybeare is determined to educate his 15-year-old daughter Julian as if she were a man. The girl takes lessons from Robert Herrick, rector of the parish, until Herrick is driven out for sheltering an old woman accused of witchcraft. Julian goes to Cambridge, where she has private coaching from the don John Cleveland. Cleveland, however, is more interested in her virginity than in her mind, and seduces her – and she finds herself as entranced by sex as by the heady religious and intellectual atmosphere of Cambridge. Then her brother finds out about the seduction, and tragedy ensues.

Macaulay's other novels include (from the 1920s) Dangerous

READ ON

- *The Towers of Trebizond.*
- ▶ **To the satires:** Compton Mackenzie, *Vestal Fire*; Nancy Mitford, *Love in a Cold Climate*; ▷Muriel Spark, *The Ballad of Peckham Rye.*
- ▶ **To *They Were Defeated*:** ▷Robert Graves, *Wife to Mr Milton.*
- ▶ **To Macaulay's work in general:** ▷Willa Cather, *The Song of the Lark*; ▷Elizabeth Bowen, *The Death of the Heart*; A.S. Byatt, *The Virgin in the Garden*; ▷Elizabeth Jolley, *The Sugar Mother.*

Ages, Orphan Island, Keeping Up Appearances *and* Staying with Relations, *and (from the 1930s)* I Would be Private *and* No Man's Wit. *She also wrote poetry, essays on literature and religion, and a book combining travel, archaeology and autobiography,* The Pleasure of Ruins.

McBAIN, ED (BORN 1926)

US novelist.

'Ed McBain' is one of the pseudonyms of ▷Evan Hunter. He writes fast, tough police-procedurals set in New York; many of them (including the 87th Precinct series) are woven out of several simultaneous investigations, in the manner of such TV series as *Hill Street Blues.* McBain also describes the private lives of his hard-talking, street-wise cops: this humanises the violence. His books include *Cop Hater, Give the Boys a Great Big Hand, Calypso* and *Eighty Million Eyes.*

READ ON

- ▶ Chester Himes, *Blind Man With a Pistol.* Dell Shannon, *Date With Death.* Lesley Egan, *The Hunters and the Hunted.* Joseph Wambaugh, *The Choirboys.* Martin Cruz Smith, *Gorky Park* (a police-procedural novel set in Moscow).

McCAFFREY, ANNE (BORN 1926)

US novelist.

Although McCaffrey has written novels, romances, a thriller and books on music and cookery, she is best-known for SF (often, eg in *The Crystal Singer,* with a musical background) and fantasy. Her most substantial work is the 'Pern' sequence of novels. Pern is a distant, medieval world where the élite ride and telepathically control – or are controlled by – dragons; the dragons are the only beings which can destroy Thread, a devastating space-virus which would otherwise engulf all other life. The series details the fragile balance of society on Pern, and in particular the symbiosis – by turns comic, tragic and movingly poetic – between humans and dragons on which all life depends.

The Pern books (self-contained but linked) are Dragonflight, Dragonquest, The White Dragon, Dragonsong, Dragonsinger, Dragondrums *and* Moreta. *McCaffrey's other SF books include* The Ship Who Sang, Restoree *and* Dinosaur Planet. Get off the Unicorn *is a collection of short stories.*

READ ON

- • *The Crystal Singer; Restoree* (about a girl who finds herself transported to an unknown body on another planet).
- ▶ ▷Piers Anthony, *Vicinity Cluster.* ▷Robert Heinlein, *Glory Road.* ▷Ursula Le Guin, *The Word for World is Forest.* ▷Tom de Haan, *The Child of Good Fortune.*

McCARTHY, MARY (1912–89)

US novelist and non-fiction writer.

As well as novels, McCarthy has published books on Venice

READ ON

- • *Birds of America.*

and Florence, political essays (especially on the US involvement in Vietnam) and an admired – and fictionalised – autobiography, *Memoirs of a Catholic Girlhood.* (She set the record straight in 1987 with the more factual *How I Grew.*) Each of her half-dozen novels simultaneously discusses and satirises major issues of its day. The heroine of *The Company She Keeps*, from the 1940s, tries to reconcile being a free spirit with her longing to find Mr Right. *The Group*, a 1960s best-seller, is about eight women making their way in society and demanding equal shares in the sexual and social revolution. The hero of *Birds of America* (1971) is a naive young American in Europe, worrying himself sick over small matters like dirty toilet-bowls, and over such large ones as ecological balance, the awfulness of US package-tourists and the fact that no one in Europe seems to share America's high opinion of itself. In *Cannibals and Missionaries* (1980) a group of wealthy, cultured people is held hostage by terrorists. One US critic (Brady Nordland) called *Birds of America* 'sweet, funny and very clever'; the description fits all McCarthy's work.

THE GROVES OF ACADEME (1952)

Henry Mulcahy is an inefficient, unreliable teacher in the English Department of Jocelyn College. He is also a married man with children, and a left-wing activist. The President of the College decides not to renew Mulcahy's tenure, and the department immediately starts politicking in Mulcahy's defence. The book's once-topical background (it was published during the anti-left witch-hunts of Senator Joe McCarthy – no relation of Mary McCarthy, and certainly no soul-mate) has faded, leaving a sparkling, malicious campus comedy in which everyone gets their due come-uppance; the final irony, discomforting Mulcahy's woolly liberal colleagues, is particularly neat.

McCarthy's other novels are The Oasis/A Source of Embarrassment *and* A Charmed Life. Cast a Cold Eye *is a collection of short stories.*

- **To *The Groves of Academe*:** D.J. Enright, *Academic Year*; Howard Jacobson, *Coming from Behind*.
- **To *The Group*:** Rona Jaffe, *Class Reunion* (and its sequel *Mazes and Monsters*).
- **To McCarthy's novels generally:** Alice Thomas Ellis, *The Other Side of the Fire*; ▷A.N. Wilson, *The Sweets of Pimlico*; ▷Frederic Raphael, *The Graduate Wife*; ▷Alison Lurie, *The War Between the Tates*.

McCULLERS, CARSON (1917–53)

US novelist.

Reading McCullers is like visiting a freak-show: her characters are repulsive but fascinating, kin to the more macabre human figures in modern horror videos. The hero of *The Heart is a Lonely Hunter* (1940) is a deaf-mute, distracted by his inability to communicate either his sensitivity or his generosity of spirit. The awkward, ugly heroine of *The Ballad of the Sad Café* (1951) runs a haven in the Georgia swamps for tramps, lunatics and other social misfits – and

READ ON

- **To McCullers' more freakish books:** ▷Ian McEwan, *The Comfort of Strangers*; ▷Paul Bailey, *At The Jerusalem*; ▷Émile Zola, *Nana*.

her world is shattered when she falls in love with a malign homosexual dwarf. *Reflections in a Golden Eye* (1941) describes boredom and sexual obsession among the wives in a wartime army camp. *Clock Without Hands* is about racism. Only in one book, *The Member of the Wedding*, does McCullers transcend such nightmarish imaginings. Her heroine is a young adolescent in a household bustling with preparations for a wedding: fascinated but totally ignorant about what is going on, she feels as locked out of 'real' (ie adult) society as the freaks and emotional cripples of McCullers' other books.

▶ **To *The Member of the Wedding*:** ▷Eudora Welty, *Delta Wedding*; ▷Katherine Anne Porter, *The Leaning Tower* (short stories).

McEWAN, IAN (BORN 1948)

British novelist and short-story writer.

McEwan's 1970s short stories (collected in *First Love, Last Rites* and *In Between the Sheets*) were tales of lust, violence and despair, written in coldly brilliant prose, as macabre as video nasties. His first two novels were in the same mode. *The Cement Garden* (1978) is a story of creepy adolescents with a murderous secret; *The Comfort of Strangers* (1981) is a bizarre tale of kidnapping and brutality set in Venice. He also wrote the script for the enigmatic, erotic 1980s film *The Ploughman's Lunch*. Then, in 1987, he published a novel of a completely different kind, *The Child in Time*. This is about the effects on a young father's emotional equilibrium of the loss of his beloved child. McEwan's prose is as steely as ever, but his subject allows him to describe tenderness and affection in a way which warms his work.

READ ON

▶ **To the early stories and novels:** Iain Banks, *The Wasp Factory*; Deborah Moggach, *Porky*; Madison Smartt Bell, *Straight Out*.

▶ **To *The Child in Time*:** ▷Hermann Hesse, *Rosshalde*; ▷David Cook, *Crying Out Loud*; ▷Anne Tyler, *The Accidental Tourist*.

MADNESS

▷Richard Condon, *Any God Will Do*
Margaret Forster, *The Bride of Lowther Fell*
▷Susan Hill, *The Bird of Night*
Ken Kesey, *One Flew Over the Cuckoo's Nest*
Sylvia Plath, *The Bell Jar*
▷Jean Rhys, *Good Morning, Midnight*
▷Evelyn Waugh, *The Ordeal of Gilbert Pinfold*

Depression and Psychiatry (p 59); On the Edge of Sanity (p 190)

MAILER, NORMAN (BORN 1923)

US writer.

As well as novels, Mailer has published both non-fiction (eg *Marilyn*, about Marilyn Monroe) and 'faction', a blend of real events and fiction (eg *The Executioner's Song*, 1979, an examination of the character and crimes of the murderer Gary

READ ON

▶ **To Mailer's contemporary fiction:** ▷Ernest Hemingway, *For*

Gilmore). Most of his novels are set in the present day, and deal with a single theme: maleness. He regards violence and competitiveness as essential components of masculinity, related to sexual potency – and claims, further, that capitalist society will only succeed if it models itself on the aggressive, cocky male. The world being what it is, Mailer is often forced – like ▷Hemingway before him – to describe the failure of these macho fantasies, and because so many of his books are about the failure of the American dream, despair gives his writing stinging political relevance. *The Naked and the Dead* (1948) is about the brutalisation of a group of bewildered young airmen in the second world war. In *Why Are We in Vietnam?* (1967), a savage Hemingway parody, a man takes his son on a bear-hunt as an 18th birthday celebration, and this quintessential US manhood-ritual is linked, in a devastating final paragraph, with the mindless, gung-ho crowing of the gook-slaughtering US army in Vietnam, to which the boy will be drafted now that he is adult. *An American Dream* (1965), an equally pungent satire, shows a man at the end of his tether who commits murder and then tries to cudgel from his increasingly insane mind the reasons why his country should have conditioned him to kill, why someone else's violent death should be the outcome of the American dream.

Whom the Bell Tolls; ▷John Cheever, *Falconer*; Henri de Montherlant, *The Bullfighters*; William Styron, *The Long March*.

▶ **To *Ancient Evenings*:** James Clavell, *Shōgun*; L.P. Myers, *The Near and the Far*; ▷Thomas Mann, *Joseph and His Brothers*.

ANCIENT EVENINGS (1983)

Pharaoh Rameses IX of Egypt, perplexed by his failure as a ruler, asks his minister Menenhetet to think back to a former existence as charioteer to the great warrior pharaoh Rameses II, and to explain the secrets of Rameses' success. Menenhetet's account is the bulk of the book, a dazzling description of a society dependent on belief in magic and on a (not unconnected) view of its own powers of rejuvenation, of constantly being able to deconstruct and reconstruct its past.

A good sampler of Mailer's work is Advertisements for Myself, *an anthology of his early writings with a fascinating autobiographical commentary. His other novels include* Barbary Shore, The Deer Park *and the thriller* Tough Guys Don't Dance.

MANN, THOMAS (1875–1955)

German novelist and non-fiction writer.

Although Mann was not a political writer, the themes of his work reflect northern European politics of the last 100 years. His first great novel, *Buddenbrooks* (1901), shows the decline of a powerful German industrial family over three decades – and although it is superficially a Forsyte-like

READ ON

- *Buddenbrooks*; *The Confessions of Felix Krull, Confidence Man*.

▶ **To *The Magic***

family saga, its strength comes from the persistent impression that the Buddenbrooks are characteristic of the decadent 'old Germany' as a whole. The hero of *The Magic Mountain* (1924) spends much of the book learning about Europe's moral, artistic and philosophical heritage – and then goes to fight in the first world war. In *Joseph and His Brothers* (1933–43), based on the Bible and written under the shadow of nazism, Joseph, the figure symbolising progress, is a plausible rogue, a Hitler-figure, and his brothers, symbolising barbarism, are as gullible as they are honest. The composer-hero of *Doctor Faustus* (1947) can unlock his creativity only by entering ever deeper into the morass of his own mind, and by accepting that to be 'ordinary' is to opt not for cultural calm but for chaos. The con-man central character of *The Confessions of Felix Krull, Confidence Man* (1954), Mann's only comic novel, preys on the expectations of those who still believe in the old rules of religion, society and politics.

Mountain: ▷Johann Wolfgang von Goethe, *The Apprenticeship of Wilhelm Meister*; Robert Musil, *The Man Without Qualities*.

▶ **To *Buddenbrooks***: ▷I.B. Singer, *The Family Moskat*; ▷Honoré de Balzac, *Cousin Bette*.

▶ **To *Joseph and His Brothers***: ▷Gustave Flaubert, *Salammbô*

THE MAGIC MOUNTAIN (DER ZAUBERBERG) (1924)

Castorp, a rich, unimaginative young man, spends seven years in a Swiss TB sanatorium. The sanatorium is full of endlessly talkative intellectuals, who educate Castorp in music, philosophy, art and literature. The book shows him growing in both knowledge and moral stature, until at last he is cured both of TB and of the greater disease (in Mann's eyes) of ignorant complacency. As the novel ends, however, he strides out to fight in the first world war – and Mann invites us, in the light of hindsight, to ponder his probable fate and that of the European culture he has so laboriously acquired.

Mann's shorter works include Mario the Magician *(about demonic possession),* Death in Venice *(Tod in Venedig) (about a dying writer galvanised by longing for a beautiful boy),* Lotte in Weimar *(a historical novel about the young ▷Goethe), and* The Holy Sinner *(a beautiful – and poker-faced, despite the ridiculousness of its events – retelling of a medieval religious legend involving incest, communion with angels and magical transformations).* Stories of a Lifetime *is a collection of short stories.*

MANNING, OLIVIA (1908–80)

British novelist.

Manning is best known for the 6-novel sequence *Fortunes of War* (*The Balkan Trilogy*, 1960–65 and *The Levant Trilogy*, 1977–80). The central characters, Guy and Harriet Pringle, are English expatriates during the early years of the second world war. They settle in Bucharest, where Guy teaches

READ ON

▶ ▷Elizabeth Bowen, *The Heat of the Day*. Jennifer Johnston, *The Captains and the*

English; then, as the Axis powers advance, they move to Athens and from there to Cairo, where they 'hole up' during the desert campaign of 1942. Like the rest of Manning's characters, English, Middle Eastern or European, the Pringles dwell on the fringes, not at the centre, of great events; their lives are bounded by bread-shortages, electricity-cuts and squabbles over status. The civilisation which bred them is collapsing, and they are themselves symbols of its decadence: they are effete and powerless, able only to run before events. None the less, Harriet's character does contain the seeds of change. When she marries Guy she is an unawakened personality, a genteel 1930s 'English rose'. Events draw from her emotional and intellectual strength she never knew she had – and the effects are to alienate the rest of the stuffy British community and to put stress on her marriage to Guy, an honourable, unimaginative man trapped in pre-war attitudes. He wanted a wife who was a companion not an equal, a pupil not a friend; although he is the same age as Harriet, he is as typical of the 'old' generation as she is of the 'new'. None of this is openly declared. At first sight Manning seems to be offering no more than a series of artless anecdotes about the muddle and horror of life in exotic cities engulfed by war. It is not till the mosaic is complete that her underlying scheme becomes apparent: the description of a whole culture in a state of unwished-for, panic-stricken change.

The novels in The Balkan Trilogy *are* The Great Fortune, The Spoilt City *and* Friends and Heroes; *those in* The Levant Trilogy *are* The Danger Tree, The Battle Lost and Won *and* The Sum of Things. *Manning's other novels are* Artist Among the Missing, School for Love, A Different Face, The Doves of Venus, The Play Room *and* The Rain Forest. Growing Up *and* A Romantic Hero *are collections of short stories.*

Kings. Isabel Colegate, *The Shooting Party*. ▷Evelyn Waugh, *Sword of Honour*.

MANSFIELD, Katherine (1888–1923)

New Zealand short-story writer.

Mansfield went to London at 14, and spent the rest of her life in Europe. When she wrote of New Zealand it was either with childhood nostalgia (for example in 'Prelude' and 'At The Bay') or with distaste for the lives its adults led in the outback ('Ole Underwood'; 'The Woman at the Store') or in dingily genteel suburbs ('Her First Ball'; 'How Pearl Button was Kidnapped'). She admired ▷Chekhov's stories, and sought to write the same kind of innocent-seeming anecdotes distilling single moments of human folly or aspiration. Many of her stories are about small children. In 'Sixpence', for example, she describes a little boy's sudden in-

READ ON

► ▷Anton Chekhov, *The Lady With the Little Dog and Other Stories*. ▷John Cheever, *Collected Stories*. Jean Stafford, *Collected Stories*. William Saroyan, *Best Stories of Saroyan*. ▷Elizabeth Bowen,

explicable naughtiness, and the guilt his father feels when he beats him; in 'The Little Girl', she shows a young child's feelings for her father. Her favourite characters were shallow, silly and desperate people: an unemployable film-extra ('Pictures'), a snobbish mother and her unmarried daughters ('The Garden-party'), a hen-pecked singing-teacher ('Mr Reginald Peacock's Day'), expatriates on the continent ('The Man Without a Temperament'; 'Je ne parle pas français'). She polished and refined her prose, often spending months on a single story – and the feeling of craftsmanship in her work, of slightly self-conscious artistry, greatly enhances the impression she seeks to give, that tragedies are not diminished because the lives they affect are small.

Mansfield's story-collections are In A German Pension, Bliss, The Garden Party, The Dove's Nest *and* Something Childish. *Her* Journals *give fascinating glimpses both of her character and of the events and conversations which she drew on in her work.*

The Dream Lover.
▷V.S. Pritchett, *Collected Stories.*

MANY GENERATIONS

▷Isabel Allende, *The House of the Spirits*
▷Gabriel García Márquez, *One Hundred Years of Solitude*
▷Winston Graham, *Poldark*
▷Thomas Mann, *Buddenbrooks*
▷Maisie Mosco, *Almonds and Raisins*
Richard Peck, *This Company of Women*
Rosamunde Pilcher, *The Shell Seekers*
▷I.B. Singer, *The Family Moskat*
Nicola Thorne, *A Place in the Sun*
Jan Webster, *Colliers Row*

All-engulfing Families (p 5); Eccentric Families (p 73)

MANZONI, ALESSANDRO (1785–1873)
Italian writer.

Manzoni was Italy's leading 19th-century poet, playwright and novelist, a writer of the stature of ▷Goethe or ▷Tolstoy. His one novel, *The Betrothed* (I promessi sposi, 1842), is ranked with ▷Tolstoy's *War and Peace* both as imaginative fiction and as a study of a whole society from top to bottom. The heart of the story is a series of somewhat operatic events surrounding the engagement, in 17th-century Lombardy, of two young peasants. Their innocent plans create ripples of involvement which draw in landowners (good and bad), priests (saintly and venal), village gossips, gipsies,

READ ON

▶ Eucleides da Cunha, *Revolution in the Badlands* (a similarly panoramic view of a whole society, this time that of Brazil, town and country, during an uprising).
▷Sigrid Undset,

children and the aged – an entire society, revealed in magnificent, poet's prose. One of the book's set pieces, describing plague in Milan, has an imaginative power rivalled only in ▷Zola or by the low-life scenes in ▷Hugo's *Notre Dame de Paris*.

Kristin Lavrandsdatter (set among the peasants and landowners of medieval Norway). ▷Boris Pasternak, *Doctor Zhivago* (matching Manzoni's counterpointing of private and public affairs).

▶ Shiva Naipaul, *Fireflies* is a panorama of a more modern kind, a tragi-comedy showing the pull between people of different races and religions in Jamaica.

MÁRQUEZ, Gabriel García (born 1928)

Colombian novelist and short-story writer.

In Márquez' invented South American town of Macondo, a place isolated from the outside world, 'magic realism' rules: there is no distinction between magic and reality. At one level, life is perfectly ordinary: people are born, grow up, work, cook, feud and gossip. But there is a second, irrational and surrealist plane to ordinary existence. The Macondans (unless they murder each other for reasons of politics, sex or family honour) live for 100, 150, 200 years. Although they are as innocent of 'real' knowledge as children – they think ice miraculous and they are amazed to hear that the world is round – they know the secrets of alchemy, converse with ghosts, remember Cortez or Drake as 'uncles'. Macondo is a rough-and-tumble Eden, a paradise where instinct rules and nothing is impossible – and Márquez spends his time either describing its enchantment or detailing the savage results when people from the outside world (jackbooted generals; con-men; lawyers; bishops) break through to 'civilise' it. For Márquez, Macondo stands for the whole of South America, and his stories are barbed political allegories. But he seldom lets this overwhelm the books. Instead of hectoring, he opens his eyes wide, puts his tongue in his cheek and tells us wonders.

READ ON

- *Love in the Time of Cholera*.

▶ ▷Salman Rushdie, *Shame*. ▷Isabel Allende, *The House of the Spirits*. Carlos Fuentes, *The Old Gringo*. ▷Virginia Woolf, *Orlando*. ▷Italo Calvino, *Our Ancestors*. Gerald H. Morris, *Doves and Silk Handkerchieves*. Mike Nicol, *The Powers That Be*.

One Hundred Years Of Solitude (1967)

As Colonel Aurelio Buendia faces the firing squad, the whole history of his family flashes before his eyes. They begin as poor peasants, in a one-roomed hut on the edge of a swamp. They proliferate like tendrils on a vine: Aureliano himself has 17 sons, all called Aureliano. The family-members absorb knowledge, people and property until they and Macondo seem indissoluble. Finally, led by Aureliano senior, they defend the old, innocent values against invasion by a government which wants to impose the same laws in Macondo as everywhere else, and the dynasty disappears from reality, living on only in fantasy, as a memory of how human beings were before the whole world changed.

Márquez' other novels are No One Writes to the Colonel, In Evil Hour, Chronicle of a Death Foretold, The Autumn of the Patriarch *(the stream-of-consciousness monologue of a dying dictator),* Love in the Time of Cholera *(a mesmeric love-story spanning 60 years) and* The General in his Labyrinth *(about the last days of Simón Bolívar). His short stories are collected in* Leaf-storm and other Stories, Big Mama's Funeral *and* Innocent Erendira and other Stories.

MARSH, NGAIO (1899–1982)

New Zealand novelist.

Few writers use 'classic' detective-story ingredients as magnificently as Marsh. Her murder-methods are ingenious and unexpected. Her locations are fascinating: backstage (and onstage) at theatres; during a village-hall concert; in the shearing-shed of a sheep-farm; at a top-level diplomatic reception. Her characters are exotic and her detection is scrupulously fair, with every clue appearing to the reader at the same time as to Alleyn, Marsh's urbane and hawk-eyed sleuth. Above all, her books move at a furious pace, fuelled by her effervescent glee at the follies of humankind.

FINAL CURTAIN (1947)

Shortly after the second world war, Agatha Troy (Alleyn's artist wife) is persuaded to spend a week painting the portrait of Sir Henry Ancred, a distinguished actor now retired. She goes to his country mansion, and finds it a lowering old house in the best whodunnit tradition. One wing has been taken over by an evacuated prep school, and the rest is filled with eccentric relatives who have been plunged into twittering alarm by the arrival of Sir Henry's young, vulgar and nubile mistress, who may just become his wife and cut the rest of the family off from their inheritance. Sittings for the painting proceed – Sir Henry is costumed as for his most famous role, Macbeth – and are interrupted first by a series of unpleasant practical jokes, and then by the old man's murder. Scotland Yard must be called in, and Alleyn arrives back from war-service just in time to take the case

READ ON

- *Enter a Murderer*; *Overture to Death*.
- ▶ ▷Margery Allingham, *The Beckoning Lady*. H.R.F. Keating, *Zen There Was Murder*. Emma Lathen, *When in Greece*. Margaret Millar, *Wall of Eyes*. ▷Peter Dickinson, *The Poison Oracle*.

and sort out the murderer from half a dozen candidates, each with a cast-iron alibi and a very good reason for wishing Sir Henry dead.

Marsh's three dozen novels include Hand in Glove, Died in the Wool, Clutch of Constables, Vintage Murder, Spinsters in Jeopardy, Surfeit of Lampreys, Black as He's Painted *and* Death in Ecstasy. Black Beech and Honeydew *is an autobiography, especially interesting on her childhood and her fascination with theatre.*

MASTERS, JOHN (BORN 1914)

British novelist.

Masters, an army officer in India, wrote a series of books setting fictional characters in the context of real historical events. The Raj background and the interplay between two incompatible cultures are brilliantly evoked, and the foreground action is fast, thrilling and plausible. The best-known books in the sequence are *Nightrunners of Bengal* (1951), set during the Indian 'Mutiny', and *Bhowani Junction* (1954), about the plot to blow up a train during the struggle for independence.

Masters' other books include Far, Far the Mountain Peak, The Road Past Mandalay, The Breaking Strain, Thunder at Sunset *and* The Himalayan Concerto.

READ ON

- Paul Scott, *The Raj Quartet*; ▷J.G. Farrell, *The Siege of Krishnapur*.
- **Similar books, about different periods and continents:** James Clavell, *Shōgun* (17th-century Japan); ▷Robert Graves, *Sergeant Lamb of the Ninth* (the American War of Independence); Timothy Mo, *An Insular Possession* (the British and Hong Kong).

MAUGHAM, W. SOMERSET (WILLIAM) (1874–1965)

British writer of novels, short stories and plays.

A tireless traveller (especially in the Far East), Maugham wrote hundreds of short stories based on anecdotes he heard or scenes he observed en route. Many of them were later filmed: 'Rain', for example (about a missionary on a cruise-liner in Samoa struggling to reform a prostitute, and losing his own soul in the process), was made half a dozen times. Maugham's novels used true experience in a similar way, shaping it and drawing out its meaning but keeping close to real events. *Liza of Lambeth* (1897) is about a London slum girl tormented by her neighbours for conceiving a bastard child. *Of Human Bondage* (1915) is the story of an orphan, bullied at school because he has a club foot, who struggles to find happiness as an adult, is ravaged by love for a worthless woman, and settles at last to become a

READ ON

- **To *Liza of Lambeth*:** ▷Émile Zola, *The Boozer* (L'Assommoir).
- **To *Of Human Bondage*:** ▷C.P. Snow, *Strangers and Brothers*; ▷Jerome Weidman, *Fourth Street East*.
- **To *The Moon and Sixpence*:** Joyce Cary, *The Horse's Mouth*.

country doctor. The stockbroker hero of *The Moon and Sixpence* (1919) gives up career, wife and family to become a painter in the South Seas, as Gauguin did. *Cakes and Ale* (1930) is an acid satire about the 1930s London literary world; Maugham avoided libel suits only by claiming that every writer it pilloried was just another aspect of himself.

Maugham's other novels include The Trembling of a Leaf, The Casuarina Tree, The Razor's Edge *and* Catalina. *His* Complete Short Stories *and* Collected Plays *(from 1907–32 he wrote two dozen successful plays, mainly comedies) were published in the 1950s.* A Writer's Notebook *and* The Summing Up *give fascinating insights into the balance between his life and work.*

▶ **To *Cakes and Ale*:** ▷Rose Macaulay, *Crewe Train*; ▷J.B. Priestley, *The Image Men*.

▶ **To the short stories:** Guy De Maupassant, *Boule de Suif*; ▷R.L. Stevenson, *Island Nights' Entertainment*; ▷Rudyard Kipling, *Wee Willie Winkie*; ▷Paul Theroux, *World's End*.

MAURIAC, François (1885–1970)
French novelist.

Mauriac's books, all set among rich families in the Bordeaux wine country at the start of this century, are based on Roman Catholic doctrines of guilt and repentance. They show people tormented by conscience (often quite justified: his characters include murderers, embezzlers, adulterers and family tyrants). Some are never challenged; others are outcasts, reviled by neighbours and relatives as unpleasant as they are themselves. A few repent, and the move from moral darkness to light irradiates their souls. The quest for redemption is, however, always left to the individual: no one is saved against his or her own will. Despite the religious starting-point of Mauriac's books, they are anything but churchy: they are psychological case-studies rather than religious tracts. Like ancient Greek tragedy, his work can seem remorselessly gloomy – and it has a similar hypnotic power.

The Nest Of Vipers (Le Nud de vipères) (1932)
The book is the confession of a dying man, trying to explain to his grown-up children how his wife's infidelity, many years before, shrivelled his soul and led him to hate both her and them. For 30 years he has plotted to rob them of their inheritance, taking pleasure in the prospect of their distress when he dies and leaves them penniless. Then his wife unexpectedly dies, and he begins a reassessment of his moral situation, and a painful process of rehabilitation.

Mauriac's other novels include Thérèse Desqueyroux *(a chilly investigation of the mind of a woman who has poisoned her husband),* Genetrix *(about a young couple whose love is blighted by the man's monstrous, possessive mother),* The

READ ON

▶ ▷Georges Simenon, *The Shadow Falls* (Le testament Donadieu). ▷Carson McCullers, *Reflections in a Golden Eye*. ▷Graham Greene, *Brighton Rock*. Theodore Dreiser, *Sister Carrie*. ▷Patricia Highsmith, *The People Who Knock on the Door*. John Hergesheimer, *The Three Black Pennies*.

▶ **The idea of the stifling, overbearing family is sent up in:** ▷Ivy Compton-Burnett, *Brothers and Sisters* and ▷Tom Sharpe, *Ancestral Vices*.

Desert of Love *(in which a father and son fall in love with the same woman), and* The Woman of the Pharisees *(about religious bigotry, and the way the middle-aged resent the young).*

MELVILLE, HERMAN (1819–91)

US novelist.

As a teenager, Melville educated himself by reading the Bible, Shakespeare, Milton and Sir Thomas Browne. He served at sea until he was 23, and later worked as a customs officer. His books take their style from the grand literature he read, and their stories from his own seafaring adventures or from travellers' tales. His novels are long, and read at times as if Genesis or Job had been revised to include whaling, smuggling, shipwreck and naval war. But their epic thought and style easily match the magnificence of the books which influenced him.

MOBY-DICK (1851)

Moby Dick is a huge sperm-whale, and the novel tells of Captain Ahab's obsessive attempts to hunt it down and kill it. Melville's whaling-lore is exhaustive, his action-scenes are breath-taking, and he gives an unforgettable picture of Ahab: lonely, driven, daunting as an Old Testament patriarch, a fitting adversary for the monster he has vowed to kill.

Melville's other novels include Typee *and* Omoo, *based on his own experiences after being shipwrecked among cannibals in Polynesia;* Redburn: his First Voyage*;* White-jacket, or The World in a Man-o'-War*; the bitter satire* The Confidence Man *and* Billy Budd, *the story of an inarticulate young sailor who kills a sadistic petty officer.*

THE MIDDLE AGES

▷Italo Calvino, *Our Ancestors*
▷Umberto Eco, *The Name of the Rose*
▷William Golding, *The Spire*
▷Victor Hugo, *Notre Dame de Paris*
Pär Lagerkvist, *The Dwarf*
▷Thomas Mann, *The Holy Sinner*
Ellis Peters, *A Morbid Taste for Bones*
▷Jean Plaidy, *The Bastard King*
Nicolai Tolstoy, *The Coming of the King*
Helen Waddell, *Peter Abelard*

Other Peoples, Other Times (p 192); Renaissance Europe (p 207)

READ ON

- ▷Nathaniel Hawthorne, *The Scarlet Letter*. ▷Victor Hugo, *Toilers of the Sea*. ▷Joseph Conrad, *The Nigger of the Narcissus*.
- **Novels about dark obsessions of other kinds:** ▷Thomas Mann, *Doctor Faustus*; ▷Norman Mailer, *The American Dream*; ▷John Fowles, *The Collector*.

MILLER, WALTER M. (BORN 1922)

US novelist.

In Miller's best-known book, *A Canticle for Leibowitz* (1960), the human race has survived the nuclear holocaust (or 'Great Fallout') at the expense of having to retrace its steps towards 'civilisation'. In the twelfth century of the new era, the curators of knowledge are a group of monks, the Blessed Order of Leibowitz. They pore over their sacred writings, Leibowitz's jottings and research-notes, and try to turn what they read into actuality. Their experiments – which even they view with alarm, tampering with powers beyond their comprehension – will (we know from hindsight) parallel the discoveries of alchemists and scientists from our own time, repeating the cycle which led to the Great Fallout in the first place. In the meantime, in all ignorance, the monks are just making their first experiments with electricity.

Miller's main work consists of short stories, collected in The Darfsteller, Conditionally Human *and* The View from the Stars.

READ ON

- *The Darfsteller* (short story, from the book of the same name, about a human actor who takes the place of an android in the electronic theatre of the future).
- ▶ ▷Russell Hoban, *Riddley Walker*. ▷James Blish, *Black Easter*. ▷Philip K. Dick, *A Maze of Death*. Bamber Gascoigne, *Cod Strewth* (a similar, but comic story: the surviving book is not science but scraps of ▷Rabelais).

MILNE, JOHN (BORN 1952)

British writer.

After three conventional novels (*London Fields*, *Out of the Blue* and *Tyro*) Milne began a series starring Jimmy Jenner, a one-legged, streetwise London private eye – and one of the best crime thriller heroes since Philip Marlowe last hung up his hat. Whenever Jenner picks up his phone, he enters a labyrinth of betrayals, beatings-up, quadruple bluff and equivocal encounters with beautiful girls, world-weary cops and corpses not quite so dead as they ought to be. The books fizz along, propelled not by Chandleresque wisecracks but by a peculiarly English, peculiarly 1990s combination of irony and irritability. Milne's Jenner novels, so far, are *Dead Birds*, *Shadow Play* and *Daddy's Girl*.

READ ON

- ▶ ▷Sara Paretsky, *Indemnity Only*. Robert B. Parker, *The Judas Goat*. Robert Crais, *The Monkey's Raincoat*.

MITCHELL, MARGARET (1900–49)

US novelist.

Gone with the Wind, Mitchell's only book (published in 1936; filmed three years later with Clark Gable and Vivien Leigh) was aptly described in its day as 'the greatest love-story ever told'. In Atlanta, Georgia, at the outbreak of the 1860s American civil war, Scarlett O'Hara falls in love with Ashley Wilkes, the foppish son of a neighbouring plantation-owner,

READ ON

- ▶ ▷Boris Pasternak, *Doctor Zhivago*. ▷Daphne Du Maurier, *Rebecca*. Colleen McCullough, *The Thorn Birds*.

only to discover that he is having an affair with her sister. Heartbroken, she turns to other men, including the cynical, rakish Rhett Butler. The civil war proceeds, the South loses, Atlanta is burned and Scarlett's beautiful house, Tara, is plundered. The devastation of war mirrors the suffering in her heart. She tells Rhett of her hopeless love for Ashley, Rhett leaves her (with a blunt 'Frankly, my dear, I don't give a damn'), and she realises that he was really the man she loved all the time.

M.M. Kaye, *The Far Pavilions.*

MONEY

▷John Galsworthy, *The Forsyte Saga*
Brian Glanville, *The Financiers*
▷Maxim Gorky, *Yegor Bulitchev and Others*
▷Judith Krantz, *Scruples*
Emma Lathen, *Banking on Death*
▷Christina Stead, *House of All Nations*
▷Jerome Weidman, *A Family Fortune*
Donald Westlake, *Bank Shot*

MOORCOCK, MICHAEL (BORN 1939)

British novelist.

In the 1960s Moorcock edited the SF magazine *New Worlds*, pioneering and encouraging 'new wave' writing. The underlying ideas of this are traditional: time-travel, space-opera, sword-and-sorcery. But the literary style is free-wheeling, psychedelic, experimental and poetic. Moorcock's own 'new wave' work is at its peak in his Jerry Cornelius books (eg *The English Assassin*; *The Final Programme*), which are less straightforward novels than firework displays of ideas, magical mystery tours round one man's overheated brain. In later books Moorcock returned to a more sober style, still crammed with ideas but much easier to read. Many of his novels offer alternative versions of the present (*Warlord of the Air*, for example, imagines a 20th century where the first world war never happened and the old 19th century empires, British, Austrian, Russian and German, are still jockeying for power). Others (*Gloriana*; *The Jewel in the Skull*) are satires about societies which are dark and decadent perversions of our own. A good starting-point to his multifarious, dazzling work is the 1970s series 'Dancers at the End of Time' (*An Alien Heat, The Hollow Lands, The End of All Songs* and a cluster of less closely related novels). The time is the very last days of the universe. The few hundred surviving members of the human race control vast energies: anything desired can be obtained by twisting a 'power ring'. Jerek Cornelian (the last human being ever

READ ON

- *The Jewel in the Skull.*
- ▶ ▷Robert Heinlein, *The Number of the Beast*. Robert E. Vardeman and Victor Milan, *The War of Powers*. ▷J.G. Ballard, *The Day of Creation*. ▷Robert Silverberg, *Tom O'Bedlam.*

to be born, an avatar of Jerry Cornelius from the earlier novels) falls in love with a strait-laced Victorian time-traveller, Mrs Amelia Underwood. He follows her back in time, and is promptly stranded in the slums of Victorian London: a typical Moorcock idea, allowing him to collapse history, fantasy, social comment and literary parody – Cornelian gives ▷H.G. Wells the idea for *The Time Machine* – into a single mesmeric and unpredictable experience.

Many of Moorcock's novels are grouped in series: The Chronicles of the Black Sword, The High History of the Runestaff, The Chronicles of Castle Brass, The Books of Corum, The History of the Eternal Champion. *His single novels include* The Ice Schooner, Breakfast in the Ruins *and* Condition of Muzak. The Singing Citadel, Voyage on a Dark Ship *and* The Time Dweller *are collections of short stories.*

MOORE, Brian (BORN 1921)

Irish novelist.

Moore's novels explore personal anguish and unease in a similar way to ▷Graham Greene's, though his characters are quite different. He is particularly good at describing feelings of rootlessness and sexual longing in lonely women (*The Lonely Passion of Judith Hearne*; *The Great Victorian Collection*; *The Doctor's Wife*; *The Temptation of Eileen Hughes*), and the torments of firm Roman Catholic believers in threatening situations (*Catholics*; *Mary Dunne*; *Black Robe* – set, unusually for Moore, in the 17th century, and about a Jesuit missionary captured by North American Indians).

The Colour Of Blood (1987)

Cardinal Bem, head of the Church in an unnamed eastern European communist state, survives an assassination attempt only to be taken into 'protective custody'. He must escape, to make a vital speech at a forthcoming religious celebration – and the book concerns his attempts to shed his physical identity in order to evade police checks, while maintaining the blazing religious and political certainty by which he has always lived his life.

Moore's other novels include Cold Heaven, The Feast of Lupercal, The Mangan Inheritance, An Answer from Limbo *and* Lies of Silence.

READ ON

- *The Doctor's Wife.*
- **To *The Colour of Blood*:** ▷Saul Bellow, *The Dean's December*; ▷Morris West, *The Clowns of God*.
- **To Moore's work in general:** ▷Frederic Raphael, *The Graduate Wife*; ▷Kazuo Ishiguro, *The Remains of the Day*; ▷Peter Carey, *Oscar and Lucinda*.

MOORHOUSE, Frank (BORN 1938)

Australian short-story writer.

Moorhouse's stories are character-sketches: he is less in-

READ ON

- Robert Coover,

terested in plot than in showing states of feeling, emotion and (particularly) psychological disturbance. His complex style (short scenes, jump-cut as in films; dialogue with little indication of who is speaking; no distinction between the description of thoughts and actions, the subjective and the objective), quickly builds up a sense of randomness, of disorientation. Some of his 1960s stories were published in girlie magazines, and their sexual explicitness was considered shocking at the time. His collections are *Futility and Other Animals* (1969, anthropologist's reports on the 'urban tribe' of small-town Australia), *The American Baby* (1972, parodying Australia's infatuation with US culture), *Conference-ville* (1976, set among university students and teachers), *Tales of Mystery and Romance* and *The Everlasting Secret Family and Other Secrets*, both about the obsessions and rituals of 'ordinary' family life. *Forty-Seventeen* (1988) is a set of linked stories forming a 'discontinuous narrative', as Moorhouse puts it: a narrative viewed as if by flashes of lightning.

Pricksongs and Descants. ▷J.D. Salinger, *Nine Stories/For Esmé, with Love and Squalor.* ▷Keri Hulme, *The Windeater.* Anaîs Nin, *Under a Glass Bell.* Richard Brautigan, *Willard and His Bowling Trophy* (novel).

▶ **To *Forty-Seventeen*:** Sherwood Anderson, *Winesburg, Ohio*; ▷Alice Munro, *Who Do You Think You Are?/The Beggar Maid.*

MORRIS, WILLIAM (1834–96)

British craftsman and writer.

At the end of his life Morris (hitherto an artist, designer and philosopher) turned to fiction, writing historical novels and two future-fantasies, *A Dream of John Ball* (1888) and *News From Nowhere* (1891). *News from Nowhere* has the distinction of being one of the very few fantasies to predict a happy future for the human race. Its hero drifts off to sleep during a political meeting in the 1890s, and wakes up to find that he has been transported 60 years forwards in time, and that every socialist dream has been fulfilled. The worker's paradise exists: war, fear, disease and poverty have been eradicated, along with money, prisons and politicians. Everyone is equal, and the harmony between human beings and their environment (the banks of the Thames) is as perfect as it was in Eden before the arrival of the Serpent. Morris' vision is poetic rather than sickly-sweet, and he writes without a twitch of irony. Whatever our hindsight-programmed cynicism a century later, *News from Nowhere* is still a fascinating and remarkable read. If its optimism had been based on Christian rather than humanist beliefs, it might be universally recognised as a major work of visionary literature – which is exactly what it is.

Morris' other fantasies include The House of the Wolfings *(influenced by Icelandic sagas and northern European legends such as Beowulf),* The Wood Beyond the World *and* The Sundering Flood.

READ ON

- *A Dream of John Ball.*

▶ ▷Robert Graves, *Seven Days in New Crete.* Sarah Scott, *Millenium Hall.* ▷Hermann Hesse, *The Glass Bead Game.* Michael Frayn, *Sweet Dreams* (a satire on exactly the kind of liberal-socialist paradise Morris describes – but literal: Frayn's leading character is exploring Heaven itself).

MORRISON, TONI (BORN 1931)
US novelist.

Morrison's books explore the experience of black people in America, from slavery to the present day. She uses history, however, not as a main subject but as the backdrop to a sensitive and witty description of ordinary people's emotions and relationships. What happened to their ancestors, and to black people in general, only partly determines who they are today. Morrison's novels include *The Bluest Eye* (1970), about an ill-treated girl's escape from reality into the fantasy that she has blue eyes, *Song of Solomon* (1977), about a man's attempts to find meaning in his life by exploring the past history of his people, and *Tar Baby* (1981), whose background is the tension between today's 'successful' black people (who may, some of them think, have achieved success by compromising their racial heritage) and the poorer (possibly purer) fellow-citizens from whom they now feel alienated.

READ ON

- *Beloved* (set during the period of national reconstruction after the Civil War); *Sula* (about the friendship of two black women growing up in Ohio in the 1920s–30s).
- ▶ ▷Alice Walker, *Meridian*; John Edgar Wideman, *Reuben*; ▷James Baldwin, *If Beale Street Could Talk*.

MORTIMER, JOHN (BORN 1923)
British writer.

Mortimer is best known for the Rumpole series of TV comedies, about an eccentric, endearing lawyer who wins the cases no one else wants to touch. Two of Mortimer's novels, *Paradise Postponed* (1985) and *Summer's Lease* (1988), have also won millions of friends as TV series. They are affectionate comedies of manners which also concern serious subjects – British politics since 1945 in *Paradise Postponed*; infidelity and possible murder in *Summer's Lease*. But their light-hearted, jovial style sugars the taste of Mortimer's otherwise acid satire on the way the British upper middle class behaves and thinks.

Mortimer's plays include A Voyage Round My Father *and* The Judge. *His Rumpole stories are collected in several volumes, each of which has 'Rumpole' in the title, such as* Rumpole of the Bailey *and* Rumpole's Return. *His novels include* Charade, The Narrowing Stream *and* Like Men Betrayed. Clinging to the Wreckage *is an engaging autobiography.*

READ ON

- ▶ **To the Rumpole stories:** Carter Dickson, *The Men Who Explained Miracles*.
- ▶ **To Mortimer's novels:** ▷H.G. Wells, *Tono-Bungay*; ▷Angus Wilson, *Anglo-Saxon Attitudes*; ▷A.N. Wilson, *Love Unknown*.

MOSCO, MAISIE
British novelist.

Mosco, a prolific romantic novelist, is best-known for the saga of a Jewish family, refugees from early 20th-century European pogroms, who make a new home in northern England. Her detail of Manchester slum existence in the

READ ON

- ▶ Thomas Armstrong, *The Crowther Chronicles*. Claire Rayner, *'Performers'*

first half of this century, and of the closeness of Jewish family and community life, is particularly admired. The books in the sequence (all written in the 1980s) are *Almonds and Raisins*, *Scattered Seed*, *Children's Children* and *Out of the Ashes*.

series. ▷Bernice Rubens, *The Brothers.* ▷Mrs Gaskell, *Mary Barton* and *North and South* give an earlier, even robuster, view of life in industrial Manchester.

MUNRO, ALICE (BORN 1931)

Canadian short-story writer.

Many of Munro's stories are set in the villages and small towns of British Columbia and Ontario, places she depicts as genteel, culturally negligible and bigoted, stagnant since the days of the Model T Ford. Many of her characters are young people of spirit (usually women or girls), stretching the bounds of this environment. Although her themes are modern – feminism, for example – her careful descriptions of the streets, houses, rooms and clothes of her people give the stories a strong nostalgic appeal. She is like one of the gentler Southern US writers (▷Eudora Welty, say) transported north.

Munro's story-collections include Lives of Girls and Women, Something I've Been Meaning to Tell You, The Moons of Jupiter *and* Who Do You Think You Are?/The Beggar Maid, *in which the stories are linked to form an epsisodic novel.*

READ ON

- ▶ ▷Eudora Welty, *The Golden Apples.*
- ▷Katherine Mansfield, *The Dove's Nest and Other Stories.*
- Sherwood Anderson, *Winesburg, Ohio.*
- Edna O'Brien, *A Scandalous Woman and Other Stories.*

MURDER MOST MIND-BOGGLING

John Franklin Bardin, *Devil Take the Blue-Tail Fly*
Edmund Crispin, *The Moving Toyshop*
▷Peter Dickinson, *The Lively Dead*
▷Umberto Eco, *The Name of the Rose*
H.R.F. Keating, *A Rush on the Ultimate*
Cameron McCabe, *The Face on the Cutting-room Floor*
Josephine Tey, *The Singing Sands*

Classic Detection (p 49); Great Detectives (p 104); Private Eyes (p 202)

MURDOCH, IRIS (BORN 1919)

Irish/British novelist and philosopher.

The subject of Murdoch's two dozen novels is personal politics: the ebb and flow of relationships, the way we manipulate others and are ourselves manipulated. The time is now;

READ ON

- *The Book and the Brotherhood.*
- ▶ ▷Mary McCarthy, *A*

Iris MURDOCH

AN UNOFFICIAL ROSE *(nine people, all looking for love; nine intertwined, entangled lives)*

WOMEN ALONE

Anita **BROOKNER, A MISALLIANCE**
(divorced woman, keeping up façade of busy, fulfilled existence, is troubled by chaotic emotional life of people she meets)

Jenni **DISKI, RAINFOREST**
(professor tries to stop intellectual meticulousness destroying emotional life)

Bernice **RUBENS, OUR FATHER**
(archaeologist's meeting with God in Sahara triggers a search of her past and the relationship between her charismatic, enigmatic parents)

Susan **HILL, IN THE SPRINGTIME OF THE YEAR**
(young widow 'rehabilitated' from grief by calm rhythms of country life)

Jane **GARDAM, CRUSOE'S DAUGHTER**
*(*Robinson Crusoe *gives lonely woman purpose in life and grasp on sanity)*

D.M. **THOMAS, THE WHITE HOTEL**
(case-history of disturbed woman, erotic and violent, reflects nightmarish psychic experience of all 20th-century humanity)

SEARCHING FOR SELF

Lisa St Aubin de **TERAN, THE BAY OF SILENCE**
(apparently happy, successful film actress haunted by schizophrenia)

Lawrence **DURRELL, THE DARK LABYRINTH/CEFALÙ**
(group of tourists enter Cretan labyrinth in search of psychic identity – and each quest is unexpectedly fulfilled)

Virginia **WOOLF, TO THE LIGHTHOUSE**
(thoughts and memories of large close family on holiday: projected day-trip to a lighthouse focuses each of their lives)

Eleanor **DARK, RETURN TO COOLAMI**
(four people motoring in Australian outback discover themselves)

Christopher **ISHERWOOD, A MEETING BY THE RIVER**
(two brothers, estranged and 'lost', find Buddhism, true love and tranquility of soul)

Hermann **HESSE, STEPPENWOLF**
(lonely middle-aged recluse 'rehabilitated' spiritually by three mystical, possibly fantasy young people)

LURE OF THE EXOTIC

Olivia **MANNING, THE RAIN FOREST**
(young couple, psychically 'lost', seek solace on magical, sinister tropical island)

Paul **THEROUX, THE MOSQUITO COAST**
(tired of US civilisation, man takes family 'back to nature' in Ecuadorian jungle)

Rosamond **LEHMANN, A SEA-GRAPE TREE**
(deserted wife seeks spiritual and psychic reassurance on Caribbean island)

Patrick **WHITE, VOSS**
(explorers 'find' themselves by trekking across Australia; at home in Sydney, girl waits breathlessly for news)

Isabel **ALLENDE, THE HOUSE OF THE SPIRITS**
(Trueba family women, over four generations, order their lives by magic, fantasy and psychic communion rather than as their patriarch ordains)

Angus **WILSON, THE MIDDLE AGE OF MRS ELIOT**
(widow seeks happiness by surrendering to impulse, going on haphazard Far Eastern odyssey)

the people are middle-class, professional, usually from the English Home Counties – and they are all bizarre, possessed by a demon which blurs reality and dream into a single, mesmeric state. Seduction, mysticism and moral disintegration are favourite themes, and the innocent late adolescent (whose effect on other people's lives is often devastating) is a standard character.

Charmed Life. Alice Thomas Ellis, *The 27th Kingdom*. D.M. Thomas, *Birthstone*. Mary Flanagan, *Trust*. Irene Handl, *The Sioux*.

THE BELL (1958)

Should we live our lives by the conventions of society or moment by moment, defining ourselves by our own changing moods and enthusiasms? This question perplexes every character in *The Bell*: all are waiting for a sudden inspiration or discovery which will define their existence, show them how they should behave. The setting is a lay community housed in a former convent, a refuge for an eccentric collection of inmates whose peace is disturbed by the mechanics of replacing the convent bell and by the arrival of two amoral 'innocents', Dora and Toby. *The Bell* was popular in the hippie 1960s, and still seems to catch the wide-eyed, distracted mood of those times. But its story and characters are fascinating and its images (for example that of the nude, startlingly white-bodied Toby diving, like a fallen angel, into the murky convent lake to investigate a sunken bell) are as disturbing as they are unforgettable.

Murdoch's other novels include The Flight from the Enchanter, The Sandcastle, A Severed Head, The Red and the Green, The Time of the Angels, The Sea, The Sea, The Book and the Brotherhood *and* The Message to the Planet.

MUSIC

▷Anthony Burgess, *The Piano Players*
▷Willa Cather, *The Song of the Lark*
▷Hermann Hesse, *Gertrud*
▷Jack Higgins, *Solo*
▷Thomas Mann, *Doctor Faustus*
▷H.H. Richardson, *The Getting of Wisdom*
Josef Skvorecky, *Dvořák in Love*

N

NABOKOV, Vladimir (1899–1977)

Russian/US novelist and short-story writer.

Nabokov wrote in Russian until 1940, when he settled in the USA; thereafter, he worked in English, and also translated and revised his earlier works. He was fascinated by language, and his books are firework displays of wit, purple-prose descriptions, ironical asides and multi-lingual puns: for his admirers, style is a major pleasure of his work. Several of his novels take the form of teasing 'biographies', revealing as much about their dogged biographers as their subjects. The hero of *The Defence* (1929) is a chess-champion, crippled emotionally both by his profession and by his feeling of identity with the whole Russian cultural tradition. The heroes of *The Real Life of Sebastian Knight* (1941) and *Look at the Harlequins!* (1974) play ironical games with their would-be biographers: the more they seem to reveal themselves, the more elusive they become. *Pnin* (1957) is a sad comedy about an accident-prone Russian professor at a US university, trying to keep the customs of the Old Country in a baffling new environment. *Invitation to a Beheading* (1935) and *Bend Sinister* (1947), Nabokov's most political books, are stories of oppression and nightmare in harsh totalitarian regimes. *Despair* (1934) is a dream-like psychological thriller about a man who hunts down and murders his double, only to find that he has destroyed himself. Humbert Humbert, the tragi-comic hero of *Lolita* (1955), is led by sexual infatuation for a twelve-year-old girl into a farcical kidnapping, a flight from the police through the motels and diners of grubby middle America, and finally to murder. The book's tone of obsessive erotic reverie is repeated in *Ada* (1969),

READ ON

- *Pnin.*
- ▶ **To Nabokov's elegant, games-playing style:** ▷Muriel Spark, *The Abbess of Crewe*; John Barth, *Giles Goat-boy*; ▷Frederic Raphael, *California Time*; ▷Julian Barnes, *Flaubert's Parrot.*
- ▶ **To his darker novels:** ▷Franz Kafka, *The Trial*; ▷Jerzy Kosinski, *The Painted Bird*; ▷Martin Amis, *Success.*
- ▶ **To his short stories:** Donald Barthelme, *City Life.*

about an incestuous love-affair between two rich, spoiled people in a mysterious country midway between 19th-century Russia and the 1930s USA.

PALE FIRE (1962)

Few novels can ever have had such an original form: a 999-line poem with introduction and commentary. The poet is an exiled Eastern European king; the commentator is a fool who fantasises that he is the real heir to the throne, and that he is writing under the shadow of an assassination-plot. The effect is as if ▷Anthony Hope had beefed up someone's PhD thesis: *Pale Fire* is funny, clever – and, despite its bizarre form, a delightfully easy read.

Nabokov's other novels include King, Queen, Knave*;* Glory*;* Camera Obscura/Laughter in the Dark *and* The Gift. Nabokov's Dozen, Nabokov's Quartet, A Russian Beauty, Tyrants Destroyed *and* Details of a Sunset *are short-story collections.* Speak, Memory *is a poetic account of his privileged, pre-Revolutionary Russian childhood.*

NAIPAUL, V.S. (VIDIADHAR SURAJPRASAD)

(BORN 1932)

Trinidadian novelist and non-fiction writer.

A Trinidadian Indian who settled in England in his early 20s, Naipaul identifies exclusively with none of these three communities, and has written about all of them. His early novels (culminating in *A House for Mr Biswas*) were gentle tragi-comedies, but from the late 1960s onwards his books grew darker. He wrote savage non-fiction about the West Indies, India, South America and the Middle East, a mixture of travel and harsh political and social analysis, and his novels dealt with totalitarian oppression and despair. *In a Free State* is about cultural alienation: its central characters are an Indian servant in Washington, a Trinidadian in racist London and two whites in a fanatical black-power Africa. *Guerrillas* is set in a Caribbean dictatorship, *A Bend in the River* in a 'new' African country, emerging from centuries of colonial exploitation into a corrupt, Orwellian state. For most of the 1980s Naipaul wrote no fiction, but in 1987 he published *The Enigma of Arrival*, synthesising most of his earlier themes. Its hero, a Trinidadian writer living near Salisbury, reflects on the way his ambitions and his art have changed as he has grown older, on the nature of friendship, on the passing of 'old England' and, generally, on the breakdown of the former order of the world. The book's tone is sombre, mellow and rueful; it seems more like autobiography than fiction. It is a unique and moving work.

READ ON

- *The Mystic Masseur.*
- ▶ **To the social comedies:** Shiva Naipaul (V.S.'s brother), *Fireflies* ; ▷R.K. Narayan, *Mr Sampath/The Printer of Malgudi*; Amos Tutuola, *The Palm-wine Drinkard*; Timothy Mo, *Sour-Sweet.*
- ▶ **To Naipaul's political novels:** ▷Joseph Conrad, *Nostromo*; Christopher Hope, *Black Swan.*
- ▶ **To *The Enigma of Arrival*:** ▷P.H. Newby, *Leaning in the Wind.*

A HOUSE FOR MR BISWAS (1961)

Mr Biswas is a free spirit shackled by circumstance. He is a poor Hindu in Trinidad, an educated man among illiterates, a good-natured soul who irritates everyone. He marries into an enormous extended family, the Tulsis, and spends the next 20 years trying to avoid being engulfed by their lifestyle, which he finds vulgar and ridiculous. The conflict – critics see it as an allegory about the absorption of political or ethnic minorities – is chiefly expressed in comedy. Mr Biswas is desperate to escape from the Tulsis' rambling mansion, thronged with disapproving relatives; his ambition is to live decently with his family in a home of his own. Although he succeeds, the book ends ironically and tragically: his victory, the vindication of all he stands for, turns to ashes even as he savours it.

Naipaul's other novels include The Suffrage of Elvira, Mr Stone and the Knights Companion *and* The Mimic Men. *His non-fiction books include* The Middle Passage *(on the West Indies and South America),* An Area of Darkness *and* India: a Wounded Civilisation *(two studies, a decade apart, of Indian life and politics) and* Among Believers: an Islamic Journey. The Overcrowded Barracoon *is a collection of essays and articles;* Miguel Street *and* A Flag on the Island *are collections of short stories.*

NARAYAN, R.K. (RASIPURAN KRISHNASWAMI) (BORN 1907)

Indian novelist.

Narayan's stories are set in the imaginary southern Indian town of Malgudi, or in the villages and farms of the nearby Mempi Hills. His characters are shopkeepers, peasant farmers, craftsmen, priests, money-lenders, teachers and housewives, and his theme is the way Hindu belief sustains them in the face of the bewildering or ridiculous events of daily life. Many of his books are comedies. In *The Maneater of Malgudi* (1961) a demented taxidermist works on a series of creatures of ever-increasing size until, to universal panic, he suggests killing and stuffing the town's sacred elephant. The narrator of *A Tiger for Malgudi* (1983) is a worldly-wise tiger who becomes a circus performer, a film star and a travelling guru. *The Painter of Signs* (1976) recounts the farcical relationship between Raman, an ambitious but under-employed sign-painter, and Daisy from the Family Planning Centre, a New Woman whose life is dedicated not to love-affairs but to preventing over-population. Other books replace knockabout with gentler, more bitter-sweet scenes from the human comedy. *The English Teacher/Grate-*

READ ON

- *The Financial Expert.*
- ► Rabindranath Tagore, *The Home and the World*. Anita Desai, *The Clear Light of Day*. S.N. Ghose, *And Gazelles Leaping*. ▷Kazuo Ishiguro, *An Artist of the Floating World*. ▷Tove Jansson, *The Summer Book*. Giovanni Guareschi, *The Little World of Don Camillo* (short stories).

ful to Life and Death (1945) is a beautiful story about a husband coping with grief after the death of his beloved wife. In *The Guide* (1958) a pushy young man sets himself up as a tourist-guide, becomes the manager of a brainless dancer, and finally finds fulfilment not in any such secular enterprise but as a prophet.

THE VENDOR OF SWEETS (1967)

The sweet-manufacturer Jagan is a devout Hindu, a follower of Gandhi. He lives an austere, uncomplicated and self-sufficient life. Then his wastrel son Mali arrives from Delhi with a non-Indian wife and a scheme for enriching himself by marketing a machine for writing novels. Mali and his wife take up residence in Jagan's house, and the old man is torn between love for his son, exasperation, and distress at the contrast between what Mali is doing (which he claims to be in the spirit of the 'new India') and the beliefs and rituals which have sustained Jagan all his life.

Narayan's other novels include Swami and Friends *and* The Bachelor of Arts *(which with* The English Teacher *form a trilogy),* Mr Sampath/The Printer of Malgudi, The Financial Expert *and* The Talkative Man. A Horse and Two Goats, An Astrologer's Day, Lawley Road *and* Malgudi Days *are short-story collections;* My Days *is a placid autobiography.*

NEWBY, P.H. (PERCY HOWARD) (BORN 1918)

British novelist.

The people in Newby's satires have neither the power nor the will to influence events. They are content to let things happen – and those things are unpredictable, dreamlike and bizarre. *Leaning in the Wind* (1986), set in the leafy English countryside, treats its characters like pieces in a surreal board-game. The protagonists are an insurance man who is also a poet, and the daughter of a nazi couple who emigrated to Cincinatti; he loves her, but she loves a Kenyan white settler who may or may not be descended from Shakespeare's sister. The plot revolves with remorseless, inconsequential logic round hauntings, forged manuscripts, betrayals and adulteries – and when the climax of the book demands a rabbit from the hat, out pops Idi Amin, that unlikeliest of conjurer's props.

Newby's other novels include A Journey to the Interior, Picnic at Sakkara, A Season in England, Revolution and Roses, A Guest and his Going, Something to Answer For *and* A Lot to Ask. Ten Miles from Anywhere *is a collection of short stories.*

READ ON

- Michael Frayn, *The Russian Interpreter*. ▷Alison Lurie, *Foreign Affairs*. ▷Evelyn Waugh, *Scoop*. ▷Anthony Powell *What's Become of Waring?*

NINETEENTH-CENTURY ENGLAND

Caryl Brahms and S.J. Simon, *Don't, Mr Disraeli*
Richard Cobbold, *Margaret Catchpole*
▷David Cook, *Sunrising*
▷Charles Dickens, *Hard Times*
▷John Fowles, *The French Lieutenant's Woman*
George and Weedon Grossmith, *The Diary of a Nobody*
▷William Thackeray, *Pendennis*
▷Anthony Trollope, *The Warden*

NYE, ROBERT (BORN 1939)

British writer of novels and children's books.

As well as novels, Nye has written prize-winning children's books and poetry. His best-known adult novel, *Falstaff* (1976), is the 'autobiography' of Shakespeare's fat knight, written as a series of two-or-three-page meditations on such subjects as 'Honour', 'Sherry Sack' and 'Sir John Falstaff's Prick'. Falstaff feels that he has been comprehensively betrayed – by his times, by his family, by his king and above all by his own aging flesh. He looks back on the successes (and excesses) of his life, reshaping awkward facts and warming himself on the memory of gargantuan meals, orgies, pranks and confidence tricks. Nye's wonderful flights of language are sometimes his own, sometimes shameless Shakespeare-borrowings, and his view of late Middle Ages life as a glorious, uninhibited romp – 'eat, drink, fuck, for tomorrow we die' – is swaggering and seductive, so long as you can stay the pace.

Nye's other novels include Merlin *and* The Voyage of the Destiny.

READ ON

- *The Memoirs of Lord Byron: a novel.*
- ▶ **To *Falstaff*:** ▷François Rabelais, *Gargantua*. ▷John Kennedy Toole, *A Confederacy of Dunces*.
- ▶ **To *Merlin*:** Nicolai Tolstoy, *The Coming of the King*.
- ▶ **To *The Voyage of the Destiny*:** ▷William Golding, *Fire Down Below*; Stephen Marlow, *The Memoirs of Christopher Columbus*.
- ▶ **To Nye's work in general:** Petronius, *Satyricon*, Bamber Gascoigne, *Cod Strewth*.

O

OGNIBLAT L'ARTSAU, Mrs: see FRANKLIN, Miles

O'HARA, John (1905–1970)

US novelist and short-story writer.

In 18 novels and no less than 374 short stories, O'Hara created a one-person archive of US life and thought in the first half of this century. He wrote of ordinary middle Americans coping with financial, social, religious and family crises. Many of his stories are told in the first person or in the form of letters, and are strong on irony, revealing the teller's mind or attitudes despite the words he or she uses. The prevailing mood is desperation. O'Hara's people feel that their lives and their country are like monsters out of control; all that can be done is to try to live a decent life, and even that ambition is ambushed by poverty, drink, sex, ambition or politics. This concentration on the darker side of life sometimes leads, in O'Hara's longer books, to melodrama: they deal in a soap-opera style with such issues as abortion, alcoholism or incest. His short stories, by contrast, are well-controlled, single anecdotes, remarkable for their restraint.

O'Hara's story-collections include Files on Parade, Here's O'Hara, The Great Short Stories of O'Hara, 49 Stories, The O'Hara Generation *and* Pal Joey *(which he, Rodgers and Hart made into a successful musical, about an amoral, cynical 1930s night-club owner). His novels include* BUtterfield 8, Ten North Frederick, A Rage to Live *and* The Lockwood Concern.

READ ON

- **To O'Hara's novels:** Ellen Glasgow, *The Sheltered Life*; Jean Stafford, *Boston Adventure*; John Braine, *Room at the Top*; Alberto Moravia, *The Woman of Rome*; Joyce Carol Oates, *Do With Me What You Will*.
- **To O'Hara's short stories:** Sherwood Anderson, *Winesburg, Ohio*; Ring Lardner, *You Know Me, Al*; Peter Taylor, *The Old Forest*; V.S. Pritchett, *When My Girl Comes Home*.

ON THE EDGE OF SANITY

▷Djuna Barnes, *Nightwood*
▷Lawrence Durrell, *The Dark Labyrinth/Cefalù*
▷Graham Greene, *Brighton Rock*
▷Hermann Hesse, *Steppenwolf*
▷Franz Kafka, *The Trial*
▷Malcolm Lowry, *Under the Volcano*
▷Vladimir Nabokov, *Despair*
▷R.K. Narayan, *The English Teacher/Grateful to Life and Death*

Depression and Psychiatry (p 59); Madness (p 166)

ORWELL, GEORGE (1903–50)

British writer.

'George Orwell' was the pseudonym of Eric Blair. In his 20s he worked for the Colonial Police in Burma (an experience he later used in the novel *Burmese Days*). He returned to England disgusted with Imperialism and determined never again to work for or support 'the system'. In fact most of his work thereafter was literary: articles, essays and books taking a jaundiced view of British society and attitudes. Commissioned to report on the industrial north of England, he wrote *The Road to Wigan Pier* (1937), an indictment not only of unemployment and poverty but also of the failure of idealists, of all political parties, to find a cure. *Down and Out in Paris and London* (1933) is a description of the life of tramps and other derelicts; *Homage to Catalonia* (1938) is a withering account of the failure of the International Brigade in the Spanish Civil War. During the 1930s Orwell published three ▷Wellsian novels, about people dissatisfied with the constricting middle-class or lower-middle-class lives they led. It was not until 1945, when the second world war seemed to have blown away forever the humbug and complacency which Orwell considered the worst of all British characteristics, that he published his first overtly political book, *Animal Farm*. In this Stalinist 'fairy story', pigs turn their farm into a workers' democracy in which 'all animals are equal, but some are more equal than others', and the rule of all quickly degenerates into the tyranny of the few. The success of *Animal Farm* encouraged Orwell to write an even more savage political fantasy, *1984*.

1984 (1949)

In the totalitarian future, Winston Smith's job is to rewrite history, adding to or subtracting from the record people who are in or out of Party favour. He falls in love – a forbid-

READ ON

- **To the savage politics of *1984*:** Victor Serge, *The Case of Comrade Tulayev*; Arthur Koestler, *Darkness at Noon*; ▷Franz Kafka, *The Trial*; ▷Vladimir Nabokov, *Bend Sinister*.
- **Future-fantasies of a similarly bleak kind:** Yevgeni Zamyatin, *We*; ▷Aldous Huxley, *Brave New World*; ▷Anthony Burgess, *A Clockwork Orange*. (Burgess also wrote *1985*, a right-wing riposte to *1984*.)
- ▷Mario Vargas Llosa. *The City and the Dogs/The Time of the Hero,* set in a Peruvian military academy, is that rare thing, an Orwellian political allegory which is also funny.

George ORWELL

1984 *(repression and oppression in grim totalitarian future)*

Alexander **SOLZHENITSYN, ONE DAY IN THE LIFE OF IVAN DENISOVICH** *(repression of dissidents in Stalinist labour-camp)*

Maxim **GORKY, FOMA GORDEEV**
(underbelly of Tsarist Russia in decline)

Nathaniel **HAWTHORNE, THE SCARLET LETTTER**
(religious bigotry in Pilgrim Fathers America)

Margaret **ATWOOD, THE HANDMAID'S TALE**
(grim future: totalitarian, religious oppression, anti-women)

Fay **WELDON, LIFE AND LOVES OF A SHE-DEVIL**
(betrayed wife takes macabre, comic revenge)

William **GOLDING, LORD OF THE FLIES**
(schoolboys revert to barbarism after being marooned from civilisation)

Joseph **CONRAD, HEART OF DARKNESS**
(wilderness as a satanic, engulfing force, human evil symbolised)

Paul **THEROUX, O-ZONE**
(efforts to make a viable post-nuclear society in US wilderness)

Patrick **WHITE, A FRINGE OF LEAVES**
('civilised' woman in distress, rehabilitated by contact with aboriginal, 'primitive' people)

Willa **CATHER, DEATH COMES FOR THE ARCHBISHOP**
(Catholic missionaries test their faith in 1870s Mexican wilderness)

Anthony **BURGESS, A CLOCKWORK ORANGE**
(crime and class-war in future Britain)

Graham **GREENE, BRIGHTON ROCK**
(crime and redemption in 1930s England)

Georges **SIMENON, THE MURDERER**
(criminal psychologically destroyed by guilt)

den thing, because it arises from freewill and not by order of the Party – and is betrayed to the Thought Police. He is tortured until he not only admits, but comes to believe, that the Party is right in everything: if it says that 2 + 2 = 5, then that is so. The book ends, chillingly, with the idea that Winston has won the victory over himself: he is happy because he has chosen, of his own free will, to have no choice.

Orwell's 1930s novels are A Clergyman's Daughter, Keep the Aspidistra Flying *and* Coming Up for Air. *A collection of his essays, articles and letters was published in 1968.*

OTHER PEOPLES, OTHER TIMES
(historical novels set in remote or unusual times)

Jean M. Auel, *Clan of the Cave Bear* (prehistoric Europe)
James Clavell, *Shōgun* (17th-century Japan)
▷Eleanor Dark, *The Timeless Land* (18th-century Australia)
▷Gustave Flaubert, *Salammbô* (ancient Carthage)
▷Norman Mailer, *Ancient Evenings* (ancient Egypt)
Naomi Mitchison, *Early in Orcadia* (prehistoric Orkneys)
▷Robert Silverberg, *Gilgamesh the King* (ancient Sumeria)
▷Sigrid Undset, *Kristin Lavransdatter* (14th-century Norway)
▷Mario Vargas Llosa, *The War of the End of the World* (19th-century Peru)

Ancient Greece and Rome (p 9); Bible (p 24)

P

Parents And Children

Samuel Butler, *The Way of All Flesh*
Margaret Forster, *Private Papers*
▷Hermann Hesse, *Rosshalde*
▷D.H. Lawrence, *Sons and Lovers*
▷Ivan Turgenev, *Fathers and Sons*
▷John Updike, *The Centaur*

Adolescence (p 2); All-engulfing Families (p 5); Eccentric Families (p 73); Growing Up: Teenagers (p 105); Many Generations (p 170)

PARETSKY, Sara (born 1947)

US novelist.

Paretsky is one of ▷Chandler's best present-day followers. Her private eye, V.I. Warshawski, moves in a murky world of drug-trafficking, union corruption, medical fraud and lethal religious politics. Warshawski is a crack shot, a karate expert, and has an armoury of brusingly unanswerable one-liners. She is also devastatingly beautiful, and combines contempt for masculine bravado with a willingness to go weak at the knees whenever a gorgeous hunk swims into view.

The Warshawski books are Indemnity Only, Deadlock, Killing Orders, Bitter Medicine, Toxic Shock *and* Burn Marks.

READ ON

▶ Eve Zaremba, *Beyond Hope*. Loren D. Estleman, *Every Brilliant Eye*. Rex Stout, *The Hand in the Glove*. ▷John Milne, *Shadow Play*.

PASTERNAK, BORIS (1890-1960)
Russian poet and novelist.

In the USSR Pasternak is remembered chiefly as a poet and translator (of ▷Goethe and Shakespeare). Western readers know him for his 1957 novel *Doctor Zhivago,* and for the savage reaction of the Soviet authorities of the time, who banned the book and made Pasternak renounce his Nobel prize. *Doctor Zhivago* is about a doctor, Zhivago, and a teacher, Lara, caught up in the civil war which followed the 1917 Revolution. Although each is married to someone else and has a child, they fall in love – and the feverishness of their affair is increased by knowledge that neither it nor they will survive the war, since they come from a doomed class, the bourgeoisie. Horrified and powerless, they witness the brutality, class hatred and fury which precede the establishment of the USSR. Despite the reaction of the late-1950s authorities to all this, Pasternak was not really concerned with politics. He was more interested in the idea of people out of step with their time, star-crossed by destiny, and in the way Zhivago's and Lara's relationship was an emotional counterpart to the chaos and destruction all round them. The book ends with Zhivago's poems about Lara, like faded love-letters plucked from the rubble of the past.

READ ON

- ▷Lev Tolstoy, *Anna Karenina.* ▷Ernest Hemingway, *A Farewell to Arms.* ▷Elizabeth Bowen, *The Heat of the Day.* ▷Margaret Mitchell, *Gone With the Wind.* ▷Iris Murdoch, *The Red and the Green.*

PEAKE, MERVYN (1911–68)
British novelist and artist.

Peake earned his living as an artist, drawing cartoons and grotesque, sombre illustrations to such books as *Treasure Island* and *The Hunting of the Snark.* He also made portraits of the main characters in his own novels: unsmiling freaks with distorted limbs and haunted eyes, violently cross-hatched as if with giant cobwebs. He admired ▷Poe and ▷Kafka, and his own work lopes gleefully – and hilariously – down the same dark passages of the imagination, peering into every corner and detailing the horrors that wait behind every moss-grown, rust-hinged door.

GORMENGHAST (1946–59)
The 'Gormenghast' trilogy *Titus Groan, Gormenghast* and *Titus Alone* takes place in a mist-shrouded, monstrous kingdom surrounding the crumbling Gothic castle of Gormenghast. Evil broods, ever undefined but waiting to pounce. Everyone, from Lord Sepulchrave himself to the physician Prunesquallor, from Nanny Slagg to the demented, crippled scullion Steerpike, lives every second of each day by a precise, bizarre ritual, as compulsive and pointless as the movements of the insane. *Titus Groan* describes the fearful consequences when Steerpike, to further

READ ON

- **To *Gormenghast*;** ▷Mary Shelley, *Frankenstein;* ▷Edgar Allan Poe, *The Fall of the House of Usher;* ▷Tom De Haan, *A Mirror for Princes;* ▷Stanislaw Lem, *Memoirs Found in a Bathtub;* Iain Banks, *Walking on Glass.*
- **To *Mr Pye*:** Paul Gallico, *Flowers for Mrs Harris.*

Mervyn PEAKE

GORMENGHAST *(Titus Groan uncovers his destiny in sinister castle-kingdom)*

SUPERNATURAL TERROR

Dennis **WHEATLEY, THE KA OF GIFFORD HILLARY**
(while Hillary sleeps, 'other self' leads malign independent life)

James **HERBERT, THE MAGIC COTTAGE**
(young couple move into macabre haunted house)

Bram **STOKER, DRACULA**
(vampire Count)

Stephen **KING, PET SEMETARY**
(ghosts walk in rural Maine)

Edgar Allan **POE, TALES OF MYSTERY AND IMAGINATION** *(madness, buried alive, and living dead)*

DERANGEMENT AND MADNESS

Sylvia **PLATH, THE BELL JAR**
(treatment for suicidal depressive mania)

Patricia **HIGHSMITH, THE GLASS CELL**
(man driven mad by prison, has wife been faithful?)

Ken **KESEY, ONE FLEW OVER THE CUCKOO'S NEST**
(lunatics take over the asylum)

Robert **SILVERBERG, TOM O'BEDLAM**
(are Tom's visions madness or manifestations of genuine alien gods?)

FANTASY SOCIETIES

Tom **DE HAAN, A MIRROR FOR PRINCES**
(disturbed family of 'medieval' dictator wait for his death)

Ursula **LE GUIN, MALAFRENA**
(Napoleonic Europe – or its mirror)

Robert **SILVERBERG, LORD VALENTINE'S CASTLE**
(young man – good – gathers followers to battle usurper)

Robert **IRWIN, THE ARABIAN NIGHTMARE**
(man on medieval pilgrimage is trapped in his own dreams)

Jack **VANCE, THE BLUE WORLD**
(floating worlds in water-paradise – but beware sea-monsters)

OLD, DARK HOUSES AND CASTLES

Daphne **DU MAURIER, REBECCA**
(what is the secret of Manderley?)

Angela **CARTER, THE MAGIC TOYSHOP**
(adolescent orphan goes to live with deranged puppeteer-uncle)

Michael **INNES, LAMENT FOR A MAKER**
(who killed the mad Laird of Erchany? What is the meaning behind the curse?)

Susan **HILL, THE WOMAN IN BLACK**
(ghosts walk in rural England)

Henry **JAMES, THE TURN OF THE SCREW**
(who can exorcise the ghosts which haunt the children?)

his own dark ambitions, starts fomenting social revolution. *Gormenghast* is about the growing-up of Titus, 77th Earl of Groan: how he learns about his inheritance, uncovers the castle's secrets and begins to chafe against the rituals which choke its people's lives. In *Titus Alone* Titus breaks free of the castle and explores the country outside, an arrogant knight-errant on a terrifying, pointless quest.

Peake's only other novel, Mr Pye, *is a gentler story about a man on Sark in the Channel Islands who shows distressing signs of turning into an angel. 'Peake's Progress', an anthology of his poems, plays and drawings, is a splendid introduction to his work and includes an extra Gormenghast story,* A Boy in Darkness.

PERPLEXED BY LIFE

(people battling to understand and control their destiny)

▷Saul Bellow, *Humboldt's Gift*
▷Albert Camus, *The Fall*
▷Erica Jong, *Fear of Flying*
▷Hermann Hesse, *Rosshalde*
▷Iris Murdoch, *The Sandcastle*
▷V.S. Naipaul, *A House for Mr Biswas*
▷Italo Svevo, *The Confessions of Zeno*
▷Angus Wilson, *Anglo-Saxon Attitudes*

Battling with Life (p 20); Growing Up: Teenagers (p 105); Revisiting One's Past (p 209)

PIRANDELLO, Luigi (1867-1936)

Italian writer of novels, short stories and plays.

Although Pirandello is chiefly known for such experimental plays as *Six Characters in Search of an Author*, he was also a prolific short-story writer and the author of six novels about aristocratic and peasant life in late 19th-century Sicily. His 250 stories take as their starting-point the kind of mundane crimes – adultery, fraud, murder – which figure in the 'news in brief' columns of tabloid newspapers: lip-smacking gossip about total strangers. But Pirandello regards each sensational event as the release of a long build-up of tension or psychological panic – and that build-up is his subject. He shows us people trapped by convention, by their own passions and longings, and by the malevolence of others. If you stripped the music from Puccini's operas and boiled their plots and motivation down to half a dozen pages of lucid, implacable prose, the results might be very similar.

Pirandello's novels include The Late Mattia Pascal, The Old

READ ON

► Alberto Moravia, *Roman Tales*. Cesare Pavese, *Nice Summer*. Ivan Klíma, *My First Loves*. William Saroyan, *The Insurance Salesman and Other Stories*. George Moore, *Celibate Lives*. ▷Vladimir Nabokov, *The Real Life of Sebastian Knight* (novel).

and the Young *and* One, None and a Hundred Thousand. *A good, representative story-collection is* Better Think Twice About It.

PLACES

Melvyn Bragg, *The Maid of Buttermere* (English Lake District)
▷Emily Brontë, *Wuthering Heights* (Yorkshire moors)
▷Graham Greene, *The Comedians* (Haiti)
▷Thomas Hardy, *Jude the Obscure* (rural Wessex)
▷John Irving, *The Cider-house Rules* (rural Maine)
▷Rudyard Kipling, *Kim* (rural India)
▷R.K. Narayan, *The Painter of Signs* (small-town India)

Deep South, USA (p 57); Ireland (p 131); Israel (p 133); Japan (p 136); Scotland (p 220); Small Town Life, USA (p 227); USSR (p 252); The Wilderness (p 270)

PLAIDY, JEAN (BORN 1906)
British novelist.

'Jean Plaidy' is one of the pseudonyms of Eleanor ▷Hibbert. She is the author of over 80 light historical novels, most of them based on the intrigues surrounding European royal marriages, accessions and other political and dynastic events. Several of her best-known books are grouped in series, including the 'Norman Trilogy' (beginning with *The Bastard King*, 1975, about William the Conqueror), the 'Plantagenet Saga' (based on the Wars of the Roses) and the 'Mary Queen of Scots' series.

Plaidy's other books include The Spanish Bridegroom, A Health Unto his Majesty, Flaunting Extravagant Queen, Perdita's Prince, Sweet Lass of Richmond Hill *and* The Prince and the Quakeress.

READ ON

▶ Margaret Irwin, *Young Bess*. Tyler Whittle, *The Young Victoria*. Anya Seton, *Katherine*. Caryl Brahms and S.J. Simon, *No Bed for Bacon* (an Elizabethan spoof).

POE, EDGAR ALLAN (1809–49)
US short-story writer.

Poe's miserable life is almost as well-known as his stories. He was an orphan whose foster-father hated him; he was thrown out of university, military college and half a dozen jobs because of the instability of his character; in order to earn a living he suppressed his real ambition (to be a poet) in favour of hack journalism and sensational fiction; he gambled, fornicated, and finally drank himself to death. He was like a man haunted by his own existence – and this is exactly the feeling in his macabre short stories, which are less

READ ON

▶ **To Poe's stories of the macabre:** H.P. Lovecraft, *Dagon and Other Macabre Tales*; M.R. James, *Ghost Stories of an Antiquary*; Roald Dahl, *Switch Bitch*; ▷Stephen King,

about the supernatural than about people driven crazy by their own imagination. 'The Fall of the House of Usher' and 'The Premature Burial' recount the terrifying results when people are accidentally entombed alive. The murderer in 'The Tell-tale Heart' buries his victim under the floorboards, only to be haunted by what he takes to be the thud of the dead man's heartbeat. The hero of 'The Pit and the Pendulum' is psychologically tortured by the Spanish Inquisition, first by fear of a swinging, ever-approaching blade and then by the way the walls of his cell move inwards to crush him. In 'The Black Cat' a murderer is given away by the mewing of a cat which he has accidentally walled up with his victim's body. As well as stories of this kind, Poe occasionally wrote lighter mysteries. The best-known of all ('The Murders in the Rue Morgue'; 'The Mystery of Marie Roget') centre on an eccentric investigator who solves crimes by meticulous reconstruction according to the evidence: they are the first-ever detective-stories.

Poe's stories are normally collected nowadays as Tales of Mystery and Imagination. *His other writings include poetry (*The Bells; The Raven*) and vitriolic literary criticism, savaging such contemporaries as Longfellow.*

Night Shift; ▷James Herbert, *Moon* (novel).

▶ **To the detection-stories:** ▷A. Conan Doyle, *The Adventures of Sherlock Holmes*; Edgar Wallace, *The Four Just Men*; ▷Isaac Asimov, *Tales of the Black Widowers*; John Dickson Carr, *The Men Who Explained Miracles*.

Police Procedural

Wilkie Collins, *The Woman in White*
Freeman Wills Crofts, *Death of a Train*
Nicolas Freeling, *Cold Iron*
▷Ed McBain, *Lightning*
▷Ruth Rendell, *A Guilty Thing Surprised*
Maj Sjöwall and Per Wahlöö, *The Laughing Policeman*
Martin Cruz Smith, *Gorky Park*

Politics

▷Chinua Achebe, *Anthills of the Savannah*
Jorge Amado, *The Violent Land*
▷Richard Condon, *Mile High*
Benjamin Disraeli, *Coningsby*
Martha Gellhorn, *A Stricken Field*
Arthur Koestler, *Darkness at Noon*
▷George Orwell, *Animal Farm*
Amos Oz, *A Perfect Peace*
Howard Spring, *Fame is the Spur*
▷C.P. Snow, *The Corridors of Power*
▷Gore Vidal, *Burr*

PORTER, KATHARINE ANNE (1890-1980)

US novelist and short-story writer.

Many of Porter's short stories, set in Texas, are accounts of ordinary matters – the relationship of old and young, swimming, the conversation of farm-workers, the coming of a circus – seen through the eyes of a child. They are wistful and nostalgic, depicting human existence as both beautiful and transient. Her major work, the 500-page novel *Ship of Fools* (1962), is in a harsher, allegorical vein. The ship of fools is the world, and the passengers are the human race, cruising to disaster. Porter's ship is sailing from Vera Cruz to Bremerhaven in 1931. The crew and most of the passengers are German; the other travellers are Mexican, Swedish, Swiss, American, and above all Spanish: 870 plantation-workers being sent home because of a slump in the sugar trade, and a troupe of sinister dancers. At the start of the voyage, the people are determined to be friendly; but soon divisions of class, race, nation and politics begin to surface, and the outcome is war. The lumpishness of this allegory is offset by the refinement of Porter's writing: the book reads like a collaboration by ▷Chekhov and ▷Conrad, unlikely but persuasive.

Porter's story-collections are Flowering Judas*;* Pale Horse, Pale Rider *(three short novels);* The Leaning Tower *and* The Old Order. *Her* Collected Stories *appeared in 1967.*

READ ON

- **To Porter's stories:** ▷Eudora Welty, *The Golden Apples*; ▷Willa Cather, *The Troll Garden*; Seán O'Faoláin, *Foreign Affairs*.
- **To *Ship of Fools:*** ▷Joseph Conrad, *Typhoon*; ▷Patrick White, *Voss*.

POWELL, ANTHONY (BORN 1905)

British novelist.

In the 1930s Powell wrote half a dozen novels satirising the intellectual and upper classes of the time. The optimistic, aimless young people of *Afternoon Men* drift from party to party, trying to summon up enough willpower to make something of themselves. *From a View to a Death/Mr Zouch: Superman* sets the arts and foxhunting at each other's throats. The hero of *What's Become of Waring?* has to find someone to write the biography of a best-selling travel-writer who has disappeared in circumstances which grow more mysterious, and more unsavoury, by the minute. After the second world war, during which he produced no fiction, Powell abandoned single books for a 12-novel sequence, *A Dance to the Music of Time,* a satirical portrait of 70 years of English high society and establishment life.

A DANCE TO THE MUSIC OF TIME (1951–75)

The sequence follows its characters from Edwardian schooldays to nostalgic, worldly-wise old age. The narrator, Nick Jenkins, discreet as a civil servant, goes everywhere,

READ ON

- **To Powell's 1930s books:** ▷Evelyn Waugh, *Vile Bodies*; Henry Green, *Party Going*; ▷Rose Macaulay, *Crewe Train*. The mood of elegiac, upper-class malice characteristic of *A Dance to the Music of Time* is repeated in three other novel sequences – ▷Marcel Proust, *Remembrance of Things Past* (*A la recherche du temps perdu*); Simon

knows everyone, and writes of his contemporaries (notably the ambition-racked Widmerpool) in elegant, ironic prose. The books move imperturbably from farce to seriousness, from knockabout to reverie. The first three novels, *A Question of Upbringing, A Buyer's Market* and *The Acceptance World,* concern the characters' schooldays, their Oxbridge careers and their entry into the glittering smart set of 1920s London. *At Lady Molly's, Casanova's Chinese Restaurant* and *The Kindly Ones* are about first jobs, marriages and the establishment of a network of sexual, social, financial and political alliances which will bind their lives. *The Valley of Bones, The Soldier's Art* and *The Military Philosophers* take the characters through two world wars, and *Books Do Furnish a Room, Temporary Kings* and *Hearing Secret Harmonies* show them coming to terms with post-war austerity, the white heat of the technological revolution and flower-power, reflecting on the change not only in themselves but in every aspect of British establishment life since their schooldays 50 years before.

Powell's other 1930s novels are Venusberg *and* Agents and Patients. *After finishing* A Dance to the Music of Time *he wrote an autobiography,* To Keep the Ball Rolling, *and two other (unrelated) novels,* O, How the Wheel Becomes It *and* The Fisher King.

Raven, *Alms for Oblivion*; Stuart Evans, *Windmill Hill* – and in the single novels Edward Candy, *Scene Changing;* Emma Tennant, *The House of Hospitalities* and ▷Frederic Raphael, *Orchestra and Beginners.*

POWYS, JOHN COWPER (1872–1963)

British novelist and non-fiction writer.

A university professor, Powys wrote books on ▷Dostoevski, ▷Homer and ▷Rabelais, dozens of articles, reviews and other non-fiction works, and a lively autiobiography. His early novels (*Ducdame*; *Rodmoor*; *Wolf Solent,* all written before 1930) are sombre, ▷Hardyish stories about the farmers and fishermen of the English West Country. After he retired from teaching Powys wrote a series of completely different novels: long, mystical books influenced by Homer and the Old Testament and drawing on English legend and dark ages history. In *A Glastonbury Romance* modern inhabitants of the Glastonbury area (including worshippers and clergy at the Abbey) find their lives mysteriously affected by local legends of King Arthur and of the Holy Grail. In a similar way, *Maiden Castle* describes how unearthing the distant past – some of the characters are archaeologists working on a prehistoric site – disturbs the present. *Owen Glendower* and *Porius* are historical romances, full of wizards, giants and ancient magic. *The Bronze Head* is about Roger Bacon, the first scientist (or last alchemist). In *Atlantis* the hero of Homer's *Odyssey* embarks on a quest to find the lost continent.

READ ON

- **To Powys' early novels:** ▷Victor Hugo, *Toilers of the Sea*; ▷George Eliot, *Silas Marner*; ▷Nathaniel Hawthorne, *The Scarlet Letter.*
- **To *A Glastonbury Romance*:** ▷Lawrence Durrell, *The Dark Labyrinth/ Cefalù*; Charles Williams, *War in Heaven.*
- **To the late historical novels:** ▷Sigrid Undset, *Kristin Lavransdatter*; Peter Vansittart, *Three Six Seven*; Pär

Lagerkvist, *The Sibyl*; ▷Gore Vidal, *Creation*.

PRICHARD, KATHARINE SUSANNAH (1883-1969)
Australian novelist.

Prichard was a political activist, and her best-known novels deal with matters of social concern, mainly in the 1920s and 1930s. *Working Bullocks* is the study of a community of timber workers in Western Australia, fighting the introduction of streamlined methods which will destroy their employment prospects. *Coonardoo* is about the confrontation of white people and aborigines. The 'goldfields trilogy' *The Roaring Nineties, Golden Miles* and *Winged Seeds* (1946–50) is a densely-organised multi-generation saga, also set in Western Australia, from the gold-rush days of the 19th century, through the industrialisation and political confrontation of the 1920s to post-second-world-war decline.

Prichard's other novels include Black Opal *(about a mining community threatened by big-business takeovers),* Intimate Strangers *(about a bickering couple whose marriage is saved by their shared political enthusiasms) and* Haxby's Circus *(about a husband-and-wife team struggling to run a travelling circus).* The Wild Oats of Han, *a children's book, is based on her idyllic childhood in Tasmania.*

READ ON

- ▷Émile Zola, *Germinal*. Mrs Gaskell, *Mary Barton*. Upton Sinclair, *The Jungle*. ▷John Steinbeck, *The Grapes of Wrath*.

PRIESTLEY, J.B. (JOHN BOYNTON) (1894-1984)
British novelist and playwright.

As well as plays and non-fiction books, Priestley wrote over 60 novels. They range from amiable satire (eg *Low Notes on a High Level*, 1956, sending up egghead BBC musicians) to sombre social realism (eg *Angel Pavement*, 1936, about a sleepy 1930s business firm galvanised into new activity and then destroyed by a confidence trickster). His best-loved novel, *The Good Companions* (1929), tells of three people who escape from humdrum lives to join the Dinky Doos concert party in the 1920s. The novel follows the concert party's career in theatres and seaside resorts all over England, and ends with each of the main characters finding self-fulfilment in an entirely unexpected way. The book bulges with show-biz cliché – brave little troupers; lodging-house keepers with hearts of gold; leading ladies and their tantrums; cynical, hung-over leading men – and with warm-hearted nostalgia for the provincial England of the Good Old Days. It is an armchair of a novel, a book to wallow in – and if life was never really like that, so much the worse for life.

READ ON

- *Lost Empires* (a darker story, about music-hall performers in 1913; *The Image Men* (a satire about advertising and television).
- **To *The Good Companions*:** Bamber Gascoigne, *The Heyday*; Noel Langley, *There's a Porpoise Close Behind Us*.
- **To Priestley's books in general:** ▷H.G. Wells, *Tono-Bungay*; James Hilton,

Goodbye, Mr Chips;
Eric Linklater,
Poet's Pub.

PRITCHETT, V.S. (VICTOR SAWDON) (BORN 1900)

British writer.

Although Pritchett has written books of many kinds (biography, criticism, novels, travel), he is best known for his short stories. He writes of ordinary people, middle class, middle income, middle aged, falling in love, quarrelling, cheating one another, enjoying small triumphs and suffering small disasters with as much concentration and effort as if they were living *War and Peace*. In 'The Fall', for example, a seedy salesman at a conference, boasting that his glamorous filmstar brother taught him how to do stage falls, has his moment of glory, time and time again, as people buy him drinks to demonstrate his skill. In 'The Camberwell Beauty' an antique dealer tries to rescue a woman hoarded like a piece of prize porcelain by a rival. In 'The Lady from Guatemala' a self-obsessed editor falls ludicrously for a girl who pursues him on a lecture tour. Drabness and seedy dignity are favourite themes of British short-story writers; Pritchett writes of them with steely detachment, as if he has understanding, but absolutely no pity, for his characters' small lives.

Pritchett's Collected Stories *were published in 1984. The best known of his individual collections are* You Make Your Own Life, When My Girl Comes Home *and* The Camberwell Beauty. *His novels – a similar blend of tartness and wistfulness – include* Nothing Like Leather, Dead Man Leading *and* Mr Beluncle. A Cab at the Door *and* Midnight Oil *are autobiography.*

READ ON

- **To Pritchett's short stories:** William Trevor, *The Day We Got Drunk on Cake*; ▷Katherine Mansfield, *The Garden Party and Other Stories*; ▷Elizabeth Bowen, *The Demon Lover*.
- **To his novels:** ▷Angus Wilson, *The Middle Age of Mrs Eliot*; ▷Mary Wesley, *Second Fiddle*.

PRIVATE EYES

Andrew Bergman, *The Big Kiss-off of 1944*
▷Raymond Chandler, *Farewell, My Lovely*
▷Dashiell Hammett, *The Maltese Falcon*
Ross Macdonald, *Sleeping Beauty*
▷John Milne, *Dead Birds*
Robert R. Parker, *The Judas Goat*
Jonathan Valine, *Lime Pit*

Classic Detection (p 49); Great Detectives (p 104);
Murder Most Mind-Boggling (p 181)

PROUST, MARCEL (1871-1922)
French novelist.

Proust's *Remembrance of Things Past* (A la recherche du temps perdu) (1913–27; magnificently translated by C.K. Scott Moncrieff and Terence Kilmartin) is in seven sections *Swann's Way, Within a Budding Grove, The Guermantes Way, Cities of the Plain, The Captive, The Fugitive, Time Regained)*. Each is as long as a normal novel and each can be read both on its own and as part of the whole huge tapestry. The book is a memoir, told in the first person by a narrator called Marcel, of a group of rich French socialites from the 1860s to the end of the first world war. It shows how they react to outside events – the Dreyfus case, women's emancipation, the first world war – and how, as the world moves on, their power and social position wane. Above all, it shows them reacting to each other, to friends, acquaintances and servants: the book is full of love-affairs, parties (at which gossip is hot about who is 'in' or 'out' and why), alliances and betrayals. Through it all moves Marcel himself, good-natured, self-effacing, fascinated by beauty (both human and artistic: his accounts of music and literature are as deeply-felt as those of people), and with a sharply ironical eye for social and sexual absurdity. Proust developed for the book a system of 'involuntary memory', in which each sensual stimulus – the smell of lilac, the taste of cake dipped in tea – unlocks from the subconscious a stream of images of the past. Though this technique has structural importance in the novel – Proust believed that our present only makes sense when it is refracted through past experience – its chief effect for the reader is to provide pages of languorous, detailed descriptions, prose poems on everything from the feel of embroidery under the finger-tips to garden sounds and scents on a summer evening. Proust likes to take his time: at one point Marcel spends nearly 100 pages wondering whether to get up or stay in bed. But only the length at which he works allows him scope for the sensuous, malicious decadence which is the main feature of his work.

Proust's other writings include translations of Ruskin's The Bible of Amiens *and* Sesame and Lilies, *a collection of short stories and literary parodies,* The Pleasures and the Days *Les Plaisirs et les jours, and* Jean Santeuil, *a draft of part of* Remembrance of Things Past.

PUBLISH AND BE DAMNED
(writers; publishers; agents; readers; fans)

▷Margery Allingham, *Flowers for the Judge*
▷Erica Jong, *How To Save Your Own Life*

READ ON

- **Good parallels to the sensuous childhood-evocations of the first part of *Remembrance of Things Past*:** Alain Fournier, *The Lost Domain*/(Le grand Meaulnes); ▷James Joyce, *Portrait of the Artist as a Young Man*.
- **Echoing the hedonism and decadence of some of Proust's later sections:** Joris-Karl Huysmans, *Against Nature* (A rebours).
- **Good on 'the texture of experience':** Dorothy Richardson, *Pilgrimage*; ▷Virginia Woolf, *The Waves*; John Dos Passos, *Manhattan Transfer*.
- **Novel-sequences of comparable grandeur:** ▷Anthony Powell, *A Dance to the Music of Time*; Henry Williamson, *The Flax of Dream*. (Willimson's later sequence *(A Chronicle of Ancient Sunlight)* starts well, but is hijacked half-way through by the author's fascist sympathies.)

▷Wyndham Lewis, *The Apes of God*
▷Rose Macaulay, *Crewe Train*
▷Anthony Powell, *What's Become of Waring?*
▷Philip Roth, *Zuckerman Unbound*
▷Tom Sharpe, *The Great Pursuit*

PUZO, MARIO (BORN 1920)

US novelist and screenwriter.

Puzo began his career as a writer of children's books, but in 1969 turned to adult fiction and had one of the biggest commercial successes in publishing history with *The Godfather*. The story concerns the New York mafia family the Corleones. It centres on Don Vito Corleone's handover of authority to his son Michael – a gift akin to being made successor to Genghis Khan – and on the power-struggle, both with outsiders and between members of the family, to which this leads. Present-day events are intercut with flashbacks to Don Vito's Sicilian childhood and his early days in the USA. The plot of *The Godfather* is in a direct line from those of such multi-generation family and big-business sagas as the novels of Harold Robbins. But Puzo's detail of mafia life is as exhaustive and compelling as a government research report. As ▷Le Carré does with spies, he seems to be spilling 'insider' secrets in every line, and his inventions (if they are inventions) are so plausible that it is hard to imagine how the real mafia could be run in any other way. After the 1970s success of the two Godfather films, Puzo turned to screenwriting (among other things, he co-wrote the first Superman film), and his later novels *Las Vegas*, *Fools Die* and *The Sicilian*, though fast-moving and exciting, are like novelised movies, airport-bookstall fodder lacking the documentary earnestness which makes *The Godfather* so compulsive.

READ ON

- ▶ **Good mafia follow-ups:** ▷Richard Condon, *Prizzi's Honour*; Donald Westlake, *The Mercenaries*; ▷Elmore Leonard, *Glitz*.
- ▶ **Blockbusters about big business and/or politics:** John Gregory Dunne, *The Red White and Blue*; ▷Jerome Weidman, *I Can Get it for you Wholesale*; Sally Quinn, *Regrets Only*.

PYM, BARBARA (1913–80)

British novelist.

Only ▷Jane Austen and ▷Ivy Compton-Burnett wrote about worlds as restricted as Pym's – and she is regularly compared to both of them. Her books are high-Anglican high comedies; she is tart about the kind of pious middle-class ladies who regard giving sherry-parties for the clergy as doing good works, and she is merciless to priests. Much of the charm of her books lies in their ornate, formal dialogue: her characters all speak with the same prissy, self-conscious elegance, like civil servants taught light conversation by Oscar Wilde.

READ ON

- ● *Quartet in Autumn*.
- ▶ ▷Ivy Compton-Burnett, *Pastors and Masters*. ▷A.N. Wilson, *Kindly Light*. Edward Candy, *Scene Changing*. Alice Thomas Ellis, *The Twenty-seventh Kingdom*. J.F. Powers, *Morte*

A GLASS OF BLESSINGS (1958)

Wilmet Forsyth is rich, well-bred, happy and dim. She fills her mind with fantasies about the priests and parishioners at her local church, imagining that their lives are a whirl of hidden passions, ambitions and frustrations. She imagines herself in love with a handsome evening-class teacher, and assumes that he adores her too. As the book proceeds, every one of these assumptions is proved spectacularly, ludicrously mistaken.

Pym's other novels are Some Tame Gazelle, Excellent Women, Jane and Prudence, Less than Angels, Quartet in Autumn, The Sweet Dove Died, Crampton Hodnett *and* An Academic Question.

d'Urban. ▷Anita Brookner, *Look at Me*.

PYNCHON, THOMAS (BORN 1937)

US novelist.

Reading Pynchon's satires is like exploring a maze with an opinionated and eccentric guide. He leads us lovingly up every blind alley, breaks off to tell jokes, falls into reverie, ridicules everything and everyone, and refuses to say where he's going until he gets there. *The Crying of Lot 49* (1967) begins with Oedipa Maas setting out to discover why she has been left a legacy by an ex-lover, and what it is; but it quickly develops into a crazy tour of hippie 1960s California, an exploration of drugs, bizarre sex, psychic sensitivity and absurd politics, centring on a group of oddball characters united in a secret society determined to subvert the US postal system. *Gravity's Rainbow* (1973) is a much darker fable, a savage anti-war satire set in a top-secret British centre for covert operations during the second world war. In a mad world, where actions have long ceased to have any moral point, where nothing – on principle – is ever explained or justified, the characters spend their working hours alternately doing what they're told and trying to find out the reason for their existence, and pass their leisure hours in masochistic, joyless sex. On the basis of his short stories and *The Crying of Lot 49*, Pynchon is sometimes claimed as a comic writer. But although *Gravity's Rainbow* is satirical, its jokes are knives, its farce makes us scream with despair not joy.

Pynchon's first and most experimental novel was V *(1963).* Mortality and Mercy in Vienna *is a novella, and* Low-lands *is a collection of short stories.*

READ ON

- **The satirical fury of *Gravity's Rainbow* is most nearly matched in:** ▷Joseph Heller, *Catch-22* and William Gaddis, *J.R.* (about a deranged 10-year-old genius in a reform school who trades in stocks and shares and exploits other people's greed).
- **Pynchon's more genial, loonier side is parallelled in:** ▷Mario Vargas Llosa, *Aunt Julia and the Scriptwriter*; Terry Southern, *The Magic Christian* and ▷Kurt Vonnegut, *Breakfast of Champions*.
- **Midway between despair and farce, recommended follow-ups are:** ▷John Irving, *The Hotel New Hampshire* and ▷Jerzy Kosinski, *The Devil Tree*.

R

RABELAIS, FRANÇOIS (C 1494–1553)

French satirist.

At heart Rabelais' *Gargantua* (1534) and *Pantagruel* (1532–3) are simple fairy-tales: accounts of the birth and education of the giant Gargantua and of his son Pantagruel. But Rabelais was really writing satire, sending up the whole of medieval knowledge and belief. The giants study philosophy, mathematics, theology and alchemy; they build an anti-monastery whose rules are not poverty, chastity and obedience but wealth, fornication and licence. Pantagruel's mentor is no dignified greybeard but the conman Panurge, and the two of them go on a fantastic journey (through countries as fabulous as any of those visited by Sinbad or Gulliver) to find the answer to the question 'Whom shall Pantagruel marry?' Because Rabelais' heroes are giants, every human appetite is magnified a thousand-fold. It takes 17,913 cows to provide enough milk to feed the infant Gargantua, and when he is learning to wipe his bottom he experiments with so many different substances that it takes two pages just to list them. Much of *Gargantua*'s first half is taken up with a fierce battle between the giants and their neighbours, and in particular with the exploits of the roistering, apoplectic Friar John of the Funnels and Goblets, who is later rewarded by being made Abbot of the Monastery of Do As You Like. Rabelais described his books as a 'feast of mirth', and their intellectual satire is balanced by celebration of physical pleasure of every kind: not for nothing has the word 'rabelaisian' entered the dictionary. The original French, already engorged with puns, jokes, parodies and over-the-top lists of every kind, was inflated to nearly twice the length by the

READ ON

▶ ▷Laurence Sterne, *Tristram Shandy*. ▷Jonathan Swift, *Gulliver's Travels*. Giovanni Boccaccio, *Decameron* (short stories). Anon, *The Thousand Nights and One Night/The Arabian Nights*. Alexander Theroux, *D'Arconville's Cat*. ▷J.P. Donleavy, *The Ginger Man*.

17th-century translator Thomas Urquhart. His English is funnier, filthier and even more fantastical than Rabelais' French: Rabelais would have loved (and stolen back) every word of it.

RAPHAEL, FREDERIC (BORN 1931)

US/British novelist and screenwriter.

Raphael's sourly witty TV plays and series, showing the hollow husks that brilliant Oxbridge graduates become in later life, have diverted attention from his 16 novels. These walk in darker, more sinister paths. His subject is the power of evil, whether political, moral or social. Sometimes (as in *Lindmann,* about guilt for a second-world-war atrocity, or in *Like Men Betrayed,* set in the 1940s Greek civil war, evil is an external force, the result of perverted idealism; in other books (*Richard's Things,* about erotic possession and betrayal; *Heaven and Earth,* about artistic and personal integrity, we are ourselves corrupt, battling our own urges and ambitions. The heart of darkness in Raphael's work is concealed by a firework-display of satirical, witty dialogue which some readers find intrusive, others a symptom of his characters' inability to cope with their own despair.

APRIL, JUNE AND NOVEMBER (1972)

Daniel Meyer, a film-director, has spent his youth in a dazzle of artistic, social and sexual triumph. Now, as middle age looms, he begins to suspect that under the Byronic façade his true self has all but disappeared. Affairs follow, with a younger and an older woman; he lets himself be seduced by different life-styles, in grubby, rainy London and on a sun-bleached Greek island, a rich man's paradise. Like all Raphael's main characters, Meyer is a battle-ground between genuineness and the role he plays in life – and the question of which side of him wins is left a cliffhanger until the book's last, most ironical line of all.

Raphael's other novels include The Limits of Love, Orchestra and Beginners *and* Two for the Road. The Glittering Prizes *and* After the War *are novels linked to TV series.* Sleeps Six *and* Oxbridge Blues *are collections of short stories.*

READ ON

- *Heaven and Earth.*
- ▶ ▷F. Scott Fitzgerald, *The Great Gatsby*. Vita Sackville-West, *The Edwardians*. ▷Philip Roth, *Zuckerman Unbound*. Rona Jaffe, *Class Reunion*.

RENAISSANCE EUROPE

Caryl Brahms and S.J. Simon, *No Bed for Bacon*
▷Alexandre Dumas, *The Three Musketeers*
▷Dorothy Dunnett, *Niccolò Rising*
Carlos Fuentes, *Terra Nostra*
Stephen Marlowe, *The Memoirs of Christopher Columbus*

▷Jean Plaidy, *Queen of the Realm*
Irving Stone, *The Agony and the Ecstasy*

The Middle Ages (p 175)

RENAULT, MARY (1905–83)

British novelist.

In her 30s and 40s Renault wrote several novels about hospital and wartime life, culminating in *The Charioteer*, the moving story of a homosexual serviceman. In the 1950s she began writing historical novels about ancient Greece. *The King Must Die* and *The Bull from the Sea* are based on the myth of King Theseus of Athens, who killed the Cretan Minotaur; *Fire From Heaven*, *The Persian Boy* and *Funeral Games* are about Alexander the Great. Like ▷Robert Graves, Renault treats people of the past as if they were psychologically just like us, so that even the most bizarre political or sexual behaviour seems both rational and credible.

THE MASK OF APOLLO (1966)

Niko, a Greek actor of the 4th century BC, is used as a go-between by politicians trying to replace the despotic régime in Sicily with an ideal state ruled by a philosopher-king. Political intrigue is interwoven with Niko's own complicated private life, and with his (brilliantly described) theatrical personality: he is as vulnerable, as self-centred, as dedicated and as nervously extrovert as any Broadway or National Theatre star today.

Renault's other Greek books are The Last of the Wine *and* The Praise Singer. *Her novels with 20th-century settings are* Purposes of Love/Promise of Love, Kind Are Her Answers, The Friendly Young Ladies/The Middle Mist, Return to Night, North Face *and* The Charioteer.

READ ON

- *The Last of the Wine.*
- ▶ Helen Waddell, *Peter Abelard*. John Arden, *Silence Among the Weapons*. Naomi Mitchison, *The Corn King and the Spring Queen*. ▷Gore Vidal, *Creation*. Pär Lagerkvist, *The Sibyl*. Henry Treece, *Oedipus*.

RENDELL, RUTH (BORN 1930)

British novelist.

Rendell's Chief Inspector Wexford novels are atmospheric murder mysteries in traditional style, set in the small towns and villages of the English Home Counties. Like P.D. ▷James, she spends much time developing the character of her detective, a liberal and cultured man appalled at the psychological pressures which drive people to crime. Those pressures are the subject of Rendell's other books (both under her own name and as ▷Barbara Vine): grim stories of paranoia, obsession and inadequacy. In *Judgement in Stone*

READ ON

- ▶ **To the Wexford books:** ▷P.D. James, *Shroud for a Nightingale*; Nicolas Freeling, *Love in Amsterdam*.
- ▶ **To the psychological thrillers:** Joan Fleming, *Young Man*

(1978), for example, an illiterate housekeeper is terrified that if her problem is discovered she will be sacked – and her cunning, desperate attempts to conceal it begin a ladder of consequences which leads inexorably to murder.

Rendell's Wexford books include A New Lease of Death, Wolf to the Slaughter, A Guilty Thing Surprised, Some Lie and Some Die *and* An Unkindness of Ravens. *Her psychological novels include* The Face of Trespass, The Killing Doll, The Tree of Hands, Live Flesh *and* Talking to Strange Men. The Fallen Curtain, Means of Evil *and* The Fever Tree *are collections of short stories. As Barbara Vine Rendell has written* A Dark-Adapted Eye; A Fatal Inversion; House of Stairs.

I Think You're Dying; ▷Patricia Highsmith, *The Glass Cell*; John Katzenbach, *The Traveller*.

REVISITING ONE'S PAST

▷Margaret Atwood, *Surfacing*
▷Anita Brookner, *Hôtel du Lac*
▷Bernice Rubens, *Our Father*
▷Graham Swift, *Waterland*
▷Paul Theroux, *Picture Palace*
▷Virginia Woolf, *Mrs Dalloway*

REWRITING HISTORY
(what might have happened if . . .)

▷Kingsley Amis, *The Alteration*
Martin Cruz Smith, *The Indians Won*
▷Len Deighton, *SS-GB*
▷Peter Dickinson, *King and Joker*
▷Michael Moorcock, *Warlord of the Air*
Keith Roberts, *Pavane*

RHYS, JEAN (1894–1979)
British novelist.

All Rhys' novels and stories are about the same kind of person, the 'Jean Rhys woman'. She was once vivacious and attractive (an actress, perhaps, or a dancer) but she fell in love with some unsuitable man or men, was betrayed, and now lives alone, maudlin and mentally unhinged. In Rhys' first four novels (published in the 1920s and 1930s), the heroines are casualties of the Jazz Age, flappers crushed by life itself. In her last, 1960s, book *Wide Sargasso Sea* the central character is a victim of the way men think (or fail to think) of women: she is a young Caribbean heiress in the early 1800s, who marries an English gentleman, Mr Rochester, and ends up as the demented creature hidden in the

READ ON

- *Wide Sargasso Sea.*
- ▶ **To *Good Morning Midnight*:** ▷Brian Moore, *The Doctor's Wife*; ▷Doris Lessing, *The Golden Notebook*; ▷Mary McCarthy, *The Company She Keeps*; ▷Anita Brookner, *H*
- ▶ **To *Wide Sargasso***

attics of Thornfield Hall in *Jane Eyre.*

GOOD MORNING, MIDNIGHT (1939)

Deserted by her husband after the death of their baby, Sasha would have drunk herself to death if a generous friend had not rescued her and paid for her to spend a fortnight in Paris. She 'arranges her little life', as she puts it: a cycle of solitary meals and drinks, barren conversations with strangers, drugged sleep in seedy hotel-rooms. She is a damned soul, a husk – and then a gigolo, mistaking her for a rich woman, begins to court her, and she has to gather the rags of her sanity and try to take hold of her life once more.

Rhys' other novels are Quartet/Postures, After Leaving Mr Mackenzie *and* Voyage in the Dark. The Left Bank, Tigers are Better-looking *and* Sleep it off, Lady *are collections of short stories.*

THE RHYTHM OF NATURE

(people in tune with or in thrall to the land)

▷Pearl S. Buck, *The Good Earth*
Erskine Caldwell, *God's Little Acre*
Neil M. Gunn, *The Well at the World's End*
▷Thomas Hardy, *Far From the Madding Crowd*
▷Susan Hill, *In the Springtime of the Year*
Mikhail Sholokhov, *Virgin Soil Upturned*

Down to Earth (p 67)

RICHARDSON, HENRY HANDEL (1870–1946)

Australian novelist.

'Henry Handel Richardson' was the pseudonym of Ethel Robertson. She was born and educated in Australia, but went to Europe in her late teens and remained there, with one three-month break, for the rest of her life. Her best-known books, however (*The Getting of Wisdom*, 1910, and the Richard Mahony trilogy: see below) are set in Australia and reflect her own or her parents' experience. She was interested in 'psychic outsiders', people who felt that heightened awareness or sensibilities set them apart from their fellows. *The Getting of Wisdom* is about a gifted, unhappy adolescent in a late 19th-century boarding school, who uses love of the arts as an escape from the oppressive narrowness of the régime. The battle against depressive illness is a major theme of the Mahony trilogy. *The Young Cosima* is about Liszt's daughter Cosima, her husband Hans von Bülow and her lover Wagner – all of them exemplars (at least in their own fevered imaginations) of Nietzschean 'superbe-

Sea: Lisa St Aubin de Terán, *The Keepers of the House.*

READ ON

- *Maurice Guest* (another study of depression, this time about a man ambitious to be a professional musician who finds that he has talent but no genius, and who is then further distracted by falling unhappily in love).
- ▶ **To *The Fortunes of Richard Mahony*:** ▷Gustave Flaubert, *Madame Bovary*; ▷Malcolm Lowry,

ings', who are nevertheless racked by feelings and emotions as uncontrollable as anyone else's.

THE FORTUNES OF RICHARD MAHONY (1915–29)

In this trilogy of novels (*Australia Felix, The Way Home, Ultima Thule*) Mahony, a British doctor, goes to Australia to make his fortune in the 1850s gold rush, marries and settles. His gold-prospecting fails, and he turns first to storekeeping and then back to medicine, before making a sudden fortune from shares he thought were worthless. Unable to cope with wealth, he dissipates his money, impoverishes his family and begins a long, anguished slide into depressive mania. His devoted wife takes a job as postmistress in a remote area, nursing her husband and bringing up her uncomprehending, sorrowing family. Although the trilogy is chiefly concerned with Mahony's complex character and his relationship with his family, it is also a compelling account of 19th-century Australian pioneer and outback life.

Richardson's only other novel is Maurice Guest *(see Read On).* Two Studies *contains a pair of long short stories;* The End of a Childhood *and* The Adventures of Cuffy Mahony *are collections of short stories;* Myself When Young *is autobiography.*

Under the Volcano.

- ▶ **To *Maurice Guest*:** ▷Hermann Hesse, *Steppenwolf.*
- ▶ **To *The Getting of Wisdom*:** ▷Antonia White, *Frost in May.*

RICHARDSON, SAMUEL (1689–1761)

British novelist.

A successful printer, Richardson was compiling a book of sample letters for all occasions when he had the idea of writing whole novels in letter-form. He produced three, *Pamela, Clarissa* and *Sir Charles Grandison.* They are enormously long (over a million words each), and readers even at the time complained of boredom. But the books were still best-sellers, not, as Richardson imagined, because of their high moral tone, but because his sensational theme (the way some people are drawn irresistibly to debauch the innocent) guaranteed success.

CLARISSA, OR THE HISTORY OF A YOUNG LADY (1748)

To escape from her parents, who have shut her in her room until she agrees to marry a man she loathes, the hapless Clarissa Harlowe elopes with Mr Lovelace, a rake. He tries every possible way to persuade her to sleep with him, and when she refuses he puts her into a brothel, drugs and rapes her. She goes into a decline and dies of shame. The story is told by means of letters from the main characters, to one another, to friends and acquaintances. One of Richardson's triumphs – which some critics claim justifies the

READ ON

- • *Pamela.*
- ▶ Pierre Choderlos de Laclos, *Dangerous Alliances* (Les liaisons dangereuses) is another letter-novel about moral predation, but shorter, wittier and less sentimental. A young aristocrat in pre-Revolutionary France, bored by the restrictions of polite society, devotes herself to the cynical, ice-cool shedding of all moral restraint. This book apart, Richardson's work

book's inordinate length – is to reveal Lovelace's villainy only gradually, as Clarissa herself discovers it.

has been more pilloried than parallelled. ▷Henry Fielding, for example, in *Tom Jones* mocks Richardson's moral earnestness: far from shrinking from the pleasures of seduction, Tom lives for them.

RICHLER, MORDECAI (BORN 1931)

Canadian novelist.

The heroes of Richler's vitriolic black satires are 'outsiders' (for example Jews in a gentile society), poor (they come from big-city slums) or inept (too guileless for their own good). They face a hostile world of crooks, cheats, extortionists, poseurs (often film makers or tycoons) and bullies. Sometimes, like the hero of *The Apprenticeship of Duddy Kravitz* (1959), Richler's men fight back, using the enemies' weapons and winning the battle at the expense of their own souls; others, like the middle-aged hero of *Joshua Then and Now* (1980), are so humbled by the sense of their own inadequacy that instead of fighting the slings and arrows of outrageous fortune (in Joshua's case, the false accusation that he is a sexual deviant), they welcome them. *Joshua Then and Now* and *Cocksure* (1968) (a violent farce about an honest man bewildered by the permissiveness of the 'swinging sixties') are Richler's most savage books, written to lacerate as well as to amuse.

Richler's other novels include A Choice of Enemies, The Incomparable Atuk/Stick Your Neck Out *and* St Urbain's Horseman. Shovelling Trouble *and* Home Sweet Home *are collections of essays and articles, many of them about Canada and its attitude to 'culture'.* The Street *is a memoir of his childhood in the backstreets of Montreal, a fascinating parallel to the opening chapters of* The Apprenticeship of Duddy Kravitz.

READ ON

- **To *The Apprenticeship of Duddy Kravitz*:** ▷Jerome Weidman, *I Can Get It for You Wholesale*; ▷Saul Bellow, *The Adventures of Augie March*.
- **To *Cocksure*:** Budd Schulberg, *What Makes Sammy Run?*; ▷Gore Vidal, *Myra Breckinridge*.
- **To Richler's work in general:** ▷Nathaniel West, *Miss Lonelyhearts*; ▷F. Scott Fitzgerald, *The Great Gatsby*.

ROBERTS, MICHÈLE (BORN 1949)

British poet and novelist.

Much of Roberts' work has a feminist edge, and one novel in particular, *Mrs Noah* (1987), is likely to leave the male half of the human race feeling distinctly uncomfortable. It is a dazzling fantasy, set in the present day. A woman visiting

READ ON

- *The Wild Girl* (the Gospel according to Mary Magdalene, a stunning reworking

Venice with her preoccupied husband fantasises that she is Mrs Noah. The Ark is a vast library, a repository not only of creatures but of the entire knowledge and experience of the human race. She is its curator (or Arkivist), and her fellow-voyagers are five Sibyls and a token male, the Gaffer, a bearded old party who once wrote a best-selling book (the Bible) and has now retired to a tax-heaven in the sky. Each Sibyl tells a story, and each story is about the way men have oppressed women down the centuries. For all its feminist anger, the book is a witty, imaginative tour de force.

of familiar New Testament themes)
▶ ▷Margaret Atwood, *The Handmaid's Tale*. ▷Angela Carter, *The Infernal Desire Machines of Doctor Hoffman*. ▷Keri Hulme, *The Bone People*. Joe Orton, *Head to Toe*.

Roman Catholicism (1)

▷Kingsley Amis, *The Alteration*
Georges Bernanos, *Diary of a Country Priest*
▷Anthony Burgess, *Earthly Powers*
▷Rumer Godden, *A Candle for St Jude*
▷Graham Greene, *Monsignor Quixote*
Nikos Kazantzakis, *The Greek Passion*
▷Thomas Keneally, *Three Cheers for the Paraclete*

Roman Catholicism (2) (p 213)

Roman Catholicism (2)

▷David Lodge, *How Far Can You Go?*
▷Brian Moore, *The Colour of Blood*
J.F. Powers, *Morte d'Urban*
Frederick Rolfe, *Hadrian the Seventh*
▷Muriel Spark, *The Abbess of Crewe*
▷Morris West, *The Devil's Advocate*
▷Antonia White, *Frost in May*

Roman Catholicism (1) (p 213)

ROSSNER, Judith (born 1935)

US novelist.

Rossner's novels treat human life as a straightforward battle of wits between emotional predators and their quarry – a struggle which always ends in psychological mutilation or destruction. In some books, for example *Nine Months in the Life of an Old Maid* (1969, about a ghastly family who get on each others' nerves) the chase is funny and the mode is farce. In others, for example *Looking for Mr Goodbar* (1975, about a woman cruising singles bars in search of love) the events are grim and the mode is tragedy. The theme of emotional depredation has been popular with recent US

READ ON

- *Attachments*; *August*.

▶ Joyce Carol Oates, *The Poisoned Kiss*. ▷Angela Carter, *The Infernal Desire Machines of Doctor Hoffman*. Robert Bloch, *Psycho*. ▷Susan Hill, *The*

writers of all kinds, from 'serious' novelists to the authors of big-business and family sagas. Rossner is one of its wittiest exponents.

Bird of Night.

▶ **Similar novels from an earlier period:** ▷Djuna Barnes, *Nightwood*; ▷Christina Stead, *The Man Who Loved Children.*

ROTH, PHILIP (BORN 1933)

US novelist.

One of the wryest and wittiest of all contemporary US novelists, Roth writes of Jewish intellectuals, often authors or university teachers, discomforted by life. Their marriages fail; their parents behave like joke-book stereotypes (forever making chicken soup and simultaneously boasting about and deploring their sons' brains); sexual insatiability leads them from one farcical encounter to another; their career-success attracts embarrassing fans and inhibits further work; their defences of self-mockery and irony wear ever thinner as they approach unwanted middle age. In his best-known book, *Portnoy's Complaint* (1969), Roth treated this theme as farce, heavy with explicit sex and Jewish-mother jokes. The majority of his novels are quieter, the tone is more rueful, and he generalises his theme and makes it symbolise the plight of all decent, conscience-stricken people in a world where barbarians make the running. His major 1980s work was a series of novels about a New York Jewish author, Nathan Zuckerman, who agonises over his trade, writes an immensely successful (dirty) book and is immediately harrassed by the way his fame both forces him to live the life of a celebrity and makes him even more of an enigma to his family and friends.

THE PROFESSOR OF DESIRE (1977)

David Kepesh, a brilliant young literature teacher, is trying to sort out his life. His views on art and literature, which once seemed the last word in wit and wisdom, now appear to him to have been engulfed by the subjects he studies: he feels like a dwarf trying to shift a mountain. His emotional life is dominated by an insistent craving for physical pleasure which he finds degrading but irresistible and which he longs to replace by love. His mother and father are elderly, tetchy and horrified by the way their son the genius has betrayed his Jewish roots. Kepesh's circumstances seem to him like a maze, as bewildering and terrifying as anything in ▷Kafka – and the book shows him gradually, painfully, discovering the key.

READ ON

- *When She was Good.*

▶ Bernard Malamud, *Dubin's Lives.* ▷Bernice Rubens, *Our Father.* ▷Margaret Atwood, *Cat's Eye.* ▷John Fowles, *Daniel Martin.* ▷John Updike, *Marry Me.*

Roth's other books include Letting Go, The Great American Novel *(which uses baseball as a farcical symbol for every red-blooded US tradition or way of thought),* My Life as a Man *and* Our Gang *(a ▷Swiftian satire about the Nixon presidency).* Goodbye Columbus *collects an early novella and five short stories. The Zuckerman books are* The Ghost Writer, Zuckerman Unbound, The Anatomy Lesson, The Prague Orgy *and* The Counterlife. The Facts: a Novelist's Autobiography, *a fictionalised account of Roth's life, closes with a letter from 'Zuckerman' accusing Roth of living a fake life, of describing the truth of existence only when he invents fictional characters and incidents.*

RUBENS, BERNICE (BORN 1927)

British novelist.

Rubens' heroes and heroines are people at the point of breakdown: her novels chart the escalation of tension which took them there or the progress of their cure. Some of the books are bleak: in *The Elected Member/The Chosen People* (1969), for example, a man is driven mad by feeling that he is a scapegoat for the entire suffering of the Jewish people throughout history, and the story deals with his rehabilitation in a mental hospital. In other books, Rubens turns psychological pain to comedy, as if the only way to cope with the human condition were to treat it as God's black joke against the human race. God is even a character in *Our Father* (1987): he pops up in the Sahara, in the High Street, in the parlour, in bed with the heroine and her husband, constantly nagging her to make up her mind about herself – and his persistence leads her to rummage through childhood memories (where it becomes clear that she completely misunderstood her parents' emotional relationship) and to redefine her life.

Rubens' other novels include Madame Sousatzka, I Sent a Letter to my Love, The Ponsonby Post, Sunday Best, The Brothers, A Five Year Sentence, Birds of Passage, Favours, Spring Sonata *and* Mr Wakefield's Crusade.

READ ON

- *Birds of Passage.*
- ▶ **To *The Elected Member*:** Paul Sayer, *The Comforts of Madness.*
- ▶ **To *Madame Sousatzka*:** ▷Elizabeth Jolley, *Milk and Honey.*
- ▶ **To Rubens' work in general:** ▷Paul Theroux, *Picture Palace.* ▷David Cook, *Missing Persons,* ▷Anita Brookner, *Hôtel du Lac,* Susan Fromberg Shaeffer, *Worldly Goods,* Robert Elric, *A Lunar Eclipse,* ▷Susan Hill, *A Bit of Singing and Dancing* (short stories).

RUSHDIE, SALMAN (BORN 1947)

Indian/British novelist and non-fiction writer.

Rushdie's novels are magic realism: a mesmeric entwining of actuality and fantasy. *Midnight's Children* (1981) is the story of a rich Indian family over the last 80 years, and especially of Saleem, one of 1001 children born at midnight on 15 August 1947, the moment of India's independence from

READ ON

- ▶ **To *Midnight's Children*:** ▷Gabriel García Márquez, *One Hundred Years of Solitude.*

Salman RUSHDIE

SHAME *(feud between ruling families in fantasy-state 'Peccavistan')*

Jeanette **WINTERSON, THE PASSION**
(Napoleon)

Augusto **ROA BASTOS, I THE SUPREME**
(Francia, dictator of Paraguay)

Evelyn **WAUGH, BLACK MISCHIEF**
(England-educated 1930s black African ruler)

Miguel **ASTURIAS, THE PRESIDENT**
(corruption and jackboot evil in South America)

Michael **MOORCOCK, GLORIANA**
(state and ruler one gross, monstrous entity)

DICTATORS

Chinua **ACHEBE, ANTHILLS OF THE SAVANNAH**
(emerging African totalitarian state)

Nadine **GORDIMER, A SPORT OF NATURE**
(white girl joins South African freedom fighters)

Gore **VIDAL, BURR**
('traitor' who tried to set up rival republic to Jeffersonian America)

Timothy **MO, AN INSULAR POSSESSION**
(British imperialism and Hong Kong)

Authur **KOESTLER, DARKNESS AT NOON**
(treason-trial of old-guard revolutionary in unnamed but Stalinist dictatorship)

George **ORWELL, ANIMAL FARM**
(animals declare republic which degenerates into dictatorship)

POLITICS

Isabel **ALLENDE, THE HOUSE OF THE SPIRITS**
(political and personal evolution in rich South American family over 100 years.)

Gabriel García **MÁRQUEZ, ONE HUNDRED YEARS OF SOLITUDE** *(sprawling family dominate small town in fantasy South America)*

Peter **CAREY, ILLYWHACKER**
(132-year-old Australian conman tells his story)

Gerald H. **MORRIS, DOVES AND SILK HANDKERCHIEVES** *(magic and realism in 1900s English mining village)*

Günter **GRASS, THE FLOUNDER**
(fisher-couple and talking fish live through all German history)

John **IRVING, THE WORLD ACCORDING TO GARP**
(evolution of writer in fantasy New England town)

MANY GENERATIONS

Britain. Saleem's birth time gives him extraordinary powers: he is, as Rushdie puts it, 'handcuffed' to India, able to let his mind float freely through its history and to share in the experience of anyone he chooses, from Gandhi or Nehru to the most insignificant beggar in the streets. In Saleem's experience (as relayed to us) time coalesces, 'real' politics blur with fantasy, a child's memories and magnifications are just as valid as newspaper accounts. The effect is to change reality to metaphor – and Rushdie uses this to make several sharp political points. In *Shame* (1983) he goes still further. This novel is set in a dream country, Peccavistan ('Sinned' rather than Sind), whose geography and history are like Pakistan's seen in a distorting mirror. We witness a power-struggle between members of the Harappa dynasty and their friends/rivals/enemies the Hyders. Interwoven with it all is the story of Omar Khayyam Shakil, a bloated, brilliant physician, and his wife Sufiya Zinobia, a mental defective inhabited by a homicidal demon. *The Satanic Verses* (1988) dramatises the conflict of good and evil in the persons of two actors, who fall out of a plane and are transformed (quite literally) into the angel Gibreel and Shaitan, the Devil. (The book violently offended fundamentalist Muslims, who took 'Gibreel's' sardonic, ironic dreams about the prophet Mahound in the fantasy city Jahilia as blasphemy against their religion. Copies of *The Satanic Verses* were burned, and Rushdie was sentenced to death by Ayatollah Khomeini of Iran – events whose surreal horror beggared anything in his fiction.) Describing books like these is like summarising dreams: the telling bleaches them of wit, poetry and compulsion. Like ▷Márquez, Rushdie reinvents reality, makes fantasy seem more plausible than truth itself.

Rushdie's other works include Grimus *(an early, experimental novel) and* The Jaguar Smile *(non-fiction: a politically savage report on the effect of US policies in central America in general and Nicaragua in particular).*

▶ **To *Shame*:** Augusto Roa Bastos, *I, The Supreme*. ▷Günter Grass, *The Tin Drum*.

▶ **To *The Satanic Verses*:** ▷Angela Carter, *Nights at the Circus*. Lisa St Aubin de Terán, *Keepers of the House*.

S

SALINGER, J.D. (JEROME DAVID) (BORN 1919)

US novelist and short-story writer.

Salinger's only novel, *The Catcher in the Rye* (1951), is a rambling monologue by 17-year-old Holden Caulfield. He has run away from boarding school just before Christmas, and is spending a few days drifting in New York City while he decides whether to go home or not. He feels that his childhood is over and his innocence lost, but he detests the phoney, loveless grown-up world (symbolised by plastic Christmas baubles and seasonal fake goodwill). He thinks that to be adult is a form of surrender, but he can see no way to avoid it. He wanders the city, talking aimlessly to taxi-drivers, lodging-house keepers, bar-tenders, prostitutes and his own kid sister Phoebe, whom he tries to warn against growing up. Finally, inevitably, he capitulates – or perhaps escapes, since we learn that what we have just read is his 'confession' to the psychiatrist in a mental home. Salinger pursued the question of how to recover moral innocence in his only other publications, a series of short stories about the gifted, mentally unstable Glass family. 'Franny and Zooey', the most moving of the stories, shows Zooey Glass, an actor, talking his sister Franny out of a nervous breakdown. It is a performance of dazzling technical brilliance and full of loving-kindness, but – and this is typical of Salinger's grim view of human moral endeavour – although it helps Franny momentarily, it contributes nothing whatever to the good of the world at large.

The Glass family stories are collected in Franny and Zooey*;* Nine Stories/For Esmé, with Love and Squalor *and* Raise High the Roofbeam, Carpenters.

READ ON

- **To *The Catcher in the Rye*:** ▷Carson McCullers, *The Member of the Wedding*; ▷Willa Cather, *My Antonia*; ▷John Updike, *The Centaur*; Truman Capote, *Breakfast at Tiffany's*; Alan Sillitoe, *Saturday Night and Sunday Morning*.
- **To 'Franny and Zooey':** Sylvia Plath, *The Bell Jar*; ▷Susan Hill, *The Bird of Night*.

SARTRE, JEAN-PAUL (1905–80)

French novelist, poet and philosopher.

The philosophy of existentialism, which Sartre developed in essays, plays, novels and monographs, says that Nothingness is the natural state of humanity: we exist, like animals, without ethics or morality. But unlike beasts we have the power to make choices, and these give moral status: they are a leap from Nothingness to Being. For some people, the choice is the leap of faith, and belief in God gives them moral status; for others the choice is to make no choice at all, to drift the way the world leads them without taking moral initiatives. For Sartre's characters, the leap into being involved taking responsibility, making moral decisions from which there was no turning back. His vast novel *The Roads to Freedom* (1945–9; in three volumes, *The Age of Reason, The Reprieve* and *Iron in the Soul/Troubled Sleep*) tackles this theme exactly: the questions of what moral decisions to make and how to make them. It describes a group of young people trying to sort out their personal lives and at the same time to cope with the moral and intellectual challenges of fascism, communism, colonialism and the second world war. The book is packed with intellectual, political and philosophical discussion and argument: a complex read. But few writings better give the intellectual 'feel' of the 1930s and 1940s, the matrix from which so many of today's ideas were born.

Sartre's main philosophical monograph is Being and Nothingness. *His plays include* The Flies, The Victor/Men Without Shadows, Crime Passionel *and* Huis Clos/No Exit/In Camera. Nausea/The Diary of Antoine Roquentin *is an autobiographical novel about a young intellectual in the 1920s and 1930s.* The Wall/Intimacy *is a collection of short stories.*

READ ON

- *Nausea.*
- ▶ ▷Albert Camus, *The Plague*. Arthur Koestler, *Darkness at Noon*. ▷Frederic Raphael, *Like Men Betrayed*.
- ▶ **Novels discussing similar personal dilemmas, but with different backgrounds and cultural conditions:** ▷Lev Tolstoy, *War and Peace*; ▷Ford Madox Ford, *The Good Soldier*; ▷Olivia Manning, *The Levant Trilogy*.

SAYERS, DOROTHY L. (DOROTHY LEIGH) (1893–1957)

British novelist.

The writer Colin Watson cruelly but accurately described Sayers' kind of crime fiction as 'snobbery with violence'. The fascination of her books is not only in the solving of bizarre crimes in out-of-the-ordinary locations (an advertising agency; an Oxford women's college; an East Anglian belfry), but also in the character of her detective, the supersleuth Lord Peter Wimsey. He is a languid, monocled aristocrat, whose foppish manner conceals the facts that he has a first-class Oxford degree, was in army intelligence during the first world war, collects rare books, plays the piano like Rubinstein, dances like Astaire and seems to have swal-

READ ON

- *Gaudy Night.*
- ▶ Amanda Cross, *No Word from Winifred*. ▷Michael Innes, *Hamlet, Revenge!* Robert Robinson, *Landscape with Dead Dons*. John Dickson Carr, *Poison in Jest*. Rex Stout, *Fer de Lance*.

lowed a substantial dictionary of quotations. He is aided and abetted by his manservant Bunter, a suave charmer adept at extracting confidences from the cooks, taxi-drivers, waitresses, barbers and vergers who would collapse in forelock-tugging silence if Wimsey himself ever deigned to speak to them. Seldom have detective stories been so preposterous or so unputdownable.

▷Ruth Rendell, *Some Lie and Some Die.*

HAVE HIS CARCASE (1932)

In a sleepy seaside resort, someone has cut the throat of a gigolo – and the plot thickens when it is discovered that he was romantically involved with a lonely, rich and foolish widow. But where do the men with the patently-false hair and beards come into it? Why are there no footprints in the sand? What connects the crime with the Russian ex-royal dynasty? All these mysteries are as nothing compared to the greatest cliffhanger of all: will Wimsey's persistent charm ever wear down Harriet Vane, the best-selling crime-novelist, until she agrees to marry him?

The Wimsey/Vane romance is also featured in Strong Poison, Gaudy Night *and* Busman's Honeymoon. *Sayers' other Wimsey books – which some admirers prefer to those involving Harriet Vane – include* Murder Must Advertise *and* The Nine Tailors.

SCHOOLS

Nicholas Best, *Tennis and the Masai*
▷Charles Dickens, *Nicholas Nickleby*
James Hilton, *Goodbye, Mr Chips*
▷James Joyce, *Portrait of the Artist as a Young Man*
▷John Le Carré, *Call for the Dead*
▷H.H. Richardson, *The Getting of Wisdom*
▷John Updike, *The Centaur*
▷Evelyn Waugh, *Decline and Fall*

Adolescence (p 2)

SCOTLAND

Georgey MacKay Brown, *Greenvoe*
Lewis Grassic Gibbon, *A Scots Quair*
Alasdair Gray, *Lanark*
Neil M. Gunn, *Morning Tide*
Compton MacKenzie, *The Monarch of the Glen*
▷Scott Walter, *The Heart of Midlothian*
▷Robert Louis Stevenson, *Kidnapped*
▷Jan Webster, *Colliers Row*

SCOTT, WALTER (1771–1832)
British novelist and poet.

Scott began his career not with novels but with poems, in a style similar to Scottish folk-ballads and the lyrics of Robert Burns. In 1814, piqued because his verse was outsold by Byron's, he turned instead to historical novels, and wrote 29 in the next 18 years. They are swaggering tales of love, bravery and intrigue, many of them centred on events from Scottish history and set in the brooding landscapes of the highlands and islands.

ROB ROY (1817)
In the 1710s, Osbaldistone and Rashleigh are rivals for the hand of Diana Vernon. Rashleigh embezzles money and frames Osbaldistone. Osbaldistone escapes to the highlands of Scotland, where he seeks help from Rob Roy, an outlaw who (like Robin Hood centuries before him) robs the rich to help the poor, rights wrongs and fights a usurping power (in his case, the English) on behalf of an exiled, true royal prince (James Stuart, the Old Pretender). Osbaldistone's quest to clear his name becomes inextricably bound up with the Jacobite Rebellion, and it is not until Rashleigh (who, not unexpectedly, supports the English and betrays Rob Roy to them) is killed that justice prevails and Osbaldistone and Diana at last find happiness.

Scott's other novels include Waverley, Guy Mannering, Old Mortality, The Heart of Midlothian, The Bride of Lammermoor, Ivanhoe, Kenilworth, The Fortunes of Nigel, Quentin Durward, Redgauntlet *and* Castle Dangerous.

READ ON

- *Ivanhoe*; *The Heart of Midlothian*.
- ▶ Harrison Ainsworth, *The Tower of London*. James Fenimore Cooper, *Last of the Mohicans*. ▷Victor Hugo, *Notre-Dame de Paris*. ▷Alexandre Dumas, *The Man in the Iron Mask*. Nigel Tranter, *Montrose: the Captain General*.

SEGAL, ERICH (BORN 1937)
US novelist and non-fiction writer.

Love Story (1970), Segal's first novel, was one of the most affecting romances of the century. A true three-handkerchief weepie, it tells of the idyllic, doomed love-affair between two college students, one of whom falls terminally ill. The book, and the film made from it, moved audiences to tears from Manchester to Melbourne, from Peking to Peoria. In a later romance, *Oliver's Story* (1977), Segal took up the life of one of the young people from the earlier book, eight years later. Oliver falls in love again, only to be haunted by the thought that he is betraying his earlier, 'eternal' love.

READ ON

- *Doctors*.
- ▶ *Love Story*'s ecstatic sadness is matched in ▷Boris Pasternak, *Doctor Zhivago* and ▷Margaret Mitchell, *Gone With the Wind*. Philip Roth, *Letting Go* is about a campus love-affair and the early years of marriage, similar in background to *Love Story* though by no means as sad.

Love Story's unselfconscious sentimentality is parallelled in Richard Bach, *Jonathan Livingstone Seagull*, though its plot (an 'outsider' allegory about a bird longing to fly free) could hardly be more different.

SHARPE, Tom (born 1928)

British novelist.

If, as many foreigners maintain, British humour is obsessed with the functions of the lower body, then Sharpe is our comic Laureate. In each of his books he chooses a single target – polytechnic life, publishing, Cambridge University, the landed gentry – and demolishes it magnificently, comprehensively, by piling slapstick on crudity like a demented circus clown. Sharpe's heroes live in a state of unceasing, ungoverning panic, and are usually crippled by lust, forever tripping over their own erections. His old men are gluttonous, lecherous and senile, prone to perversion and prey to strokes and heart attacks; his matrons are whooping, whip-wielding Boadiceas, scything down every beddable male in sight. If your humorous fancy is for penises trapped in briar-patches, condoms ballooning above Cambridge spires or maniacs burying sex-dolls in wet cement, Sharpe's books are for you.

Riotous Assembly (1973)

Kommandant van Heerden, police chief of the sleepy South African town of Piemburg, wants a quiet life and an invitation to join the exclusive British Country Club. His assistant Verkramp wants van Heerden's job. Konstabel Els wants to keep on playing with his electrodes and fucking kaffirs. But Miss Hazelstone phones to say that she has just shot her black cook – and that it was not a 'garbage-disposal operation' but the result of a lovers' tiff. Van Heerden, thinking that she must be covering up for her brother the bishop, sets out on an investigation which spirals into an orgy of transvestism, voyeurism, bestiality and murder. The South African setting gives this book devastating point: given the situation, even Sharpe's most slapstick satirical excess seems a model of self-restraint.

READ ON

- *Indecent Exposure*; *Blott on the Landscape*.
- ▶ Colin Douglas, *The Houseman's Tale*. Thorne Smith, *The Bishop's Jaegers*. Howard Jacobson, *Peeping Tom*. ▷J.P. Donleavy, *The Ginger Man*.

Sharpe's other books include Wilt *and its sequels* The Wilt

Alternative *and* Wilt on High; The Throwback; Porterhouse Blue; Ancestral Vices *and* Vintage Stuff.

SHELLEY, Mary (1797–1851)

British novelist.

After the death of her husband (the poet) in 1822, Shelley began a literary career of her own, editing her husband's work, writing essays, journals and travel-books, and publishing short stories and novels, many on what would now be considered SF themes. Her best-known book is *Frankenstein, or the Modern Prometheus* (1818), about a man who tries to prove the superiority of scientific rationality to the supernatural by usurping God's function and creating life. Although, thanks to Hollywood, Frankenstein's monster has nudged his creator from centre-stage, even the worst Frankenstein films keep to one of Shelley's most fascinating ideas: that the monster is an innocent, as pure as Adam before the Fall, and that its ferocity is a response learned by contact with 'civilised' human beings. Shelley developed the theme of the contrast between innocence and the corruption of civilisation in other books, most notably the future-fantasy *The Last Man* (1826), set in a world where all human beings but one have been destroyed by plague, and the survivor wanders among the monuments of the glorious past like a soul in Hell.

READ ON

- **To *Frankenstein*:** ▷H.G. Wells, *The Island of Doctor Moreau*; ▷Bram Stoker, *Dracula*; Gerald Du Maurier, *Trilby*.
- **To *The Last Man*:** ▷Daniel Defoe, *Robinson Crusoe*; Bernard Malamud, *God's Grace*.

Ships And The Sea

John Dickson Carr, *The Blind Barber*
▷Joseph Conrad, *The Nigger of the 'Narcissus'*
Paul Gallico, *The Poseidon Adventure*
▷Herman Melville, *Moby-Dick*
Nicholas Monsarrat, *The Cruel Sea*
▷Katharine Anne Porter, *Ship of Fools*
Paul Rodgers, *To Kill a God* (Captain Cook's voyages)
▷Jules Verne, *Twenty Thousand Leagues Under the Sea*
▷Herman Wouk, *The Caine Mutiny*

Shipwreck (p 223)

Shipwreck

▷Martin Boyd, *Nuns in Jeopardy*
▷Daniel Defoe, *Robinson Crusoe*
Nicholas Monsarrat, *Running Proud*
▷Muriel Spark, *Robinson*
▷Kurt Vonnegut, *Galápagos*

▷Patrick White, *A Fringe of Leaves*

Ships and the Sea (p 223)

SHUTE, NEVILLE (1899–1960)

British/Australian novelist.

'Neville Shute' was the pseudonym of Neville Shute Norway. In the 1920s he worked as an aeronautical engineer, and he later served as a second-world-war naval commander – experiences which inspired two of his finest books, *Pied Piper* (1942), about a mild-mannered man who rescues a group of children from the nazis, and *No Highway* (1948), about an aircraft engineer trying desperately to warn sceptical superiors and politicians of the existence of metal fatigue. In 1950 Shute settled in Australia, and made it the setting for most of his later books. He wrote of ordinary people in a self-effacing style; his books have the immediacy of 'in-depth' newspaper reporting. But the characters of each story are in crisis, and the plot shows them working out moral or ethical dilemmas which have implications far beyond the novel's bounds. Several of his books were filmed, and inspired a whole genre of documentary-style drama about 'issues', now also common on television. Some of Shute's themes (for example the horrific effects of bombing on civilians, the subject of his 1939 novel *What Happened to the Corbetts*, or the existence of metal-fatigue) have been overtaken by events, and his once-slangy dialogue has dated. But few popular writers have treated serious themes so grippingly. Despite their age, his novels are unputdownable.

ON THE BEACH (1957)

The book is set in the Melbourne suburbs at some unstated time in the near future. We see perfectly ordinary people (a young couple with a baby; a woman and her US sailor-lover) bustling about their mundane lives. But the background is anything but ordinary: the whole human race is facing imminent annihilation from the nuclear fallout of World War III. As the novel proceeds, and Shute explores the implications of this theme, his characters' attempts to preserve everyday decencies are shown to be not so much survival strategy as a pitiable, pointless evasion of reality.

Shute's early books include So Disdained, Lonely Road *and the excellent war-story* Landfall. *His later novels include* The Far Country, In the Wet, Requiem for a Wren *and* Trustee from the Toolroom. Slide Rule *is an autobiography up to 1938.*

READ ON

- *A Town Like Alice* (about two survivors from the Japanese occupation of Malaya who decide to develop one small settlement in the Australian outback).
- ▶ **To *On the Beach*:** John Christopher, *The Death of Grass*; ▷George Turner, *The Sea and Summer*.
- ▶ **To Shute's books involving technology and research:** Nigel Balchin, *The Small Back Room*; ▷C.P. Snow, *The New Men*.
- ▶ **To Shute's work in general:** H.E. Bates, *The Purple Plain*; ▷Morris West, *The Navigator*; Ernest K. Gann, *The High and the Mighty*; ▷Elizabeth Bowen, *The Heat of the Day*.

SILVERBERG, ROBERT (BORN 1935)
US novelist.

Silverberg has written over 300 books, both under his own name and as Walter Chapman, Ivar Jorgensen, Calvin M. Knox, David Osborne, Lee Sebastian and Robert Randall (his pseudonym when he collaborates with Randall Garrett). As well as SF and fantasy he writes children's stories and non-fiction books on science and history. Most of his SF novels – like ▷Ballard's – involve escalation towards catastrophe of the scientific or political trends of the present day. The theme of *Master of Life and Death* (1957) is over-population. *Recalled to Life* (1958) imagines a medical advance which allows us to bring the dead back to life. The hero of *Stochastic Man* (1975) is a psychic adviser to presidents who finds that he can genuinely predict the future. *A Time of Changes* (1971) imagines a planet colonised by an extreme religious group. Silverberg is also known for fantasy series set in worlds of the far future. Majipoor, for example, is a giant planet where magic and science, medieval politics and high technology, aliens and humans, co-exist. In *Lord Valentine's Castle* (first volume of the 'Majipoor' Trilogy, 1979–83), a wandering juggler discovers, by chance use of his psychic powers, that he is the rightful ruler of the planet, and gathers a company of warriors to win his inheritance. In *The Majipoor Chronicles* a boy discovers the planet's computer archives, and embarks on a psychic exploration of its teeming, magical history. In *Valentine Pontifex* the ruler of Majipoor has to undertake his most demanding task yet, a battle against the Metamorphs who are destroying crops, trying to starve Majipoor's people into submission and take over Valentine's throne.

Silverberg's other books include Lord of Darkness, Capricorn Games *and two inspired by Biblical and other ancient myths,* Shadrach in the Furnace *and* Gilgamesh the King.

READ ON

- **To the SF:** ▷Robert Heinlein, *Job*; Frederik Pohl, *The Reefs of Space*; ▷Ray Bradbury, *The Illustrated Man*.
- **To the fantasies:** ▷Piers Anthony, *Vicinity Cluster*; Iain Banks, *Consider Phlebas*; ▷Anne McCaffrey, *Dragonflight*.

SIMENON, GEORGES (1903–89)
Belgian novelist.

Simenon is best-known for some 150 crime-stories featuring the pipe-smoking, calvados-drinking Commissaire Maigret of the Paris Police. The books are short and spare; they concentrate on Maigret's investigations in bars, lodging-houses and rain-soaked Paris streets, and on his casual-seeming, fatherly conversations with suspects and witnesses. But Simenon is a far more substantial writer than this suggests. His non-Maigret novels – several hundred, since for 50 years he averaged a book every six or seven weeks – are compelling psychological studies of people distracted by

READ ON

- **To *Pedigree*:** ▷Jerome Weidman, *Fourth Street East*.
- **To Simenon's non-Maigret novels:** Julian Symons, *The 31st of February*.
- **To the Maigret books:** Nicolas Freeling, *Love in*

fear, obsession, despair or hate. *Act of Passion* (1947) is the confession of a madman who kills his lover to keep her pure, to prevent her being contaminated by the evil which he feels has corroded his own soul. The hero of *The Man Who Watched the Trains Go By* (1938), outwardly placid and controlled, is in fact so gnawed by the sense of his own inadequacy that he chooses murder as the best way to make his mark on the world. In *The President* (1958) a politician, brooding in enforced retirement, is unexpectedly offered the chance to revenge himself both politically and personally on the man who wronged him. *Ticket of Leave* (1942) is about a woman who falls in love with a paroled murderer. All these books are written in a sinewy, unemotional style, as plain as a police report. Only in one novel, *Pedigree* (1948), does Simenon break out of his self-imposed limits. It is a 500-page account of a boy's growing-up in Belgium in the first 15 years of this century, an evocation not only of trams, gaslight, cobble-stones and teeming back-street life, but of an emerging personality. A fictionalised autobiography, it is one of Simenon's most unexpected and rewarding works.

Amsterdam; Maj Sjöwall and Per Wahlöö, *The Laughing Policeman*; Friedrich Dürrenmatt, *The Quarry*.

SINGER, I.B. (ISAAC BASHEVIS) (BORN 1904)

Polish/US novelist and short-story writer.

Singer writes in Yiddish, and maintains that even when he translates his work himself, English dilutes its force. His characters are also Yiddish-speakers, either Middle European Jews – merchants, yeshiva-students, gravediggers, rabbis, drunks – from the ghettos and peasant villages of the 17th-19th centuries, or (in several of his finest stories) present-day settlers in Israel or the USA. They struggle to lead decent lives, uplifted or oppressed by the demands of orthodox Jewish belief and ritual. They are haunted by outside forces beyond their control: supernatural beings – several stories are narrated by dybbuks, ghosts and even the Devil himself – or mindless, vicious anti-semitism. Only one of Singer's novels is contemporary: *The Penitent* (1974), about a Polish-American Jew who returns to Israel and tries to come to terms with his own belief and with the tragic history of his people. The rest have historical settings – except that no Singer fiction is really historical, since everything he writes is a fable, with universal resonance. *Satan in Goray* (1955), *The Magician of Lublin* (1960) and *The Slave* (1962) are about dark forces, demonic evil breaking out in small, closed communities. In *The Manor* (1967), *The Estate* (1970) and *Enemies, a Love Story* (1972) the destructive forces are internal, as people's orthodox beliefs are challenged by love-affairs, business-deals, friendships and other such worldly claims. In *The King of the Fields* (1989), the

READ ON

- **To the short stories:** S.Y. Agnon, *The Bridal Canopy*; Isaac Babel, *Odessa Tales*; ▷Nikolai Gogol, *Arabesques*.
- **To *The Family Moskat*:** I.J. Singer (I.B.'s brother), *The Brothers Ashkenazy*.
- **To Singer's other novels:** Bernard Malamud, *The Fixer*; Nikos Kazantzakis, *The Greek Passion*; ▷Mario Vargas Llosa, *The War of the End of the World*; ▷Jerzy Kosinski, *The Painted Bird*.

destructive force is nothing less than European 'civilisation' itself, destroying the Edenic innocence of a remote group of Polish hunter-gatherers 1800 years ago.

THE FAMILY MOSKAT (1950)

This is a warm, multi-generation story about a large Jewish family in Warsaw – and Singer's finest novel. The focus is on the human relationships within the family, magnificently and movingly described; but the novel's edge comes from the constant intrusion of grim outside reality, the tormented history of Poland between the Congress of Vienna in 1815 and the second-world-war nazi storming of the Warsaw Ghetto. Counterpoint between inner and outer reality, between public and private life, between flesh and spirit, makes this book not just another family saga but a statement about Jewish (and non-Jewish) humanity at large. In that, *The Family Moskat* is characteristic of Singer's work – it is his universality, not his particularity, which makes him one of the most respected writers of the century.

Singer's short-story collections are Gimpel the Fool, The Spinoza of Market Street, Short Friday, The Séance, A Friend of Kafka, A Crown of Feathers, Passions, Love and Exile, Old Love, The Death of Methuselah *and* The Image. Collected Stories *is a fat anthology.* In My Father's Court *is a memoir of Singer's Warsaw days as the son of a rabbi, a theological student and a budding writer.*

SMALL TOWN LIFE, USA

Sherwood Anderson, *Winesburgh, Ohio*
▷John Cheever, *Bullet Park*
▷John Irving, *The Cider House Rules*
Garrison Keillor, *Lake Wobegon Days*
Arthur Laurents, *The Way We Were*
Jean Potts, *The Diehard*

Deep South, USA (p 57)

SMITH, E.E. 'DOC' (EDWARD ELMER SMITH, PHD) (1890-1965)

US novelist.

Smith's books are the quintessence of space-opera. Good guys in powerful spaceships battle villains, explore new worlds, use entire planets as weapons, arrange the rise and fall of galactic civilisations. Although his scientific invention has been overtaken by events, and his plots and situations have been endlessly pirated in trashy films and TV series, no SF writer has surpassed him as a teller of straightforward, edge-of-the-seat space yarns. *First Lensman*, the

READ ON

- *Skylark of Space* (first of the 4-novel 'Skylark' series); *The Imperial Stars* (first of the 10-novel 'Family d'Alembert' series).
- ▶ David A. Kyle, *The*

first novel of the 'Lensman' series (1950–60; *Triplanetary*, 1948, is a prologue) is a splendid introduction to his work. Faced with the ever-growing power of criminals, from space pirates to intergalactic drug barons, the police are falling further and further behind until Virgil Samms, head of the Triplanetary Service, receives word that he will find help on Arisia, a ghost-planet hitherto shunned by space-travellers.

Dragon Lensman (first of a trilogy of Lensman sequels authorised by the Smith estate). Vonda N. McIntyre, *Enterprize – the First Adventure* (a powerful book using characters from the TV series *Star Trek*). ▷Harry Harrison, *Star Smashers of the Galaxy Rangers* (a merciless spoof).

SMITH, WILBUR (BORN 1933)

South African novelist.

Smith's novels, set in South Africa, are swaggering adventure yarns in the tradition of ▷H. Rider Haggard. Their backgrounds are war (especially the Boer War), mining and jungle exploration; their heroes are free spirits, revelling in the lawlessness and vigour of frontier life. (John Wayne played their US equivalents in a hundred films.) *Shout at the Devil* (1968) is typical: the story of lion-hunting, crocodile-wrestling, ivory-poaching Flynn O'Flynn, whose Robin Hood humiliations of the sadistic German commissioner Fleischer take a serious turn when war is declared – this is 1914 – and he falls into a German trap.

Smith's other novels include Gold Mine, A Sparrow Falls *and the 'Courtneys of Africa' trilogy* The Burning Shore, Power of the Sword *and* Rage *(about the lifelong feud of two half-brothers during the last turbulent century of South African affairs).*

READ ON

- *A Time to Die* (about Sean Courtney, a white safari guide who agrees to lead his rich US clients across the border into Mozambique, where the daughter is promptly kidnapped by guerrillas).
- ▶ ▷Desmond Bagley, *Running Blind*. John Gardner, *The Secret Generation*. ▷Hammond Innes, *Campbell's Kingdom*. ▷H. Rider Haggard, *King Solomon's Mines*.

SNOW, C.P. (CHARLES PERCY) (1905–80)

British novelist.

Snow's main work is the novel-sequence 'Strangers and Brothers' (1940–74). Though many characters recur, each book is self-contained. As the series proceeds, Lewis Eliot (the narrator of all 11 novels) rises from humble provincial beginnings to become a barrister, a civil servant and a senior government official. Snow's preoccupation was power: how people influence each other, the working of committees

READ ON

- ▶ ▷Anthony Trollope, *Can You Forgive Her?* (the first novel in the 'Palliser' sequence). ▷Angus Wilson, *The Old Men at the Zoo*.

and hierarchies, the morality of office. He coined the phrase 'the corridors of power' – and he offers unrivalled glimpses of the people who tramp those corridors, of real individuals behind the establishment façade. *The Masters*, one of the key books in the sequence, describes the alliances and compromises required to elect a new master for a Cambridge college. *The New Men*, about scientists working on the first atomic bomb, is a study of responsibility: should we use our skills for ends we feel are wrong? In *The Conscience of the Rich*, about family loyalty, a rich young man rejects the future his father plans for him and becomes a doctor. *The Sleep of Reason*, the bleakest of all Snow's books, discusses our moral responsibility for others' evil; it was based on a horrific real 1960s case of multiple child-murder. Snow's themes are large, but his books are blander and less agonised than this suggests. His characters – especially the imperturbable committee-men (never women) who keep things going and the mavericks who let feelings interfere with common sense – are fascinating, and his scenes of discussion and persuasion are brilliantly done: he keeps us on the edge of our seats about such apparently trivial matters as whether someone will end up saying 'yes' or 'no'.

The books in the sequence are Strangers and Brothers, The Light and the Dark, A Time of Hope, The Masters, The New Men, Homecomings, The Conscience of the Rich, The Affair, The Corridors of Power, The Sleep of Reason *and* Last Things. *Snow's other novels include two thrillers,* Death Under Sail, A Coat of Varnish, *and* The Search, *a fascinating study of the excitement and passion of scientific research.*

Pamela Hansford Johnson (Lady Snow), *Error of Judgement*. ▷Gore Vidal, *Washington, D.C.* ▷Neville Shute, *No Highway*.

SOLZHENITSYN, ALEXANDER (BORN 1918)

Russian novelist and non-fiction writer.

Denounced for treason in 1945 (he was a Red Army soldier who criticised Stalin), Solzhenitsyn spent eight years in a labour camp where he developed stomach cancer, and after nine months in a cancer hospital was sent into internal exile. He turned this bitter experience into novels (the prison-camp books *One Day in the Life of Ivan Denisovich* (1961) and *The First Circle* (1968); *Cancer Ward)* (1968), and their publication outside the USSR made him one of the most famous of all 1960s Soviet dissidents. He was finally expelled from the USSR in 1974, for writing an exhaustive description of the location, history and methods of the Russian prison-camp system, *The GULAG Archipelago* (1974–8). Few writers have ever surpassed him as a chronicler of human behaviour at its most nightmarish: his personal history authenticates every word he wrote.

READ ON

▶ ▷Fyodor Dostoevski, *Notes from the House of the Dead*. Arthur Koestler, *Darkness at Noon*. ▷Vladimir Nabokov, *Bend Sinister*. André Brink, *Looking on Darkness*. ▷Thomas Pynchon, *Gravity's Rainbow*. William Styron, *Sophie's Choice*.

Solzhenitsyn's only other novel is August 1914, *about the stirrings of the Russian Revolution.*

SOMETHING NASTY...

Roald Dahl, *Kiss Kiss* (short stories)
Thomas Harris, *The Silence of the Lambs*
▷James Herbert, *Moon*
▷Stephen King, *Pet Sematary*
▷Ruth Rendell, *Live Flesh*

Good and Evil (p 97)

SOUTH AFRICA

J.M. Coetzee, *In the Heart of the Country*
▷Nadine Gordimer, *Burger's Daughter*
Dan Jacobson, *A Dance in the Sun*
David Karp, *The Day of the Monkey*
Mike Nicol, *The Powers That Be*
Alan Paton, *Cry, The Beloved Country*
▷Tom Sharpe, *Riotous Assembly*
Anthony Sher, *Middlepost*
Carolyn Slaughter, *The Innocents*
▷Wilbur Smith, *Rage*

SPARK, MURIEL (BORN 1918)

British novelist.

Spark made her name in the 1960s: her tart black comedies seemed just the antidote to the fey optimism of the time. Her books' deadpan world is a distorted mirror-image of our own, a disconcerting blend of the bland and the bizarre. In *Memento Mori* old people are mysteriously telephoned and reminded that they are about to die. In *Robinson* a plane-load of ill-assorted people (among them the standard Spark heroine, a Catholic with Doubts) crashes on an island where laws and customs are hourly remade at the whim of the sole inhabitant. In *The Prime of Miss Jean Brodie* an Edinburgh schoolmistress tries to brainwash her pupils into being nice, conforming gels. *The Abbess of Crewe* reworks convent politics in terms of Watergate; the hero of *The Only Problem*, a scholar working on the Book of Job, finds its events parallelling those in his own life. Spark develops these ideas not in farce but in brisk, neat prose, as if they were the most matter-of-fact happenings in the world. The results are eccentric, unsettling and hilarious.

READ ON

- *The Ballad of Peckham Rye*; *The Bachelors*.
- ▶ Ronald Firbank, *The Eccentricities of Cardinal Pirelli*. ▷Rose Macaulay, *The Towers of Trebizond*. Alice Thomas Ellis, *The 27th Kingdom*. ▷Anita Brookner, *Look at Me*. ▷John Updike, *The Witches of Eastwick*. ▷Elizabeth Jolley, *Miss Peabody's Inheritance*.

THE GIRLS OF SLENDER MEANS (1963)

A group of young ladies lives in a run-down London club for distressed gentlefolk. It is 1945, and there is rumoured to be an unexploded bomb in the garden. The girls are excited by the possibility of imminent destruction: they find it almost as thrilling as the thought of sex. They bustle about their busy, vapid lives: pining after film stars, writing (unanswered) letters to famous writers, bargaining for black-market clothing coupons. The book is an allegory about seedy-genteel, self-absorbed Britain under the threat of nuclear extinction; for all Spark's breezy humour, the novel is haunted by the questions of where we'll be and how we'll behave when the bomb goes up.

Spark's other novels include The Mandelbaum Gate *(her most serious book, about a half-Jewish Catholic convert visiting Jerusalem at the height of Arab-Israeli tension),* The Driver's Seat, Not to Disturb, The Takeover *and* Territorial Rights. The Stories of Muriel Spark *is a generous short-story collection.*

SPIES AND DOUBLE AGENTS

▷Ted Allbeury, *The Secret Whispers*
▷Joseph Conrad, *The Secret Agent*
▷Frederick Forsyth, *The Fourth Protocol*
John Kruse, *The Hour of the Lily*
▷John Le Carré, *A Perfect Spy*
▷Ruth Rendell, *Talking to Strange Men*
Hardiman Scott and Becky Allan, *Bait of Lies*

Action Thrillers (p 2); High Adventure (p 119)

STEAD, CHRISTINA (1902–83)

Australian novelist.

Although Stead was born in Australia, she lived most of her life, and set many of her books, in Europe (especially Paris) and the USA. She writes of these places, however, not as a native but as a visitor, in a detached, ironic tone. In *The Beauties and Furies*, a savage moral tale about adultery, a young wife runs off to 1930s Paris and has an affair with a handsome but ruthless sexual adventurer; in the end he drops her and goes in search of younger prey. *House of all Nations*, an 800-page blockbuster about the insidious corruption of money, centres on the customers, staff and owners of a private European bank, and especially on its chief Jules Bertillon, a man whose moral sense and conscience have atrophied in the face of 'market forces'. Stead was a socialist, and this book is a devastating, if covert, assault on

READ ON

- **To *The Beauties and Furies*:** ▷Jean Rhys, *After Leaving Mr Mackenzie*; Patrick Hamilton, *Hangover Square*; ▷Djuna Barnes, *Nightwood*.
- **To *House of All Nations*:** ▷John Galsworthy, *The Forsyte Saga*; ▷Jerome Weidman, *A Family Fortune*.
- **To *The Man Who***

the pre-second-world-war European capitalist system. *The Man Who Loved Children*, set in the USA but based on Stead's own experience, is a story of stifling family life at the turn of the century, presided over by a monstrous, bullying father; the whole thing is seen through the eyes of his daughter, Louise, as she grows from terrified, adoring childhood to rebellious adolescence and adulthood.

Stead's other novels include For Love Alone, Dark Places of the Heart/Cotter's England, The People With the Dogs, Miss Herbert (The Suburban Wife) *and the long, ironic 'romance'* Letty Fox, Her Luck. The Salzburg Tales *is a collection of macabre, satirical and bawdy short stories modelled on Chaucer's* Canterbury Tales.

Loved Children: ▷Ivy Compton-Burnett, *A Family and a Fortune*; ▷Angela Carter, *The Magic Toyshop*.

STEEL, Danielle

US novelist.

If there can be such a thing as feminist romance, that is what Steel writes. Her young women are briskly in charge of their own destinies, and regard men not as knights in shining armour but as equal partners – an attitude which some of her men find hard to take. Melting femininity is present, in that the books are about love-affairs, but so is melting masculinity: where emotion and sentiment are concerned, all human beings are one. Her books include *Golden Moments/Passion's Promise, Crossings, Loving, The Promises, Fine Things, Kaleidoscope, Season of Passion, Remembrance, Palomino, Summer's End, Zoya* and *Full Circle* (1985), whose heroine is involved with the 1970s protest movement in the USA, fighting for civil rights and the end of the Vietnam war.

READ ON

- *Star.*
- ▶ Helen Van Slyke, *The Rich and the Righteous*. ▷Mary Wesley, *The Camomile Lawn*. Charlotte Vale Allen, *Promises*. ▷Alice Walker, *Meridian*.

STEINBECK, John (1902–68)

US novelist.

Until Steinbeck settled to writing in 1935, he moved restlessly from one job to another: he was a journalist, a builder's labourer, a house-painter, a fruit-picker and the caretaker of a lakeside estate. This experience gave him first-hand knowledge of the dispossessed, the unemployed millions who suffered the brunt of the US Depression of the 1930s. Their lives are his subject, and he writes of them with ferocious, documentary intensity and in a style which seems exactly to catch their habits of both mind and speech. The ruggedness of his novels is often enhanced by themes borrowed from myth or the Old Testament. *To A God Unknown* (1933) is about an impoverished farmer who begins worshipping ancient gods and ends up sacrificing himself for rain. *Tortilla Flat* (1935) about 'wetbacks' (illegal Mexican

READ ON

- *Of Mice and Men* (a tragedy about the friendship between two ill-matched farmworkers, Lennie – a simple-minded giant of a man – and the weedier, cleverer George).
- ▶ Erskine Caldwell, *God's Little Acre*. ▷Edith Wharton, *Ethan Frome*. ▷William Faulkner,

immigrants to California) uses the story of Arthur, Guinevere and Lancelot from British myth. *East of Eden* (1952) is based on the story of Cain and Abel. Though Steinbeck never thrusts such references down his readers' throats, they add to the grandeur and mystery which, together with documentary grittiness, are the overwhelming qualities of his work.

The Hamlet. Upton Sinclair, *The Jungle*. ▷Victor Hugo, *Toilers of the Sea*. ▷Somerset Maugham, *Liza of Lambeth*.

THE GRAPES OF WRATH (1938)

The once-fertile Oklahoma grain-fields have been reduced to a dust-bowl by over-farming, and the Joad family are near starvation. Attracted by leaflets promising work in the fruit-plantations of California, they load their belongings into a battered old car and travel west. In California they find every plantation surrounded by destitute, desperate people: there are a thousand applicants for every job. The plantation-owners pay starvation-wages and sack anyone who objects; the workers try to force justice by strike action – and are beaten up by armed vigilantes. When Tom Joad, already on the run for murder, is caught up in the fight for justice and accidentally kills a man; it is time for Ma to gather the family together again and move on. There must be a place for them somewhere; there must be a Promised Land.

Steinbeck's shorter novels include Cannery Row, The Pearl *and* The Short Reign of Pippin IV. *His short stories, usually about 'wetbacks', share-croppers and other victims of the US system, are in* The Red Pony *and* The Long Valley. The Acts of King Arthur and his Noble Knights *is a straightforward retelling of British myth;* The Portable Steinbeck *is a packed anthology.*

STENDHAL (1783-1842)

French novelist and non-fiction writer.

'Stendhal' was a pseudonym used by the French diplomat Henri-Marie Beyle. As well as fiction (four novels; a dozen short stories) he published essays on art, literature and philosophy and several autobiographical books. Unlike most early 19th-century writers – even ▷Balzac and ▷Dickens – who concentrated on surface likenesses, painting word-pictures of events, people and places without introspection, Stendhal was chiefly interested in his characters' psychology. The main theme of his novels was the way outsiders, without breeding or position, must make their way in snobbish, tradition-stifled society by talent or personality alone. His books give the feeling that we are watching the evolution of that personality, that we are as intimate with his people's psychological development as if they were relatives or friends.

READ ON

- *The Charterhouse of Parma*.
- ▶ **To *Scarlet and Black***: ▷André Gide, *Strait is the Gate*; ▷Nikolai Gogol, *Dead Souls*; ▷George Eliot, *Middlemarch*; ▷Honoré de Balzac, *Lost Illusions*: John Braine, *Room at the Top*; ▷Jerome Weidman, *I Can Get it for You Wholesale*.

SCARLET AND BLACK (LE ROUGE ET LE NOIR) (1830)

The book is a character-study of Julien Sorel, a carpenter's son who rises in the world by brains, sexual charm and ruthlessness. He becomes first tutor to the children of the local Mayor, then the Mayor's wife's lover, and finally secretary to an aristocratic diplomat whose daughter falls in love with him. In ten years he has travelled from humble origins to the verge of a dazzling marriage and a brilliant career. But then the Mayor's wife writes a letter denouncing him as a cold-hearted adventurer, his society acquaintances reject him, and he returns to his native town to take revenge.

▶ **To *The Charterhouse of Parma*:** ▷Umberto Eco, *The Name of the Rose*.

Stendhal's other completed novels are Armance, The Abbess of Castro *and* The Charterhouse of Parma. The Life of Henri Brulard *and* Memoirs of an Egoist *are fictionalised autobiography.*

STERNE, LAURENCE (1713–68)

British novelist.

Sterne's only novel, *The Life and Opinions of Tristram Shandy, Gentleman* (1760–7) is less a story than a gloriously rambling conversation. Tristram sets out to tell his life-story (beginning with the moment of his conception, when his mother's mind is less on what she is doing than on whether his father has remembered to wind the clock). But everything he says reminds him of some anecdote or wise remark, so that he constantly interrupts himself. It takes 300 pages, for example, for him to get from his conception to the age of seven, and in the meantime we have had such digressions as a treatise on what the size and shape of people's noses tells us about their characters, an explanation of how the boy came to be called Tristram by mistake for Trismegistus (and what each name signifies), accounts of the Tristapaedia (the system devised for Tristram's education), the curse of Ernulphus of Rochester and the misfortunes of Lieutenant le Fever; we have also had the novel's preface (placed not at the beginning but as the peroration to Book III), and many musings on life, love and the pursuit of happiness by Tristram's father, Uncle Toby and Corporal Trim. The reader is constantly exhorted, nudged and questioned; there is even a blank page in case you have urgent thoughts of your own to add. We never know how Tristram's life turns out; instead, we are copiously informed about Uncle Toby's love-affair, Tristram's travels in France and the adventures of the King of Bohemia. Sterne himself called *Tristram Shandy* 'a civil, nonsensical, good-humoured book'; it is the most spectacular shaggy-dog story ever told.

READ ON

▶ ▷François Rabelais, *Gargantua*. Miguel de Cervantes Saavedra, *Don Quixote*. Tobias Smollett, *The Expedition of Humphry Clinker*. ▷John Kennedy Toole, *A Confederacy of Dunces*. Flann O'Brien, *At Swim-Two-Birds*. ▷Saul Bellow, *Henderson the Rain King*.

Sterne's other writings include sermons – he was a Yorkshire parson – and A Sentimental Journey, *a discursive, half-fictionalised account of the towns and people he saw and the tales he heard during six months' travelling in France.*

STEVENSON, R.L. (ROBERT LOUIS) (1850–94)

British writer of novels, short stories and non-fiction.

Apart from the brief psychological thriller *Dr Jekyll and Mr Hyde* (1886), about a man who uses drugs to change himself from kindly family doctor to deformed killer and back again, Stevenson's chief works are historical adventure-stories. They have been hijacked by child readers, but (except perhaps in *Treasure Island*, 1883) there is also plenty to interest adults: Stevenson's evocation of scenery (especially Scotland), the psychological complexity of his characters, and the feeling (which he shared with ▷Tolstoy) that each human life is part of a vast historical, moral and cultural continuum.

Stevenson's historical novels include The Black Arrow *(a story of the Wars of the Roses),* Weir of Hermiston *(about an Edinburgh 'hanging-judge' in the early 19th century) and the Jacobite trilogy* Kidnapped, Catriona *and* The Master of Ballantrae. *His lighter fiction includes* The Wrong Box, The Wrecker *and* The Ebb-tide. The Merry Men *and* Island Nights' Entertainment *contain short stories. He also wrote poetry, travel books (eg* Travels with a Donkey*) and plays.*

READ ON

- **To *Dr Jekyll and Mr Hyde*:** ▷H.G. Wells, *The Invisible Man*; Gaston Leroux, *The Phantom of the Opera*; James Hogg, *Confessions of a Justified Sinner*.
- **To the adventure stories:** ▷Daniel Defoe, *Robinson Crusoe*; ▷Walter Scott, *The Heart of Midlothian*; John Masefield, *Jim Davis*; ▷John Buchan, *Castle Gay*; ▷A. Conan Doyle, *The Valley of Fear*; ▷Desmond Bagley, *Running Blind*.

STEWART, MARY (BORN 1916)

British novelist.

Stewart's romantic adventure stories are set in magnificently-evoked, exotic parts of Europe and the Mediterranean. Her books include *Madam Will You Talk?*, *Wildfire at Midnight*, *Thunder on the Right*, *Nine Coaches Waiting*, *The Moon-spinners*, *Airs Above the Ground*, *The Gabriel Hounds*, *Touch Not the Cat* and *This Rough Magic* (1964), in which a girl, holidaying on Corfu, is caught up not only in sorcery – Corfu is the 'magic island' of Shakespeare's *The Tempest* – but in a gun-running conspiracy between Greece and Albania. Stewart also wrote a trilogy based on the legends of Merlin and King Arthur; the first volume is *The Crystal Cave* (1970).

READ ON

- *The Gabriel Hounds*.
- Anne Bridge, *Illyrian Spring*. Helen MacInnes, *The Venetian Affair*. ▷Dorothy Dunnett, *Dolly and the Cookie Bird*.

STOKER, Bram (1847–1912)
Irish writer.

Forget all sendups and tawdry horror-film exploitation. *Dracula* (1897) is still one of the most blood-curdling novels ever written. The reader may begin by counting off the clichés – foggy cemeteries, vaults under the madhouse, the blazing crucifix, the bat-count climbing down the castle walls – but the sheer power of the story, its conviction and its exotic (and erotic) eeriness soon grip like tiny pointed teeth. Stoker was not a genius, but *Dracula* is a work of genius, the Gothic novel (written in the form of diaries and letters to give added authenticity) to end them all.

READ ON

▶ ▷Edgar Allan Poe, *Tales of Mystery and Imagination*. Dennis Wheatley, *The Ka of Gifford Hillary*. ▷James Herbert, *Moon*. ▷Stephen King, *Salem's Lot*.

STONE, Irving (1903–89)
US novelist.

Stone's 'biographical novels' tell real lives in a swaggering, melodramatic fictional style. His historical research is exact, and he gives a magnificent impression of the period his characters lived in and of their character and relationships. His books, many of them successfully filmed, include *Lust for Life* (1934, about Van Gogh), *The Agony and the Ecstasy* (1971, about Michelangelo), *The Passions of the Mind* (1971, about Freud) and *The Origin* (1980, about Darwin).

READ ON

▶ Josef Skvorecky, *Dvořák in Love*. Lloyd C. Douglas, *The Big Fisherman* (about St Peter). Alan Brien, *Lenin: the Novel*.

Sunday Times Top Twelve

In 1989, a letter in the *Sunday Times* of London asked readers to list the twelve classics of world literature which were enjoyable reading as well as essential. Over 1000 books were suggested. The top twelve, in order of popularity, were:

▷Jane Austen, *Pride and Prejudice*
▷Charles Dickens, *David Copperfield*
▷Emily Brontë, *Wuthering Heights*
▷George Eliot, *Middlemarch*
▷Thomas Hardy, *Tess of the d'Urbervilles*
▷Graham Greene, *The Power and the Glory*
Lewis Carroll, *Alice in Wonderland*
▷Fyodor Dostoevski, *Crime and Punishment*
▷J.R.R. Tolkien, *The Lord of the Rings*
▷John Steinbeck, *The Grapes of Wrath*
▷Anthony Trollope, *Barchester Towers*
▷Evelyn Waugh, *Brideshead Revisited*

Indulging in book-writer's privilege, I should like to add:

▷Daphne du Maurier, *Rebecca*

▷William Golding, *Rites of Passage*
▷Hermann Hesse, *Rosshalde*
▷Gabriel García Márquez, *One Hundred Years of Solitude*
▷I.B. Singer, *Short Stories*
▷R.K. Narayan, *The Vendor of Sweets*

SVEVO, ITALO (1861-1928)
Austrian/Italian novelist.

Svevo was a businessman in Trieste; his firm made underwater paint. Despite encouragement from his friend ▷James Joyce, he never took his writing seriously until the last year of his life, when a French translation of *The Confessions of Zeno* (1922) brought him European fame. His books are ironical comedies. Their ineffective, bewildered heroes blunder about in society, looking for some point to their existence – and the chief irony is that they are genuinely the 'zeros' they think they are, their existence has no point at all. *The Confessions of Zeno* is the autobiography of a man who wants to give up smoking. He explains that his addiction is actually psychological, since every cigarette he smokes reminds him, in ▷Proustian fashion, of some past experience, so that to give up smoking would be to surrender his own history; he writes of his Oedipal relationship with his father (whom he accidentally killed), of his prolonged, ludicrous courtship of the wrong woman, and of his treatment by a psychiatrist sicker than himself. The book is as dreamlike and terrifying as ▷Kafka's novels – indeed, Svevo exactly shared Kafka's vision of the world as an absurd, endless and sinister labyrinth.

Svevo's other novels are A Life, As A Man Grows Older *and the shorter* Tale of the Good Old Man and the Pretty Girl.

READ ON

- ▷Franz Kafka, *The Castle*. ▷Saul Bellow, *Herzog*. Alberto Moravia, *The Conformist*. Joaquin Machado de Assis, *The Heritage of Quincas Borba*. William Cooper, *Scenes from Married Life*. ▷William Boyd, *The New Confessions*. ▷Gabriel Garciá Márquez, *Love in the Time of Cholera*.

SWIFT, GRAHAM (BORN 1949)
British novelist.

Swift's novels centre on apparently ordinary people – shopkeepers, housewives, clerks – under psychological stress. They have reached turning-points in what have seemed boring, routine lives, and the novels show them mentally rerunning the past to find explanations for their feelings, either to themselves or to others. In *Waterland* (1983) the main character is an elderly history teacher, and the event he is remembering is the discovery, forty years before, of a boy's body in a drainage-ditch in the English Fens. In front of a bored, cheeky class, he begins thinking aloud about the reasons for the boy's death – and his monologue ranges

READ ON

- *Out of This World* (in which, in alternate monologues, the son and grand-daughter of a first-world-war hero, an arms manufacturer, reflect on the way the old man's obsessive love for them has

through the history of the Fens (one of the remotest and most mysterious English regions), the story of several generations of his own family, and, not least, an account of the rivalry between his mentally subnormal brother Dick and Freddie Parr, the boy found drowned.

Swift's other novels are The Sweet Shop Owner, Shuttlecock *and* Out of This World. Learning To Swim *is a collection of short stories.*

poisoned both their lives).

▶ Peter Benson, *The Levels*. Gerald H. Morris, *Doves and Silk Handkerchieves*. ▷John Irving, *The Cider House Rules*.

SWIFT, JONATHAN (1667-1745)

British/Irish satirist and journalist.

Swift was a savage satirist, pouring out poems, articles and essays attacking the follies of his time. *Gulliver's Travels* (1726) differs from his other work only in that the edge of its satire is masked by fairy tale – indeed, the satire is often edited out so that the book can be sold for children. Gulliver is a compulsive explorer, despite the moral humiliation he suffers after every landfall. In Lilliput the people (who are six inches high) regard him as an uncouth, unpredictable monster – particularly when he tells them some of the ideas and customs of his native England. In Brobdignag he becomes the pet of giants, and tries without success to convince them of the value of such civilised essentials as lawcourts, money and guns. He visits Laputa and Lagado, cloud-cuckoo-lands where science has ousted common sense; on the Island of Sorcerers he speaks to great thinkers of the past, and finds them in despair at what has become of the human race. Finally he is shipwrecked among the Houynhyms, horses equipped with reason who regard human beings as degenerate barbarians, and who fill him with such distaste for his own species that when he returns to England he can hardly bear the sight, sound or smell of his own family. Throughout the book, Gulliver doggedly preaches the glories of European 'civilisation' (that is, the customs and beliefs of the Age of Enlightenment), and arouses only derision or disgust.

READ ON

▶ Voltaire, *Candide*. Samuel Butler, *Erewhon*. ▷Nathaniel West, *A Cool Million*.

▶ **Equally lacerating satires on aspects of late 20th-century life:** Michael Frayn, *A Very Private Life*; ▷Thomas Pynchon, *The Crying of Lot 49*; ▷Angela Carter, *The Passion of New Eve*.

T

TAYLOR, ELIZABETH (1912–75)

British novelist and short-story writer.

A large part of Taylor's art consists in appearing to have no art at all: few authors have ever seemed so self-effacing in their work. As each novel or story begins, it is as if a net curtain has been drawn aside to reveal ordinary people in a normal street. The setting is the outskirts of some large English town; the people are housewives, bus-conductors, labourers, schoolchildren; there seems to be no drama. But as the story proceeds, an apparently unfussy chronicle of ordinary events and conversations builds up enormous psychological pressure, which Taylor then releases in a shocking or hilarious happening which opens speculation wide about whatever will happen when the book is closed. Her artistry – subtle, gentle and unsettling – is at its peak in short stories; her novels, thanks to larger casts, more varied settings and longer time-schemes, tend more to wry social comedy than to the sinister.

THE DEVASTATING BOYS (1972)

The people in this story collection are typical Taylor characters: an elderly couple in the countryside who decide to offer a holiday to two black children from the city slums; a young West Indian, utterly alone in London on the eve of his birthday; an 11-year-old child taking a bus home from a hateful piano lesson; a blue-rinsed widow with an orderly routine of life. Something unexpected happens to each of them, a psychological bombshell. They were as unremarkable as our neighbours – but after these stories, our neighbours will never seem the same again.

READ ON

- *Hester Lilly*; *The Wedding Group* (novel).
- ▶ **To the stories:** ▷V.S. Pritchett, *The Camberwell Beauty and Other stories*; William Trevor, *Angels at the Ritz*; Mary Gordon, *Temporary Shelter*; Joyce Carol Oates, *Crossing the Border*.
- ▶ **To the novels:** ▷Susan Hill, *A Change for the Better*; ▷Barbara Pym, *Excellent Women*; ▷Angus Wilson, *Late Call*; Theodor Fontane, *Effi Briest*.

Taylor's short stories are collected in Hester Lilly, The Blush *and* A Dedicated Man. *Her novels include* At Mrs Lippincote's, A View of the Harbour, A Game of Hide-and-seek, The Wedding Group, Blaming, A Wreath of Roses, Mrs Palfrey at the Claremont *and* The Soul of Kindness.

TERRORISTS/FREEDOM FIGHTERS

Jerzy Andrzeyewski, *Ashes and Diamonds*
▷Joseph Conrad, *Under Western Eyes*
Rosalind Laker, *This Shining Land*
▷John Le Carré, *The Little Drummer Girl*
▷Doris Lessing, *The Good Terrorist*
Primo Levi, *If Not Now, When?*
▷Frederic Raphael, *Like Men Betrayed*
Idries Shah, *Kara Kush*

War: Behind the Lines (p 259)

THACKERAY, WILLIAM MAKEPEACE (1811-63)

British novelist and journalist.

Until the success of *Vanity Fair*, when he was 36, Thackeray earned his living as a journalist and cartoonist (especially for Punch magazine) and as a humorous lecturer. His first intention in his novels was to write 'satirical biographies', letting the reader discover the follies of the world at the same time as his naive young heroes and heroines. But the characters took over, and his books now seem more genial and affectionate than barbed. He invented characters as grotesque as ▷Dickens', caricatures of human viciousness or folly, but he wrote of them with a kind of disapproving sympathy, a fellow-feeling for their humanity, which Dickens lacks. Humbug, ambition and the seven deadly sins are Thackeray's subjects – and so are friendship, kindness and warm-heartedness. At a time when many English novels were more like sermons, clamorous for reform, he wrote moral comedies, showing us what fools we are.

VANITY FAIR (1847–8)

The book interweaves the lives of two friends, gentle Amelia and calculating, brilliant Becky Sharp. Becky is an impoverished orphan determined to make her fortune; Amelia believes in love, marriage and family life. Each of them marries; Amelia's husband has an affair with Becky, and dies at Waterloo with her name on his lips; Becky's husband finds her entertaining a rich, elderly admirer and abandons her. In the end, each girl gets what she longed for, but not in the way she hoped. Amelia, after ten years pining for her dead husband, is cruelly told by Becky of his infidelity, and

READ ON

- *Pendennis.*
- ▶ ▷Jane Austen, *Emma*. ▷Arnold Bennett, *The Card*. ▷H.G. Wells, *Tono-Bungay*. ▷Eudora Welty, *The Ponder Heart*. ▷Barbara Pym, *No Fond Return of Love*.

turns for comfort to a kind man who has worshipped her from afar, and who now offers her marriage, a home and all the comforts of obscurity. Becky's son inherits his father's money and gives her an annuity on condition that she never speaks to him again; we see her at the end of the book, queening it in Bath, an idle, rich member of the society she has always aspired to join and whose values Thackeray sums up in the title of the book.

Thackeray's other books include Pendennis *(the story of a selfish young man, spoilt by his mother, who goes to London to make his fortune as a writer) and its sequel* The Newcomes, Henry Esmond *and its sequel* The Virginians, *and a number of shorter tales and stories including* Barry Lyndon, The Great Hoggarty Diamond *and the spoof fairy-tale* The Rose and the Ring.

TRAINS

▷Agatha Christie, *Murder on the Orient Express*
Freeman Wills Crofts, *Death of a Train*
▷Graham Greene, *Stamboul Train*
▷Jaroslav Hašek, *The Good Soldier Švejk*
▷Patricia Highsmith, *Strangers on a Train*
▷John Masters, *Bhowani Junction*

TOLKIEN, J.R.R. (JOHN RONALD REUEL)

(1892–1973)
British novelist.

In 1939 Tolkien, a teacher of Anglo-Saxon literature at Oxford University, published a children's book (*The Hobbit*), about a small furry-footed person who steals a dragon's hoard. Bilbo Baggins was a hobbit, and his quest was the prologue to an enormous adult saga in which elves, dwarves, wizards, ents, human beings and hobbits unite to destroy the power of evil (embodied by the Dark Lord Sauron and his minions the Ring-wraiths and the orcs). The three volumes of *The Lord of the Rings*, published in the mid-1950s, started a vogue for supernatural fantasy-adventure which has spread world-wide and taken in films, quizbooks and role-play games as well as fiction. Tolkien outstrips his imitators not so much because of his plot (which is a simple battle between good and bad, with the moral issues explicit on every page) as thanks to his teeming professorial imagination. He gave his made-up worlds complete systems of language, history, anthropology, geography and literature. Reading him is like exploring a library; his invention seems inexhaustible.

READ ON

▶ ▷Stephen Donaldson, *The Chronicles of Thomas Covenant.* ▷Piers Anthony, *A Spell for Chameleon.* ▷David Eddings, *The Belgariad Quintet.* Terry Pratchett, *The Colour of Magic* is a spectacular spoof, hardly less fantastical and engrossing than Tolkien's original.

Although The Hobbit *and* The Lord of the Rings *are self-contained, Tolkien published several other volumes filling in chinks of their underlying history, explaining matters only sketched in the main narrative, and adding even more layers of linguistic, historical and anthropological fantasy. The chief books are* The Silmarillion *and* Unfinished Tales. Lost Tales *(three volumes) and* The History of Middle Earth *(five volumes) contain notes and drafts, chiefly of interest to addicts.* Farmer Giles of Ham *and* The Adventures of Tom Bombadil *are short stories for children.*

TOLSTOY, LEV NIKOLAEVICH (1828–1910)

Russian novelist.

In his 60s and beyond Tolstoy became famous as a kind of moral guru or secular saint: he preached the equal 'value' of all human beings, and suited actions to words by giving away his wealth, freeing his serfs and living an austere life in a cottage on the edge of his former estate. A similar view underlies his fiction. His ambition was to enter into the condition of each of his characters, to show the psychological complexity and diversity of the human race. His books are not tidily organised, with every event and emotion shaped to fit a central theme, but reflect the sprawl of life itself. The result was a psychological equivalent of ▷Balzac's 'snapshots' in *The Human Comedy*. Whether Tolstoy is showing us a coachman who comes and goes in half a page, or a major character who appears throughout a book, he invites us to feel full sympathy for that person, makes us flesh out his or her 'reality' in terms of our own.

READ ON

- *Anna Karenina*.
- ▶ **To *War and Peace*:** ▷Émile Zola, *The Downfall*, (La débâcle). ▷I.B. Singer, *The Family Moskat*; André Malraux, *Man's Estate*.
- ▶ **To *Anna Karenina*:** ▷Ivan Turgenev, *On the Eve*; ▷George Eliot, *Romola*; ▷Gustave Flaubert, *Madame Bovary*; ▷Boris Pasternak, *Doctor Zhivago*.

WAR AND PEACE (1869)

The book begins with people at a St Petersburg party in 1805 discussing the political situation in France, where Napoleon has just been proclaimed emperor. Tolstoy then fills 100 pages with seemingly random accounts of the lives and characters of a large group of relatives, friends, servants and dependants of three aristocrats, Andrey Bolkonsky, Pierre Bezuhov and Natasha Rostov. Gradually all these people become involved both with one another and with the gathering storm as Napoleon's armies sweep through Europe. The story culminates with the 1812 French invasion of Russia, Napoleon's defeat and his retreat from Moscow. The war touches the lives of all Tolstoy's people, and in particular resolves the triangle of affection between his central characters. The effects of war are the real subject of *War and Peace*. It contains 539 separate characters – the range is from Napoleon to the girl who dresses Rostov's hair, from Bolkonsky to an eager young soldier sharpening his sword on the eve of battle – and Tolstoy shows how their individual nature and feelings are both essential to and validated by the vast tapestry of human affairs of which they are part.

Tolstoy's other novels include Anna Karenina *(in which an adulterous and tragic love-affair is used to focus a picture of the stifling, morally incompetent aristocratic Russian society of the 1860s),* The Death of Ivan Illich, The Kreutzer Sonata, Master and Man *and* Resurrection. *His autobiographical books include* Childhood, Boyhood, Youth *and* A Confession.

TOOLE, JOHN KENNEDY (1937–69)

US novelist.

A Confederacy of Dunces (1980), Toole's only novel, was published posthumously: it had collected so many rejection-slips that he killed himself. It is a no-holds-barred comic grumble against the 20th-century world in general and the city of New Orleans in particular. Its anti-hero, Ignatius J. Reilly, is a narcissistic, hypochondriacal, towering genius who regards himself as too good for the world. He has successfully avoided working for 30 years, living in a fetid room in his mother's house and alternately masturbating, playing the lute and scribbling brilliant thoughts on a succession of supermarket notepads. At last his mother sends him out to find a job – with catastrophic results. Bored after one hour in a trouser-factory, he sets about destabilising staff-management relations; hired to sell hot-dogs, he eats his stock; in all innocence, he takes up with drug-addicts, whores and corrupt police. If Ignatius were likeable (say, like Voltaire's Candide), the satire might seem more genial and sympathetic; but he is a revolting example of how, in Toole's view, there is no excuse for the clinical brilliance of the brain being shackled to such a bag of guts as the human body. *A Confederacy of Dunces* is witty, slapstick, Rabelaisian, Falstaffian – and offers the human species no reason at all for self-congratulation or for hope.

READ ON

- Robert Coover, *The Universal Baseball Association*. Frederick Rolfe, *Hadrian the Seventh*. ▷Peter Carey, *Illywhacker*. B.S. Johnson, *Christie Malry's Own Double-Entry*. ▷Martin Amis, *The Rachel Papers*.

THEROUX, PAUL (BORN 1941)

US novelist and non-fiction writer.

Some of Theroux's most enjoyable books are about travelling: *The Great Railway Bazaar, The Old Patagonian Express, The Kingdom by the Sea, The Iron Rooster*. In all of them the narrator, the writer himself, feels detached, an observer of events rather than a participant – and the same is true of the people in Theroux's novels. They live abroad, often in the tropics; like the heroes of ▷Graham Greene

READ ON

- **To *My Secret History*:** ▷John Fowles, *Daniel Martin*; ▷Graham Greene, *The Honorary Consul*.
- **To Theroux's novels**

Lev TOLSTOY

Jeanette **WINTERSON, THE PASSION**

Anthony **BURGESS, THE NAPOLEON SYMPHONY**

NAPOLEON

'ALL HUMAN LIFE IS HERE'

STENDHAL, SCARLET AND BLACK *(middle- and upper-class life in Napoleonic France)*

Miguel de **CERVANTES SAAVEDRA, DON QUIXOTE** *(fantasy knight-errantry in Renaissance Spain)*

Johann Wolfgang von **GOETHE, THE APPRENTICESHIP OF WILHELM MEISTER** *(young man travels 18th-century Europe, learning about life and love)*

Charles **DICKENS, DAVID COPPERFIELD** *(English city society in the 1830s)*

Mark **TWAIN, THE ADVENTURES OF HUCKLEBERRY FINN** *(small-town life on Mississippi before American Civil War)*

Ivan **TURGENEV, FATHERS AND SONS** *(landed class resist fashionable revolutionary ideas, 1860s)*

Nicolai **GOGOL, DEAD SOULS** *(conman tours rural estates, buying up dead serfs' 'souls')*

Fyodor **DOSTOEVSKI, THE IDIOT** *(psychological disintegration of count dismissed by family as simpleton)*

Maxim **GORKY, FOMA GORDEEV** *(brutal upbringing in barge-owning family on 19th-century Volga)*

TSARIST RUSSIA

WAR AND PEACE *(tapestry of Russian life during Napoleonic Wars)*

NAPOLOENIC WARS

Bernard **CORNWELL, SHARPE'S REGIMENT**

C.S. **FORESTER, THE GUN**

William **THACKERAY, VANITY FAIR**

FALLOUT OF WAR

Boris **PASTERNAK, DOCTOR ZHIVAGO**
(tragic love in chaos of Russian revolution)

Ernest **HEMINGWAY, A FAREWELL TO ARMS**
(love-affair overshadowed by World War I)

Olivia **MANNING, FORTUNES OF WAR**
(World War II: effects on civilians in Balkans and Egypt)

William **STYRON, SOPHIE'S CHOICE**
(US woman haunted by memory of nazi concentration camps)

Kazuo **ISHIGURO, A PALE VIEW OF HILLS**
(Japanese woman coping with memories of Hiroshima)

(the author Theroux most resembles) they feel uneasy both about the society they are in and about themselves; they fail to cope. The hero of *Saint Jack* (1973), a US pimp in Singapore, hopes to make a fortune providing R and R for his servicemen compatriots, but the pliability of his character makes him the prey for every conman and shark in town. In *The Mosquito Coast* (1981) an ordinary US citizen, depressed by life, uproots his family and tries to make a new start in the Honduran jungle, with tragic, farcical results. *Picture Palace* (1978) is the life-story of a famous photographer who has hidden all her life behind her camera, reduced existence to images on film, and now, in withered old age, agonisingly contrasts her memories of youth, warmth and affection with the dusty prints which are all she has to show for them.

MY SECRET HISTORY (1989)

André Parent is an American writer, born at the time of the second world war, randy for women and hot for every experience the world can offer. He teaches in Africa, writes novels and stories, makes a fortune from a travel book. He fulfils his adolescent ambition, 'to fuck the world', only to find that he has lost moral identity. The book is wry, funny, and no comfort to Americans, intellectuals, writers, the middle-aged, or indeed anyone else at all.

Theroux's other novels include Waldo, Fong and the Indians, The Black House, The Family Arsenal, Doctor Slaughter *and the acid science-fiction fantasy* O-Zone. Sinning With Annie, The Consul's File *and* The London Embassy *are collections of short stories.*

in general: ▷P.H. Newby, *Leaning in the Wind*; Timothy Mo, *Sour-Sweet*; ▷William Boyd, *Stars and Bars*.

- **To *O-Zone*:** Robie Macauley, *A Secret History of Time to Come*.
- **To the short stories:** ▷Lawrence Durrell, *Antrobus Complete*.
- **To the travel books:** Jonathan Raban, *Coasting*.

TROLLOPE, ANTHONY (1815–82)

British novelist.

Until Trollope was 52 he worked for the Post Office, travelling in Europe, the USA, north Africa and all over the British Isles. He turned his foreign experience into travel books, and used his British observations in 47 novels, many of them written, in the fashion of the time, for serial publication in magazines. His style is genial and expansive, and his books deal with such characteristic Victorian themes as class, power, money and family authority. His favourite characters are the upper-middle class of small towns and the surrounding estates. His plots involve the exercise of authority by the older generation and, by the young, all kinds of pranks, kicking over the traces, unsuitable love-affairs and mockery of their elders' stuffiness. Trollope's best-loved novels are in two six-book series, the 'Barsetshire' books (1855–67), about intrigue and preferment in a cathe-

READ ON

- **To the Barsetshire books:** Angela Thirkell, *High Rising* (first of a series set in Barsetshire and borrowing Trollope's characters); Elizabeth Goudge, *Cathedral Close*; Hugh Walpole, *The Cathedral*; ▷Barbara Pym, *Crampton Hodnett*.
- **To the Palliser books:** ▷John

dral city, and the 'Palliser' books (1864–80), about politics on the wider stages of county and country. Each novel is self-contained, but recurring characters and cross-references between the books, added to Trollope's easy-going style, give the reader a marvellously comfortable sensation, as of settling down to hear about the latest scrapes of a group of well-loved friends.

BARCHESTER TOWERS (1857)

The second novel in the Barsetshire sequence is high comedy. Imperious Mrs Proudie, wife of the timid new Bishop of Barchester, brings the Reverend Obadiah Slope into the Palace to help dominate her husband and run the diocese. But Slope is a snake in the grass, determined to make a rich marriage for himself, to win preferment in the church, even to defy Mrs Proudie if that will advance his cause. Their power-struggle is the heart of the book, a stately but furious minuet which soon sweeps up all Trollope's minor characters: rich, pretty Widow Bold, apoplectic Archdeacon Grantly, flirtatious Signora Vesey-Negroni, saintly Mr Harding, bewildered Parson Quiverful and his 14 squalling brats.

The Barsetshire novels are The Warden, Barchester Towers, Doctor Thorne, Framley Parsonage, The Small House at Allington *and* The Last Chronicle of Barset. *The Palliser novels are* Can You Forgive Her?, Phineas Finn, The Eustace Diamonds, Phineas Redux, The Prime Minister *and* The Duke's Children. *Trollope's other novels include* The Bertrams, Orley Farm, The Belton Estate, The Way We Live Now *and* Mr Scarborough's Family.

Galsworthy, *The Forsyte Saga*; Benjamin Disraeli, *Coningsby*; ▷Christina Stead, *House of All Nations*.

▶ **To Trollope's work in general:** Oliver Goldsmith, *The Vicar of Wakefield*; Louis Auchincloss, *The Great World and Timothy Colt*; ▷Barbara Taylor Bradford, *A Woman of Substance*.

TURGENEV, Ivan Sergeevich (1818–83)

Russian novelist and playwright.

A rich man, Turgenev spent much of his life travelling in Europe, and was welcomed abroad as the leading Russian writer of his time. He was less popular in Russia itself. Although his limpid style (influenced by his friend ▷Flaubert) and his descriptions of nature were admired, his wistful satire, treating all human endeavour as equally absurd, won favour with neither conservatives nor radicals. His favourite characters are members of the leisured class, and his stories of disappointed ambition, failed love-affairs and unfocussed dissatisfaction anticipate not so much later revolutionary writings as the plays of ▷Chekhov.

FATHERS AND SONS (1861)

Arkady, a student, takes his friend Bazarov home to meet his father. The old man is impressed by Bazarov's vigorous

READ ON

- *Torrents of Spring* (the story of a man torn by love for two women, a beautiful girl and the wife of an old school friend).

▶ ▷Gustave Flaubert, *Sentimental Education*. George Moore, *The Lake*. ▷L.P. Hartley, *The Go-Between*. ▷Willa Cather, *The Professor's House*.

character and outspoken views – which are that none of the old moral and social conventions have intrinsic validity, and that people must decide for themselves how to live their lives. (This attitude to life, 'nihilism', was widespread among Russian intellectuals in the 1860s and 1870s.) The novel soon leaves politics to explore the effects of Bazarov's character on his own life. He falls in love, and disastrously misinterprets his beloved's wish for friendship as the proposal of a 'free' liaison; he visits his parents, who cannot reconcile their admiration for their son with bewilderment at his ideas; he quarrels with the traditionalist Pavel, Arkady's uncle, and fights an absurd duel with him; he nurses serfs during a typhus epidemic and becomes fatally infected. Although Bazarov always regarded his own existence as futile, after his death it becomes apparent that he has changed the lives and attitudes of every other person in the story.

▷Anton Chekhov, *The Lady With the Little Dog* (and other short stories).

Turgenev's novels include Rudin, A Nest of Gentlefolk, On the Eve, Smoke *and* Virgin Soil. A Hunter's Notes/A Sportsman's Sketches *contains short stories and poetic descriptions of country scenes.* A Month in the Country, *a Chekhovian comedy, is his best-known play.*

TURNER, George (born 1916)

Australian novelist.

Turner's novels, set in the near future, are unsparing about human folly and barbarity. But their grimness is warmed by a feeling of hope, and by a distinction of style, rare in dystopian books of this kind. His best-known work, the trilogy *Beloved Son*, *Vaneglory* and *Yesterday's Men* (1978–83), describes the rebuilding of human civilisation after a global nuclear holocaust a century from now.

The Sea and Summer (1987)

The novel is set in New Melbourne, Australia, three generations hence. The human race has pillaged the environment to the point where the atmosphere itself is in revolt: the ice caps are melting and water is lapping at the lower floors of the kilometre-high tower blocks where the Swill live. The Swill are unemployed and unemployable, an urban underclass surviving on state handouts, denied education and kept in check by army patrols and razor wire: ninety per cent of the population. The Sweet, by contrast, have privilege, wealth and culture – so long as they keep their jobs. The novel tells how Billy Kovacs, a Swill 'tower boss' (gang ruler) forms an unlooked-for relationship with a Sweet family fallen on hard times – and details the effects of that relationship on both him and them.

READ ON

- *Beloved Son*.
- ▶ **To *The Sea and Summer*:** ▷Anthony Burgess, *A Clockwork Orange*; ▷Ray Bradbury, *Fahrenheit 451*.
- ▶ **To the *Beloved Son* books:** ▷Angela Carter, *Heroes and Villains*; John Brunner, *The Sheep Look Up*.
- ▶ **To Turner's work in general:** ▷Paul Theroux, *O-Zone*; Keith Roberts, *Pavane*; ▷David Cook, *Sunrising*.

Turner's other novels are Young Man of Talent, A Stranger and Afraid, The Cupboard Under the Stairs, A Waste of Shame, The Lame Dog Man *and* Transit of Cassidy.

TWAIN, MARK (1835–1910)

US novelist and journalist.

'Mark Twain' was the pseudonym of Samuel Clemens. A former steam-boat captain on the Mississippi, soldier, gold-miner and traveller, he wrote breezy, good-humoured accounts of his experiences, with an eye for quirky customs, manners and characters. His favourite form was the short story or comic, factual 'sketch' of half a dozen pages, and several of his books are collections of such pieces. He wrote three historical novels, *Personal Recollections of Joan of Arc* (serious: the biography of Joan by a former page and secretary), *The Prince and the Pauper* (about a beggar-boy changing places with King Edward VI of England, his exact double) and *A Connecticut Yankee in King Arthur's Court* (in which a man, transported back in time, startles Camelot with such 'magic' items as matches, a pocket watch and gunpowder). In Twain's best-loved books, *The Adventures of Tom Sawyer* (1876) and *The Adventures of Huckleberry Finn* (1886), he wove reminiscences of boyhood and of life on the Mississippi into an easy-going, fictional form. *Tom Sawyer* is about the scrapes, fancies and fears of boyhood. The heroes of *Huckleberry Finn*, a boy and a runaway slave, pole a raft down the Mississippi, beset by conmen, bounty-hunters and outraged citizens, and fall into slapstick adventures each time they land. Twain is regarded in the USA as a founding father of American literature, and dismissed in Europe as a children's author; he offers far slyer, far gentler, pleasures than either view suggests.

Twain's satires include Pudd'nhead Wilson *and* Extract from Captain Stormfield's Visit to Heaven *(funny) and* The Mysterious Stranger *(serious).* Tom Sawyer Abroad *and* Tom Sawyer Detective *are novels, following Tom's adventures in adult life. Twain's short stories are collected in* The Celebrated Jumping Frog of Calaveras County and Other Sketches *and* The Man That Corrupted Hadleyburg. *His books of travel and reminiscence include* The Innocents Abroad, Roughing It, A Tramp Abroad *and* Life on the Mississippi.

READ ON

- **To *Huckleberry Finn*:** Alphonse Daudet, *Tartarin of Tarascon*; ▷Henry Fielding, *Tom Jones*; H.E. Bates, *The Darling Buds of May*.
- **To Twain's travel-books:** ▷Robert Louis Stevenson, *Travels With a Donkey* (and its sibling, ▷John Steinbeck, *Travels with Charlie*); ▷Laurence Sterne, *A Sentimental Journey*; Laurie Lee, *As I Walked Out One Midsummer Morning*.

TYLER, ANN (BORN 1941)

US novelist.

Tyler writes, in cool, stylish prose, of the anguish of people caught up in the pains of everyday emotional life. She is es-

READ ON

- *Dinner at the Homesick*

pecially good on relationships: between husbands and wives, brothers and sisters, parents and children. Her plots are as simple as those of any romantic novelist: people finding one another, drifting apart, coming together again. But the elegance of her writing, and the extraordinary lifelikeness of her characters, take her into the literary company of ▷Lurie or ▷Updike, worlds away from most romance.

Restaurant.

▶ ▷Alison Lurie, *The War Between the Tates*. ▷John Updike, *Rabbit, Run*. Susan Fromberg Shaeffer, *The Injured Party*.

THE ACCIDENTAL TOURIST (1985)

Ethan, the 12-year-old son of Macon and Sarah Leary, is brutally murdered, and his death destroys his parents' marriage. The story centres on Macon, a writer of rueful travel books, as he struggles against the need to rebuild his life, and in particular against the possibility of finding happiness with Helen (a dog-trainer many years his junior). Just as emotional scar tissue begins to form, Sarah comes back into his life, reopening the wound and confronting him once more with the need for choice.

Tyler's other novels include The Clock Winder, Celestial Navigation, Searching for Caleb *and* Earthly Possessions.

U

UNDSET, SIGRID (1882–1949)

Norwegian novelist.

Outside Norway, Undset is best-known for *Kristin Lavransdatter* (1920–22), a novel-trilogy set in medieval times. It follows the life of Kristin, a landowner's daughter who flies in the face of convention by insisting on marrying the man she loves. He is arrogant and unyielding, even when his political enemies imprison him and strip him of wealth and lands. Only Kristin stands by him: the book's subject is the growth of her soul, the way her Christian devotion transcends humiliation and despair. The book's bleak subject-matter is offset by Undset's warm feeling for her characters, and by her detailed, perceptive picture of 14th-century life and thought.

READ ON

- *The Master of Hestviken.*
- ▶ Helen Waddell, *Héloise and Abelard*. ▷Umberto Eco, *The Name of the Rose*. Janet Lewis, *The Trial of Sören Kvist.*

UNLOOKED-FOR FRIENDSHIPS

▷David Cook, *Winter Doves*
▷Tove Jansson, *The Summer Book*
▷Alison Lurie, *Foreign Affairs*
Joseph Olshan, *A Warmer Season*
▷C.P. Snow, *The Light and the Dark*
▷John Steinbeck, *Of Mice and Men*
▷Morris West, *The World is Made of Glass*

UPDIKE, JOHN (BORN 1932)

US novelist and short-story writer.

Updike's short stories (most of them written for the *New Yorker*) are witty anecdotes about the snobberies and love-affairs of ambitious Long Island couples, or single,

READ ON

- *Of the Farm.*
- ▶ ▷Philip Roth, *The Ghost Writer*. Arthur

brilliant jokes (for example treating bacteria under a microscope as if they were guests at a trendy cocktail party). Some of his novels are in a similarly glittering, heartless style. In *Couples* (1968) a small group of bored Connecticut commuters changes sex-partners as carelessly as if playing a party game. In *The Witches of Eastwick* (1984) three bored young widows set themselves up as a coven of amateur witches, only to become sexually ensnared by a devilishly charming man. The hero of *A Month of Sundays* (1975) is a 'progressive' clergyman tortured by lust. Updike's other novels are deeper, concentrating more on the underlying pain than on the ludicrous surface of his characters' lives. The 'Rabbit' trilogy (*Rabbit, Run*; *Rabbit Redux*; *Rabbit is Rich,* 1960–81) tells the life of an ex-school sports champion who finds emotional maturity and happiness almost impossible to grasp. The hero of *Roger's Version* (1986), a middle-aged professor, is thrown into moral turmoil by the possibility of devising a computer-program to prove the existence of God. *Marry Me* (1976), one of Updike's most moving books, is a tragi-comedy about an adulterous affair.

THE CENTAUR (1963)

George Caldwell, an eccentric, ineffective science teacher at Olinger High School in the 1950s, deflects his feelings of inadequacy by fantasising that he is Chiron, the centaur who taught the heroes of Greek myth (which makes his headmaster Zeus and his colleagues Athene, Hephaestus and Hercules), and that he has terminal stomach cancer. The book describes three days in his life, during which he is forced to come to terms with himself and with his adolescent son Peter, who idolises him. Myth-reminiscences start and end the book; its heart is more straightforward, a moving account of small-town life and of the inarticulate love between Peter and his perplexed, exasperating father.

Updike's other novels include The Poorhouse Fair, Of the Farm, The Coup, S, *and two made from stories about a neurotic writer,* Bech, a Book *and* Bech is Back. *His story-collections include* The Same Door, Pigeon Feathers, Museums and Women, The Music School *and* Trust Me. Self-consciousness *contains six autobiographical essays, fascinating background to his fiction.*

Laurents, *The Way We Were.* ▷Anne Tyler, *Dinner at the Homesick Restaurant.* ▷Frederic Raphael, *Heaven and Earth.* ▷Angus Wilson, *Hemlock and After.* ▷Brian Moore, *The Great Victorian Collection.*

USSR

Martin Cruz Smith, *Gorky Park*
▷John Le Carré, *The Russia House*
▷Maxim Gorky, *Mother*

▷Boris Pasternak, *Doctor Zhivago*
Victor Serge, *The Case of Comrade Tulayev*
Mikhail Sholokhov, *And Quiet Flows the Don*
Vladimir Zinoviev, *The Yawning Heights*

V

VARGAS LLOSA, MARIO (BORN 1936)
Peruvian novelist.

An admirer of ▷Márquez, Vargas Llosa uses magic realism to give a similarly mordant view of South American life and politics. His books with contemporary settings are his sharpest: *Aunt Julia and the Scriptwriter* (1983) sends up big-city life; *The City and the Dogs/The Time of the Hero* (1962) is a satire on fascism set in a gung-ho, brutal military academy. His finest book, *The War of the End of the World* (1981), is quieter. Ostensibly a historical novel about the setting-up (and savage dismantling by the authorities) of a religious community for drop-outs and derelicts – the kind of people Christ himself might have chosen to wait for the apocalypse at the turn of the 19th/20th centuries – it spreads tendrils of fantasy into every area of social, religious, military and political life.

Vargas Llosa's other novels include The Green House, Conversation in the Cathedral *and* Captain Pantoja and the Special Service. The Cubs *is a collection of short stories.* The Perpetual Orgy *is a book-length musing about ▷Flaubert's* Madame Bovary, *part literary criticism, part reconstruction, part anthology: it is magic realism and non-fiction, hand in hand.*

READ ON

- **To Vargas Llosa's fiction:** ▷Isabel Allende, *Of Love and Shadows*; ▷Gabriel García Márquez, *The Autumn of the Patriarch*; Augusto Roa Bastos, *I the Supreme*.
- **To *The Perpetual Orgy*:** ▷Julian Barnes, *Flaubert's Parrot*.

VERNE, JULES (1828–1905)
French novelist.

Verne began writing in the 1860s, the heyday of both exploration and popular science – and his inspiration was to mix the two. His stories mimic the memoirs of real-life explor-

READ ON

- ▷A. Conan Doyle, *The Lost World*. ▷H.G. Wells, *The*

ers of the time, fabulous adventures narrated in sober, business-like prose – and, by stirring in scientific wonders impossible or unlikely at the time, he tips them into fantasy. His heroes are not tethered to the surface of the Earth: they tunnel towards its core (*Journey to the Centre of the Earth*), live underwater (*Twenty Thousand Leagues Under the Sea*) and ride rockets into space (*From the Earth to the Moon*; *Round the Moon*). Alternately with these 'scientific' adventure-stories, Verne produced tales of more orthodox derring-do: *Michel Strogoff*, for example, is a gentleman-adventurer whose bravery saves Civilisation as We Know It; in *Round the World in Eighty Days* Phileas Fogg embarks on a crazy journey to win a bet. Modern science has outstripped most of Verne's inventions, but few later SF writers have bettered him in straight-down-the-line, thrill-in-every-paragraph adventure.

First Men in the Moon. ▷H. Rider Haggard, *She*. C.S. Lewis, *That Hideous Strength*. Edgar Rice Burroughs, *Pirates of Venus*. ▷E.E. 'Doc' Smith, *The Imperial Stars*. ▷Kurt Vonnegut, *The Sirens of Titan*.

VIDAL, GORE (BORN 1925)

US novelist and non-fiction writer.

Vidal made his name as a tart-tongued, witty commentator on 1960s and 1970s life, a favourite chat-show guest. Whatever the topic, from the rotation of crops to the horror of nazi concentration camps, from zen to flower-arranging, he had something interesting to say. The same protean brilliance fills his novels. Whether their subject is homosexuality (*The City and the Pillar*, 1948/65), the excesses of the film industry (*Myra Breckinridge*, 1968) or US politics (the series *Burr*, *1876*, *Washington DC*, *Empire* and *Hollywood: a Novel of The Twenties*, 1967–89), they are original, stimulating and engrossing. This is particularly so in his historical novels, where he makes his alternative view of past events seem more attractive than reality itself. *Julian* is a study of the last pagan Roman emperor, who tried to stop the rush of Christianity in the name of (as Vidal sees it) the more humane, more generous Olympian religion. *Creation* is the memoirs of an imaginary Persian nobleman of the 5th century BC, who went as ambassador to India, China and Greece and knew Confucius, Buddha and Socrates. *Lincoln* refocuses our view of the thoughts and achievements of the 16th US president.

KALKI (1978)

Teddy Ottinger, a test pilot, is summoned to the Tibetan ashram of the mysterious Kalki. Born an American, James Kelly, Kalki has settled in the Himalayas after the Vietnam war and announced that he is the tenth avatar of the god Vishnu and that his coming to earth means the end of the present cycle of human existence. The book, a witty intellectual thriller, shows how Kalki's prophecy is fulfilled, and

READ ON

- *Duluth*.
- ▶ **To *Kalki*:** ▷Richard Condon, *Winter Kills*; ▷Kurt Vonnegut, *Galápagos*.
- ▶ **To Vidal's historical novels:** Peter Green, *The Sword of Pleasure* (set in republican Rome); John Hersey, *The Wall* (about US missionaries in China); John Barth, *The Sot-weed Factor* (set in Maryland in the time of the Pilgrim Fathers).
- ▶ **To Vidal's novels in general:** ▷Kingsley Amis, *The Alteration*; ▷Patrick White, *The Twyborn Affair*; ▷Muriel Spark, *The Ballad of Peckham Rye*.

what happens to Teddy and the few other survivors in a world left unchanged except that all human life has ceased.

Vidal's other novels include Williwaw, In a Yellow Wood, The Season of Comfort, Two Sisters, Myron *and* Duluth. *He also wrote detective stories (including* Death in the Fifth Position*) under the name* Edgar Box. A Thirsty Evil *is a collection of short stories.*

VINE, Barbara: see RENDELL, Ruth

VONNEGUT, Kurt (born 1922)

US novelist.

SF ideas shape Vonnegut's novels – and so do autobiography, political and social satire, loonish humour and a furious, nagging rage at the way the human race is pillaging the world. *Galápagos* (1985) begins at the moment of nuclear apocalypse (which is triggered by a bomber-pilot fantasising that firing his missile is like having sex). A group of people, gathered in Ecuador for the 'Nature Cruise of the Century', find that their ship has become a Noah's Ark: they are the sole survivors of humankind. They land in the Galápagos Islands, equipped with no technology except a computer whose memory is stuffed with 1,000 dead languages and a million quotations from the world's great literature, and set about survival. At first they are hampered, as (Vonnegut claims) the human race has been handicapped throughout its existence, by the enormous size of their brains, attics of unnecessary thought. But Galápagos is the cradle of the evolutionary theory – and that may be humanity's last hope.

Vonnegut's other novels are Player Piano*;* The Sirens of Titan*;* Mother Night*;* Cat's Cradle*;* God Bless You, Mr Rosewater*;* Slaughterhouse Five*;* Breakfast of Champions*;* Slapstick*;* Jailbird*;* Palm Sunday *and* Deadeye Dick. Canary in a Cathouse *and* Welcome to the Monkeyhouse *contain short stories.*

READ ON

- *Cat's Cradle*; *The Sirens of Titan*.
- ▶ ▷Brian Aldiss, *The Primal Urge*. Frederik Pohl, *The Coming of the Quantum Cats*. ▷Michael Moorcock, *The Final Programme*. ▷Russell Hoban, *Riddley Walker*. ▷Walter M. Miller, *A Canticle for Leibowitz*. Bamber Gascoigne, *Cod Strewth*.

WALKER, ALICE (BORN 1944)
US novelist, poet and non-fiction writer.

The background to Walker's books is the struggle for equal rights in the US over the last 30 years, first by blacks and then by women. Radical politics are not, however, her main concern. She writes wittily, ironically, about the follies of human life, and she is as merciless to her idealistic, college-educated activists as she is to their slobbish, mindless opponents. If ▷Mary McCarthy or ▷Alison Lurie had written about black, feminist politics, these might have been their books. *Meridian* (1976), Walker's second novel, is the splendidly ironical study of a southern black activist, educated to be a 'lady' (in the 1920s white meaning of the term), who becomes a leader in the equal-rights movements of the 1960s. When we see Meridian years later, all battles won, holed up in the small southern town of Chickokema where apart from the coming of equality nothing momentous has ever happened, she is totally confused about where all her energy, her driving-force, has gone. Was this really what her life was for?

Walker's other novels are Third Life of Grange Copeland, The Color Purple *(also a film) and* The Temple of My Familiar. In Love and Trouble *and* You Can't Keep a Good Woman Down *are short-story collections. She has also published poetry (*Once; Revolutionary Petunias; Willie Lee, I'll See You in the Morning*) and a book of essays,* In Search of Our Mother's Garden.

READ ON

- *The Color Purple.*
- ▶ **To Walker's elegant, tart style:** ▷Mary McCarthy, *The Group*; ▷Muriel Spark, *The Girls of Slender Means.*
- ▶ **To her view of the bizarreness lurking inside perfectly ordinary-seeming human beings:** ▷John Irving, *The World According to Garp*; ▷Tove Jansson, *Sun City.*
- ▶ **To her politics:** ▷Gayl Jones, *Corregídora*; Lisa Alther, *Kinflicks*; Ralph Ellison, *Invisible Man.*

Lew WALLACE

BEN-HUR *(Christian and pagan antagonism in ancient Rome)*

BIBLE OLD TESTAMENT

Jeanette **WINTERSON, BOATING FOR BEGINNERS**
(Noah's flood)

Thomas **MANN, JOSEPH AND HIS BROTHERS**
(- seen as allegory of 1930s fascist Europe)

Joseph **HELLER, GOD KNOWS**
('memoirs' of King David)

THE FIRST CHRISTIANS

George **MOORE, THE BROOK KERITH**
(Joseph of Arimathea)

Pär **LAGERKVIST, BARABBAS**
(- before, during and after Christ's crucifixion)

Lloyd C. **DOUGLAS, THE ROBE**
(effects on Roman centurion and others who inherit Christ's robe at crucifixion)

Frank **SLAUGHTER, THE SHOES OF THE FISHERMAN**
(Peter)

Henryk **SIENKIEWYCZ, QUO VADIS?**
(first Christian converts, first martyrs)

Anthony **BURGESS, THE KINGDOM OF THE WICKED**
(missionary journeys of Paul, Luke and Barnabas)

JOSEPH, MARY AND JESUS

Pasquale Festa **CAMPANILE, FOR LOVE, ONLY FOR LOVE** *(Joseph)*

Severia **HURÉ, I, MARY, DAUGHTER OF ISRAEL**
(Mary)

Robert **GRAVES, KING JESUS**
(fulfilment of all Old Testament prophecy)

Michèle **ROBERTS, THE WILD GIRL**
(Gospel according to Mary Magdalene)

WALLACE, Lew (1827-1905)

US novelist.

Ben-Hur (1880), the best-known of Wallace's historical romances, is set in Palestine in the reign of the Roman Emperor Nero. The Jewish aristocrat Judah Ben-Hur and the Roman general Messala, once friends, quarrel over politics. Messala falsely accuses Ben-Hur of treason; Ben-Hur's lands are confiscated, his wife and mother are thrown into prison (where they contract leprosy) and he himself is condemned to the galleys. He escapes, leads a resistance-movement against the Romans, wreaks vengeance on Messala during a chariot-race in the Coliseum (the book's action-climax), rescues his mother and wife and takes them to be healed by the preacher Jesus. They are converted to Christianity, and the book ends with a moving scene as they witness Christ's crucifixion. Wallace's Christianity is somewhat preachy, but his depiction of the grandeur and decadence of ancient Rome, of the resistance-movement in Palestine and of the fervour of early Christian converts is unsurpassed.

Wallace's other novels include The Fair God, *a novel of Cortez' invasion of Mexico, and* The Prince of India, *which culminates in a magnificent description of the Turkish siege of Constantinople in 1453. Wallace's* Autobiography *is almost as swaggering as his fiction, particularly about his time as a general during the American Civil War.*

READ ON

- ▶ **To *Ben-Hur*:** Henryk Sienkiewicz, *Quo Vadis?*; Lord Lytton, *The Last Days of Pompeii*.
- ▶ **To Wallace's work in general:** ▷Walter Scott, *Ivanhoe*; ▷Victor Hugo, *Notre Dame de Paris*.

War: Behind The Lines

▷Noel Barber, *A Woman of Cairo*
▷Elizabeth Bowen, *The Heat of the Day*
Elizabeth Darrell, *At the Going Down of the Sun*
▷Jaroslav Hašek, *The Good Soldier Švejk*
▷Ernest Hemingway, *A Farewell to Arms*
▷Thomas Keneally, *Schindler's Ark*
▷Neville Shute, *What Happened to the Corbetts*
▷Lev Tolstoy, *War and Peace*

Terrorists/Freedom Fighters (p 240); War: Front Line (p 259)

War: Front Line

Stephen Crane, *The Red Badge of Courage*
▷Len Deighton, *Bomber*
Emma Drummond, *Forget the Glory*
William Fairchild, *The Poppy Factory*
▷Joseph Heller, *Catch-22*

▷Ernest Hemingway, *For Whom the Bell Tolls*
Alistair Maclean, *The Guns of Navarone*
▷Norman Mailer, *The Naked and the Dead*
Erich Maria Remarque, *All Quiet on the Western Front*

War: Behind the Lines (p 259)

WAUGH, EVELYN (1903–66)

British novelist.

Waugh's main work was a series of tart satires on 1930s attitudes and manners. His vacuous, amiable heroes stumble through life, unsurprised by anything that happens. By chance, they land in the centre of affairs (political, business and sexual) and their presence triggers a sequence of ever more ludicrous events. Innocence is their only saving grace: Waugh's views were that the world is silly but dangerous, and that those who think they understand it are the most vulnerable of all. He was particularly venomous about British high society, depicting the ruling class as a collection of alcohol-swilling Hooray Henries or Henriettas, whose chief pastimes are partying (if young) and interfering in public life (if old). That class apart, the range of his scorn was vast. *Decline and Fall* sends up (among other things) the English prep school system, *Black Mischief* mocks tyranny in an African state emerging from colonialism, *Scoop* satirises gutter journalism and *The Ordeal of Gilbert Pinfold* (1957) mercilessly details the hallucinations of an alcoholic author on a detestable ocean cruise. The second-world-war trilogy *Sword of Honour* (1965) sets Waugh's foolish heroes in the context of truly dangerous, genuinely lunatic real events, and *Brideshead Revisited* (1945) is a more serious book still, the study of an aristocratic Catholic family collapsing under the weight of centuries of unconsidered privilege.

A HANDFUL OF DUST (1934)

The book begins with standard Waugh farce: a pin-headed society wife, Brenda Last, takes a lover to occupy her afternoons. But the effect on her husband Tony and son John is devastating, and the book moves quickly from farce to tragedy. Waugh never abandons the ridiculous – no one else would have placed his hero in impenetrable tropical jungle, the slave of a megalomaniac who makes him read *Edwin Drood* aloud – but he also writes with compassion for his characters, involving us in their loneliness as his shallower novels never do.

Waugh's other novels are Vile Bodies, Put Out More Flags *and* The Loved One. *His travel-books include* Remote Peo-

READ ON

- *Scoop*.
- ▶ ▷William Boyd, *A Good Man in Africa*. ▷Malcolm Bradbury, *Eating People is Wrong*. ▷David Lodge, *How Far Can You Go?* ▷P.H. Newby, *The Picnic at Sakkara*. ▷John Updike, *The Coup*. Paul Micou, *The Music Programme*.

ple *and* Waugh in Abyssinia. *His* Diaries *and his autobiography* A Little Learning *are a revealing blend of pity for himself and mercilessness to others.*

WEBSTER, Jan (born 1924)

British novelist.

Webster writes family sagas, spanning many generations. Her best-known books are the sequence *Colliers Row, Saturday City* and *Beggarman's Country,* set in the Glasgow slums.

READ ON

- ▶ Christine Marion Fraser, *Blue Above the Chimneys.* ▷Maisie Mosco, *Almonds and Raisins.* Helen Forrester, *Twopence to Cross the Mersey.* Sarah Shears, *Louise.*

Weepies

▷Charlotte Brontë, *Jane Eyre*
▷Daphne Du Maurier, *Rebecca*
▷Brenda Jagger, *A Song Twice Over*
▷Norah Lofts, *The Brittle Glass*
▷Margaret Mitchell, *Gone With the Wind*
▷Boris Pasternak, *Doctor Zhivago*
▷Erich Segal, *Love Story*
Mrs Henry Wood, *East Lynne*

WEIDMAN, Jerome (born 1913)

US novelist.

The typical Weidman hero is a successful banker or businessman. Forced by some crisis to look back over the past, he recounts the story of his life and the influences which have made him what he is. Many of the men are Jewish, the sons of poor European immigrants in the early years of the century; the novels are warm-hearted, Dickensian stories of the struggle for existence in the sweat-shops and backstreets of 1930s New York, and of young men rising, by brains, luck or adroitness – some of them are crooks – to the positions they hold today. Without exception, Weidman's characters are creations of the American dream – and every one of them feels compromised, as if material success has eroded the moral value-system which helped their parents in their first years in the USA, and which supported their own childhood and growing up.

READ ON

- ● *Fourth Street East* (and its sequels *Last Respects* and *Tiffany Street*).
- ▶ Budd Schulberg, *What Makes Sammy Run?* ▷Mordecai Richler, *The Apprenticeship of Duddy Kravitz.* ▷Saul Bellow, *The Adventures of Augie March.* E.L. Doctorow, *World's Fair.* Louis Auchincloss, *Venus in Sparta.*

OTHER PEOPLE'S MONEY (1967)

In 1915, three-year-old Victor is made the foster-son of rich Walter Weld and his wife. Five years later another orphan, Philip Brandwine, joins the household. The novel recounts the boys' childhood, their young manhood, their service in the second world war – and their rivalry for the love of Harriet Weld, their foster-sister. Its subsidiary theme is the character-clash between the two men: Philip is charismatic, dazzling and untrustworthy, Victor is meticulous, earnest and unquestioningly loyal. Their relationship collapses during the second world war, only to be rebuilt afterwards, in the agonising reunion which starts and ends the book. Over everything hovers an enigma, unsolved until the book's last page: what was there about the boys that made the Welds take them as foster-sons in the first place?

Weidman's novels include I Can Get it for You Wholesale, Your Daughter Iris, The Enemy Camp, The Center of the Action, The Temple *and* A Family Fortune. *His short-story collections include* The Horse That Could Whistle Dixie, My Father Sits in the Dark *and* The Death of Dickie Draper. Praying for Rain *is autobiography.*

WELDON, FAY (BORN 1933)

British novelist and screen-writer.

A TV dramatist, Weldon writes novels in short, screenplay-like scenes full of dialogue: her books are like sinister sitcoms turned into prose. In the 1970s she was regarded as a leading feminist writer, and 'women's experience' is a major theme. Her heroines are ordinary people resisting the need to define themselves as someone else's wife, lover or mother, and missing the traditional cosiness such roles afford. Individuality can only be bought at the cost of psychic discomfort – and this is often intensified by the malice of others and by the hostility of the environment: witchcraft and the venomousness of nature add spice to Weldon's plots. Her books are fast, funny and furious; but their underlying ideas, especially for male chauvinist pigs, are no joke at all.

READ ON

- *The Hearts and Lives of Men.*
- ▷Margaret Atwood, *Life Before Man*. Marge Piercy, *The High Cost of Living*. Mary Gordon, *The Company of Women*. Penelope Mortimer, *Long Distance*. Alice Thomas Ellis, *Unexplained Laughter*. Maggie Gee, *Light Years*.

PUFFBALL (1980)

Liffey, married to boring, ambitious Richard, longs to live in a country cottage; Richard wants a child. They strike a bargain, move to the wolds near Glastonbury and do their best to get Liffey pregnant. Almost at once the idyll turns to nightmare. The cottage has few facilities; there are no commuter-trains to London; their neighbour is a child-beater and an amateur witch. As the baby grows in Liffey's womb and Richard, alone in London for five days a week, consoles himself, Mabs (the neighbour) tries every trick of witchcraft, from potions to pin-stuck wax models, to make Liffey abort her child. *Puffball* is a romantic novel for grown-up people – and the games Weldon plays with our longing for a happy ending give the plot some of its most devastating, satisfying twists.

Weldon's other novels include Down Among the Women, Female Friends, The President's Child, Little Sisters, Praxis, Watching Me Watching You, The Life and Loves of a She-Devil, The Shrapnel Academy, The Heart of England, The Hearts and Lives of Men *and* Leader of the Band. The Rules of Life *is an SF novella.*

WELLS, H.G. (HERBERT GEORGE) (1866–1946)

British writer of novels, short stories and non-fiction.

Wells' early novels were science fantasies, imagining what it would be like if people could travel in time (*The Time Machine*, 1895) or space (*The First Men in the Moon*, 1901), or how the Earth might defend itself against extra-terrestrial attacks (*The War of the Worlds*, 1898). Like ▷Verne, Wells predicted many inventions and discoveries now taken for granted: in *The War in the Air* (1908) for example, he forecast fleets of warplanes and bombers in the days when the Wright brothers were still headline news. For all their scientific wonders, these novels are full of pessimism about society: wherever people go, they find barbarism, oppression and misery. *The Island of Doctor Moreau* (1896), about a mad scientist hybridising humans and animals on a lonely island, brings the pessimism nearer home. Side by side with such morbid fantasies, Wells wrote a series of utterly different books. They are genial social comedies, about ordinary people (shop-assistants, clerks) who decide that the way to find happiness is to break out and 'make a go of things'. Sometimes (as in *Ann Veronica*, 1909, about a girl determined on emancipation despite the wishes of her family) Wells' message is polemical; but most of the books – *Love and Mr Lewisham* (1900), *Kipps* (1900), *The History of Mr Polly* (1910) – replace propaganda with an indulgent, enthusiastic view of human enterprise.

TONO-BUNGAY (1909)

George Ponderevo goes to live with his uncle Toby. He helps Toby market a marvellous new elixir, Tono-Bungay: it is the answer to the world's problems, the health, wealth and happiness of humankind in a bottle. The Tono-Bungay fortune swells by the minute – and then George discovers that the product is 99% distilled water. The discovery presents George with unresolvable moral dilemmas of all

READ ON

- **To Wells' SF:** ▷Jules Verne, *Twenty Thousand Leagues Under the Sea*; C.S. Lewis, *Out of the Silent Planet*; H.P. Lovecraft, *The Shadow over Innsmouth*.
- **To his social comedies:** ▷Arnold Bennett, *The Card*; Hugh Walpole, *Mr Perrin and Mr Traill*; ▷David Cook, *Missing Persons*.

kinds. Does it matter what Tono-Bungay is made of, if it does what it claims to do? Is Toby a crook or does he genuinely believe he is benefiting humankind? How can George bankrupt those he loves – and in the process destroy his own chances of a happy marriage and a prosperous home? He puts off the decision, and in the meantime continues his hobby: pioneer aviation. In the end, technology – the lighter-than-air-machine itself – comes to the rescue: a charming example of Wells' view that all moral and social dilemmas can be solved by science.

Wells' other science-fantasies include When the Sleeper Wakes, The Food of the Gods *and the story-collections* Tales of Space and Time *and* The Country of the Blind and Other Stories. *His other novels include* Mr Blettsworthy on Rampole Island, *a savage anti-totalitarian satire.*

WELTY, EUDORA (BORN 1909)

US novelist and short-story writer.

Unlike such writers as ▷Faulkner or ▷McCullers, who saw the southern United States as a kind of hell tenanted by freaks and degenerates, Welty treated them as paradise. The countryside is lush; birds and animals teem; all nature is in harmony. Human beings are at the heart of the idyll – and Welty shows them as uncomprehending innocents. The 'Negroes' – she is writing about times long gone – are children of nature, at peace with their environment. The 'White Folks', by contrast, feel edgy. They sense that they are corrupt, that their presence threatens Eden; but they have no idea what the matter is, and all they can do is live as they always have and hope that things will be all right, that nothing will change. The surface events in Welty's books are a mosaic of ordinariness – parties, children's games, chance meetings in town or at the bathing-station – but underlying them all is a sense of fragility, of impending loss. Her characters are living in a dream, comfortable and comforting, but it is only a dream, and already we, and they, sense the first chill of wakefulness.

DELTA WEDDING (1946)

In the 1920s, nine-year-old Laura travels to her uncle's plantation in the Mississippi Delta, to help in preparations for her cousin's wedding. She revels in the eccentric, affectionate rough-and-tumble of cousins, great-aunts, visitors (and dozens of blacks, as friendly and unconsidered as household pets); she climbs trees, bakes cakes, guesses riddles, listens to gossip as the wedding-dress is sewn. Welty also shows the preparations through the eyes of the bride's parents, the bride and groom themselves, and an as-

READ ON

- *Losing Battles* (more farcical, set not among cotton barons but in a sleepy, dim-witted farming-community, but with the same undertone of devastating moral condemnation).
- ▶ ▷Randall Jarrell, *Pictures from an Institution*. ▷L.P. Hartley, *The Go-Between*. ▷Colette, *The Ripening Seed*. ▷Evelyn Waugh, *Brideshead Revisited*. Robert Penn Warren, *All the King's Men*. Lillian Hellman, *Pentimento*.

sortment of servants, friends and neighbours. The wedding brings a whole community into focus – and we are shown, with persistent, gentle irony, that it is not just the bride and groom who must undergo a rite of passage, but the South itself.

Welty's other novels are The Robber Bridegroom, The Ponder Heart, The Optimist's Daughter *and* Losing Battles. *Her short stories are collected in* A Curtain of Green, The Wide Net, The Golden Apples *and* The Bride of Innisfallen.

WESLEY, Mary (1912)

British novelist.

Wesley's first adult novel, *Jumping the Queue*, was published when she was 70, and since then she has had runaway success. She writes of elegant elderly people, usually women, whose efficient outward lives depend on unsuspected and eccentric thoughts, rituals or long-held secrets. Her stories tell what happens when some chance event – often falling in love with a younger person – brings eccentricity to the surface, rippling the apparently tranquil pool in ways which are bizarre, hilarious and very, very sad.

Not That Sort Of Girl (1987)

Rose is 69, recently widowed, and hard as nails. For 50 years her 'ideal' marriage had been a polite fiction, sustained (for her) by an intermittent, passionate and secret love affair. Sex has been the calm centre of her existence, her reason for living – a matter usually of music-hall farce, but here treated seriously and sensitively, and no joke at all.

Wesley's other books include Harnessing Peacocks, The Vacillations of Poppy Carewe, The Camomile Lawn *and* Second Fiddle.

READ ON

- *Jumping the Queue* (about a middle-aged woman, a would-be suicide, who gives refuge to a charming murderer, and finds that his presence makes her life flower anew).
- ▷Elizabeth Jolley, *Palomino*. Joanna Trollope, *A Village Affair*. ▷Anita Brookner, *Look at Me*.

WEST, Morris (born 1916)

Australian novelist.

West's books are fast-moving moral thrillers, stories not of espionage or crime but of the solution of ethical dilemmas. The hero of *The Shoes of the Fisherman* is a saintly iron-curtain prelate who is elected Pope. *The Clowns of God* is about another Pope forced to abdicate because he has seen a vision predicting the imminent end of the world, and proposes to publicise the fact. In *The Navigator* (1981) a group of people sails to find the Polynesian paradise to which all human souls, the myth says, go after death; they are led by a man who is either a visionary, a charlatan or mad. *The*

READ ON

- *The Devil's Advocate*.
- ▷Jerome Weidman, *The Temple*. Frank Slaughter, *Epidemic*. ▷Neville Shute, *Requiem for a Wren*. ▷C.P. Snow, *The Sleep of Reason*. ▷Thomas Keneally,

Ambassador (1965) is about a conscientious US ambassador who resigns over his country's policy in South Vietnam.

THE WORLD IS MADE OF GLASS (1983)

In Vienna in 1913, the psychiatrist Jung treats a woman who regards him more as a confessor than a healer – and the experience brings him hard up against his sense of his own moral failure, both as a doctor and as a man.

West's other novels include Children of the Sun, The Devil's Advocate, Daughter of Silence, The Tower of Babel, Summer of the Red Wolf, The Salamander *and* Harlequin.

Three Cheers for the Paraclete. ▷Brian Moore, *The Colour of Blood.*

WEST, NATHANIEL (1906–40)

US novelist and screenwriter.

West wrote rubbishy films for a living: their titles include *Rhythm in the Clouds, Born to be Wild* and *Hallelujah I'm a Bum.* To please himself, he wrote four satirical novels, dark black comedies a million miles from Hollywood. The hero of *Miss Lonelyhearts* (1933) is a cynical newspaperman assigned to the agony column. He begins by despising the wretches who write for advice, but soon begins to pity them and finally leaves his desk to intervene in one case personally, with fatal but farcical results.

West's other novels are The Dream Life of Balso Snell, A Cool Million *and* The Day of the Locust.

READ ON

- *The Day of the Locust* (a bleakly funny send-up of Hollywood).
- ▶ Joe Orton, *Head to Toe.* Budd Schulberg, *What Makes Sammy Run?* ▷Aldous Huxley, *After Many a Summer.* ▷Mordecai Richler, *Cocksure.* Thorne Smith, *The Bishop's Jaegers.*

WESTLAKE, DONALD (BORN 1933)

US novelist

Westlake's comedy thrillers are some of the funniest in the business. *The Busy Body* (1966) is typical: the story of a bushy-tailed New York mafioso forced to dig up a body on which half a million dollars' worth of heroin has been hidden – only to have the body stolen from under his nose. What follows, as in most Westlake books, is a 'chase comedy' as breathlessly preposterous as any silent film.

Westlake's farces include Spy in the Ointment, Who Stole Sassi Manoon?, Bank Shot, Brothers Keepers, Two Much, A New York Dance/Dancing Aztecs, Gangway! *and* Nobody's Perfect. *He also writes serious thrillers, both under his own name (*The Mercenaries; Killy*) and as* 'Richard Stark' (The Rare Coin Score, The Blackbird, Lemons Never Lie) *and* 'Tucker Coe' *(A Jade in Aries).*

READ ON

- ▶ ▷Richard Condon, *Prizzi's Honour.* Greg MacDonald, *Fletch.* ▷Margery Allingham, *The Beckoning Lady.* ▷Harry Harrison, *Bill, the Galactic Hero.*

Edith WHARTON

THE HOUSE OF MIRTH *(woman rebels against 1900s New York high society)*

'PLAYTHINGS OF DESTINY'

Thomas HARDY, FAR FROM THE MADDING CROWD
(tragic life and love in 19th-century rural England)

William THACKERAY, VANITY FAIR
(two girls' ambitions to conquer 1810s English high society)

Theodore DREISER, AN AMERICAN TRAGEDY
(ambition, crime and punishment in lower-class 1920s New York)

Nathaniel HAWTHORNE, THE HOUSE OF THE SEVEN GABLES *(New England family cursed for generations because of religious intolerance)*

STIFLING COMMUNITIES

Gustave FLAUBERT, MADAME BOVARY
(mid-19th-century small-town France)

Margaret ATWOOD, THE HANDMAID'S TALE
(21st-century fundamentalist Republic of Gilead)

Olivia MANNING, THE RAIN FOREST
(retreat for psychological misfits on island 'paradise')

Alison LURIE, THE WAR BETWEEN THE TATES
('progressive' US university)

AGAINST THE ODDS

Emily BRONTË, WUTHERING HEIGHTS
(1800s Yorkshire: a woman loves brutal, 'child-of-nature' foster-brother)

Helen WADDELL, PETER ABELARD
(12th-century Paris: a monk falls in love with beautiful pupil)

Victor HUGO, NOTRE DAME DE PARIS
(14th-century Paris: hunchback tries to protect beautiful gipsy from men who would debauch her)

Hermann HESSE, GERTRUD
(1890s German university: two students, friends, love the same woman)

PRESSURE TO CONFORM

Anthony TROLLOPE, DOCTOR THORNE
(snobbery, illegitimacy and inheritance among 19th-century English landed gentry)

Sinclair LEWIS, BABBITT
(wealthy, morally empty merchant tries to break free of sterile small-town conformity)

Angus WILSON, LATE CALL
(widow lives with uncongenial son in soulless 1960s British 'new town')

John UPDIKE, RABBIT, RUN
(ex-high-school sports star tries to adjust to adult mediocrity)

WHARTON, Edith (1862–1937)

US writer of novels, short stories and non-fiction.

A society hostess, Wharton caused outrage by writing with ironical rage about the complacency and shallowness of her own class. (She later described high society as 'frivolous..., able to acquire dramatic significance only through what its frivolity destroys'.) In 1907 she moved to Europe and broadened her scope, writing two Hardyesque rural tragedies (*Ethan Frome, Summer*), several books set in Europe (including *The Reef*, which her friend ▷Henry James admired) and some atmospheric ghost stories. But she regularly returned to her favourite theme, the stifling conventions of 1870s-1920s New York high life – and it is on this that her reputation rests. Her enemies put her down as a clumsy imitator of James. But whereas he showed his characters' psychological innerness, she was interested in manners, in events. She also wrote shorter, wittier sentences, and crisper dialogue. Except that her subject-matter is so sombre, she is more like Oscar Wilde than James.

THE HOUSE OF MIRTH (1905)

Lily Bart, a beautiful, sharp-witted girl, has been conditioned to luxury from birth. Unfortunately she is an orphan, living on a small allowance. She gambles at cards, loses, and because of her moral scruples (she refuses to work off her debts by becoming the mistress of a wealthy creditor), she ends up poorer and more desperate than ever. Faced with the choice of marrying either a rich man she despises (not least because he is a Jew, something her WASPish upbringing has taught her to abhor) or the penniless man she loves, she chooses neither – and soon afterwards, as the result of scandalous accusation, loses her position in society. She moves into cheap lodgings and sinks into despair. She has achieved moral integrity, broken free of her upbringing, but in the process, because of that upbringing, she has destroyed herself.

Wharton's other New York books include the novels The Custom of the Country, The Age of Innocence *and* Old New York, *and the short-story collections* The Descent of Man, Xingu, Certain People *and* Human Nature. Ghosts *contains ghost-stories, and* A Backward Glance *is autobiography, interesting on her friendship with Henry James.*

READ ON

- *The Custom of the Country*.
- ▶ Ellen Glasgow, *Barren Ground*. Louis Auchincloss, *A World of Profit*. ▷George Eliot, *Middlemarch*. ▷William Thackeray, *Vanity Fair*. ▷Elizabeth Taylor, *The Wedding Group*. ▷Mary Wesley, *Not That Sort of Girl*.

WHITE, Antonia (1899-1979)

British novelist.

A journalist and translator (notably of ▷Colette), White is remembered for four deeply-felt autobiographical novels.

READ ON

- ▶ **To *Frost in May*:** ▷James Joyce,

Frost in May (1933) is the story of a child at a grim convent boarding school. The nuns' mission is to 'break' each pupil like a horse – to tame her for Christ – and the book remorselessly charts the series of small emotional humiliations they inflict on the heroine, which have entirely the opposite effect to the one they planned. In the later novels White's heroine works as an actress (*The Lost Traveller*, 1950), tries to combine serious writing with work as a copy-writer (*The Sugar House*, 1952), and finally (*Beyond the Glass*, 1954), in the course of a terrifying mental illness, exorcises the ghosts of Catholicism and her relationship with her father, the influences which have both defined and deformed her life.

White's other books include the short-story collection Strangers, *and* The Hound and the Falcon, *an account in letter-form of her return to Catholicism.*

Portrait of the Artist as a Young Man; Jane Gardam, *Bilgewater*; ▷Thomas Keneally, *Three Cheers for the Paraclete.*

▶ **To *Beyond the Glass*:** Sylvia Plath, *The Bell Jar.*

▶ **To White's work in general:** ▷Rosamond Lehmann, *Dusty Answer*; ▷Rose Macaulay, *The World My Wilderness.*

WHITE, PATRICK (1912–90)

Australian novelist and playwright.

White was interested in Nietzsche's idea of 'superbeings', people endowed with qualities or abilities which set them apart from the rest of the human race. But White's characters are cursed, not blessed, by difference: their chief attribute is a cantankerous individuality which makes it impossible for them to adjust to society or it to them. In some books (eg *Riders in the Chariot*, 1961, about anti-semitism, or *The Vivisector*, 1970, about a convention-defying painter) the 'enemy' is the stifling gentility of lower-middle-class Sydney suburbanites. In others (eg *The Tree of Man*, 1956, about a young farmer in the 1900s, or *A Fringe of Leaves*, 1976, see right), the battle is more symbolic, against the wilderness itself. But wherever conflict takes place, it is of epic proportions: White's craggy prose puts him in the company of such past writers as ▷Melville or ▷Conrad, and in the 20th century only ▷Golding equals his blend of fast-paced story-telling and brooding philosophical allegory.

VOSS (1957)

In 1857, financed by a group of Sydney businessmen, a group of explorers sets out to cross Australia. The expedition is led by the German visionary Voss: physically awkward, ill-at-ease in towns and houses, speaking a tortured, poetic English which sounds as if he learned it by rote, phrase by painful phrase. The other members include an ex-convict and a dreamy aboriginal boy, Jackie, torn between the white people's culture and his own. White balances reports of the expedition's struggle against the desert and to understand one another with accounts of the life of Laura

READ ON

- *A Fringe of Leaves* (about a woman shipwrecked in Queensland in the 1840s, who is captured by aborigines and brought to terms not only with an alien culture but with her feelings about the 'civilisation' she knew before).

▶ **To *Voss*:** ▷William Golding, *Darkness Visible*; ▷H.H. Richardson, *The Fortunes of Richard Mahony*; ▷Peter Carey, *Oscar and Lucinda*; Paul Bowles, *The Sheltering Sky*; ▷Joseph Conrad, *The Nigger of the 'Narcissus'.*

▶ **To *A Fringe of Leaves*:** ▷D.H. Lawrence, *The*

Trevelyan, a young woman fascinated by Voss (at first as a larger-than-life character, an epic personality, and then as a vulnerable human being) as she waits in Sydney, like a medium hoping for spirit-messages, for news of him.

White's other novels are Happy Valley, The Living and the Dead, The Aunt's Story *(a comedy about an indomitable spinster travelling alone),* The Solid Mandala, The Eye of the Storm *and* The Twyborn Affair. The Burnt Ones *and* The Cockatoos *are collections of short stories.* Flaws in the Glass *is an autobiography, good on White's own battles against the wilderness (he was an outback farmer) and against convention (he was homosexual).*

Plumed Serpent; ▷Katharine Susannah Prichard, *Coonardoo.*

► **To White's work in general:** ▷Christina Stead, *The Man Who Loved Children*; Joyce Cary, *The Horse's Mouth*; ▷Elizabeth Taylor, *Blaming.*

WILDER, THORNTON (1897–1975)

US novelist and playwright.

Wilder is known for plays as well as novels: *The Matchmaker* (source of the musical *Hello, Dolly*), *Our Town, The Skin of Our Teeth* and many others. His works explore an idea he called 'simultaneity'. Time is not progressive but circular, our destinies move in cycles, and when people's cycles coincide (like the overlapping Olympic rings), that is the moment of simultaneity, of crisis, in all their lives. In his best-known novel, *The Bridge of San Luis Rey* (1927), the moment of simultaneity is the collapse of a bridge in 18th-century Peru; the book tells the lives of each of the five people killed in the disaster, reaching a climax at the exact instant when the bridge falls in.

THE IDES OF MARCH (1948)

This historical novel charts, in a series of imaginary letters, the converging destinies of a group of people in ancient Rome; it ends on the morning of the Ides of March, 44 BC, as Julius Caesar leaves for the senate-house where (history tells us) he was due to be assassinated. The letter-writers are Caesar himself, Brutus, Cassius, Mark Antony, the poet Catullus, the dissolute aristocrats Clodius and Clodia (symptomatic of the decadent old ruling families Caesar was hoping to replace), and Wilder's purpose is to show how, given those people and circumstances, Caesar's death and the ensuing civil war were inevitable.

Wilder's other novels are The Cabala, The Woman of Andros, Heaven's My Destination, The Eighth Day *and* Theophilus North.

READ ON

- *The Bridge of San Luis Rey.*

► **To *The Ides of March*:** ▷Marguerite Yourcenar, *Memoirs of Hadrian*; John Arden, *Silence Among the Weapons*; ▷Mary Renault, *The Last of the Wine*; Hilda Doolittle ('H.D.'), *Hedylus.*

► **Other books, of different periods and on different themes, but all concerned with our perception of time:** ▷James Joyce, *Ulysses*; ▷Lawrence Durrell, *Tunc* and *Numquam*; ▷Salman Rushdie, *The Satanic Verses.*

► **To Wilder's work in general:** ▷Günter Grass, *The Flounder*; Osbert Sitwell, short stories.

THE WILDERNESS

▷Willa Cather, *Death Comes for the Archbishop*

▷Joseph Conrad, *Heart of Darkness*
Fenimore Cooper, *The Last of the Mohicans*
▷Eleanor Dark, *The Timeless Land*
▷Brian Moore, *Black Robe*
▷Paul Theroux, *The Mosquito Coast*
▷Patrick White, *Voss*

WILSON, A.N. (ANDREW NORMAN) (BORN 1950)

British novelist.

Wilson's early books (*The Sweets of Pimlico*; *Unguarded Hours*) were comic novels in the style of ▷Evelyn Waugh, and just as funny. Then, in the mid-1980s, he began to write more serious books, tragi-comedies about the fears and despair of educated, upper-class people, usually women. Their sad hilarity, and a slightly donnish touch in the writing, are reminiscent of the books of ▷Barbara Pym.

LOVE UNKNOWN (1986)

Three women who shared a London flat in the 1960s have gone their separate ways in the 20 years since. One has flitted from man to man like a wind-up butterfly. Another inherited money and has lived a celibate life in Paris. The third has made an 'idyllic' marriage to the man they all once idolised. Now, as the novel begins, adultery is discovered and the three women's lives intersect once more, unstoppably and painfully.

Wilson's tragi-comedies include The Healing Art, Who Was Oswald Fish, Wise Virgin *and* Gentlemen in England. *He has also written non-fiction; books about Anglicanism and eminent Victorians, and biographies of Milton, ▷Scott and Belloc.*

READ ON

- *Kindly Light.*
- ▷Barbara Pym, *A Glass of Blessings*. ▷Bernice Rubens, *Our Father*. ▷Muriel Spark, *The Girls of Slender Means*. ▷Alison Lurie, *Foreign Affairs*.

WILSON, ANGUS (BORN 1913)

British novelist and short-story writer.

Wilson is a nuclear-age successor to the great Victorian novelists. His plots are expansive, his pages teem with characters and his style is pungently satirical. His middle-class heroes and heroines, often members of the professions, have large, quarrelsome families; adultery, homosexuality, shady dealing and the conflict between public and private duty shape their lives. The 'public' plot of *Hemlock and After* (1952) is about a novelist trying to establish a writers' centre in a large, old house; the 'private' plot concerns his anguish about his own homosexuality. *The Old Men at the Zoo* (1961) is a satire set in a future Britain threatened by a united Europe and defeated by its own penchant for replac-

READ ON

- *As If By Magic.*
- **To Wilson's novels:** ▷Iris Murdoch, *The Sandcastle*; ▷Willa Cather, *The Professor's House*; Peter Taylor, *A Summons to Memphis*.
- **To the short stories:** ▷V.S. Pritchett, *The Camberwell Beauty*;

ing action with committee rhetoric. The heroine of *The Middle Age of Mrs Eliot* (1958), unexpectedly widowed, throws off the home-counties mask and embarks on a raffish odyssey across the world, a quest to find herself. In *Late Call* (1964) another lower-middle-class matron, forced to live with her widowed, unloved son, has to come to terms with the soulless New Town he lives in, a reflection both of his own inner desolation and of the emotional wasteland between them where once was love. *Setting the World on Fire* (1980) is a study of the lives and relationships of two brothers, one a finicky lawyer, the other an artist (an experimental theatre director). As well as his novels, Wilson's short stories are much admired. They are sharp anecdotes of emotional ineptness, often involving the clash between middle-aged parents and their children or between ill-matched lovers.

Mary Gordon, *Temporary Shelter.*

ANGLO-SAXON ATTITUDES (1956)

Gerald Middleton is a rich, successful academic (a historian of Anglo-Saxon England). His personal life is a shambles: he lives apart from his wife, dislikes his children and grandchildren, squabbles with his colleagues and has lost touch with his friends. Faced with the need to accept or reject an important academic task, he begins to think again about the greatest, and oddest, archaeological discovery of his youth 50 years before: an obscene pagan statue in the tomb of a 7th-century Christian missionary. Was it a hoax – and if so, if this is yet another lie on which he has built his life, what can he do now to set things right?

Wilson's other novels are No Laughing Matter *and* As If By Magic. The Wrong Set, Such Darling Dodos *and* A Bit Off the Map *are collections of short stories.*

WINTERSON, JEANETTE (BORN 1959)

British novelist

Winterson's tart, magic-realist fables set characters with modern sensibilities (feminism; pacifism; vegetarianism) in riotously chaotic historical settings: Noah's Ark (filled with grumbling women) in *Boating for Beginners*, the rank back-canals of Venice and the battlefields of Napoleonic France in *The Passion*, the mud-flats and brothels of 17th-century London in *Sexing the Cherry*. The books are short and funny, as hardboiled as rock videos and as tantalising as overheard gossip. If the past was really like this, a lot is explained about why modern people are the way they are.

READ ON

- *The Passion.*
- ▶ ▷Michèle Roberts, *Mrs Noah.* ▷Angela Carter, *The Magic Toyshop.* ▷Italo Calvino, *The Cloven Viscount* (in *Our Ancestors*). ▷Günter Grass, *The Flounder.*

SEXING THE CHERRY (1989)

A giantess known as the Dog Woman rescues an infant from the Thames, names him Jordan and brings him up until he is apprenticed to the naturalist John Tradescant and starts to travel the world in search of exotic plants. The place is London, in the grip of Puritans whose Christian fervour has no truck with compassion or even with simple truth. Jordan's dreams of far countries, and of a princess who exists beyond the grasp of gravity, are intertwined, page by page, with his mother's account of her brutal daily life, as fundamentalist to its violent principles as the Puritans she preys on are to theirs.

Winterson's first novel was Oranges Are Not the Only Fruit.

WODEHOUSE, P.G. (PELHAM GRENVILLE)

(1881–1975)
British novelist.

In the 1920s and 1930s Wodehouse wrote Broadway shows, and he once described his novels as 'musical comedy without the music'. There are over 100 of them, gloriously frivolous romps set in high society 1920s England or among dyspeptic US newspaper magnates and film tycoons. Wodehouse's gormless heroes are in love with 'pips' and 'peacherinos'. Before they can marry they must persuade dragon-like relatives (usually aunts) to give reluctant consent or to part with cash – and the persuasion often involves stealing valuable jewels (to earn undying gratitude when they are 'found' again), smuggling the girl into the house disguised (so that the radiance of her personality will charm all opposition) or blackmail (threatening to reveal embarrassing secrets of the relative's misspent youth). There are two main novel-series, the Jeeves books (in which Bertie Wooster consistently makes an ass of himself, usually by being the fall-guy in Jeeves' machiavellian schemes), and the Blandings books (in which Lord Emsworth's prize pig bulks large). Other books tell of the multifarious members of the Mulliner family and the Drones Club, of golfers, cricketers and incompetent crooks; in all of them the season is high summer, every cloud is lined with silver, and happy endings are distributed 'in heaping handfuls' (to quote Wodehouse's own immortal phrase).

READ ON

- *Summer Lightning.*
- ▶ Ben Travers, *Rookery Nook* (novel version). Richard Gordon, *Doctor in the House*. Patrick Dennis, *Auntie Mame*. The same kind of gormless farce, transplanted to California, updated to the 1980s and set among incompetent crooks and gangsters is in ▷Donald Westlake's Dortmunder books, eg *Bank Shot* or *Who Stole Sassi Manoon?*

LEAVE IT TO PSMITH (1923)

Before Eve Halliday will marry him, Freddie Threepwood needs £1,000 to start a bookmaker's business. He goes to Blandings Castle to ask his father Lord Emsworth. But Lord Emsworth has no access to his own fortune: that route is guarded by Lady Constance Keeble and her sidekick the Efficient Baxter. The plot spirals to include poets who are not everything they seem, stolen jewels, a purloined pig – and above all the machinations of the endlessly, irritatingly good-humoured Psmith.

Wodehouse's Blandings books include Galahad at Blandings, Heavy Weather, Pigs Have Wings *and* Uncle Fred in the Springtime. *His Jeeves books include* Joy in the Morning, The Inimitable Jeeves, Jeeves in the Offing *and* The Code of the Woosters. *His other novels include* Money in the Bank, Uncle Dynamite, The Luck of the Bodkins *and* Quick Service. The Man Upstairs, The Clicking of Cuthbert, Eggs and Crumpets *and* Meet Mr Mulliner *are short-story collections, and* Performing Flea *is autobiography.*

WOLFE, THOMAS (1900–38)

US novelist.

Wolfe's life's work was an incoherent, multi-million-word torrent of autobiographical prose, an attempt to make epic fiction of ordinary US life. His models were ▷Homer, Shakespeare and ▷Dickens – and his work is every bit as grand as that suggests. He and his publishers organised some of the material into two long novels, telling the story of Eugene Gant, a young Carolina writer, from boyhood to first success. The first and most accessible book, *Look Homeward, Angel* (1929), tells of Eugene's childhood as the youngest member of a sprawling, bickering slum family, of his awakening to culture and of his heart-breaking realisation that to 'follow art' he must abandon his family and everything it stands for and chop off his own roots. *Of Time and the River* (1935) continues the story, following Eugene through college and to Paris, charting his artistic friendships, his learning about sex and love, and his first attempts at writing. After Wolfe's death two other novels, *The Web and the Rock* and *You Can't Go Home Again*, were assembled from his manuscripts. They follow another writer, George Weber – an adult version of Eugene Gant – through marriage, divorce, disillusion with the USA and hostility to European fascism in the 1930s.

READ ON

▶ ▷John O'Hara, *From the Terrace*. ▷Lawrence Durrell, *The Black Book*. ▷H.H. Richardson, *The Fortunes of Richard Mahony*. James Jones, *From Here to Eternity*.

WOOLF, VIRGINIA (1882-1941)

British novelist and non-fiction writer.

As well as novels, Woolf published two dozen non-fiction books: biographies (one of Flush, Elizabeth Barrett Browning's pet dog), diaries, essays on feminism and on literature. She was fascinated by psychology, and her nine novels set out to show, in prose, the workings of the subconscious mind. Instead of narrating strings of events she lets her

READ ON

▶ ▷Marcel Proust, *Swann's Way* (the first part of *Remembrance of Things Past*). ▷Jean Rhys, *Good*

characters run on in a 'stream-of-consciousness' style which gradually builds a clear picture of their personalities. She developed the technique from Freud's case-histories, but her characters are not psychologically damaged, as Freud's patients were: she tells us the jumble of thoughts and memories in ordinary men and women, and she is particularly good at showing moments of radiant inner happiness. *Mrs Dalloway* (1925), the interior monologue of a middle-class woman preparing to give a dinner-party, reveals her feelings about herself and her past as well as the urgent claims of the coming evening. In *To the Lighthouse* (1927) a group of adults and children is shown on a summer holiday – the trip to the lighthouse is a promised birthday treat for one of the children – and then in the same place ten years later, when the trip is finally made. Despite war and death in the intervening years, the influence of the dead mother is as strong as in her lifetime. *The Waves* (1931), Woolf's most complex book, traces six people's reactions to experience from childhood to maturity, showing how apparently small 'real' past events continue to affect the personality as waves shape and reshape the shore.

Woolf's other novels are The Voyage Out, Night and Day, Jacob's Room, Orlando, The Years *and* Between the Acts. Haunted House *and* Mrs Dalloway's Party *are collections of short stories.*

Morning, Midnight. D.M. Thomas, *The White Hotel*. Dorothy Richardson, *Pilgrimage*. Anaîs Nin, *Seduction of the Minotaur*. ▷Margaret Atwood, *Surfacing*. Gertrude Stein, *Three Lives*. ▷Iris Murdoch, *The Sea, the Sea*.

WOUK, HERMAN (BORN 1915)

US novelist and playwright.

Wouk's best-known novel, *The Caine Mutiny* (1951), is a tense study of life on a second-world-war US minesweeper whose crew judge the captain unfit for command. Its culminating sequence, a court-martial of the mutineers during which the captain is tricked into revealing his paranoia, was made into a hit Broadway play and a Humphrey Bogart film – and the book itself inspired a score of other novels, films and plays about the craziness not only of war but of the hierarchies of command: they range from the James Cagney/Henry Fonda film comedy *Mr Roberts* to ▷Heller's novel *Catch-22*. Wouk himself wrote two other powerful second-world-war books, *The Winds of War* and *War and Remembrance* His other novels, several made into blockbuster films, include *Marjorie Morningstar* (1955, the story of a young woman who goes to New York to make her way in show-business and who finds romance instead), *Youngblood Hawke* (1962, a tragic-comic satire about a genius-novelist – based on ▷Thomas Wolfe – who is corrupted as soon as he begins meeting agents, publishers and publicists), and *The City Boy* (1948, a wisecracking story about a poor but

READ ON

- **To *The Caine Mutiny***: Erich Maria Remarque, *All Quiet on the Western Front*; Nicholas Monsarrat, *The Cruel Sea*; Pierre Boulle, *The Bridge Over the River Kwai*; ▷Norman Mailer, *The Naked and the Dead*.
- **To *Marjorie Morningstar***: ▷Willa Cather, *The Song of the Lark*.
- **To *The City Boy*:** ▷Jerome Weidman, *Fourth Street East*; ▷Mordecai Richler,

cheerful New York Jewish family during the Depression).

The Apprenticeship of Duddy Kravitz.

WYNDHAM, John (1903–69)

British novelist and short-story writer.

'John Wyndham' was one of the pseudonyms of John Wyndham Lucas Beynon Harris, who wrote straightforward SF and thrillers under the names 'John Wyndham Parkes' and 'Lucas Beynon'. The 'John Wyndham' novels are less SF than thrillers, set on Earth, with SF overtones: he called them 'logical fantasies'. In *The Midwich Cuckoos* (1957) an alien race seeks to colonise Earth not by force of arms but by fertilising women – and the story begins, in the quiet English countryside (a favourite Wyndham location) as the half-alien children approach puberty. In *Chocky* (1968) a small boy has an invisible confidant – not a figment of his imagination, but a being from outer space. *The Day of the Triffids* (1951) begins with two simultaneous disasters, the sudden blinding of all human beings and the growth of enormous, mobile, predatory plants; the novel concerns the hero's attempts to organise resistance and save the human race.

Wyndham's other novels include The Chrysalids, The Kraken Wakes *and* Trouble With Lichen. *His short stories are collected in* The Seeds of Time, Consider Her Ways *and* Web.

READ ON

- ▶ Bob Shaw, *Night Walk*. ▷James Herbert, *The Magic Cottage*. ▷H.G. Wells, *The Time Machine*.

Y

YERBY, Frank (born 1916)
US novelist.

Yerby's early books, serious novels about racism, were published in the second world war, and found few readers. In 1945 he changed his style, began to write historical romances – and became one of the best-selling authors of the century. Superficially his books are straightforward 'bodice-rippers', passion-and-crinoline melodramas set in the American Deep South. But his persistent underlying theme is the equality of all people, white or black, and this gives his work an edge unusual in romance. In the 1960s he broadened his scope, writing books set in ancient Greece, Biblical Palestine, Victorian England and present-day Washington, D.C.

Yerby's romances include The Foxes of Harrow, The Golden Hawk, Floodtide, A Woman Called Fancy, The Devil's Laughter, Bride of Liberty, Griffin's Way *and* A Darkness at Ingraham's Crest. *His other novels include* The Saracen Blade, The Serpent and the Staff, Goat Song, Judas My Brother *and* Hail the Conquering Hero.

READ ON

- ▶ **To the romances:** ▷Margaret Mitchell, *Gone with the Wind*; Kathleen Winsor, *Forever Amber*; Colleen McCullough, *The Thorn Birds*.
- ▶ **To Yerby's other books:** Lloyd C. Douglas, *The Big Fisherman*; ▷John Galsworthy, *The Man of Property*; Allen Drury, *A Shade of Difference*.

YOURCENAR, Marguerite (1903–88)
French writer.

Yourcenar is best known for her novel *Memoirs of Hadrian* (1951), a study of the urbane, civilised man who ruled the Roman Empire in the second century AD. Unlike ▷Robert Graves' *I, Claudius*, which is chiefly the tale of an outrageous family power struggle, *Memoirs of Hadrian* is a philosophical autobiography, concerned not only with politics and

READ ON

- *The Abyss* (about a similar philosophical journey, this time by a Flemish scholar wandering Renaissance Europe

conquest but with Hadrian's intellectual and emotional growth. It is a quiet, understated book, balancing Hadrian's descriptions of his search for tranquillity of soul with the torments and ecstasies of his passion for the beautiful boy Antinous.

in search of 'knowledge untrammelled by doctrine').

► ▷Mary Renault, *The Mask of Apollo*. ▷Gore Vidal, *Julian*. ▷Thornton Wilder, *The Ides of March*.

Z

ZOLA, ÉMILE (1840-1902)

French novelist and non-fiction writer.

Zola won scandalous fame at 27 with his novel *Thérèse Raquin*, about a pair of lovers who murder the woman's husband. The book's financial success let him take up fiction full-time, and he began a 20-novel series designed to show – in a scientific way, he claimed, as species are described – every aspect of late 19th-century French life. Although each novel is self-contained, their main characters are all members of the two families which give the series its name, *The Rougons and the Macquarts*. Zola's scheme echoed ▷Balzac's in *The Human Comedy*, and like Balzac he was interested in exact description, what he called 'naturalism'. But his morbid and pessimistic nature led him to concentrate on the harsher aspects of human existence, so that his characters often seem less like real human beings than the people dragged into sermons to illustrate the effects of drink, lust or poverty. Outside France, Zola's best-known books are *Germinal* (1885, about conditions in the coal-mines, and including a strike and a major accident), *Earth* (La Terre) (1887, about subsistence farming), *The Belly of Paris* (Le ventre de Paris) (1873, about the food-markets of the city), *The Boozer* (L'assommoir) (1871) and *For Women's Delight* (Pour lę bonheur des dames) (1883, about the staff and customers of a department store).

READ ON

- *Thérèse Raquin*.
- ▶ ▷Somerset Maugham, *Liza of Lambeth*. Theodor Fontane, *Effi Briest*. Frank Norris, *The Pit*. Theodore Dreiser, *An American Tragedy*. ▷John Steinbeck, *The Grapes of Wrath*. George Gissing, *New Grub Street*.

NANA (1880)

The subject is sex. Nana's mother was a country girl who went to Paris to seek her fortune, became a laundress but was destroyed by drink – this is the story of *The Boozer*. Nana grows up as a street-urchin, and later becomes an actress and singer. She is beautiful but corrupt, morally brutalised by her childhood. She sets out systematically to destroy men: Zola thinks of her first as one of the Sirens in myth, drawing men irresistibly to her by the beauty of her voice, and then as a spider, preying on them even as she mates with them. He pities neither Nana nor her victims: like his other novels, this panorama of big-city life is painted entirely in shades of black.

Other books in the series include The Human Beast (La bête humaine) *(about the gangs of navvies who built railroads),* Money *(set among financiers) and* The Downfall (La débâcle) *(a devastating picture of the 1870 Commune and siege of Paris, which Zola saw as a cleansing operation, ridding the city of the corruption which had led to the misery described in his other books). In his last years he finished the first three books of another series,* The Four Gospels*: their titles are* Fertility, Work *and* Truth.

INDEX

A

B

C

D

E

H

I

J

K

L

M

N

O

P

S

T

U

V

W

X

Y

Z

OTHER REFERENCE BOOKS FROM BLOOMSBURY PUBLISHING

BLOOMSBURY GUIDE TO ENGLISH LITERATURE
Edited by Marion Wynne-Davies
The new authority on English Literature, combining essays outlining the development of each genre with over 5,000 A-Z entries.

BLOOMSBURY GOOD WORD GUIDE
Edited by Martin H. Manser
Consultant editors Betty Kirkpatrick, John Silverlight and Jonathon Green. Now in its second edition, the book gives clear and practical advice on the many questions which puzzle speakers and users of English.

BLOOMSBURY THEATRE GUIDE
Trevor R. Griffiths and Carole Woddis
Now in paperback. Over 300 entries with extensive cross-references, covering playwrights, directors, companies and theatres.

BLOOMSBURY GOOD MOVIE GUIDE
David Parkinson
The new guide for all film and video fans. Includes details and summaries of over 4,000 films.

BLOOMSBURY GOOD MUSIC GUIDE
Neville Garden
Covers over 300 composers and thousands of musical works. A must for anyone who enjoys listening to music.